Theories Terroris..

Theories of Terrorism explains and advances the major theories of terrorism that address issues of becoming a terrorist, being a terrorist, and leaving terrorism, in a clear and accessible format.

Readers will gain an understanding of the most promising explanations of terrorism that have been developed to date and how they can be used to explore core substantive issues related to the topic. The content is delivered with a scholarly depth, though still accessible by students at different levels. The book offers explanations from prominent scholars for the three phases of radicalization, covering emerging topics such as women's involvement in terrorism, fear of terrorism, the code of the terrorist, and suicide terrorism. This is the first book in the *Advances in Criminological Theory* series to address the issue of terrorism and emphasizes the use of theory to direct research development in the future.

The style and content coverage of the book make it appropriate as a supplemental text in undergraduate courses on terrorism and political violence. The inclusion of current empirical literature and guidance for future research efforts gives the text appeal for graduate students and academics in the disciplines of criminology/criminal justice, political science, sociology, and interdisciplinary terrorism studies. The emphasis on theory and the radicalization process throughout the text will also make the book useful as a reference for general graduate-level theory courses within these areas.

Murat Haner is a Lecturer of Criminology at the Department of Criminology at the University of South Florida. He received his PhD from University of Cincinnati. He is author of *The Freedom Fighter: A Terrorist's Own Story*. His current research is focused on examining the issue of radicalization into terrorist organizations and understanding public opinion on terrorism, counterterrorism policies, and other pressing social issues. His research has been published in journals such as *British Journal of Criminology*, *Crime & Delinquency*, *Terrorism & Political Violence*, and *Justice Quarterly*.

Melissa M. Sloan is an Associate Professor of Sociology and Interdisciplinary Social Sciences at the University of South Florida. She received her PhD in Sociology from Vanderbilt University. Her research interests include the sociology of emotion, with a particular focus on fear of terrorism and psychological well-being, and the interdisciplinary research process. Her research has been published in journals such as *Social Psychology Quarterly*, *Socius: Sociological Research for a Dynamic World*, and the *American Review of Public Administration*.

SERIES EDITORS

Advances in Criminological Theory

Francis T. Cullen
University of Cincinnati

William S. Laufer
University of Pennsylvania

Freda Adler
University of Pennsylvania

Theories of Terrorism

Contemporary Perspectives

Edited by

**Murat Haner &
Melissa M. Sloan**

NEW YORK AND LONDON

First published 2022
by Routledge
605 Third Avenue, New York, NY 10158

and by Routledge
2 Park Square, Milton Park, Abingdon, Oxon OX14 4RN

Routledge is an imprint of the Taylor & Francis Group, an informa business

© 2022 Taylor & Francis

The right of Murat Haner & Melissa Sloan to be identified as the authors of the editorial material, and of the authors for their individual chapters, has been asserted in accordance with sections 77 and 78 of the Copyright, Designs and Patents Act 1988.

All rights reserved. No part of this book may be reprinted or reproduced or utilised in any form or by any electronic, mechanical, or other means, now known or hereafter invented, including photocopying and recording, or in any information storage or retrieval system, without permission in writing from the publishers.

Trademark notice: Product or corporate names may be trademarks or registered trademarks, and are used only for identification and explanation without intent to infringe.

Library of Congress Cataloging-in-Publication Data
Names: Haner, Murat, editor.
Title: Theories of terrorism : contemporary perspectives /
Murat Haner & Melissa M. Sloan [editors].
Description: New York, NY : Routledge, 2022. |
Series: Advances in criminological theory |
Includes bibliographical references and index.
Identifiers: LCCN 2021016523 (print) | LCCN 2021016524 (ebook) |
ISBN 9780367457617 (hbk) | ISBN 9781032104232 (pbk) |
ISBN 9781003026303 (ebk)
Subjects: LCSH: Terrorism–esearch. | Bombers (Terrorists) | Criminology.
Classification: LCC HV6431 .T5635 2022 (print) |
LCC HV6431 (ebook) | DDC 363.32501–dc23
LC record available at https://lccn.loc.gov/2021016523
LC ebook record available at https://lccn.loc.gov/2021016524

ISBN: 978-0-367-45761-7 (hbk)
ISBN: 978-1-03-210423-2 (pbk)
ISBN: 978-1-00-302630-3 (ebk)

DOI: 10.4324/9781003026303

Typeset in Times New Roman
by Newgen Publishing UK

Contents

List of Contributors vii

Preface xi

Part I. Becoming a Terrorist

1. The Psychological Processes of Terrorism 3
   Orla Lynch and Carmel Joyce

2. Explaining Political Terrorism 34
   Michael Stohl and Peter Grabosky

3. Explaining Religious Terrorism 55
   Nilay Saiya

4. Explaining White Supremacy and Domestic Terrorism 78
   Amanda Graham

Part II. Being a Terrorist

5. Gender and Terrorism 119
   Kathy Laster and Edna Erez

6. Terrorist Target Selection 151
   Max Abrahms and Joseph Mroszczyk

7. Explaining Suicide Bombings 172
   Susanne Martin

8. Code of the Terrorist 199
   Murat Haner, Michael L. Benson, and Francis T. Cullen

Part III. Beyond Terrorism

9. Desistance from Terrorism 239
   Daren Fisher

10. Terrorism and Deterrence — 262
    Pauline L. Moore and Brian A. Jackson

11. Situational Crime Prevention and Terrorism — 284
    Joshua D. Freilich, Jeff Gruenewald, and Steven Chermak

12. Fear of Terrorism: Extent, Sources, and Reactions — 315
    Heejin Lee, Brooke Miller Gialopsos, and Cheryl Lero Jonson

13. How Terrorism Ends — 345
    Leonard B. Weinberg

Index — 376

Contributors

Max Abrahms is an Associate Professor in the Department of Political Science at Northeastern University and a non-resident fellow at the Quincy Institute for Responsible Statecraft and Observer Research Foundation.

Michael L. Benson is Professor Emeritus and Senior Research Associate in the School of Criminal Justice at the University of Cincinnati.

Steven Chermak is a Professor in the School of Criminal Justice at Michigan State University.

Francis T. Cullen is Distinguished Research Professor Emeritus and Senior Research Associate in the School of Criminal Justice at the University of Cincinnati.

Edna Erez is Professor in the Department of Criminology, Law, and Justice at the University of Illinois in Chicago.

Daren Fisher is an Assistant Professor in the Department of Criminal Justice at The Citadel.

Joshua D. Freilich is Professor in the Department of Criminal Justice at John Jay College.

Peter Grabosky is Professor Emeritus in the School of Regulation and Global Governance at the Australian National University

Amanda Graham is an Assistant Professor in the Department of Criminal Justice and Criminology at Georgia Southern University.

List of Contributors

Jeff Gruenewald serves as Director of the Terrorism Research Center (TRC) and Associate Professor in the Department of Sociology & Criminology at University of Arkansas.

Murat Haner is Lecturer of Criminology in the Department of Criminology at University of South Florida.

Brian A. Jackson is a Senior Physical Scientist at the RAND Corporation and a Professor of Policy Analysis at the Pardee RAND Graduate School.

Cheryl Lero Jonson is an Associate Professor in the Department of Criminal Justice at Xavier University.

Carmel Joyce was Post-Doctoral Research Fellow at The Centre for the Study of Terrorism and Political Violence, St Andrews, Scotland and is a graduate student in the Department of Social Work at Salem State University.

Kathy Laster is Professor and Director of Sir Zelman Cowen Centre at Victoria University, Melbourne, Australia.

Heejin Lee is Post-Doctoral Research Fellow in the School of Criminal Justice at the University of Cincinnati.

Orla Lynch is Senior Lecturer in Criminology and Associate Dean of Graduates Studies at University College Cork, Ireland.

Susanne Martin is Associate Professor in the Department of Political Science at University of Nevada, Reno.

Brooke Miller Gialopsos is an Assistant Professor in the Department of Criminal Justice at Seattle University.

Pauline L. Moore is an Associate Political Scientist at the RAND Corporation and a Professor of Policy Analysis at the Pardee RAND Graduate School.

Joseph Mroszczyk is a Defense Contractor working as a War Gaming Specialist at the US Naval War College. He also serves as an Officer in the US Navy Reserve.

Nilay Saiya is Assistant Professor in the Department of Political Science at Nanyang Technological University, Singapore.

Melissa M. Sloan is an Associate Professor in the Department of Sociology at University of South Florida.

Michael Stohl is Professor in the Department of Political Science at the University of California, Santa Barbara.

Leonard B. Weinberg is Foundation Professor of Political Science at the University of Nevada.

Preface

Terrorism is an area of urgent global concern. While its analytical study dates back to the late seventies, academic attention to terrorism dramatically increased following the terrorist attacks of September 11, 2001 (Sandler, 2014). Since this time, the number of terrorism and homeland security-focused academic programs, think tanks, and research centers has proliferated worldwide. These research programs have produced insights regarding the nature of terrorism (e.g., extent, global spread, and methods) and have developed measures aimed at controlling its origins, spread, and impact. Many universities now offer courses on issues related to terrorism at both the undergraduate and graduate levels within the social science disciplines and house interdisciplinary terrorism research centers.

Accordingly, the topic of terrorism (and the collateral issue of homeland security) is now included as a standard course in many criminology and criminal justice curriculums at universities worldwide. This attention to terrorism within the field of criminology is relatively recent, however, as terrorism research was initiated primarily by political scientists, psychologists, and economists. In recognition of the growth of interest in terrorism among criminologists, Joshua Freilich and Gary LaFree edited a special issue of *Terrorism and Political Violence* on Criminology Theory and Terrorism in 2015 and that same year helped to establish a division of the American Criminological Society on Terrorism and Bias Crimes.

As interest in terrorism studies among criminologists continues to increase, it is our goal with this volume—the first in the *Advances in Criminological Theory* series to be devoted to terrorism—to present the most promising themes and theories in terrorism research to date for use by students and academics seeking to advance theoretically driven research in the area. Prominent scholars in the field have written chapters that illuminate major theories and discuss how they can be used to explore core substantive issues related to (1) becoming a terrorist, (2) being a terrorist, and (3) leaving terrorism. We are grateful to these contributors and look forward to the research that will surely build on the work presented in this volume. With the recently elevated threat of domestic terrorism within the United States alone, following the January 6, 2021 storming of the US Capitol, we certainly expect advances in criminological understandings of terrorism to play a critical role in developing effective homeland security policies.

Murat Haner & Melissa M. Sloan
August, 2021
University of South Florida

References

Freilich, J.D., & LaFree, G. (2015). Criminology theory and terrorism: Introduction to the special issue. *Terrorism and Political Violence*, 27(1), 1–18.

Sandler, T. (2014). The analytical study of terrorism: Taking stock. *Journal of Peace Research*, 51(2), 257–271.

Part I

Becoming a Terrorist

1

The Psychological Processes of Terrorism

Orla Lynch and Carmel Joyce

Psychology as a discipline is comprised of an eclectic body of work ranging from psychoanalytic psychology to cognitive psychology, from social psychology to psychometrics (Hergenhahn & Henley, 2014). To evaluate how psychology contributes to our knowledge on terrorism and political violence, we have to consider both research that speaks to the issue of terrorism alongside bespoke psychological research on terrorism—in other words, the psychology of terrorism and *a* psychology of terrorism. In the case of the former, given that terrorism is composed of a range of observable behavior impacted by interpersonal and intra/intergroup factors, then one could say that *all* psychological research is relevant for how we think about terrorism and political violence; however, not all research on terrorism is psychological.

The aim of this chapter is to examine the questions we, as psychologists, are asking about psychology and psychological processes when undertaking research on terrorism and political violence (Taylor, 2014). As such, in seeking to understand the state of the research area we are asking if psychological research is challenging or replicating the politicized and securitized assumptions inherent in the field (Stampnitzky, 2013). To this end, we will critically assess the role and strengths of psychological research in how we think about and carry out research on terrorism. In addition, we examine how psychology as a discipline can contribute to understanding and addressing, in an evidence-based and ethical manner, the big social issues of our time. Never has this been so relevant, given the revelations that emerged around the role of psychologists in the CIA enhanced interrogations (Marks, 2018) program in the USA and the statutory obligation of psychologists in the UK with regard to Prevent reporting (Lynch, 2021) on extremism. This chapter begins by reflecting on the state of play of psychological research in the field of terrorism and political violence, and continues with a review of the most recent psychological research in the field.

A Psychological Problem?

It may seem self-evident to say that the discipline of psychology should have a lot to say about terrorism. Terrorism is after all an observable act; an act often inspired by extreme cognitions and one that serves a communicative purpose (Schmid & Jongman, 1988). In addition, the impact of terrorism has tangible psychological consequences for victims and survivors (Argomaniz & Lynch, 2016). However, psychology is not the dominant framework used to understand terrorism, nor is it comprehensively used by researchers. This can be qualified by pointing to the very significant increase in the application of psychological theory to the case of terrorism, and the rapid increase and improvement in the quality of material produced in this area over the past 15 years (Horgan, 2017). However, we still have some way to go to achieve the potential that is possible in applying psychology to terrorism (Lynch and Joyce, 2018).

Despite the improvements in the field, much of the psychological research on terrorism could be described as tokenism; a reflection on the relevance of psychology after the fact, or the retrospective framing of findings in psychological terms (Bouhana & Wikström, 2011; Lynch & Joyce, 2018). These issues emerge due to a general failure to identify what elements of terrorism are psychological problems (and what are not!); a failure to start at a psychologically focused and informed research question; and a failure to define, not the term "terrorism," but what the problem appears to be (Lynch and Joyce, 2018).

However, the current state of psychological research on terrorism is not merely an artifact of psychological science, but also due to the controversial ethical and political issues inherent in the study of terrorism and political violence (Schuurman, 2018). Indeed, there are several challenges to the study of terrorism and political violence that are experienced across a range of disciplines, including (but not limited to) the definitional issues that exist around terrorism (Schmid & Jongman, 1988); any relationship to radicalization (Neumann, 2013); the reactionary nature of the field (Bouhana, 2019); the somewhat arbitrary delineation between state and substate terrorism (Wilkinson, 2011); a preoccupation with delineating ideological motives; the reciprocity between terrorism and counterterrorism (Soule, 1989) and the promise of what has become known as CVE/PVE—countering/preventing violent extremism (Williams, 2020).

However, psychological researchers must be mindful of the unique issues that emerge in our discipline as we attempt to study terrorism, a field that is very much in its infancy. As an area of research that is, on the one hand, heavily attended to (Silke, 2007) yet relatively new to the processes of empirical investigation, the temptation in psychology is to take concepts like "terrorism," "political violence," "radicalization," etc., at face value without deconstructing how these concepts are understood by those most affected by them, or those with the power to apply them (Jackson et al., 2009). Indeed, to date, much of the effort in psychology, has been related to the identification of a "typical terrorist"—a one-size-fits-all interpretation of the characteristics and behaviors of "terrorists" (Horgan, 2017). This, of course, demonstrates the very particular interpretation that psychological science has constructed of terrorism and the terrorist, namely that knowing about the individual actor has a significant role to play in how we understand terrorism. Thankfully, researchers in psychology are no longer preoccupied with this red herring. However, researchers must not lose sight of the fact that, as new labels and definitions emerge in terrorism, so too does the way in which these labels/terms are mobilized, both within and outside of the discipline. Psychology still has a lot to say in relation to terrorism and related phenomena, however the onus of responsibility is on researchers to reflect on the issues which plague this discipline and, rather than ignore these issues, they must be brought into relief during the scientific inquiry.

Recently, Stephen Reicher (2021) addressed the issue of how problems are framed from a psychological point of view and pointed to the separation of the study of behavior and the study of psychology, highlighting that they are two fundamentally different processes. He pointed out that any behavior we witness can not only be understood by understanding the motivation to act, but also the constraining (and facilitating) social and material forces. According to Reicher (2021), any effort on the part of researchers to attribute behavior purely to internal criteria, can only result in the psychologizing of behavior. This psychologizing is more a reflection of the internal states of the researcher (their values, perceptions, judgment, and their need to create an objective fact) rather than a reflection on the subject of investigation. Reicher (2021) also points out that not all phenomena can or should be subject to psychological explanations. Importantly, and highly relevant in the case of terrorism studies, he points out that the fundamental attribution error (the tendency to attribute causality to internal criteria, that is, characteristics of the person rather than characteristics of the situation) is as much an artifact of ideology as it is psychology (Reicher, 2021).

The fundamental attribution error is rife in terrorism research, it can manifest in the blatant way we speak about mental health and personality types. It can also be more insidious and be reflected in the assumption that people engage in terrorism because they can be placed on a "sub-clinical" scale and are somehow psychologically fragile or vulnerable (Corner & Gill, 2015). Taking this approach means that the nuance and complexity of the individual as a social and political being is lost. Importantly, it also harms efforts to ensure that psychology contributes in a meaningful way to research on terrorism (Gill & Corner, 2017).

Psychology as a Science

"Psychology appears to progress by removing the obstacles it has placed in its path"

Stern (Rozen, 2001, p. 2)

Psychology as a discipline has always suffered somewhat from an inferiority complex. In order to have a seat at the table and to be considered for publication by the major scientific journals, psychological research has mirrored the scientific methods of the hard sciences (Perez-Alverez, 2018). Psychology, in an effort to meet the requirements of a science (clearly defined terminology, quantifiability, controlled conditions, predictability, generalizability, transferability, and testability) adopted a dominant focus on lab-based methods (Stevens, 2017).

Indeed, psychologists have attempted for many years to replicate the processes of the hard or natural sciences and increasingly researchers are considering the relevance of the subject for such treatment (Rozen, 2001). However, this is as much about the limitations in how we think about the production of scientific knowledge as it is about the process of doing social science research. Solomon Asch, a famous psychologist known for his methodological innovation, emphasized that in order to come to know about the psychological phenomenon we are studying, we must describe it faithfully, look freely at it, and examine its foundations (Rozen, 2001). In effect, Asch was pointing out that psychological research is a unique undertaking and must account for the context, for free will, and for agency, and not succumb to the limits of prescribed scientific methods in matters of human behavior. This, of course, is not conducive to the production of definitive results in the traditional model of science. Rozen (2001) also points out that psychological knowledge must focus on the collation of large amounts of evidence drawn from a variety of different sources and a multiplicity of approaches—stating that description cannot be a narrow phenomenon. The implications of this for fields that focus on exceptional and extreme outliers of behavior is, of course, obvious—we may never have large amounts of data in the manner Rozen describes. This leaves us to (re)consider how we should think about the psychology of terrorism and the issue of specialization, evidence, and the universality of human behavior. This brings us back to the two key issues raised earlier—what we perceive the general problem to be with regard to terrorism, and what it is about terrorism that is a psychological problem. We will now deal with each in turn.

Problematizing Terrorism Research

In our efforts to research terrorism, the phenomenon is often simplified beyond recognition. It is depicted in binary terms—good versus evil, us versus them; groups are given clear identifiable boundaries and individuals are presumed to share mono-dimensional roles. The processes underpinning the choice to engage in terrorist violence, however, are some of the most complex social and psychological issues imaginable. In addition, terrorism most often means substate terrorism, further simplifying the phenomenon to exclude certain actors and motives. Terrorism, as we predominantly use the term in academia, is rooted in Western understandings of international relations and it is understood most readily in legal bounded terms (Bankoff, 2003). Of course, the complexity of terrorism has long been recognized in the heated academic arguments around definitions (Botticher, 2017; Kaczkowski et al., 2019; Schmid & Jongman, 1988) but only within existing narrow parameters. There have always been calls for a recognition of the harm that states are capable of, but this is not reflected in the field (Wright, 2020). And while there is a recognition that terrorism as a label is most often applied as a term to demonize the social other (Lynch, 2013), this is often overlooked in our analysis.

As might be expected, the psychological research that focuses on terrorism incorporates many of these problematic assumptions; it focuses primarily on substate terrorism, it predominantly addresses narrow and isolated issues of individual differences and psychopathology, and it examines social categories without deference to the power that maintains them. However, these issues are not issues that are unique to psychological research, they are issues that are part of both psychological research and terrorism research, respectively. While these issues do not reflect the sum total of the field, they need to be attended to in order to ensure psychological science can meaningfully contribute to our knowledge on terrorism and political violence.

If we were to broadly summarize the work on the psychology of terrorism, it would be fair to say it revolves around, as Horgan (2017) puts it, the "big bang questions" of who becomes a terrorist, as well as why they choose to do so. If these are the key questions and the mainstay of psychological research into terrorism, then it is fair to say we have failed to adequately answer the question. In reality, however, this is not about a failure to answer the big bang questions, but in fact a recognition that we are asking the wrong questions in the first place.

To understand how we came to be focused on the wrong question, we have to start at a time when psychoanalytic explanations of terrorism were more commonplace (see Hacker, 1976; Kampf, 1980; Volkan, 1988, 1997). In the earliest days of research into modern terrorism, psychoanalytic psychology was more visible. The body of work debated the role of Freud's basic concepts (e.g., the repetition compulsion) and their relevance for terrorism, but also referred to issues of trauma, attachment, voice (or lack of), and the communicative nature of terrorism (Kleinot, 2017). Interestingly, the work of psychoanalysts emphasized the issue of vulnerability and environmental triggers long before it was incorporated into frameworks on extremism in recent times. In addition, issues of group boundaries, group identity, and historical traumas all emerged in the psychoanalytic literature on terrorism, as did issues of shame, alienation, and complex grievance (Kleinot, 2017; Volkan, 1988). In effect, psychoanalytic psychology pointed to the complexity of terrorism; the equifinality of terrorism; the interactivity between the person, the group, and society; and the importance of history (both personal and political) in how we understand the person's choice to engage in terrorism. However, while these insights, given what we know today, are useful, and largely accurate they are, due to the nature of psychoanalytic research, very much unverifiable and ungeneralizable.

In its reflections on terrorism and political violence, the psychoanalytic literature predominantly drew on existing concepts and hypotheses from a general population, taking the approach that human nature is human nature (Victoroff, 2005) and avoiding exceptionalizing terrorist behavior. This meant that the specificity of terrorism was not a priority for this subdiscipline, nor was there any significant data or evidence to speak of. While the universality of human behavior is, of course, considered a valid approach, ultimately the field fell out of favor. This was due in large part to the demands for policy answers—the drive to find psychological solutions for counterterrorism and policing measures (Victoroff, 2005), a move which highlighted where political decision makers saw the problem of terrorism to lie—not in the complexity of society, history, or the interaction of the individual with their environment, but again with the behavior of the individual.

Despite the sidelining of these early approaches to understanding terrorism in the aftermath of 9/11, these issues (particularly the focus on the individual) were revisited in an effort to come to terms with terrorism that was portrayed as an existential threat to Western societies. Issues of mental ill health, personality profiles, and individual differences re-emerged albeit in slightly different guises (Victoroff, 2005). While the evidence still did not exist to support the hypothesis of a terrorist personality or a significant role for mental ill health in terrorist activity, these convenient ideas could not be shaken. It should be said that we do not have the evidence to support or refute the idea of a terrorist personality, or a significant role for mental ill health in the case of terrorist actors. We do, however, have evidence from other related fields (psychological criminology, clinical psychology, and forensic psychology, for example) that focusing on the internal characteristics of an individual is neither a comprehensive nor a methodologically sound way to understand and conceptualize human behavior (LaFree & Freilich, 2017).

Yet again, however, we were focusing on the wrong question. Deciphering whether mental ill health is related to terrorist activity is less relevant than asking what it means to say that an individual suffering from mental ill health is responsible for a terrorist act. If we strip this issue back to first principles the issue really is, can we talk about a causal relationship between mental ill health and terrorism—which of course we cannot. Evidence from decades of psychological and psychiatric research demonstrates the interactivity of a multiplicity of factors in determining the choice to engage in any behavior, and mental ill health, in many cases, might not be at all relevant (Evans et al., 2013). While it might be simpler conceptually and psychologically for researchers to "other" those involved in terrorism as separate from those in "normal" society, the uncomfortable reality is that there appears to be very little separating "us" from "them."

Further complicating matters, there is the issue of the chicken or the egg scenario; is an individual more likely to have a mental health disorder before joining a terrorist group or develop a mental health disorder because they joined a terrorist group? Basically, the underlying issue is what does it actually mean when an individual simultaneously has a mental health disorder and is also involved in terrorism. Of course, we should add, it depends on the disorder, but at a basic level does the pathology functionally impact on their behaviour choices? And if so, how does it impact on these choices? And does the group impact these choices? Can the group have a positive or negative impact? And what might this mean for rehabilitative efforts? Researchers in Northern Ireland found that the conflict environment acted as a psychological buffer, strengthening social ties, solidifying identity categories, and lowering suicide rates (Muldoon & Downes, 2007). However, and this is something we will return to later, we know from other contexts that involvement in violence has significant psychological costs for the perpetrator. Could being part of a terrorist organization provide meaning and social support, effectively buffering against the risk of psychological ill health? Or does it cause trauma due to participation in interpersonal violence? We know from gang research that young people who are involved in gangs are more likely than their peers to have higher levels of mental ill health, but the cause–effect relationship is not definitive (Frisby-Osman & Wood, 2020) These questions effectively problematize any assumption that mental ill health is causally linked to involvement in terrorism, despite our best attempt not to draw these hasty conclusions.

Importantly, this brings up the issue of where we should start when we are thinking about an individual who gets involved in terrorism. Should we consider the individual's personal clinical history over their lifespan, any adverse childhood experiences, their criminal record, their interpersonal relationships? Should we consider their efforts to engage with mental health services or perhaps their neglect by local mental health services? Should we look at their failure and expulsion from school? Should we look at their employment options, or lack thereof, and their history of victimization? How should we understand the life-history of the individual if we are looking to meaningfully understand the process of engaging in terrorist activity? Importantly, how we deem parts of the story relevant or not, is ideological not psychological. Excluding social issues, welfare issues, trauma, and victimhood serve not to clarify the story, only once again to simplify it beyond recognition.

Probability and Prediction in Terrorism Research

Currently, when seeking to address the big bang question of terrorism studies—who becomes a terrorist?—we often seek to answer it via a retrospective analysis of the available demographic data (Horgan, 2017). However, we are now confident that, in the case of terrorism, the decision to get involved is not quantifiable by deciphering a range of combinations of characteristics (Bouhana, 2019). This approach has a long history dating back to the 1960s and 1970s when researchers and police (e.g., the FBI) sought to categorize members of terrorist groups as a means of understanding them (Victoroff, 2005). However, we now know that involvement in terrorism cannot merely be known by looking at past examples of terrorist actors and creating an algorithm based on this (often incomplete) data; the combinations of possible personal characteristics are infinitesimal (Bouhana, 2019), and that is before we even look at environmental triggers and barriers. We know now that those who choose to get involved do so for many idiosyncratic reasons, both personogenic and situational, but we also know that the environment is a key factor in the opportunity and choice to engage. It goes without saying that the issue of the prediction of behavior is complex. There is a significant body of work in existence that looks at a range of categories of human behavior including addiction, health behaviors, conservation/climate change behaviors etc., and attempts to understand patterns and to potentially predict patterns. However, in the case of terrorism research, risk and to a lesser degree prediction, focus heavily on the relationship between ideology, beliefs, and violence. This is an issue that dominates the field, in terms of the link between both cognitions and action.

Much like the approach to individual differences and psychopathology in terrorism research, the issue of prediction, be it prediction of personality dimensions or prediction of the risk of violent behavior, suffers from a lack of data. However, the lack of data is ultimately not the issue; the issue is that the assumptions exist that we can somehow come to know about risk of involvement in terrorism based on a particular set of data. If we look at the type of work being done around what is arguably much simpler phenomena, we get an idea of the issue in question. Fascinating research is currently being undertaken that focuses on the general prediction of personality characteristics and personality dimensions in the general population. In one study by Stachl et al. (2020) the authors collected comprehensive data from participants' smartphones (location, music, communication, mobility, social behavior, etc.) and used a machine learning algorithm to examine which of the big five personality dimensions are predictable based on this data and subsequently administered psychological tests as part of the study. Despite the overwhelming (and worrying) amount of data collected in this study (24/7 data from phones over one month) the authors were only able to infer trait information on openness, conscientiousness, and extraversion, less for emotional stability, and none for agreeableness. While these are significant findings, it does show the limitations of predictability even with staggering amounts of personal data. Comparing this, for example, to the work of Tschantret (2020) using a small sample (n = 24) and textual analysis to infer predetermined personality features in a terrorist sample, it highlights how the value we place on personality characteristics and prediction may be misplaced.

Personality characteristics are but one focus and the issue of the relationship between these characteristics, beliefs, attitudes, intentions, and behavior is commonly addressed in a range of research areas including health psychology, and the underlying principles are relevant to the case of terrorism studies. Research on needs is prominent in terrorism studies and much can be learned from research in other domains (Jasko et al., 2020; Kruglanski et al., 2020). Research on meeting needs, for example health needs, focuses on the malleable elements of individual behavior and, as such, these are the social-cognitive aspects of behavior. The underlying assumptions of approaches that focus on these elements, for example the prototype willingness model (PWM), are that behavior is planned by weighing up the costs and benefits of behavioral outcomes. A significant aspect of this model is the relationship between *intention and behavior*. However, researchers demonstrate that individuals do not always behave as they intend, even when it is in their best interests to do so. Other models introduce further complexity to such models by incorporating intuitive or heuristic elements to account for variations in behavior over and above a rational actor approach (Todd et al., 2016). In addition, these approaches deal with planned behavior but also unplanned behavior.

Researchers have demonstrated some success in, for example, modeling risk behavior in adolescence using the PWM (Todd et al., 2016).

Importantly for research into terrorism, the predictive utility is limited in most research studies to specific and less complex behaviors, for example, smoking and unsafe sex. This raises the issue again regarding what questions we should be asking: which parts of the problem of terrorism are psychological problems and how should we break down and define the problem—what should we be focusing on?

This gets to the very heart of a significant problem with terrorism research related to so-called de-radicalization or disengagement (increasingly referred to as Countering Violent Extremism, CVE). Very simply put, the problem in this domain comes down to elaborating on what we are actually hoping to achieve. Are we hoping that individuals stop doing violence (Lynch, 2015), or are we looking for some cognitive affective change that we presume is directly related to the decision to engage in the act of terrorism (specifically violence)? Todd et al. (2016) point to some interesting limitations that might inform how we think about predicting behavioral outcomes and the nuances are highly relevant for terrorism and extremism. First, they point to the differences between adult and adolescent behavior, particularly for risky behavior; they also refer to the need to examine gender differences in decision-making; furthermore, they refer to the role of drugs and alcohol in influencing behavior, along with the importance of willingness and intention in determining outcomes. Importantly, they also point to the changes in behavioral choices as the behavior becomes more routine, implying of course that the longer a person engages in the risky behavior, the more complex, or at least nuanced, the decision-making process becomes. Applied to the case of terrorism, the behavior and intention of those who engage in terrorist acts might need to be viewed using a wide-angle lens. This would involve taking a time-series approach but also considering all the social, political, ideological, intra- and intergroup factors that make up the story of engagement in such acts, but analyzed in a more defined, specific, and narrow way.

Problem Framing and Problem Definition

If we think about terrorism as a unified, identifiable phenomenon, it is reasonable to suggest that it is overwhelmingly complex. In an effort to simplify how we can think about terrorism for the purpose of research, but more specifically for the purpose of psychological research, it is worth considering that terrorism as a phenomenon involves two frames: the political and the individual. The political carries with it all of the assumptions that we outlined earlier, but the individual should be the focus of psychological analysis. Now, that is not to isolate the individual from their environment, and we draw on the ecological framework advocated by Bronfenbrenner (Ashiabi & O'Neal, 2015) to demonstrate the complex interactions that are a part of the individual. But separating the political from the personal in the context of terrorism research is, in effect, making the space for a psychological analysis of the relevant actors. The aim of this approach is to strip the subject of the political baggage and jargon that so often accompanies it with the aim of understanding the subject in its own right, separate from the politicized labels, limitations, boundaries, and expectations of higher order definitions (Lynch & Joyce, 2018)

As a first step, this dual process of narrowing the focus and identifying/defining the problem needs to be informed by our desired outcome—what we are looking to achieve in the research process. For example, are we looking to categorize observable behavior or are we looking to inform or develop behavior change initiatives? Are we seeking to understand decision-making by terrorist actors or are we looking to critique existing psychological approaches to understanding terrorism? The starting point is, however, not the research question, but the problem framing—what are we talking about when we talk about terrorism and what is the specific problem we need to address?

A useful example of how we might define the problem of terrorism, both as a universal behavioral phenomenon and a specific psychological process, is to consider extremism as a framework. The actions of individuals who participate in terrorism and terrorism-related activities can reasonably be defined as extreme (Kruglanski et al., 2017). Involvement in terrorism is rare, as such, it is best thought of as a behavioral outlier; involvement in the violence of terrorism is even rarer. This means that access to meaningful data on these individuals and groups is limited both by the low incidence of terrorist activity as well as by the difficulty in collecting data on individuals involved in clandestine activity. Given these inherent problems of the field, this is where the focus on the individual actor (in context) and a *definition of the problem* approach become relevant. The problems we associate with data collection in the case of terrorism are problems of conceptual boundaries, exceptionalism around terrorism, and the construction of the terrorist actor as a societal other. If we consider our research population to consist of those individuals involved in terrorism, we will never overcome the data deficit that exists in the field. However, if we consider that the behaviors we are talking about are witnessed in abundance in other areas of human activity then we can expand both how we think about the terrorist actor and how we can make meaning of extremism and political violence. In addition, if we expand how we think about the terrorist actor and their interpersonal interactions, understanding terrorist activity becomes more about the interactions of the individual than the individual themselves.

To use a simplified example, if we look again at Bronfenbrenner's (Ashiabi & O 'Neal, 2015) ecological model of human development that positions the individual at the center of a sphere of influence that includes family, community, society, political, and religious institutions, then understanding the individual as the core of that process means understanding the dynamics of the interactions between the person and their immediate and remote social worlds. Such an approach means that even for the extremist actor, and even in the case of so-called lone actors, the individual is not truly isolated and understanding this individual then means understanding their interactions in and with this social world (Gill, 2015).

Importantly, while Bronfenbrenner's model is instructive it also raises the issue of the lifespan—where do we start the story? what elements of the person's life-history are relevant? is the contemporaneous reality the only relevant one? and how does the process of interpersonal interactivity change over time? Taking the example of extremism, and using Kruglanski's needs-based model as an example (Kruglanski et al., 2017, 2020), the authors address the process element of their framework by examining needs, and recognizing that needs change over time.

Finally, it is important to note that positioning terrorism in a framework of extremism, firmly situates it as a psychological problem that can be understood as the interaction of individual, group, and societal components. The recognition that extremism is a norm-based label gives hope that it will be generalizable as a principles-based approach to understanding terrorism rather than a definitional based approach.

We Are Where We Are

There has been a range of comprehensive reviews conducted that examine the state of play of terrorism research over the past 20 years, and a number of these were conducted by psychologists or serve to review psychological contributions to the field (Kleinot, 2017; Ranstorp, 2007; Schuurman, 2018; Silke, 2001, 2003; Victoroff, 2005). The aim of this chapter is not to revisit these analyses, because the key points are already well made, but to look at the very recent trends in the literature and to think about where we are going, considering where we have been.

If we look back over the past five years at research conducted specifically on terrorism and psychological processes, there are three themes that emerge.[1] One is a 'resurgence' (relatively speaking) of arguments that advocate for an increased role for psychoanalytic approaches to terrorism, another is a clinical psychological focus on mental health and measurement, and the third is an interdisciplinary perspective on terrorism that incorporates psychological research alongside disciplines like politics and criminology. With a view to understanding the current state of play of psychological research into terrorism, the remainder of the chapter will focus on these three trends and consider how they are (or are not) changing how we frame the problem of terrorism.

Psychoanalytic Psychology—Coming in from the Cold?

Psychoanalytic psychology is a field of studies that has made significant contributions to our understanding of human behavior, particularly aggression and violence, and importantly in the case of terrorism research, interventions for these problem behaviors. However, as mentioned, due to a widespread rejection of the non-scientific nature of the output from the field, there is currently little input from this area into our understanding of terrorism and political violence (see Horgan, 2017). Psychoanalytic psychology was also poorly represented in our understanding of terrorism due, as Cohen (2019) points out, to the process of individualization that occurred in psychoanalytic work whereby behavior was increasingly understood as an intra-psychic condition rather than one that incorporated social, political, and ideological conditions.

And while psychoanalytic psychology has contributed somewhat to the field of terrorism studies, even when psychoanalytic researchers attended to terrorism and political violence, the output has rarely attracted attention given what might be seen as an overreliance on circular speculations concerning the "terrorist psyche" and "unfalsifiable theories," which are widely rejected among academics and practitioners (Cohen, 2019). However, recently researchers have pointed to the complementarity of psychoanalytic psychology and its relevance for cognitive and social psychological models of TPV, especially considering the degree of what is unknown about emotionality, as well as unconscious and symbolic aspects of intergroup behavior and ideological driven violence (Cohen, 2019).

Increasingly in psychoanalytic work, researchers have pointed to the limitations of focusing on the individual and assumptions about individual motive and motivation. For example, El Din Aysha (2017) points to the need to understand seemingly irrational terrorist behavior (e.g., suicide terrorism) as a reaction to modernity, the prevailing cultural mood, and the role of political actors seeking to achieve some strategic goal. He astutely points out that individual psychological issues may also be a part of the story, but they are background issues of less concern than might have been previously thought. Importantly, the author points to the lack of individual psychopathology highlighted in the work of Ariel Merari (2010), among individuals who planned to or engaged in suicide attacks (and survived). This is, of course, not to say that individual pathology does not have a role in our understanding of terrorism, only that simplistic reductionist approaches to the application of psychology to TPV need to be treated with caution.

Recent literature points to the fact that lessons from psychoanalytic research and practice may open interesting avenues for investigation into terrorism and political violence. This is particularly the case with the therapeutic group or the large group. The "large group" is a term that is often referred to in psychology practice and research. There can be a therapeutic large group (e.g., an AA meeting) or there can be a transformative large group where members come together to resolve some issue. In addition, there can be a more general appraisal of the large group whereby it describes an undetermined amount of people who share the same sentiment about their large group identity. Examples of large groups include tribal group identity, most commonly expressed as a nationality, a religious group, an ethnicity (Volkan, 2018). This identity is something individuals are socialized into and while it is relevant as a group process, it is also profoundly relevant at an individual level. Theorists have long reflected on the relationship between mass movements and individual psychological processes. One of the most significant factors is the relationship between external challenges to the large group identity and a sense of social cohesion that manifests as anxiety chaos and panic (Volkan, 2018); this is highly relevant when we consider the riots in Washington DC on 6th 2021 as an example. In addition, the psychology of the large group brings history, patterns of thinking, chosen traumas (Pemberton & Aarten, 2017), and leader–follower relationships to bear on individual processes. In effect, the large group makes the past relevant and meaningful for individuals, thus the social identity of individuals serves to bring history, trauma, emotionality, culture, and meaning to an individual's interpretation of the world.

Large group psychoanalytic processes have particular relevance for the issue of boundaries and borders. For example, Volkan (2018) reflects on how a threatened group becomes preoccupied with both physical and psychological borders. He discusses the need to create significant differences between groups, so that the group distinctly identifies in opposition to the outgroup. This leads to a cascade process whereby the dehumanization of the outgroup occurs, a process of avoidance is normalized and, ultimately, the set up and maintenance of a psychological border. This barrier or border allows the creation of the other, an outsider status that is bestowed with characteristics that are at odds with the ingroup, thus representing a threat to the group. A key example of this is the immigrant other and the increasingly xenophobic reaction to immigration in politics but also more widely among the population.

In terms of how the problem is framed, this recent psychoanalytic research contributes to how we might conceive of the personal and the social, how we concern ourselves with the impact of history, culture, and trauma on the individual, along with how social groups become fragmented and borders created. Taking such an approach is somewhat similar to the concerns expressed by Moghaddam (Martin, 2017) whereby he points to the real problem of terrorism as being the divisions emerging in society due to the creation of borders and in-/outgroups rather than the specific and limited instances of violence. The sustainability of the problem of division is increasingly witnessed in US politics, and while the relationship to terrorism is more an issue of ideological than a psychological framing, the nature of the ingroup/outgroup divide is of concern.

Clinical Forensic Psychology and Research into Terrorism

Terrorism studies has always had a love/hate relationship with the issue of mental ill health but psychopathology has long been in the background as a key factor in how we understand and talk about terrorism (Khoshnood, 2017; Weatherston & Moran, 2003). However, preferences have swung from a blanket rejection of the role of mental health due to a lack of data, to a rejection of the causality inherent in a mental health explanation (Corner et al., 2016). There is an increasing recognition that, similar to the rest of the population, mental health is part of the story of involvement in terrorism. However, the issue with a focus on mental ill health and terrorism is the presumption that it serves to account, in some way, for the choice to engage in terrorism in a causative manner. This is to say that some form of vulnerability or altered cognitions facilitate involvement in terrorist activity. This approach, regardless of the severity of the clinical condition, is flawed. Any evidence to support such claims is absent from the large bodies of literature on clinical and forensic psychology from other domains. We know that behavior is complex, that mental illness is complex, and that involvement in terrorism is not a one-off event; it involves interpersonal relationships, planning, choices, etc. The role of mental ill health is but one component that may or may not be relevant.

This is largely recognized by those involved in the field as the literature on terrorism does point out that, on the whole, of the studies conducted on individuals who carried out suicide terrorism (perhaps the example more relevant when we are discussing mental health), there was no evidence of diagnosed individual psychopathology. Similarly, evidence from research with paramilitary groups points to the fact that psychopathology, where it is identified, is seen as a risk factor for the group and their mission (Horgan, 2006). However, there are significant research issues with many of the earlier publications on mental health and terrorism, including issues around selection effects, the prevalence of diagnosis at a distance, using nonclinical data as evidence of a mental health disorder, reliance on court data, assumptions of causality linking psychopathology and violence, and poor and incomplete data. These issues are still the main limiting factors for researchers in this area, but these problems with early research efforts very much tarnished the field. Recent work by Corner et al. (2016) sought to address these issues and has led to the production of a more nuanced and comprehensive analysis of how we might think about mental health and terrorism regarding prevalence, relevance, and the availability of data; however, limitations still exist.

Apart from the issues mentioned above, two further major issues exist with the approach that has long been taken around mental health and terrorism: one is that in the case of terrorism and mental health, there is a tendency to prioritize the severe end of the spectrum, for example, personality disorders/schizophrenia, and the other is the assumption that mental health can be causatively linked to violence. In the case of the former this focus on specific disorders has been generalized in the literature beyond what the data supports, and in the latter, there is no evidence to support any link between violence and psychopathology in the general population and certainly none in the terrorist population (Wehring & Carpenter, 2011). It is important to note that the only reliable evidence that does exist regarding violence and individuals with severe mental health issues, is that these individuals are significantly more likely to be the victims of violence than the rest of the population (Wehring & Carpenter, 2011). And this brings us to an important point which is that we are not talking about a population! When we speak about mental health in a general way, we are usually referring to things like prevalence in the population—the entire population of say children, or teenagers or those in psychiatric institutions or male adults etc. Terrorist actors are not a population, they do not share characteristics such as personality or demographic characteristics nor do they participate in the same activities. Corner et al. (2016) point out that a significant flaw in the research is the assumption that the terrorist population is coherent and can be theorized as such. At the simplest level, there is significant role differentiation in a terrorist group, and this approach also fails to account for state terrorism as it focuses specifically on the substate group; also the issue of lone wolves versus members of a hierarchical organization exists; the overlap with organized crime membership is relevant; and the significant differences that exist between and within groups should be attended to.

Another issue of relevance in the case of mental ill health and terrorism is that of negative function and diagnosis. In the terrorism literature the preoccupation is with finding evidence of mental health disorders, the holy grail of course being an actual previous clinical diagnosis, with data from court reports following closely behind. The issue of functioning is important because in the case of mental health diagnosis, the diversity of functioning even within the same category of disorder is substantial. Among clinicians a diagnosis based on clinical criteria from the DSM is but one piece of information used to assess a client, and a hugely relevant part of the story is the *functional impact* of the condition on the individual's day-to-day life. This is missing from the research on terrorism both because we do not have the relevant data from clinicians and because the literature is often isolated from the main bodies of work in the field.

The literature that exists on mental ill health and terrorism has a general consensus around the (non-)issue of causality—however, this is not the end of the debate. As with other areas of terrorism research, the issue of how we frame the problems is still highly relevant. Rather than attempting to understand any causative relationship, the question becomes: given that an extremist population is an outlier from the general population (Kruglanski et al., 2020), is there some significant difference in the relevance of mental ill health among this population? In other words, what mental ill health diagnosis predisposes individuals to, or arises from, involvement in a terrorist group and/or terrorist activity? If the data supports the significance of any such findings, what does this mean in terms of behavior functioning and the *doing* of terrorist violence?

We do know from significant research on police and the military from criminological research, that there is a psychological cost to violence for the perpetrator and that harming or killing another person leads to an increased risk of developing a psychiatric condition. Research on police who killed or injured someone while on duty demonstrates a significant association with PTSD symptoms (Komarovskaya et al., 2011) and research with members of the military show similar findings (Grossman, 2014). Importantly, both refer to the impact of the context of the violence and refer to the degrees of trauma based on the identity of the victim. For example, the killing of noncombatants, the injuring of women and children, and a lack of social support in the aftermath of the violence all have a role to play in the manifestation, or not, of symptoms of psychological distress in the perpetrator. This, of course, has implications for how we think about interventions with these perpetrators after the fact, but it should also be part of the debate on mental health and terrorism more broadly.

Research that examined the mental health of individuals who participated in the Rwandan genocide pointed out that perpetrators exhibited a high degree of psychiatric morbidity, particularly PTSD and related disorders, as well as depression after the fact (Schaal et al., 2012). Interestingly, this article had a large female perpetrator sample, which is rare, and the findings demonstrated that female perpetrators were equally likely (but not more so) to demonstrate psychiatric symptoms. However, the severity of trauma for these women was dose dependent (i.e., the more trauma, the more severe the symptoms). These research endeavors further problematize the presumed correlation between mental ill health and the decision to become involved in terrorism. Research suggests that it is their involvement in terrorist acts that may (in certain instances) be corrosive to mental health. This brings us back to the age-old question of what came first—the chicken or the egg? Or in this case, did mental ill health lead to involvement in terrorism or did involvement in terrorism contribute to mental ill health? Unfortunately, we simply do not have the datasets large enough to unpack this question. The best that can be hoped for, in terms of ethical research, is to refrain from the joining of dots in the absence of data points.

Ultimately what recent research on the psychology of terrorism tells us is that there is a substantial role for clinical and forensic psychological research. However, to date, the work that has focused specifically on the perpetrators of terrorism and political violence has fallen victim to the exceptionalism that is inherent in the field of terrorism studies. Focusing again on the big bang questions, the field has sought answers that would separate the terrorist actor from the mainstream population, and similarly sought to identify the exceptional elements of those individuals. There is huge potential in this subfield to contribute to our understanding of the processes of terrorism, from issues of trauma and recovery, to prison intervention and managing individual needs and expectations. Lessons from forensic psychology are particularly relevant here. Again, in thinking about the questions we are asking, we need to consider the strengths of the field, the evidence base available, the framing of the problem of terrorism, and to ensure that the politicization of the phenomenon does not further impact on the analysis.

Lessons from Other Domains, Psychological Research, and Interdisciplinarity

As mentioned, the key psychological questions in terrorism research relate to why and what kind of people become members of a terrorist organization. We have also repeatedly pointed to the issue of determining what parts of terrorism research should be seen as psychological problems. The natural conclusion from the discussions above must first be that not all elements of what we refer to as terrorism are amenable to psychological analysis and so contributions from other disciplines are essential. From what we know about process of involvement in terrorism, the pathway involves opportunity, peer network involvement and influence, a family history of involvement, elements of chance, etc. (Horgan, 2008). Despite the bespoke research on terrorism addressing these issues, there are substantial bodies of work from other disciplines that are of direct relevance. For example, there are decades of useful data from criminological research that can speak to the issue of involvement in deviant, subversive, and clandestine groups, not terrorist in nature, but psychologically and sociologically similar organizations (LaFree & Freilich, 2017).

Much like psychology, criminology was slow to attend to the issue of terrorism, and is only recently starting to attend directly to it. However, recently criminological research on gangs and violence is increasingly being referenced in relation to terrorism (LaFree & Freilich, 2017). In addition, foundational work in criminology is of substantial use for psychologists researching involvement in terrorism. For example, criminological work on violence was carried out in the 1980s by the Criminologist, Terence Thornberry, who proposed the Interactional Theory to explain the violence carried out by streetgang members. In an effort to understand both the violence and the choice of individuals to engage in violence, he spoke of the issue of "selection"—the fact that the groups chose members who were already delinquent. He also drew attention to the issue of "facilitation" where the group provides opportunities for violence, and "enhancement" where the gang encourages increased delinquency. These selection and situational framings of gang memberships and violence are of considerable interest in the case of terrorism. It provides an antidote to the personogenic explanations that dominate the field. This approach has emerged in the terrorism studies field under the guise of the crime terror nexus (Globsec, 2019) where there have been efforts to identify those actors who are simultaneously involved in terrorism and crime, or have progressed from crime to terrorism (or vice versa). However, here again, the issue is more fundamental than crime or terrorism. The issue is more likely to be that identified by Thornberry of "facilitation" due to socioeconomic status, educational opportunities, grievance, victimhood etc. Understanding the psychological component of this approach and being involved in multidisciplinary research undertaking is key to ensuring a meaningful psychological analysis of the issue.

As mentioned earlier, lessons from research into gangs also has additional insights that are relevant in the case of terrorism and political violence, in particular in relation to the issue of mental health. We already know that there is a high prevalence of mental ill health in gangs (MacFarlane, 2019). A large-scale study evaluating psychiatric morbidity using standardized measures was carried out in 2013 (n = 4664) and it was discovered that by comparison with violent non-gang members, gang members were significantly more likely to have a mental health disorder. While similar data is not available in the case of terrorism, the work of Corner et al. (2016) and Gill (2015) has pointed to the necessity to consider that, in the case of terrorism, many of the same issues may be at play.

Expanding on this issue, we know that involvement in extreme groups, for example terrorist groups or violent street gangs, has implications for mental health after the fact. This often takes the form of substance abuse or trauma-related symptomology (MacFarlane, 2019). We also know that populations exposed to terrorism have increased morbidity and mortality attributable to substance use disorders in the long term (Kerridge et al., 2014). However, we know less about the specific predisposing factors. In the literature on terrorism, drug use after the fact is discussed both in relation to the victims/survivors of the violence, but also the perpetrators. However, there is limited knowledge about the use of illicit drugs by active members of a terrorist organization. We know that drug use by members of paramilitary groups and the general public was frowned upon by terrorism groups in Northern Ireland (Higgins & Kilpatrick, 2005). This, of course, does not mean that substance abuse was not an issue. Knowing the type and extent of drug use among group members might also provide us with important information in relation to group dynamics and the leadership processes that could be applied to the case of terrorism and political violence.

In the case of terrorism and political violence, drug use has been written about in theaters of war (e.g., Syria and Iraq, Afghanistan) and we know of paramilitary group involvement in the drug trade more generally. However, we know much less about individual drug use. Given the research on perpetrators of violence and mental ill health, and the anecdotal evidence of self-medication with illicit drugs in the aftermath of involvement in violence, it is reasonable to assume that there is a significant prevalence of drug use during and after involvement in terrorism. We know, for example, that paramilitaries in Northern Ireland closely controlled the drug trade (Higgins & Kilpatrick, 2005), they doled out punishment beatings, firebombed houses and targeted the friends and family of heroin users. Among some of the terrorist groups, there was no tolerance of heroin use, however, the groups were active in the control of the drug trade (Silke, 2000). Similarly, drugs like Fenethylline (Captagon) have long been trafficked by groups in the Middle East and Southeast Asia, but there are reports that it is used by paramilitary groups like ISIS/ISIL because of its psychostimulant properties (Al-Iman et al., 2017). Al-Wataify and Al-Dahmoshi (2019) point out that consumption of Captagon is linked to increased ferocity. Barker (2015) claimed that the ISIS Paris attackers in 2015 used Captagon, but it was unknown if they were under its influence at the time of the violence.

In addition, the use of such drugs, apart from the acute impact on violent behavior, has stark social consequences: loss of life, morbidity, increase in the incidence of crime etc. (Barker, 2015). For the individual, the costs are also severe; withdrawal symptoms may include depression and somatic symptoms and the long-term impacts of use include psychosis and hallucinations (Al-Iman et al., 2017). However distasteful it may appear to be to have to consider a compassionate approach to the needs of the perpetrators of terrorism, if we are to focus on a psychological approach (as opposed to a retributive approach) to preventing harm and aiding societal recovery then it needs to be considered as part of our response.

Borrowing from criminological research, it is clear that participation in violence toward others, and in particular, fatal acts of violence, has a devastating effect on the mental health of perpetrators of such acts. Research on mental ill health must not be used solely to "other" those involved in acts of terrorism as this approach brings us further away from identifying both the problem and the solution. Instead, it is possible to view the consequences of involvement in terrorism from a psychological perspective, and taking a person centred approach, by considering the effects of violence on those who perpetrate such acts. If we refuse to consider the possibility that those involved in violence are deserving of psychological understanding, we also refuse to consider the possibility of meeting their needs. Addressing the psychological effects of participation in terrorism can provide avenues to circumventing transgenerational transmission of political violence. Put simply: we cannot change what we do not acknowledge.

Extremism as a Psychological Process

Earlier we mentioned Kruglanski et al.'s (2020) use of *extremism* as a concept that encompasses the behaviors and processes we recognize as terrorism. This is one of the more useful developments in the field of terrorism studies in recent years as it represents a shift away from the use of political concepts, with vague psychological undertones, to more useful concepts that root behavior in the relevant societal norms. If we look at the emergence and usage of the term "radicalization," we can see how the analytical utility of such a term from a psychological perspective was overshadowed by the political and securitized assumptions inherent in its use. The term which emerged with a vengeance in the aftermath of 9/11 really told us everything and nothing at all. As Neumann (2013) pointed out, radicalization is what happens before the bomb goes off, but it does nothing to help us understand the choices and events that lead an individual to engage in extreme violence. More recently, the use of the term extremism has been increasingly used to refer to involvement in terrorist activity. This is both a reflection of the limitations of the use of the term terrorism, a recognition of the link between terrorist and non-terrorist behavior, and a realization that the legal, moral, and behavioral boundaries that have dominated terrorism research may not be so firm. As a psychological concept, extremism is much more appropriate. Extremism is a range of behaviors judged in comparison to the mainstream, and so captures the dynamics, degree, and idiosyncrasies of political violence in context.

Kruglanski et al. (2020) have embraced extremism as a psychological concept and an explanatory concept in the case of terrorism. The authors define extremism as the occurrence of "infrequent phenomena whose rarity results from a pronounced intensity or magnitude of their underlying motivation" (p. 2). Importantly, the antithesis of extremism is moderation, a state or occurrence that is determined by the consensus of the majority population. Importantly this has implications for how we think about the *end of terrorism* as well as *deradicalization* and what desistance might look like, but more about that later.

Extremism, whether it is related to political violence or not, is constructed as a psychological phenomenon. According to Kruglanski et al. (2020), extremism is represented as the failure of an individual to fulfill the entirety of their basic needs through moderation, thus failing to achieve motivational balance. Simply put, when an individual fails to meet their basic needs, behavior that is prohibited yet serves to fulfill the unmet need is prioritized. The exceptional nature of this behavior may undermine the ability of the individual to meet other needs and this imbalance is undesirable for the individual, explaining why extremism is rare.

This approach differs from other explanations of terrorist behavior because it is normative, needs based, and universal. This means that the choice to engage in terrorism serves to meet a distinct individual need. Those involved in terrorist acts/organizations are no exception. All humans are driven to meet needs because meeting the need serves a purpose for them psychologically. The activity is only judged extreme in comparison to a reference group. Importantly, in this model, the authors point out that extremism can be as a result of one decision in which a particular need is prioritized over others, but also can be an ongoing state of being. However, they point out that the intensity and longevity of the choices are important. In one-off instances of extremism balance can be easily restored, but less so with prolonged ongoing instances of extremism. However, that is not to say that one choice to prioritize a particular need does not count as extremism. Importantly, because the imbalance is a cognitive process, rather than necessarily a behavioral act, narratives, social networks, and shared reality are all extremely relevant to understanding the process. Oftentimes the shared nature of a group-inspired/supported motivation can be long lasting.

However, the issue of motivation is somewhat moot without references to the behavioral actions that are taken to satisfy that need. In the case of Kruglanski et al. (2020), the means of achieving satiation are linked to values and expectancies, immediacy and effectiveness. Here again the narrative that supports the motivation to meet a need and the social network that informs it is relevant to the choice of behavior. However, research from other psychological subdisciplines points out that motivation and intent are not guarantees of action (Todd et al., 2016).

The implications of Kruglanski et al.'s (2020) model have significant consequences for how we think about intervening with individuals who have chosen extremism. For example, the cognitive consequences of motivational imbalance in the case of terrorism are selective attention, cognitive preoccupation, projection of the need onto others, and a focus on satisfying the need in multiple ways. What this means is that the individual can become focused on goal fulfillment, while sacrificing other personal and social goals (e.g., relationships etc.), and breaking social norms (e.g., laws) to achieve the goal. However, the cost of neglecting basic needs does mean that extreme behavior will always be a low prevalence phenomenon. Importantly, however, the supportive role of particular narratives and group support should be seen as potential tools for elongating the motivational imbalance.

While the focus on extremism does not address the entirety of the issue of terrorism, it certainly does frame it in a manner that is conducive to psychological analysis. Earlier we referred to the process of behavior change and the PWM model and how this might inform how we think about decision-making, motivation, intent, and behavior. The focus on extremism and, in particular, needs-based analysis of decision-making fits in part into the existing frameworks within psychology on decision-making and thus there is significant potential to develop our understanding of the phenomenon in this domain.

Conclusion

Much research in social sciences is concerned with the research of the gaps, we speak of gap analysis, bridging the gaps, and overcoming gaps in knowledge, and this is, of course, a noble venture, for knowledge is always needed. However, when combined with the academic aspiration for uniqueness, innovation, and novelty this search for the gaps becomes not about creating knowledge but carving out a space where one's research is exclusive. There is an element of this in all research areas, and the nature of academic higher degrees and the competitive nature of academia overall facilitates this, but the gaps are not always the place where knowledge can be developed in a conceptually well-grounded manner. In terrorism research we often see novel contributions from one-time authors (Silke, 2003), who contribute a unique piece to a terrorism journal and then return to their own field. Equally we see a proliferation (although less so now) of individual case studies examining outlier cases of terrorism and political violence that add to the field, but not in a sustainable way (see for example the 2011 REA from Bouhana and Wikström). However, the process of *doing* psychology does not lie in the novelty but in the mundane research into human behavior; it lies in the conceptual development based on well-thought-out research questions and problem framing; and it lies in the interdisciplinarity that is essential in order to allow psychology to attend to the big social issues of our time—in our case, terrorism. This is not to dismiss terrorism research and researchers, but it is to point out that the process of doing research on the psychology of terrorism is fundamentally about going back to first principles and describing and conceptualizing the phenomenon under investigation as a psychological problem.

Research on psychology serves numerous purposes from clinical assessment to cross-cultural research. The special burden experienced by psychological research is that of having to explain, and intervene in, complex social phenomena that are both cognitive and behavioral in origin and manifestation. However, psychology also has the tools available to it in the form of research methods to address the issues inherent in dealing with human participants (Rozen, 2001). The aim of this chapter is not to claim that where we have arrived at is incorrect, but to take a moment to consider where we are going. Most importantly, how do we as psychologists speak to the big social issues of our time?

In 1934, Shepard Dawson pointed out that social problems are partly material and partly mental. She further stated that the really serious problems in life are about the interpersonal cooperation between individuals in a society. Nearly 80 years later Professor Steve Reicher (2021) pointed out that, along with the material and the mental, the structural and the social are key to understanding the dynamics in society that lead to major social issues. Groups are not groups due to some innate process but due to macro societal factors that are manipulated to various ends.

With this in mind it must be noted that psychology is not value neutral. Psychology is not the objective quantification of observable behavior in a vacuum, but a reflection of all the societal dynamics that contribute to individual and group behavior. That said, the psychology of terrorism must capture that complexity and conceptualize any relevant processes in a meaningful and honest manner.

Note

1 A search for all output type from 2015 to 2020 was conducted using ONESEARCH. The search criteria were: Psychology/psychological AND Terrorism AND Processes in all combinations.

References

Al-Iman, A., Santacroce, R., Roman-Urrestarazu, A., Chilcott, R., Bersani, G., Martinotti, G., & Corazza, O. (2017). Captagon use and trade in the Middle East. *Human Psycho-pharmacology*, 32(3).

Al-Wataify, A.F., & Al-Dahmoshi, H.O.M. (2019). Rapid screening of addiction associated drug among long term prisoners. *Drug Invention Today*, 12(3), 572–576.

Argomaniz, J., & Lynch, O. (2016). *Victims and perpetrators of terrorism*. London: Routledge.

Ashiabi, G.S., & O'Neal, K.K. (2015). Child social development in context: An examination of some propositions in Bronfenbrenner's bio-ecological theory. *Sage Open*, 5(2), DOI 10.1177/2158244015590840.

Bankoff, G. (2003). Regions of risk: Western discourses on terrorism and the significance of Islam. *Studies in Conflict & Terrorism*, 26(6), 413–428.

Barker, A. (2015). Captagon: Evidence Paris attackers used 'jihadist's drug' favoured by Islamic State fighters. Available at: www.abc.net.au/news/2015-11-24/captagon-the-drug-that-kept-the-paris-attackers-calm/6970464. Accessed December 10, 2020.

Botticher, A. (2017). Towards academic consensus definitions of radicalism and extremism. *Perspectives on Terrorism*, 11(4), 73–77.

Bouhana, N. (2019). The moral ecology of extremism: A systematic perspective. Prepared for the *UK Commission for Countering Extremism Paper Series*. Available at: https://assets.publishing.service.gov.uk/government/uploads/system/uploads/attachment_data/file/834354/Bouhana-The-moral-ecology-of-extremism.pdf. Accessed January 1, 2021.

Bouhana, N., & Wikström, P.H. (2011). *Al Qaida influenced radicalisation: A rapid evidence assessment.* Occasional paper 97, the Home Office UK. Available at: https://assets.publishing.service.gov.uk/government/uploads/system/uploads/attachment_data/file/116724/occ97.pdf.

Cohen, S.J. (2019). The unconscious in terror: An overview of psychoanalytic contribution to the psychology of terrorism and violence radicalisation. *International Journal of Applied Psychoanalytic Studies*, 16(4), 216–228.

Corner, E., & Gill, P. (2015). A false dichotomy? Mental illness and lone-actor terrorism. Law and Human Behavior, 39(1), 23–34.

Corner, E., Gill, P., & Mason, O. (2016). Mental health disorders and the terrorist. *Studies in Conflict and Terrorism*, 39(6), 560–568.

Dawson, S. (1934). Psychology and social problems. *Nature*, 134, 517–520. Available at: www.nature.com/articles/134517a0. Accessed February 15, 2021.

El Din Aysha, E. (2017). Islamist suicide terrorism and Erich Fromm's social psychology of modern times. *Journal of Social and Political Psychology*, 5(1), 82–106.

Evans, S.C., Reed, G.M., Roberts, M.C., Esparza, P., Watts, A.D., Correia, J.M., Ritchie, P., Maj, M., & Sazena, S. (2013). Psychologists' perspectives on the diagnostic classification of mental disorders: Results from the WHO-IUPsyS Global Survey. *International Journal of Psychology*, 48(3), 177–193.

Frisby-Osman, S., & Wood, J.L. (2020). Rethinking how we view gang members: An examination of affective behavioural and mental health predictors of UK gang involved youth. *Youth Justice*, 20(1–2), 93–112.

Gill, P. (2015). *Lone actor terrorism: A behavioural analysis*. London: Routledge.

Gill, P., & Corner, E. (2017). There and back again: The study of mental disorder and terrorist involvement. *American Psychologist*, 72(3), 231–241.

Globsec (2019). From criminals to terrorists and back. Report available at: www.globsec.org/projects/criminals-terrorists-back/. Accessed November 10, 2020.

Grossman, D. (2014). *On killing*. London: Open Road Media.

Hacker, F.J. (1976). *Crusaders, criminals, crazies: Terror and terrorism in our time*. New York: W.W. Norton.

Hergenhahn, B.R., & Henley, T.B. (2014). *An introduction to the history of psychology*. Stamford, CA: Wadsworth Cengage Learning.

Higgins, K., & Kilpatrick, R. (2005). The impact of paramilitary violence against heroin user community in Northern Ireland: A qualitative analysis. *International Journal of Drug Policy*, 16(5), 334–342.

Horgan, J. (2006). *The psychology of terrorism*. London: Routledge.

Horgan, J. (2008). From profiles to pathways and roots to routes: Perspectives from psychology on radicalization into terrorism. *The Annals of the American Academy of Political and Social Science*, 618, 80–94.

Horgan, J. (2017). Psychology of terrorism: Introduction to the special issue. *American Psychologist*, 72(3), 199–204.

Jackson, R., Smyth, M.B., & Gunning, J. (Eds.). (2009). *Critical terrorism studies: A new research agenda*. Abingdon: Routledge.

Jasko, K., Webber, D., Kruglanski, A.W., Gelfand, M., Taufiqurrohman, M., Hettiarachchi, M., & Gunaratna, R. (2020). Social context moderates the effects of quest for significance on violent extremism. *Journal of Personality and Social Psychology*, 118(6), 1165–1187.

Kaczkowski, W., Lokmanoglu, A., & Winkler, C. (2019). Definitions matter: A comparison of the global terrorism database and the U.S. governmental reports of terrorist incidents in Western Europe, 2002–2016. *Cambridge Review of International Affairs*, DOI: 10.1080/09557571.2019.1705246.

Kampf, H.A. (1980). On the appeals of extremism to the youth of affluent, democratic societies. *Terrorism: An International Journal*, 4, 161–193.

Kerridge, B.T., Khan, M.R., Rehm, J., & Sapoka, A.M. (2014). Terrorism, civil war and related violences and substance use disorder morbidity and mortality: A global analysis. *Journal of Epidemiology and Global Health*, 4(1), 61–72.

Khoshnood, A. (2017). The correlation between mental disorders and terrorism is weak. *British Journal of Psychology Bulletin*, 41(1), 56.

Kleinot, P. (2017). One man's terrorist is another man's freedom fighter: A selected overview of the psychoanalytic and group analytic study of terrorism. *Psychoanalytic Psychotherapy*, 31(3), 272–284.

Komarovskaya, I., Maguen, S., McCaslin, S.E., Metzler, T.J., Madan, A., Brown, A.D., Galatzer-Levy, I.R., Henn-Haase, C., & Marmar, C.R. (2011). The impact of killing and injuring others on mental health symptoms among police officers. *Journal of Psychiatric Research*, 45(10), 1132–1336.

Kruglanski, A.W., Jasko, K., Chernikova, M., Dugas, M., & Webber, D. (2017). To the fringe and back: Violent extremism and the psychology of deviance. *American Psychologist*, 72(3), 217–230.

Kruglanski, A.W., Szumowska, E., Kopetz, C.H., Vallerand, R.J., & Pierro, A. (2020). On the psychology of extremism: How motivational imbalance breeds intemperance. *Psychological Review: Advance Online Publication.* https://doi.org/10.1037/rev0000260.

LaFree, G., & Freilich, J.D. (2017). *The handbook of the criminology of terrorism*. London: Wiley and Sons.

Lynch, O. (2013). British Muslim youth: Radicalisation, terrorism and the construction of the "other." *Critical Studies on Terrorism*, 6(2), 241–261.

Lynch, O. (2015). Desistance and deradicalization: The case of Northern Ireland. In S. Zeiger & A. Aly (Eds.), *Countering violent extremism: Developing an evidence base for policy and practice*. Sydney: Curtin University, pp. 111–119.

Lynch, O. (2021). Terrorism. In D.A. Crighton & G. Towl (Eds.), *Forensic psychology*. London: Wiley-Blackwell, pp. 372–390.

Lynch, O., & Joyce, C. (2018). *Applying psychology: The case of terrorism and political violence*. London: Wiley-Blackwell.

MacFarlane, A. (2019). Gangs and adolescent mental health: A narrative review. *Journal of Child and Adolescent Trauma*, 12, 411–420.

Marks, D.F. (2018). American psychologists the Central Intelligence Agency and enhanced interrogation. *Health Psychology Open*, 5(2).

Martin, S. (2017). 4 questions for Fathali M. Moghaddam. *Monitor on Psychology*, 48(4), 25–26.

Merari, A. (2010). *Driven to death: Psychology and social aspects of suicide terrorism.* Oxford: Oxford University Press.

Muldoon, O., & Downes, C. (2007). Social identification and post-traumatic stress symptoms in post-conflict Northern Ireland. *British Journal of Psychiatry*, 191, 146–149.

Neumann, P.R. (2013). The trouble with radicalisation. *International Affairs*, 89(4), 873–893.

Pemberton, A., & Aarten, P.G.M. (2017). Narrative in the study of victimological processes in terrorism and political violence: An initial exploration. *Studies in Conflict and Terrorism*, 4, 541–556.

Perez-Alvarez, M. (2018). Psychology as a science of subject and comportment beyond the mind and behaviour. *Integrative Psychological and Behaviour Science*, 52, 25–51.

Ranstorp, M. (Ed.). (2007). *Mapping terrorism research.* London: Routledge.

Reicher, S. (2021). For psychologists the pandemic has shown peoples capacity for cooperation. *The Guardian*, January 2. Available at: www.theguardian.com/commentisfree/2021/jan/02/psychologists-pandemic-cooperation-government-public-britain. Accessed January 3, 2021.

Rozen, P. (2001). Social psychology and science: Some lessons from Solomon Asch. *Personality and Social Psychology Review*, 5(1), 2–14.

Schaal, S., Weierstall, R., Dusingizemungu, J.P., & Elbert, T. (2012). Mental health 15 years after the killings in Rwanda: Imprisoned perpetrators of the genocide against the Tutsi versus a community sample of survivors. *Journal of Traumatic Stress*, 25, 446–453.

Schmid, A., & Jongman, A. (1988). *Political terrorism: A new guide to actors, authors, concepts, data bases, theories and literature.* Oxford: North Holland.

Schuurman, B. (2018). Research on terrorism, 2007–2016: A review of data, methods, and authorship. *Terrorism and Political Violence*, 32(5), 1011–1026.

Silke, A. (2000). Drink drugs and rock n'roll: Financing loyalist terrorism in Northern Ireland. Part two. *Studies in Conflict & Terrorism*, 23(2), 107–127.

Silke, A. (2001). The devil you know: Continuing problems with terrorism research. *Terrorism and Political Violence*, 13(4), 1–14.

Silke, A. (2003). Cheshire cat logic: The recurring theme of terrorist abnormality in psychological research. *Psychology Crime and Law*, 4(1), 51–69.

Silke, A. (2007). The impact of 9/11 on research on terrorism. In M. Ranstorp (Ed.), *Mapping terrorism research.* Abingdon: Routledge.

Soule, J.W. (1989). Problems in applying counterterrorism to prevent terrorism: Two decades of violence in Northern Ireland reconsidered. *Terrorism*, 12(1), 31–46.

Stachl, C., Ramona Schoedel, Q.A., Gosling, S.D., Harari, G.M., Buschek, D., Volkel, S.T., Schuwerk, T., Oldemeier, M., Ullman, T., Hussman, H., Bischl, B., & Buhner, M. (2020). Predicting personality from patterns of behaviour collected with smartphones. *PNAS*, 117(30), 17680–17687.

Stampnitsky, L. (2013). *Disciplining terror.* Cambridge: Cambridge University Press.

Stevens, J.R. (2017). Replicability and reproducibility in comparative psychology. *Frontiers in Psychology*, 8(862) https://doi.org/10.3389/fpsyg.2017.00862.

Taylor, M. (2014). It I were you I wouldn't start from here: Response to Marc Sageman's "The stagnation in terrorism research." *Terrorism and Political Violence*, 26(4), 581–586.

Todd, J., Kothe, E., Mullan, B., & Monds, L. (2016). Reasoned versus reactive prediction of behaviour: A meta-analysis of the prototype willingness model. *Health Psychology Review*, 10(1), 1–24.

Tschantret, J. (2020). The psychology of right wing terrorism: A text-based personality analysis. In *The psychology of violence*, online publication. Available at: http://dx.doi.org/10.1037/vio0000362.supp.

Victoroff, J. (2005). The mind of the terrorist: A review and critique of psychological approaches. *Journal of Conflict Resolution*, 49(1), 3–42.

Volkan, V.D. (1988). *The need to have enemies & allies: From clinical practice to international relationships*. Northvale, NJ: Jason Aronson.

Volkan, V.D. (1997). *Blood ties: From ethnic pride to ethnic terrorism*. New York: Farrar, Straus, & Giroux.

Volkan, V.D. (2018). Refugees as the other: Large group identity, terrorism and border psychology. *Group Analysis*, 51(3), 343–358.

Weatherston, D., & Moran, J. (2003). Terrorism and mental illness: Is there a relationship? *International Journal of Offender Therapy*, 47(6), 698–713.

Wehring, H.J., & Carpenter, W.T. (2011). Violence and schizophrenia. *Schizophrenia Bulletin*, 37(5), 877–878.

Wilkinson, P. (2011). *Terrorism versus democracy: The liberal state response*. London: Routledge.

Williams, M. (2020). *Preventing and countering violent extremism*. London: Routledge.

Wright, J. (2020). State terrorism: Are academics deliberately ignoring it? *Journal of Global Faultlines*, 6(2), 204–214.

2

Explaining Political Terrorism

Michael Stohl and Peter Grabosky

The attacks on September 11, 2001 virtually guaranteed that terrorism would become a dominant issue confronting governments in the twenty-first century, inevitably concentrating the attention of journalists and scholars. And so it has. The 9/11 attacks also effectively guaranteed that it would be insurgent terrorism that dominated the framing of the problem. And indeed, it has continued to be the case that state terrorism remains both the less discussed and the deadlier form of terrorism. Unfortunately, much that has been written about terrorism, recently as well as in the past, has been impressionistic and/or polemical in nature. Thus, for example, Lum et al. (2006) found that of the more than 20,000 articles on non-state terrorism published between 1971 and 2003, less than 4 percent were based on an empirical analysis of terrorism data.

This chapter will examine *political* terrorism: violent acts aimed at, and communicated to, audiences for the purpose of realizing public policy goals or collective aspirations. It will necessarily allude to forms of terrorism canvassed in other chapters in this volume, because of their inherently political nature. For example, religious terrorism may have political ends, such as the establishment of a caliphate by Islamic fundamentalists. Equally, it may be used by governments or by non-state actors to intimidate or displace religious minorities. This neither began nor ended with Hitler, and has recently been evident in Myanmar, India, and Bosnia. Suicide terrorism originated long before the attacks of 9/11: The Assassins, who lived in the mountains of Syria and Persia nearly 1000 years ago, were known to sacrifice their lives to achieve their goals of eliminating political adversaries. Lynching was employed in the United States to control and intimidate former slaves and their descendants well into the twentieth century. Homophobic violence will not succeed in eliminating alternative sexualities, but it continues to discourage their public expression in many places around the world. Terrorism can be "home-grown" as well as international or exported: The Oklahoma City bombing of 1995, and the Mogadishu market bombing in 2017, with the latter claiming approximately 600 lives, are but two examples.

We seek in this chapter to summarize evidence-based research in answering the following questions:

1. What is terrorism?
2. Who engages in terrorist activity?
3. Why do they become engaged?
4. Is terrorism a successful method of attaining political goals?

Conceptualizing Terrorism

Terrorism has suffered from deficient and contested conceptualization and from its politicization as a tool of opprobrium. In addition to the many casual definitions of the term employed loosely in political discourse and journalistic accounts, Easson and Schmid (2011, pp. 99–200) have cataloged more than 250 different definitions employed in the academic and governmental literature. Hence, terrorism means different things to different people. Derived from the Latin word *terrere*, meaning to frighten, the term terrorism was originally employed during the French Revolution to describe intimidation by *government* (the Reign of Terror). Today, the term has been "captured" to some extent by those who use it exclusively in reference to insurgent violence by non-state actors. More generally, it has been used loosely as a term of disparagement by those who would discredit their adversaries. The social construction and selective application of the label has thus resulted in the debatable adage "one person's terrorist is another's freedom fighter." As one critic noted,

> The idea that one person's "terrorist" is another's "freedom fighter" cannot be sanctioned. Freedom fighters or revolutionaries don't blow up buses containing non-combatants; terrorist murderers do. Freedom fighters don't set out to capture and slaughter schoolchildren; terrorist murderers do. Freedom fighters don't assassinate innocent businessmen,

or hijack and hold hostage innocent men, women, and children; terrorist murderers do. It is a disgrace that democracies would allow the treasured word 'freedom' to be associated with acts of terrorists.

(Senator Henry Jackson, cited by Shultz, 1986, pp. 18–19)

We favor the following definition, as it focuses on the essence of terrorism rather than the institutional auspices or one's approval of the declared or presumed ends and justification of its perpetrator or target: "An act or threat of *violence* to create *fear* and/or *compliant behavior* in a victim or wider audience for the purpose of achieving *political ends*" (Stohl, 1988, p. 3). According to this definition, terrorism can be employed by governments, by non-state entities acting independently, and by state-sponsored actors or proxies.

We also wish to emphasize the core communicative constitution of terrorism which distinguishes it from other forms of political violence. Within almost all the definitions of terrorism (as illustrated by the examples provided by Easson & Schmid, 2011) there are key communication-related concepts that distinguish terrorism from other violent acts. These include *a message* of fear and/or power, the *purposeful intent of the sender* (the perpetrator), and two types of *receivers*: victim and audience. In terrorism, the actual victims (or inanimate objects, e.g., a building, airplane, or dam) of the violence are not the only targets of the perpetrator. The audience is almost always the significant target of the violence or the threat, and there are almost always multiple audiences. The purpose of the act of violence on a victim is to communicate a message. Further, the victims of the violent act must be distinguished from the multiple targets of the act, that is, the audience(s) of that violence. Second, the perpetrator/sender is employing the violence (or threat of violence) of that act to purposefully communicate/send a message, a message that contains not only violence but the threat of even more violence and, hence, fear and the power to harm.

Whether we examine insurgent or state terrorism, how the multiple audiences of the terror react is perhaps more important than the act itself and the instrumental victims who are direct casualties. Clearly, then, terrorists are primarily interested in communicating with the audience—not the victims. To reiterate, that is the core of what distinguishes the terrorist act from the violent act whose purpose is simply to harm the target itself (see Schelling, 1966, pp. 16–17).

At the same time, terrorists are also interested in creating or reinforcing the boundaries between and among the groups in the audience.

Terrorists employ their violence and the anticipated reactions of the audience to assist the process of boundary creation and maintenance. The victims are in the outgroup and the terrorist communicates that they are employing their violence on behalf of the ingroup. Therefore, the reactions of the audience are the most important part of the process in determining the actual success of both producing fear and creating boundaries. They are far more important than the original act of violence by the terrorist. The vast majority of those who receive that message in the contemporary global environment are not eyewitnesses in the event's locale; they are a member of the audience. As a consequence of the global media environment the anticipated reactions of the audience assist the process of boundary creation and maintenance. The result is that the reactions of the audience are the most important part of the process in determining the actual success of both producing fear and creating boundaries, and they are far more important than the original act of violence by the terrorist.

Institutional Auspices

Non-State Actors

Numerous terrorist groups in various locations around the globe have been active since the turn of the twentieth century. Most prominent among these in the public mind are the various Islamic fundamentalist groups such as the Islamic State of Iraq and Syria (ISIS), Al-Shabaab in the Horn of Africa, Boko Haram in West Africa, the Taliban in Afghanistan and Pakistan, Al-Qaeda in the Middle East, Lashkar-e-Taiba in Pakistan, Jamaa Islamiya (JI) in Indonesia, and Abu Sayyaf in the Philippines. But terrorism is by no means monopolized by Islamists. Until their demise in 2009, the Liberation Tigers of Tamil Eelam sought independence from Sri Lanka. In Europe, the Irish Republican Army and its offshoots have been less active since the Good Friday Accords and 9/11 attacks, which created a hostile environment for political violence in Western democracies. Nevertheless, there continue to be occasional incidents by the Real IRA. Similarly, the Basque separatist group ETA declared a permanent ceasefire in 2006, although occasional violent incidents were recorded as recently as 2009. A rising threat has also been seen in Europe and the United States from radical right, neo-Nazis, White nationalists, and Christian fundamentalists whose actions are most often characterized not as terrorism but under the particular criminal code violation that is designated by authorities. In the United States, these "right-wing" terrorists have posed the largest threat and committed the greatest number of attacks and plots during the period 1994–2020 (Jones et al., 2020). The attack on the US Capitol in January 2021 was consistent with this trend.

Non-state actors can also be individuals, unconnected to any movement or organization. So-called "lone wolf" terrorists may have a political agenda, whether explicit or diffuse. Timothy McVeigh's extreme indignation over the 1993 siege by Federal law enforcement officials in Waco, Texas resulted in the Oklahoma City bombing exactly two years later. A reclusive mathematician named Theodore Kaczynski sent carefully prepared package bombs through the post to selected individuals in the United States between 1978 and 1995. The "Unabomber" was protesting what he saw as the loss of human autonomy arising from modern organizations and technology. The neo-Nazi London nail bomber David Copeland, embarked on a solo bombing spree in 1999 aimed at the Black, Bengali, and Gay communities that left three people dead and 140 injured. Anders Breivik, killed 77 people in 2011, targeting the Norwegian Prime Minister and a camp for the children of the Norwegian Labor Party.

State Actors

The Soviet Union during the Stalin era (1922–1953), and Germany under Hitler (1933–1945), were terrorist states that dominated their subjects by the threat of extreme coercive force. In the twentieth century, they served as models for many subsequent examples of despotic rule, from Albania to Zimbabwe. They combined the underlying logic of Sun Tzu who suggested in *The Art of War*, "kill one and frighten ten thousand" (Sun Tzu, 1963, p. 76) with a bureaucratic approach to controlling their population. In addition to serving as a tool of domestic political repression, state terrorism can also occur across national frontiers. The 1983 attack on visiting South Korean officials in Rangoon (now Yangon) was the work of North Korean government agents. In July, 1985, officers of the French intelligence services sought to discourage protest against French nuclear testing in the Pacific. They sabotaged the Greenpeace vessel Rainbow Warrior, then berthed in Auckland, New Zealand, killing a photographer in the process. Libyan government operatives were responsible for the bombing of an airliner (Pan Am 103) over Lockerbie, Scotland in 1988. During the Apartheid regime,

South African assassins targeted officers of the African National Congress in Europe and elsewhere in Africa. Over the past decade, Russian agents have been active in the poisoning of dissident citizens in various locations. We will discuss further examples of state terrorism in the section on explaining terrorism below.

Hybrid Entities

Simply to classify terrorism as undertaken by state *or* by non-state actors is illusory. Just as a great deal of public activity today is the work of public–private partnerships, contemporary terrorism often takes a hybrid form. The degree of engagement can be represented by a continuum, from terrorist activity undertaken entirely under state auspices at one pole, to activity that is exclusively private at the other. The ordering of examples below will help illustrate this variation.

During the late 1950s and early 1960s the CIA engaged organized crime leaders in the United States to arrange the assassination of Cuban leader Fidel Castro. Cuban security proved impenetrable, and the partnership was unsuccessful (Central Intelligence Agency, 1967). Taiwanese intelligence agencies engaged a member of the Bamboo United organized crime group to kill a US resident opposed to the Taipei regime (Chin, 2003, p. 59).

In some cases, private actors may engage in terrorist activity without the knowledge or encouragement of state institutions. Such arms-length activity may evolve into a cooperative partnership under favorable circumstances. So it was that the Inkatha Freedom Party was assisted by South African State Security to assassinate members of their archrival, the African National Congress, during the Apartheid regime (Gottschalk, 2002).

As the above examples suggest, terrorism can be practiced by state, non-state, or hybrid actors against domestic and foreign targets. Organizational auspices may themselves be fluid. Insurgents who prevail in political struggles may become dictators, as the career trajectories of Mussolini, Mao, and Mugabe suggest (see also Mincheva & Gurr, 2013).

Crime and Terrorism

Certain forms of "ordinary" criminal behavior may entail terrorism; others may not. There are those criminal acts that are only incidentally terroristic. For example, violence between members of competing criminal organizations may result in the unintended death of, or injury to, bystanders. As fearsome as this may be, such collateral damage lacks political intent. Conventional extortionists create fear in their victims, but their objectives comprise self-enrichment, not political ends. Serial killers who remain at large may arouse widespread public anxiety, but their predatory behavior reflects personal, not political motivations. Some violent actors may have diffuse nihilistic goals, rather than explicit political objectives. The Japanese *Aum Shinrikyo* sect is one example. Likewise, criminal organizations may use acts of terror against other criminals. Gambetta reports on the Aryan Brotherhood, an infamous US prison gang, which would carry out a "demonstration" killing or stabbing when entering a new prison to terrorize the inmate population and assert their place in the hierarchy (Gambetta, 2011, p. 141).

By contrast, traditional criminal organizations may engage in terrorism to facilitate their core business. The symbolic communicative dimension of much Mafia violence is certainly obvious (Saviano, 2019). The violent acts of many organized criminals have been designed to intimidate law enforcement or judicial officials, or members of the public who might impede an organization's normal criminal activity. In March, 1952, a Brooklyn clothing salesman named Arnold Schuster recognized a notorious fugitive criminal, Willie Sutton, on a New York City bus, and informed the police. Schuster received some media publicity as a result. Within days, he was murdered outside his home, having been shot twice in the groin and once in each eye. In two separate incidents during the 1990s, the Sicilian Mafia assassinated investigating magistrates Giovanni Falcone and Paolo Borsellino, using explosive devices of astonishing ferocity. The assassinations were as expressive as they were instrumental, the message being that government officials who valued their own lives should be more tolerant of organized criminal activity. In the early twenty-first century, the Zetas, a notorious Mexican drug gang, eliminated uncooperative public officials and concerned citizens alike by means of indescribably brutal acts, and posted images of dismembered corpses on the World Wide Web to discourage prospective adversaries. Ruthless organized criminals may just as easily orchestrate the unobtrusive disappearance of a target, and often do so. But, when appropriate, explicit slaughter tends to reach a wider audience, and the message is unambiguous.

Who are the Terrorists?

Desire for status and respect resides in persons of both affluent and underprivileged backgrounds. While many terrorist recruits are "nobodies who want to be somebody," the relationship between economic disadvantage and terrorism is weak. Sageman's (2008, p. 48) systematic study of contemporary terrorists revealed that, as with historic revolutionary movements, a large majority came from middle-class backgrounds. One can be relatively comfortable in a material sense, but still feel profoundly disempowered. Umar Farouk Abdulmutallah, who was charged with the attempted bombing of an airliner in December 2009, came from one of the wealthiest families in Nigeria. Osama bin Laden himself was a rich man. A significant proportion of *Aum Shinrikyo* members were middle-class professionals. It is also important to note that while the majority of the foot soldiers of organizations that employ violence and terrorism are not well educated or middle class, they share with their leaders the disaffection and alienation associated with marginalization. When coming from diaspora communities, they perceive themselves removed from the certainties provided by being embedded in their homeland, real or imagined, contemporary or historical.

One can appreciate the attraction, especially for someone from fairly ordinary circumstances, of joining the vanguard of a revolution or holy war. Sageman (2008) suggests that glory may be a motivating factor behind suicide terrorism, although Merari (2010) found that there are no defining or predictive psychological or demographic characteristics of suicide bombers. The attraction of joining a powerful and (in the eyes of some) prestigious entity has proven no less seductive than that of joining a conventional military service. The desire for fraternity, camaraderie, or fellowship can also be an important factor in explaining why one joins a terrorist group Sageman (2004). This is particularly significant in modern pluralistic societies where migrants or members of ethnic or religious minorities may feel excluded from the dominant culture. One official attributed the attraction of the Philippine terrorist group Abu Sayyaf to "religion, thrills and joblessness" (quoted in Rosenthal, 2008, p. 64).

Explaining Terrorism

In this section, we explore political terrorism through two different lenses. The first focuses on the conditions that explain terrorist behavior by state actors. The second will analyze terrorism from the standpoint of the terrorist.

State Terrorism

Following Gurr (1986, pp. 62–67) one may identify three sets of conditions that affect the decision-making calculus of threatened elites: the situational, the structural, and the dispositional. *Situational* conditions include the political traits of challenges to the regime (the relative status and strategies of the state and its opponents) and the elites' own political resources for countering their adversaries' challenges, that is, the regime's strength and its police and military apparatus). *Structural* conditions are those that define elites' relations with their opponents and determine or constrain their response options. These include the state's position in the international system and the nature of social stratification and the elite's position within it. *Dispositional* conditions are those which can be expected to influence how elites regard the acceptability of strategies of violence and terrorism. Norms supporting the use of violence are shaped by elites' own direct or mediated experience with violent means of power; they are most effectively inhibited when the society has a strongly developed history of democratic values.

Duvall and Stohl (1983) and Stohl (1984) explored the considerations that states may make in choosing to employ terror against their own citizens and in assisting other states to do so. The underlying argument was that state decision makers pursued what Weiner (1972) refers to as an "Expectancy X Value" theory or expected-utility theory of motivation. Here "the direction and intensity of behavior is a function of the expectation that certain actions will lead to the goal, and the incentive value of the goal object." The argument assumes that an actor behaves in accordance with a basic calculation which consists of three main elements: (1) the benefits that the actor would receive from some desired state of affairs; (2) the actor's beliefs about the probability with which the desired state of affairs would be brought about if the actor were to engage in a particular action; and (3) the actor's beliefs about the probable costs or negative consequences that it would have to bear as a result of its engaging in that action. It assumes, therefore, that the greater the relative expected utility of terrorist action for an actor as compared to other forms of governance, the greater the probability that the actor will engage in terrorist action.

When governments consider the costs of engaging in terrorist behaviors, two kinds of costs can be distinguished: response costs and production costs. Response costs are costs which might be imposed by the target group and/or sympathetic or offended bystanders. When governments consider various means of governance, they are also attentive to the expected responses of others. What others are likely to do in reaction affects the utility of a particular strategy. Most relevant to a consideration of terrorism are what might be called punitive or retributive response costs to bystanders. The bystanders in the foreign-policy realm may include domestic and foreign audiences, while the target in international as in domestic affairs may be wider than the attacking party may have intended. Governments are sensitive to the costs imposed by other governments for their behaviors. Foreign-government diplomatic condemnations, sanctions, and trade embargoes push governments to caution or secrecy in terms of their "unacceptable" behaviors, such as state terrorism, repression, and other forms of human-rights violations.

In general, one does not think of governments and governmental decision makers as inaccessible in these terms, except to the extent that they completely insulate themselves from popular contacts, and to the degree that they are immune to international pressure. They tend to rely more on the second means of invulnerability, that is, secrecy of action. State terrorism can often be expected to be covert action because in this way the government effectively reduces its vulnerability to retaliation even below its vulnerability to the (otherwise lesser) response costs expected for other means of governance. This implies that, in general, state terrorism will not have publicity of its cause as an objective; this does not suggest that the government wishes the terror to be unknown, but rather that the government does not publicize its role and relies on the communication of the threat through word of mouth and rumors. Also, it means that as public accessibility to governmental officials is greater, and/or as regime vulnerability to international pressure is greater, terrorism is more likely to be secretive or carried out by paramilitaries whose connections to the government are officially denied. Both secrecy and proxies may facilitate plausible deniability by the responsible state.

States (and other terrorist actors) might choose terrorism paradoxically, both when they perceive themselves powerless—the sense that other policy instruments of rule are unavailable or less useful, and when they are in a situation that may be labeled confident strength—when the costs are perceived as low and the probability of success believed high in relation to other means (Duvall & Stohl, 1983). If terrorism is to be believed to be a relatively more effective means of governance, then, the government must estimate that terrorism will perform better than alternative means in eliminating or quieting some actual or perceived potential challenge or threat. This is a first important principle for explaining state terrorism.

Production costs are the costs of taking the action regardless of the reactions of others. In addition to the economic cost—paying the participants, buying weapons, and the like—there is the psychological cost of behaving in a manner that most individuals, under normal conditions, would characterize as unacceptable. The psychological costs that an actor can expect from perpetrating violence on an incidental, instrumental victim involves two conjoining factors. The first factor is the extent to which human life is valued (or, conversely, the strength of internalized prohibitions against violence in general). The second is the extent to which the victim can be or has been dehumanized in the mind of the violent actor. Where moral/normative prohibitions are weak, and especially where victims can be viewed in other than human terms, the self-imposed costs of terrorist actions are apt to be low and hence the choice of terrorist actions more frequent (Duvall & Stohl, 1983, p. 209).

The extent to which victims and potential victims can be dehumanized is affected by two important variables (for an extended discussion of this point see the seminal piece by Herbert Kelman, 1973). The first is the perceived social distance between the government and the victim population. The second is the extent to which action is routinely and bureaucratically authorized, so that personal responsibility is perceived by all actors in the decisional chain to be lower for governments (a) in a conflict situation with those they define as "inferior" and/or (b) with a highly bureaucratized coercive machinery. Thus, when violence against "the other" is routinely described in terms of attacks on "animals" or described in ethnic slurs and is bureaucratized, concerns of individual responsibility for those actions are dramatically reduced and "orders" are more easily carried out.

We are not accustomed to thinking of state behaviors beyond their border in terms of terrorism, but it is only by convention with respect to the language that is employed within the international relations literature that this is the case. Coercive diplomacy, which involves the threat of violence, provides a good entry point to understand state terror in international affairs. The idea of coercive diplomacy was recounted two and a half millennia ago in the Melian Dialogue within Thucydides' *History of the Peloponnesian War*, as the Athenians coerced the Melians to align with them against Sparta in the Peloponnesian War. After the Athenians threaten the Melians and the Melians complain that they don't want to go to war, the Athenian envoys remind the Melians that,

> "The strong do as they can and the weak suffer what they must".
> (Thucydides, 1988, p. 352)

The defining characteristic of coercive diplomacy as distinct from both diplomacy and traditional military activity is that the force of coercive diplomacy is used "in an exemplary, demonstrative manner, in discrete and controlled increments, to induce the opponent to revise his calculations and agree to a mutually acceptable termination of the conflict" (George, 1971, p. 18). We may speak of terrorism as a subset of coercive diplomacy when violence or its threatened use are present. Not all coercive diplomacy employs violence and thus not all coercive diplomacy is terrorism. For example, one may employ economic sanctions in an avowedly coercive manner, as did the members of the United Nations with respect to South Africa, or the United States with respect to Syria and North Korea, and the European Union placed on Russia for their Ukraine actions without employing violent tactics. Here, we wish to draw attention to the violence or the threat of violence within coercive diplomacy whose central task has been described as "how to create in the opponent the expectation of unacceptable costs of sufficient magnitude to erode his motivation to continue what he is doing" (George, 1971, pp. 26–27).

Thus, it is quite clear that certain forms of coercive diplomacy involve the threat and often the use of violence for what would be described as terroristic purposes were it not states who were employing the very same tactic. Thomas Schelling reminds us:

> The power to hurt is nothing new in warfare, but for the United States modern technology has dramatically enhanced the strategic importance of pure unconstructive, unacquisitive pain and damage, whether used against us or in our own defense. This in turn enhances the importance of war and threats of war as techniques of influence, not of destruction; of coercion and deterrence, not of conquest and defense, of bargaining and intimidation.
> (Schelling, 1966, p. 33)

One of the most notorious examples of coercive diplomacy was the Christmas bombings of North Vietnam by the Nixon administration in

1972. The Christmas bombing involved massive saturation runs over Hanoi and the rest of North Vietnam, and were code-named "Operation Linebacker II." They were ordered by Nixon after negotiations with the North Vietnamese had stalled because of South Vietnamese objections to the Kissinger–Tho proposed peace treaty. For 12 days, American B52s flew sortie after sortie "at levels of intensity and sustainment never before achieved in the history of warfare" (Kendrick, 1974, p. 383). Each B-52 carried about two dozen 500 lb. bombs and about 100 B-52s and 500 fighter-bombers flew round-the-clock raids. This was not a military attempt to secure territory or destroy military targets:

> Nixon's logic was that he was bombing for peace. He was trying to bomb Hanoi back to the negotiating table and trying to convince Saigon by this show of force, that he was loyal to his ally. Both parts of Vietnam, Nixon reasoned, would be ready to sign with the United States once the shock treatment was over. By this reasoning, much of Hanoi and Haiphong was reduced to rubble.
>
> (Stoessinger, 1976, p. 73)

Another example occurred in May 1975; the merchant freighter Mayaguez was seized by Cambodia within its territorial waters. Rather than employ traditional diplomacy and bargaining to end the problem, President Ford was persuaded by Henry Kissinger to coerce the Cambodians into releasing the ship and crew. Kissinger persuaded Ford to order air strikes against the port of Kompong Som and an amphibious assault on the island of Koh Tang (Gaddis, 1982, p. 333), and as a result the crew was released.

Non-State Terrorism

We can also apply Gurr's formulation to the correlates of non-state terrorism for insights into the conditions that relate to the occurrence of terrorism. Structural causal explanations for terrorism are those features of a society that constrain the behavior of the people living within it; they establish roles and define the allowable range of choices people have in how they can interact, and delimit their power to change the environment in which they fund themselves. "The structural variables in our theory include the nature of social stratification and the elite's position in it ... and the state's position in the international system" (Gurr, 1986, p. 65). Modifying Gurr's theory of state terrorism to apply it here, we focus on economic and political structures that establish and constrain regime and citizen. These are the fundamental "root-causes" behind the decision to employ political violence. Looking for a "root-cause" of terrorism suggests there is a causal relationship between underlying social, economic, political, and demographic conditions and terrorist activity. According to this proposition, certain underlying conditions and grievances help explain how, where, and why terrorism occurs. As a corollary, failing to understand the linkages between these underlying conditions and terrorist violence may result in inadequate counterterror strategy. More, according to this argument, an approach to counterterrorism that ignores this relationship may even exacerbate those conditions that gave rise to terrorism and could then intensify, or substantively change, the threat of terrorist violence.

According to Newman (2006) a consensus has developed around a cluster of "root-causes" that can either create permissive environments for terrorist violence, or directly contribute to the radicalization of a segment of a population. These are, generally: high unemployment, economic inequality, and social exclusion among heterogeneous groups; rapid population growth (with a "bulge" of young people) accompanied by rapid urbanization; and a clash of values. No single factor can be identified as "causing" terrorism and the mix of contributing factors can vary in different circumstances. However, sufficient evidence exists to recommend studying "root-causes" in conjunction with other contributing factors such as political stability. Political stability and the ability of a government to actually govern and resolve political crises are cited as belonging to its own category of attending causes (Piazza, 2008).

Situational variables describe the moves political forces make within a given structure. Sometimes these choices are explicit and implemented with authority, but sometimes—as in failed or failing states—these actions are the result of an inadequate capacity to govern effectively. The consequent relationships between political actors can be contentious, with adversaries free to act independently. The situations in which people find themselves can be differentiated from the structures that can constrain their behavior.

Dispositions

Dispositional conditions influence how individuals regard the acceptability of strategies of violence and terrorism. Frederick Hacker's (1976) shorthand, first published almost a half-century ago, describing terrorists as either criminals, crusaders, or crazies is a useful means of thinking about possible dispositional conditions. However, the dispositions by themselves have not proved efficacious in predicting the choice to employ terrorism. Summarizing the results of studies that explored these questions a decade ago, Victoroff (2005) remains the single best source of information on the lack of useful profiles or personality types arising from individual psychological approaches to the causes of terrorism. His conclusion is stark:

> The leading psychological theories of terrorism include a broad spectrum of sociological, psychological, and psychiatric approaches. Strikingly, virtually none of them has been tested in a systematic way. They are overwhelmingly subjective, speculative, and, in many cases, derived from 1920s-era psychoanalytic hypotheses that are not amenable to testing. Students of terrorism might justifiably conclude from the peer reviewed literature that the total number of published theories exceeds the number of empirical studies—an imbalance that may be of more than academic import. Even the small amount of psychological research is largely flawed, rarely having been based on scientific methods using normed and validated measures of psychological status, comparing direct examination of individuals with appropriate controls, and testing hypotheses with accepted statistical methods.
> (Victoroff, 2005, pp. 33–34)

Recognizing the limitations of the focus on the psychological profile in building knowledge of suicide bombers Merari (2010, p. 4) suggests an approach that should be more useful through the recognition that there are

> three main elements in the production of suicide bombers: the community from which the suicide bombers emerge, the group that decides to use suicide attacks as a tactic, and the individuals who are willing to sacrifice themselves in the attacks.

This approach is echoed in the recent examinations of the many different paths to radicalism (McCauley & Moskalenko, 2011). Lindekilde (2014) suggests that we also know "from the extant literature on radicalization that small group dynamics alone rarely leads to radicalisation (Horgan, 2008; Schmid, 2013) and thus the paths are not easily modelled." We also know that there are both many more people who approve of radical movements than participate in them and that both within radical movements and those that support them many fewer still who participate in violent acts.

Motives for terrorism can vary widely, and are not mutually exclusive. Terrorist groups tend to come into being as a result of intense political grievances. These can be varied and numerous. They need not be rational and justifiable to outsiders, or widely shared. What matters is their intensity. Members of a polity may perceive that they are being treated unfairly. They may see themselves as being denied political freedoms, civil rights, economic opportunities, respect, and other benefits enjoyed by others.

Other grievances may be experienced more widely within a society. Among the most familiar is the presence of unwelcome outsiders, usually in the form of military forces. Pape's (2005) study of suicide terrorists identified the common factor of indignation arising from the occupation of one's homeland by a foreign force. Colonial rule in general, and military occupation in particular, have been consistent sources of resentment. One can easily appreciate how an individual residing in a land governed by an oppressive and unaccommodating colonial power may resort to terrorist activity in furtherance of national liberation.

Experience of oppression need not always be personal or direct. Moral indignation may be aroused by vicarious experience, by legend, and by exposure to explicit depiction, the latter to an unprecedented extent in the digital age. Innes (2004) observes that even lesser slights, occurring closer to home, may create an environment for festering grievances. Knowledge of hate crime or discrimination may entail lasting damage. Perceived local injustice may be intensified by perceived global injustice, and vice versa.

Ironically, moral indignation may lead to a cascade. Moral indignation gave rise to the 9/11 attacks, which in turn produced the feelings of outrage that facilitated torture and assassination by US and allied interests. Images of blindfolded prisoners at Guantanamo and Abu Ghraib, or of women's and children's corpses in Iraq, served to mobilize hatred and to inspire action on that sentiment—at least on the part of those who identified with the victims.

Terrorism can also result from a desire for revenge, retaliation for some explicit harm or injustice. We have noted above the connection between the Waco Siege and the Oklahoma City bombing.

Strategic Calculations

Actors have many strategic and tactical reasons for choosing terrorism. The first (and according to many, the principal) purpose of terrorism is advertising the cause. The violence of the terrorist act is not intended simply to destroy but also to be heard. For a regime, the terror may be a message of strength (at least relative strength), a warning designed to intimidate and to demonstrate the willingness to use violence and thus to engender compliance without the need to physically touch each citizen. For insurgents, the terror is a message: we exist, we must be heard, and you may choose not to listen only at great risk. The impact of the violent act thus extends far beyond the immediate victims and the moment. It is a message wide in time and space. The more extensive the message, the more successful the act. Terrorists of the left and the right, governments and insurgents, are thus likely to choose their victims and targets with care to achieve maximum impact. This does not mean that they will not target "innocents" or avoid mass casualties, but rather that they will make their choice on the basis of what will create maximum impact with a maximum chance of success.

In discussions of insurgent terrorists, it is often remarked that these terrorists attempt to make themselves invulnerable. There are at least two means to this end. One is inaccessibility. Retaliators may know in general, or even in particular, who the terrorist is but be unable to locate him. The anonymity of refugee camps or urban areas, and physical mobility, provide this inaccessibility for insurgent terrorists. Insurgents seek safe havens among supporters or within populations (or states) which are unwilling to confront them and make the calculation to acquiesce to the presence of terrorists within their midst. One of the key elements of any counterterrorism strategy is the struggle to convince populations that the costs of offering safe haven—or simply allowing safe havens—are greater than the cost of assisting governments in eliminating such havens.

Terrorism may be intended to achieve explicit strategic objectives. Because it tends to be inherently newsworthy, terrorism can call attention to a grievance. Causes that might otherwise be ignored can receive extensive publicity, with a view toward mobilizing support. The cause of Palestine liberation first received widespread public attention because of dramatic terrorist attacks by the Palestine Liberation Organization and other groups. However, this may have proven to be counterproductive in the longer term (see La Free & Freilich, 2019).

Terrorism may also be used strategically by insurgent groups to provoke overreaction by a repressive state, leading to a loss of state legitimacy. This, too, poses risks of adverse unintended consequences for the terrorist.

States may also employ terrorism as strategies of warfare. The targeting of civilian populations by combatant groups pre-dates the rise of the modern state. The threat or use of indiscriminate violence against non-combatants became a core strategy during WWII, with attacks on English cities during the Blitz, and strategic bombing by the US and allies of population centers in Germany and Japan. Postwar US nuclear strategy was based on the threat of annihilating both the Soviet Union and the People's Republic of China. The details may have been secret, but the overall policy was not.

Does Terrorism Work?

Political terrorism is a high-stakes undertaking. From the standpoint of the insurgent, it has led, or at least contributed to, triumph—the outright seizure of power. The Cuban and Nicaraguan revolutions come immediately to mind; terrorism was central to their respective revolutionary strategies.

In other settings, terrorism has contributed to achieving a degree of accommodation that would not have been realized through gentler methods. The Northern Ireland Peace Accords are perhaps the most prominent recent illustrative example.

Nevertheless, history is littered with the remnants of terrorist groups who have failed miserably. From the Red Brigades in Italy, the Shining Path in Peru, the Organisation Armée Secrète in France, to the Aum sect in Japan, their existence was short-lived.

Similarly, state terrorism has also achieved mixed results. The Soviet Union remained formidable under Stalin; its eventual demise was driven by economic mismanagement combined with its futile attempts to compete with the United States in an arms race. The Democratic People's Republic of Korea has endured for half a century. Short of total victory, terrorist states may also be able to achieve concessions from, or accommodation with, their adversaries.

States that rely principally on terrorism for their viability can destroy themselves. The genocidal regime of Pol Pot, having eliminated a quarter of Cambodia's population, was sufficiently weakened, by this and by discord within the ranks of the military, that it left itself vulnerable to invasion by Vietnamese forces in 1978. Regime change followed.

Counterproductive Terrorism

Whether employed by state or non-state actors, terrorism can backfire. The Mafia assassinations of Judges Falcone and Borsellino precipitated an outpouring of rage on the part of the public, who quickly embraced government proposals for more intense pursuit of Mafia activities. The hospitality accorded by the Taliban government to Al- Qaeda provoked the US invasion of Afghanistan after 9/11. Today, terrorism in support of the Palestine liberation cause tends to provoke retaliatory action by the state of Israel. Indeed, terrorism has been employed by insurgents as a tactic for the express purpose of provoking overreaction on the part of the state.

The Prevention and Control of Terrorism

Non-State Terrorism

In recent years, state responses to terrorism have tended toward a "kitchen-sink" approach, involving general enhancement of state power at the expense of individual liberties. The People's Republic of China has undertaken the mass incarceration of a Muslim minority and has mobilized a system of surveillance without precedent in human history. Liberal-democratic states have enhanced powers of surveillance, arrest, and detention.

This flurry of activity serves a number of functions. By invoking the specter of external threat, then delivering draconian measures for prevention and control, democratic states seek to assure the public that their government is protecting them. In the years since 9/11 the Parliament of Australia has enacted over 75 separate laws relating to security. Cynics can be forgiven for concluding that some of these policies are mere tools of domestic politics.

Given the billions of dollars spent annually around the world on the prevention and control of terrorism, it is surprising that there has been a dearth of scientific research on the effectiveness of counter-terrorism strategies. A systematic review by Lum et al. (2006) identified over 20,000 purported evaluation studies, of which only *seven* were deemed to have been of sufficient scientific rigor for further scrutiny.

Of these, some reported measures that were ineffective, and others reported strategies that were shown to have *increased* the likelihood of terrorism or related harm. The introduction of metal detectors at airports reduced hijackings, but may have led to a displacement effect entailing increases in other terrorist tactics such as bombing and assassination. Resolutions enacted by the United Nations, fortification of embassies, and increasing the penalties imposed on hijackers appeared to have no effect. Retaliatory attacks by states against terrorists significantly increased terrorist attacks in the short term.

References

Central Intelligence Agency (US). (1967). *Report on plots to assassinate Fidel Castro* (1967). Available at: www.history-matters.com/archive/jfk/cia/80T01357A/pdf/104-10213-10101.pdf.

Chin, K.L. (2003). Black gold politics: Organized crime, business, and politics in Taiwan. In R. Godson (Ed.), *Menace to society: Political-criminal collaboration around the world*. New Brunswick, NJ: Transaction Publishers, pp. 257–283.

Duvall, R.D., & Stohl, M. (1983). Governance by terror. In M. Stohl (Ed.), *The politics of terrorism*. New York: Marcel Dekker, pp. 179–219.

Easson, J.J., & Schmid, A.P. (2011). 250-plus academic, governmental and intergovernmental definitions of terrorism. In A.P. Schmid (Ed.), *The Routledge handbook of terrorism research*. London and New York: Routledge, pp. 99–200.

Gaddis, J.L. (1982). *Strategies of containment*. New York: Oxford University Press.

Gambetta, D. (2011). *Codes of the underworld: How criminals communicate*. Princeton, NJ: Princeton University Press.

George, A. (1971). The development of doctrine and strategy. In A. George, D. Hall & W.R. Simons (Eds.), *The limits of coercive diplomacy*. Boston, MA: Little, Brown, pp. 1–35.

Gottschalk, K. (2002). The rise and fall of apartheid's death squads. In B. Campbell & A.D. Brenner (Eds.), *Death squads in global perspective: Murder with deniability*. New York: Palgrave Macmillan, pp. 229–260.

Gurr, T. (1986). The political origins of state violence and terror: a theoretical analysis. In M. Stohl & G. Lopez (Eds.), *Government violence and repression: An agenda for research*. Westport, CT: Greenwood Press, pp. 45–71.

Hacker, F. (1976). *Crusaders, criminals, crazies*. New York: W.W. Norton.

Horgan, J. (2008). From profiles to pathways and roots to routes: Perspectives from psychology on radicalization into terrorism. *The Annals of the American Academy of Political and Social Science*, 618, 80–94.

Innes, M. (2004). Signal crimes and signal disorders: Notes on deviance as communicative action. *British Journal of Sociology*, 55(3), 335–355.

Jones, S.G., Doxsee, C., & Harrington, N. (2020). The escalating terrorism problem in the United States. Center for International and Strategic Studies Issue Brief. Available at: www.csis.org/analysis/escalating-terrorism-problem-united-states. Accessed December 1, 2020.

Kelman, H.C. (1973). Violence without moral restraint: Reflections on the dehumanization of victims and victimizers. *Journal of Social Issues*, 29(4), 26–61.

Kendrick, A. (1974). *The wound within*. Boston, MA: Little, Brown.
La Free, G., & Freilich, J. (2019). Government policies for counteracting violent extremism. *Annual Review of Criminology*, 2, 13.1–13.22.
Lindekilde, L. (2014). Abu Shaubul's study group: Small group dynamics and radicalisation. Paper presented at the Group Attitude Formation, Group Centrism and Extremism Workshop Orfalea Center for Global and International Studies, University of California, Santa Barbara.
Lum, C., Kennedy, L., & Sherley, A. (2006). The effectiveness of counter-terrorism strategies. *Campbell Systematic Reviews*, 2(1), 1–50. Available at: https://onlinelibrary.wiley.com/doi/pdf/10.4073/csr.2006.2.
McCauley, C., & Moskalenko, S. (2011). *Friction: How radicalization happens to them and us*. Oxford: Oxford University Press.
Merari, A. (2010). *Driven to death: Psychological and social aspects of suicide terrorism*. Oxford: Oxford University Press.
Mincheva, L., & Gurr, T. (2013). *Crime–terror alliances and the state: Ethnonationalist and Islamist challenges to regional security*. London: Routledge.
Newman, E. 2006. Exploring the "root causes" of terrorism. *Studies in Conflict and Terrorism*, 29, 749–772.
Pape, R. (2005). *Dying to win: The strategic logic of suicide terrorism*. Chicago, IL: University of Chicago Press.
Piazza, J.A. (2008). Incubators of terror: Do failed and failing states promote transnational terrorism? *International Studies Quarterly*, 52(3), 468–488.
Rosenthal, J.A. (2008). For-profit terrorism: The rise of armed entrepreneurs. *Studies in Conflict & Terrorism*, 31(6), 481–498, 493.
Sageman, M. (2004). *Understanding terror networks*. Philadelphia, PA: University of Pennsylvania Press.
Sageman, M. (2008). *Leaderless Jihad*. Philadelphia, PA: University of Pennsylvania Press.
Saviano, R. (2019). Meaning and mayhem. *New York Review of Books*, 19 December.
Schelling, T. (1966). *Arms and influence*. New Haven, CT: Yale University Press.
Schmid, A.P. (2013). Radicalisation, de-radicalisation, counter-radicalisation: A conceptual discussion and literature review. *ICCT Research Paper*, March. Available at: www.icct.nl/download/file/ICCT-Schmid-Radicalisation-De-Radicalisation-Counter-Radicalisation-March-2013.pdf.
Shultz, G. (1986). The challenge to democracies. In B. Netanyahu (Ed.), *Terrorism: how the West can win*. New York: Farrar, Straus, Giroux, pp. 16–24.
Stoessinger, J. (1976). *Henry Kissinger: The anguish of power*. New York: Norton.
Stohl, M. (1984). National interests and state terrorism. *Political Science*, 36(1), 37–52.
Stohl, M. (1988). Demystifying terrorism: The myths and realities of contemporary terrorism. In M. Stohl (Ed.), *The Politics of Terrorism*. New York: Marcel Dekker, pp 1–19.
Sun Tzu (1963). *The art of war*. Oxford: Oxford University Press.
Thucydides (1988). *The landmark Thucydides: A comprehensive guide to The Peloponnesian War*. Translated by R.B. Strassler (Ed.). New York: Touchstone.
Victoroff, J. (2005). The mind of the terrorist: A review and critique of psychological approaches. *Journal of Conflict Resolution*, 49(1), 3–42.
Weiner, B. (1972). *Theories of motivation*. Chicago, IL: Markham.

3

Explaining Religious Terrorism

Nilay Saiya

Twenty years ago, 19 terrorists hijacked four civilian airliners and skillfully guided them into two of the most recognizable buildings in the world—the World Trade Center in New York City and the Pentagon in Washington DC—taking the lives of nearly 3,000 innocent civilians. While the attention of the world turned to violence rooted in Islam after the 9/11 terrorist strikes, terrorism in other faith traditions has been increasing as well. In India, the rise to power of the Hindu nationalist Bhartiya Janata Party has corresponded to a startling increase in attacks by Hindu militants against religious minorities. In Burma, radical Buddhist monks have collaborated with the state in waging a genocidal campaign against Rohingya Muslims, spurring a refugee crisis in neighboring Bangladesh. Christian terrorism in the countries of the West has witnessed a sharp rise in recent years, prompted by perceived demographic threats to the religious heritage of Christian-majority countries. Finally, Jewish terrorism in the form of "price tag" attacks and "settler terrorism" has seen an uptick in the Holy Land.

Even though attacks by religious militants have increased exponentially over the past 20 years and concerns over religious terrorism have driven the foreign policies of the world's most important states, analysts continue to struggle to understand the intersection of religion and terrorism. Thus, understanding this unique form of violence remains an urgent project. This chapter discusses how religion can matter in terrorism, covers some common explanations for religious terrorism, highlights some key findings that have emerged with respect to religious terrorism, and offers some avenues for future research.

How Religion Matters in Terrorism

Religious terrorism is a difficult term to define, for it is comprised of two parts that both evade precise classification. On one hand, that religion is a notoriously nebulous concept with imprecise boundaries makes defining it a difficult task. On the other hand, one terrorism expert has counted over 100 definitions of terrorism in the scholarly literature (Laqueur, 1999, p. 6). For these reasons, defining "religious terrorism" is doubly difficult. Still, though, it is possible to delineate some recurrent features common to most definitions of religious terrorism. In general, religious terrorism (1) involves violence and destruction, (2) has political objectives, (3) is premeditated, (4) is carried out by subnational actors, (5) primarily targets civilians, and (6) is committed by actors claiming to be driven by transcendent goals or in defense of a religious community. In this chapter, then, religious terrorism is defined as premeditated political violence perpetrated against noncombatants by subnational actors who are driven by a discernible religious motivation or ideology or in defense of a religious community.

From this definition, it is apparent that religion can matter in terrorism in two ways. First, a common religion can serve as the basis for group identity. Terrorists may coalesce around a common religious identity when they perceive a threat to that identity stemming from forces external to the faith, especially the presence of religious outsiders. The establishment of group solidarity through the identification of common religious characteristics can serve as an especially powerful tool when a group finds itself threatened by an enemy outgroup. As explained by Moghadam (2009, p. 46), "The out-group is identified with a certain behavior that, according to the narrative offered by the ideology, undermines the wellbeing of the in-group." Threats to religious identity helped motivate the activities of groups like the Tamil Tigers in Sri Lanka and the Irish Republican Army in Northern Ireland. Modern-day examples of identity-based religious terrorism include the Anti-balaka militias in Central African Republic and the 969 movement in Burma. The fighting in Sri Lanka, Northern Ireland, Central African Republic, and Burma occurred (or is presently occurring) along communitarian lines defined by the participants' religion—Hindu Tamils vs. Buddhist Sinhalese in Sri Lanka, Protestants vs. Catholics in Northern Ireland, Christians vs. Muslims in Central African Republic, and Buddhists vs. Muslims in Burma (de Soysa & Nordås, 2007; Fox, 2004). At other times, the fighting takes place between opposed camps within the same religion.

In these struggles and many others, religious terrorists employ religious history, rhetoric, and symbols in establishing group identity, but they do not necessarily have theologically motivated goals or motivations.

The second way that religion matters in terrorism is by providing a meta-narrative that justifies violent actions—usually built upon a selective reading and interpretation of sacred texts (Hoffman, 1995; Juergensmeyer, 2003; Ranstorp, 1996; Sageman, 2004; Stern, 2003). For the religious terrorist, violence is a holy act undertaken with the sanction of a higher power. It is violence for which religion supplies "the motivation, the justification, the organization, and the worldview" (Juergensmeyer, 2003, p. 7). This ideology serves to create a set of beliefs about the nature of reality (including political reality) that members of the group internalize, leading combatants to perceive their acts of political violence against enemy outgroups as a divine duty.

Faith beliefs can motivate militants to pursue a range of religiously defined goals. For terrorism rooted in religious fundamentalism, the goal is to return religion, state, and society to a proper "golden age" that existed at some point in the past. For example, Al-Qaeda and related Islamist groups seek to overthrow corrupt "apostate" governments in the Muslim world and implement religious regimes in their place, returning the world of Islam to its glory days before it was overtaken by the West. For terrorism rooted in apocalypticism, by contrast, the goal is not to return to the past as in fundamentalist terrorism, but rather to hasten the "end of days" through the initiation of "cosmic war" (Juergensmeyer, 2003). In this worldview, the final battle will be followed by a time of peace for humanity, during which all inhabitants of Earth will live harmoniously under the rule of the "one true faith." For example, in 1984, a Jewish millenarian group called Gush Emunim devised a plot to destroy one of the holiest sites in all of Islam, the Dome of the Rock and Al-Aqsa Mosque in Jerusalem. The group hoped that the attack would spark a cosmic confrontation between Israel and its Muslim neighbors, which would hasten the coming of the Jewish messiah. A third way that theology can motivate terrorism is by informing nationalist and ethnic violence. For example, violent White supremacists in the United States, Canada, and Europe draw on a theology of "Christian Identity" that considers White Anglo-Saxons to be God's true chosen people and people of color to be children of Satan in justifying attacks against racial and religious minorities as a means to purify their lands from these foreign influences. So, then, there exists tremendous variety among the world's religious terrorist movements. Yet, despite the range of beliefs and pursuits, what ties them together is that they coalesce around a common religious identity and believe that they have divine sanction to carry out acts of violence, rooting their bloodshed in their particular faith tradition's texts, traditions, and history.

Explanations for Religious Terrorism

How is it that religions which proclaim a message of peace and love can become weaponized in the murder of innocent civilians? Policymakers and academics have long struggled to understand how religion becomes evil (Kimball, 2008). Religions are dynamic and complex systems; while peace and love represent one facet of religion, every one of the world's faith traditions also carries the potential for violence. What, then, explains religious terrorism?

Explanations for religious violence—and by extension religious terrorism—can be grouped into four general categories: those claiming that religion itself lies at the root of faith-based terrorism in the modern world, those focusing on particular theological beliefs, those stressing the interaction between religious and political institutions, and those downplaying the religious rationale for terrorism and instead attributing "religious" terrorism to nonreligious factors.

The first explanation for religious terrorism holds that religion itself is responsible for religious terrorism. Especially influential here are the arguments of the "new atheists" like the late Christopher Hitchens, Richard Dawkins, and Sam Harris. In books with titles such as *The God Delusion*, *The End of Faith*, and *God is Not Great*, they argue that religion necessarily leads to absolutism, division, irrationality, extremism, and violence (Dawkins, 2006; Harris, 2005; Hitchens, 2008). As Dawkins put it in an op-ed written for *The Guardian* four days after the attacks of September 11, 2001: "To fill a world with religion, or religions of the Abrahamic kind, is like littering the streets with loaded guns. Do not be surprised if they are used" (Dawkins, 2001). Echoing the theme of religion's inherent proneness to conflict is the influential "clash of civilizations" thesis championed by the late Harvard scholar Samuel Huntington. Writing in response to those who believed that liberal democracy and free-market capitalism would flourish with the end of the Cold War, Huntington argued that the "the principal conflicts of global politics will occur between nations and groups of different civilizations" rather than between peoples within civilizations (Huntington, 1993, p. 22). In Huntington's framework, these civilizations are based primarily on predominant religious traditions. Thus, the theory of clashing civilizations holds that religiously plural countries will be at greater risk for religiously based conflict, including religion-related terrorism. The clash thesis necessarily recommends that civilizations should maintain their unity by promoting intra-civilizational cooperation and limiting multiculturalism and immigration. After 9/11, the clash of civilizations gained a newfound respect among certain policymakers who used Huntington's logic to understand the roots of terrorism.

These explanations take particular aim at Islam. The neo-atheists highlight various violent passages in the Qur'an as evidence that Islam is prone to violence. In their view, Islam's foundational doctrines and sacred texts mandate violence against non-Muslims. Accordingly, individuals such as Osama bin Laden, Ayman al-Zawahiri, and Abu Bakr al-Baghdadi are not necessarily marginal figures in the Muslim world as much as they are representatives of innate Muslim hostility to the West. The clash of civilizations thesis traces the roots of Muslim rage to residual animosity from the Crusades and the downfall of the Ottoman Empire and to Islam's inability to separate religion and politics in the way that Christianity did following the Peace of Westphalia (Lewis, 1990). "In Islam ... God is Caesar," Huntington (1993, p. 70) explained. Despite numerous scholarly works debunking the thesis that Islam is more prone to violence than other faith traditions (de Soysa & Nordås, 2007; Fox, 2003), this myth continues to remain influential in political analyses of terrorism and in popular discourse.

A second explanation for religious terrorism makes a more nuanced argument, asserting that particular religious beliefs motivate terrorism, rather than claiming that religion itself is inherently violent (Hoffman, 1995, 2006; Juergensmeyer, 1993, 2003, 2008; Kimball, 2008). Scholars in this school refute the idea that terrorism is the inevitable upshot of sacred texts and religious teachings as the neo-atheists claim. Instead, they emphasize a range of motivations for religious violence rooted in particular interpretations of a religious tradition's scriptures, stories, doctrines, and history. These understandings of religion can serve as a powerful resource in justifying violence in the name of faith by emphasizing metaphysical battles of good versus evil, martyrdom, and eternal rewards. Scholars in this camp argue that religious militants are different from secular combatants insofar as the former believe they are waging a spiritual battle for transcendent truth sanctioned by a divine authority. For example, apocalyptic terrorism—the gravest form of terrorism today—is a subset of religious terrorism whose perpetrators, motivated by transcendent aims, carry out attacks uninhibited by the political, moral, or pragmatic constraints that guide most other terrorists (Lifton, 2000). While specific apocalyptic beliefs vary from religion to religion, at its core, apocalypticism involves complex theologies of the end of days, emphasizing ubiquitous corruption and depravity at a global level, the belief that the universe needs to be cleansed through a cataclysmic series of events, and the return to Earth of a messiah who ushers in a reign of peace in a new age of holy utopia after a prolonged struggle or tribulation period. Apocalyptic terrorists believe they have a divine mission to help bring about the end of the present evil age by sparking a global catastrophe that will lead to a cosmic showdown between the forces of good and evil. Essentially, such groups seek to force God's hand by speeding up the divine timetable for the ultimate final battle through a practice known as "catastrophic messianism" (Gregg, 2016). In short, the second explanation for religious terrorism emphasizes the importance of certain religious beliefs like apocalypticism in terrorism.

A third explanation for religious terrorism emphasizes the "malleability" of religion. One of the most important concepts in the study of religion and politics is the "ambivalence of the sacred" (Appleby, 1999; Philpott, 2007). To say that religion is politically ambivalent means that it is fundamentally malleable and can be used to support any number of political positions—even contradictory ones like violence and peace. Religion is ambivalent because spiritual beliefs and practices cannot be reduced to a reified ontological category from which political worldviews are determined *a priori*. For religion to become politically salient, latent spiritual views must somehow become activated. Thus, in different contexts, religion can be used to support pacifism or militarism, conflict or cooperation, autocracy or democracy. Whether or not a religion is congenial to a particular political vision depends in large part on how and by whom that faith is interpreted. All great faiths are multivocal and contain within them numerous doctrinal currents and interpretations. Thus, even those of the same faith tradition can hold a range of dramatic and contradictory religiously derived responses to their environments (Appleby, 1999).

What kinds of environments encourage or discourage religious terrorism? Of particular importance here is the interaction between religious and political institutions. In a pioneering work, Philpott (2007) argued that the "political theologies" of religious groups interacted with governmental treatment of religion to produce religious terrorism. He argued that religious actors who remain independent from the state and hold a political theology conducive to tolerance and liberalism were likely to support democracy, peace, and reconciliation. On the other hand, religious actors in a close relationship with the state and holding theologies conducive to violence were likely to support authoritarianism and violence, including terrorism. Drawing on the theory of "religious economies," other scholars examining the causes of religious conflict and terrorism have arrived at the conclusion that contexts marked by a commitment to pluralism and religious freedom tend to experience fewer problems with religious terrorism (Grim & Finke, 2010; Saiya, 2017, 2019). They argue that extremist ideas tend not to flourish in open religious systems marked by healthy religious economies where religious actors and ideas enjoy protection and access to political and social life, where states and societies do not attempt to impose a religious monopoly, and where governments do not selectively subsidize religious groups in a partial manner (Grim & Fink, 2011; Hafez, 2003; Henne et al., 2020; Saiya, 2015; Saiya & Scime, 2015; Satana et al., 2013; Toft et al., 2011). Countries which refuse to systematically discriminate against religious groups in society, thereby protecting pluralism, allow for a wide range of religious practices and doctrinal interpretations to flourish. The need to put out a "good product" in these religious marketplaces makes religious groups less likely to turn to the gun, which would repulse existing members of that faith and deter potential converts. On the other hand, the restricting of religious pluralism and religious freedom through legal and social structures serves to create an environment of ignorance, superstition, prejudice, and distrust, leading to less communal harmony and social stability and more violence (Abdullah, 2016, 2017; Farr, 2008; Grim & Finke, 2011; Saiya, 2018). In short, it is not religion *per se* that generates terrorism, but rather its restriction.

A fourth explanation for religious terrorism is skeptical of the idea that religious terrorism can be effectively differentiated from other forms of terrorism. In contrast to the first school of thought, which holds that religion itself is the cause of much of the violence and terrorism in the contemporary world, these scholars argue the opposite: religion is a secondary consideration in terrorist violence, masking the "real" underlying causes of violent conflict like endemic poverty, foreign military occupation, or the innate desire for "brotherhood" (Atran, 2010; Pape, 2005). This secularist viewpoint tends to exonerate religion of culpability in promoting and perpetuating social conflicts, insofar as the "character and causes" of religious terrorism cannot be effectively differentiated from those of "political terrorism" (Nardin, 2001). As such, religious terrorism does not constitute a distinct category of political violence. This logic is summarized succinctly by former American ambassador Michael Sheehan: "A number of terrorist groups have portrayed their causes in religious and cultural terms. This is often a transparent tactic designed to conceal political goals, generate popular support, and silence opposition" (Sheehan, 2000). This line of thinking holds that terrorists are rational actors who are motivated by tactical or strategic goals and that it is more important to pay attention to what terrorists do instead of what they say (Bloom, 2007; Crenshaw, 1981; Kydd & Walter, 2006; Pape, 2005). These studies do not dismiss religion's role in violence altogether, but instead claim that leaders of terrorist groups exploit religion in order to make the use of violence acceptable to a wider constituency in the service of achieving political objectives; theology is not, however, the main source of terrorism. In this vein, even for ostensibly religious terrorist groups like Hamas and Al-Qaeda, the main objectives are political and strategic in nature: the liberation of Palestine, the withdrawal of Western troops from the Middle East, and ending American support for Israel (Esposito, 2003). Thus, religion is used instrumentally by violent political opportunists (Isaacs, 2016).

Some scholars within this camp argue that, because religion is an inherently nebulous concept with imprecise boundaries, the distinction between "religious" and "secular" terrorism is artificial and unjustifiable on both conceptual and empirical grounds, and that the religious–secular dichotomy is best avoided altogether. They would also point out that any attempt to define religion would either leave behind particular belief systems that are generally recognized as religions or include certain traditions that most would classify as nonreligious. Religion, in other words, is a social and modern construction; in the end, there is no such thing as "religion" (Asad, 1993). For these reasons, these scholars claim that it is impossible to distinguish religious from secular violence insofar as both share certain characteristics (Cavanaugh, 2009; Gunning & Jackson, 2011; Nardin, 2001; Spencer, 2006). Cavanaugh (2009, p. 7) maintains that "the very distinction between secular and religious violence is unhelpful, misleading, and mystifying." He argues that religious violence is a "myth," born of the idea that "religion is a transhistorical and transcultural feature of human life, essentially distinct from 'secular' features such as politics and economics, which has a peculiarly dangerous inclination to promote violence" (Cavanaugh, 2009, p. 3). A common thread among scholars in this group is that describing terrorism as "religious" serves to delegitimize religious actors and justify questionable counterterrorism practices against entire religious groups.

What Have We Learned About Religious Terrorism?

While scholars in the fourth school of thought on the causes of religious terrorism downplay religion's role in modern terrorism—or reject the term "religious terrorism" altogether—a majority of terrorism scholars agree that religious terrorism comprises a discrete form of political violence. What have we learned about religious terrorism since the 9/11 attacks from their studies? How does religious terrorism differ from secular terrorism? The existing literature on religious terrorism has revealed that religious terrorism is a unique form of terrorism that is more *recent*, more *ruthless*, and more *resilient* than nonreligious forms of terrorism.

First, while acknowledging that terrorism in the name of religion has ancient roots, some believe that religion's role in modern terrorism is a relatively *recent* phenomenon. Rapoport (2004) observes that modern terrorism has transpired in several different "waves" since the 1800s. Until 1980, virtually all terrorism was secular in nature, encompassed in three types of organizations: (1) independence movements struggling against colonial occupiers in places like Algeria and Kenya; (2) separatist groups seeking territorial autonomy or national sovereignty, as in Ireland and Spain; and (3) socioeconomic revolutionaries fighting for their version of justice in places like Italy, West Germany, and South America (Fine, 2008). What tied all these movements together was that they grounded their actions in ostensibly secular ideas—Marxism, anticolonialism, social justice—rather than in religiously informed precepts. As these secular ideologies began to lose their appeal, terrorism motivated by religion began to increase.

Some terrorism experts contend that the 1990s witnessed a type of "new terrorism," distinguished by its religious or mystical character, freedom from state support, grandiose objectives, and conspicuous lethality (Laqueur, 1999; Simon & Benjamin, 2000). Hoffman (2006, p. 87) claims that the "religious imperative for terrorism is the most important characteristic of terrorist activity today." Of the 11 active international terrorist organizations in 1968, religion shaped neither the ideas nor the identities of any of them. By 1995, half of all international terrorist groups claimed a religious mantle (Hoffman 2006, pp. 90–94). This increase in religious terrorism has been met with a relative decrease in the number of secular terrorist groups. Similarly, Moghadam (2009) showed a sharp increase in religion-related suicide terrorism since the 1980s.

Why has religious terrorism increased in recent decades? A large part of the answer to that question concerns a general resurgence in religion's global political influence (Berger, 1999; Casanova, 1994; Fox, 2002; Fox & Sandler, 2004; Kepel, 2002; Marty & Appleby, 1993; Petito & Hatzopoulos, 2003; Thomas, 2005; Toft et al., 2011). Owing to processes like modernization, globalization, and democratization— the very developments that the "secularization thesis" (the idea born of the Enlightenment that religion would eventually disappear as societies modernized) predicted would kill off religion—coupled with the evident failures of secular projects and ideologies in developing countries—the major world religions have experienced a newfound relevance in the modern world (Juergensmeyer, 1993; Toft et al., 2011). Arguably, religion is today a more salient feature of international politics than at any point in the last 300 years.

A dramatic increase in religious terrorism has been an important part of this global religious resurgence. Two galvanizing events in 1979— the Iranian Revolution and the successful mujahidin resistance to the Soviet invasion of Afghanistan—demonstrated the strength of religion to achieve political objectives. The growth in religious fundamentalism since those events aimed to combat the secularism that had become the basis for global politics during the first half of the twentieth century (Toft & Shah, 2006; Toft et al., 2011). In their quest for modernity, many countries in the Islamic world, particularly those in the Middle East and North Africa, implemented aggressively secular policies that had ruinous results. National socialism produced bureaucracy and torpor rather than economic growth, even as these countries experienced massive youth bulges. Egyptian leader Gamal Abdul Nasser's dream of "pan-Arabism" suffered a tremendous setback after Israel's routing of Arab armies in the Six-Day War of 1967 and was ultimately killed off when Iraq invaded its Arab neighbor Kuwait in 1990. Oil wealth produced a new class of fantastically rich, Western-supported sheiks who used their rents to buy off large segments of the population or repress parts of the population that they feared. Ultimately, these countries degenerated into callous, corrupt, and deeply unpopular dictatorships. As levels of freedom and standards of living declined in the Arab world, the appeal of religious fundamentalism gained in strength by providing people with a sense of meaning and purpose and became the only vehicle available to oppose the state. Moreover, religious believers decried the destruction of values believed to derive from religious principles and attempts by secular autocrats to separate Islam from politics, and sought to replace corrupt and self-serving secular political orders with new ones having spiritual underpinnings that conformed to religious texts and principles. The different visions that these new religious societies would take became acrimonious points of contention that often resulted in bloodshed (Kepel, 2002).

The second major finding is that religious terrorism tends to be more *ruthless* than secular terrorism—religious belief fashions a uniquely deadly form of violence. Hoffman (2006, p. 88) observes that religious terrorism constitutes a potentially "far more lethal threat than that posed by more familiar, traditional terrorist adversaries." In a study that compared religious and secular terrorist organizations, Asal and Rethemeyer (2008) found that organizations acting on religious or ethno-religious ideologies caused more devastation than other types of terrorist groups. Piazza (2009) revealed that in terms of those wounded or killed by terrorist strikes, assaults by religious actors resulted in more than four times as many casualties as attacks by nationalist-separatist terrorists, more than four times as many casualties as attacks by leftist (anarchist, anti-globalization, communist, socialist, and environmentalist) groups, and almost sixteen times as many casualties as attacks by rightist (racist, right-wing conservative, and right-wing reactionary) groups. Simply put, religious terror is believed to be more symbolic than it is strategic (Berman, 2009; Cronin, 2011; Hoffman, 1995; Juergensmeyer, 2003; Moghadam, 2009; Rapoport, 1984; Simon & Benjamin, 2000).

Why is religious terrorism more deadly than its secular counterpart? A number of studies have found that the transcendent, utopian goals that are part and parcel of religious belief influence the nature and scope of violence undertaken by religious militants in contrast to secular terrorists who seek more circumspect and pragmatic objectives (Fox, 2004; Henne, 2012; Hoffman, 2006; Laqueur, 1999; Ranstorp, 1996; Stern, 2003; Svensson, 2007; Svensson & Harding, 2011; Toft, 2007). The reason is that religious terrorists operate under an entirely different incentive structure than do secular terrorists, and this, in turn, shapes their goals and tactics in radically different ways from their secular counterparts (Juergensmeyer, 2003, pp. 125–126). In the words of Hoffman (2006, p. 83), "terrorism motivated either in whole or in part by a religious imperative, where violence is regarded by its practitioners as a divine duty or sacramental act, embraces markedly different means of legitimization and justification than that committed by secular terrorists, and these distinguishing features lead, in turn, to yet greater bloodshed and destruction." As Juergensmeyer (2003, pp. 149–150) explains, "What makes [religious] violence particularly savage and relentless is that its perpetrators have placed such religious images of divine struggle—cosmic war—in the service of worldly political battles." In Juergensmeyer's assessment, religious terrorism is performative, expressive, and cosmic rather than strategic in nature. Religious terrorists justify their violence by framing it as a divinely sanctioned act of justice in accordance with a selective and literalist reading of religious texts (Lincoln, 2006). For believers not to partake in this divine mandate of violence puts them at risk of losing the favor of God. Conversely, obedience to the will of God is believed to be rewarded with eternal life in paradise. Because it embraces a wholly different means of legitimization and justification, religious terrorism results in far greater levels of bloodshed and devastation than other forms of terrorism. All members of "infidel societies," including the most vulnerable, are considered legitimate targets. As explained by Simon and Benjamin (2000, p. 71), religious terrorists "want a lot of people watching and a lot of people dead."

Violence in the name of God features two aspects that make it especially deadly: issue indivisibility and extended time horizons. With respect to the former, terrorist groups motivated by religious belief often perceive themselves to be engaged in a cosmic war and conflate the spiritual and temporal worlds in such a way as to prevent bargaining, compromise, and common ground between the group and the state. The issues they fight for are "indivisible" (Hassner, 2009). By contrast, groups seeking terrestrial and well-defined goals like national liberation, regime change, territorial change, policy change, social control, economic concessions, or status quo maintenance use violence strategically and target specific enemies. They are not only open to, but also desirous of, a seat at the negotiating table. With respect to the latter, religious groups employ extended time horizons when fighting for sacred causes, implying that they are ready to discount present-day costs in exchange for the hope of eternal glory. Religious terrorists understand their causes to be generations-long spiritual battles and are therefore less amenable to peaceful compromise with their enemies in the here and now.

The importance of utopian goals, issue indivisibility, and extended time horizons can be clearly seen in the ideology of Salafi-jihadism—an ideology which seeks to reverse the decadence of Islam and recapture the grandeur of the religion's past, returning to the original practices of the Prophet Muhammad and his companions (Wictorowicz, 2006). As practiced by groups like ISIS, Salafi-jihadism also champions martyrdom and mass killing, owing to the belief that Allah will reward those who sacrifice themselves in a noble mission of death with entry into paradise and an audience with God. This logic helps explain why tactics such as suicide bombings, soft target attacks, and assaults against members of the same religious or national community are more prevalent with Salafist groups. For the jihadist, violence serves a much more grandiose purpose than simply resistance to foreign occupation or socioeconomic reforms; it seeks to purify the world of evil, establish a worldwide *ummah* or community of believers, and hasten entry into paradise. Moghadam (2009) demonstrated empirically the increase and relative lethality of suicide attacks by groups motivated by a Salafist theology. Henne (2012) found that suicide missions by groups holding an Islamist (including Salafist) ideology inflicted far more death and destruction than nonreligious groups, even when accounting for group motivations and structural factors.

Secular terrorist movements, by contrast, tend to have more easily identifiable and limited ambitions such as attaining political power, redressing class-based grievances, or seeking autonomy from a central government. The perceived attainability of these objectives allows secular terrorists to use violence as a strategic tool rather than an end in itself. Unlike their religious counterparts, secular groups do care about generating public support and will generally avoid risky, high-casualty tactics that may provoke backlash from the public and consequently undercut their demands and estrange valuable constituencies. Simon and Benjamin (2001, p. 5) explain that "By avoiding egregious bloodshed, (secular) group leaders preserve their eligibility for a place at the bargaining table and, ultimately, a role in successor governments." In these cases, conflicts are seen through non-transcendent lenses, making compromise and negotiation possible. For religious terrorists, however, such actions constitute a betrayal of their divinely ordained mission. Secular conflicts, in other words, tend not to be viewed as all-or-nothing battles in which all enemies must be destroyed. Rather, once the goals of the organization have been achieved or an equitable solution has been mutually agreed upon, secular terrorists usually cease violent activity.

In such cases, we are less likely to witness capricious destruction or a wanton disregard for human life associated with religiously based terrorism (Fine, 2008).

It is also important to note that some work has offered a nonreligious rationale for the relative lethality of religious terrorism. In an important study, Berman (2009) acknowledges the relative ruthlessness of religious terrorist groups, but posits a different cause. He dismisses the idea that religious terrorists are motivated by religious ideas, and instead proposes that religious terrorists are "rational altruists" who are seeking to help their own endangered communities. Applying the economics of organizations, Berman argues that the leaders of the world's most deadly religious terrorist groups have found ways to build loyalty and cohesion by controlling defection. By weeding out "free riders" and unreliable members, these groups are able to retain those individuals most devoted to, and willing to sacrifice for, their cause.

Finally, in addition to being more recent and ruthless than non-religious terrorism, research has also shown that religious terrorism is more *resilient* in nature. Religious terrorist organizations fight harder and last longer than their secular counterparts (Asal & Rethemeyer, 2008; Jones & Libicki, 2008; Piazza, 2009). An important study by Jones and Libicki (2008) revealed that religious terrorist groups differ from those otherwise classified in their levels of resilience. Specifically, they note that while 62 percent of all terrorist groups have ended, the same can be said of only 32 percent of religious terrorist groups. They also observe that this finding cannot be attributed to the fact that religious terrorism is a recent phenomenon because the survivability of religious groups is substantially higher within cohorts examined by decade. Of the forty-five religious terrorist groups that ended, twenty-six splintered and only sixteen succumbed to state pressure, including policing and military operations. Military actions have been successful at terminating only three religious terrorist groups. "The most salient fact about religious terrorist groups," they conclude, "is how hard they are to eliminate" (Jones & Libicki, 2008, pp. 36–37). Toft and Zhukov (2015) likewise showed that jihadi militant groups in the Caucasus were more difficult to defeat than nationalist rebel groups.

Accordingly, this also means that religious terrorists commonly respond to the effects of repression differently than secular terrorists. Repression by authoritarian governments has been successful in crushing terrorist threats in countries like Argentina, Sri Lanka, Uruguay, and Peru. Notice, though, that the successes of repression against terrorism in these countries occurred against self-professed *secular* terrorist organizations—the Montoneros (in Argentina), the Tamil Tigers (in Sri Lanka), the Tupamaros (in Uruguay), and the Shining Path (in Peru). Regimes that attempt to quash or prevent religious terrorism through such brutality tend not to be as successful over the long term. Examples include Takfir wal-Hijra in Egypt, Jundallah in Iran, and the Eastern Turkistan Islamic Movement in China, all of which survived despite attempts at brutal suppression on the part of the state. At other times, "defeated" religious terrorist groups reconstitute themselves under different names like Algeria's Armed Islamic Group (AIG), which later became the Salafist Group for Preaching and Fighting, or Al-Qaeda in Iraq, which later morphed into ISIS.

Combating Religious Terrorism

The unique nature of religious terrorism presents policymakers with the difficult task of devising policies to combat it. States have employed a number of strategies in their quest to eradicate this especially pernicious form of violence. These include homeland security measures, military operations, and deradicalization efforts.

First, the reality of increasing—and increasingly lethal—attacks by religious terrorist groups has prompted states to implement an array of measures designed to make it more difficult for terrorists to carry out attacks. These include common-sense actions such as "hardening" potential targets like commercial airliners, airports, nuclear power plants, military installations, and government facilities. In some cases, entirely new departments have been created to keep countries safe from the threat of terrorism. For example, days after the 9/11 attacks, the United States created the Department of Homeland Security (DHS), an organization tasked with overseeing and coordinating a comprehensive national strategy to secure the country from future attacks. The following year, the DHS formally came into being as a stand-alone, Cabinet-level department.

More controversially, though, some countries—including liberal democracies—have responded to the threat of religious terrorism by restricting civil liberties as part of their homeland security strategies. Leaders in these countries contend that effectively averting terrorism requires their governments to limit or suspend freedoms in the name of national security. This logic rests on the assumption that liberalism shackles governments from using all of the weapons in their arsenal to optimize their counterterrorism strategies. In countries where this thinking prevails, the result is a perceived zero-sum game: restrictions on civil liberties, as morally problematic as they might be, are seen as necessary to curtail religious terrorism. Such restrictions can include enhanced government surveillance of citizens, expanded powers of detention, travel limitations, and the curtailing of public gatherings. If carried too far, however, these kinds of policies risk further embittering terrorist constituencies, making the turn to the gun more likely (Abrahms, 2007; Magen, 2018).

Of crucial importance here is the issue of religiously restrictive counterterrorism policies. History teaches, and many studies confirm, that religiously restrictive counterterrorism policies, which discriminate against entire religious groups, work at cross purposes with the desired goal of effectively combating terrorism (Saiya, 2018). This is true for three reasons. First, when states in the name of combating terrorism act indiscriminately and treat all people in a particular religious community as terrorists, they waste valuable time, energy, and resources monitoring entire religious communities when they instead should be focused very narrowly on those who actually are terrorists. Only a very small percentage of individuals in any faith tradition believe that terrorism is justifiable; many fewer still actually take up the gun. Second, such actions inevitably serve to generate sympathy for terrorism, lead people to turn to terrorist groups for protection, and end up creating more terrorists. Indiscriminate and widespread repression of religion in the name of counterterrorism raises the costs of remaining peaceful for ordinary citizens, insofar as armed resistance presents the possibility of changing the status quo. Third, repressive policies against entire religious communities makes it far less likely that individuals from those communities will cooperate with law enforcement officials on counterterrorism efforts. These logics explain why religious terrorist groups hope to provoke overreactions by states against the communities they claim to be defending.

In addition to homeland security measures, a second way states have responded to the threat of religious terrorism is through the force of arms. Military operations have attempted to root out terrorist organizations through ground wars, special operations, bombing campaigns, drone strikes, and targeted killings. The American raid on the Pakistani compound of Al-Qaeda leader Osama bin Laden and the drone strike that killed the radical cleric Anwar al-Awlaki in Yemen are oft-mentioned examples of how the use of military force can be a valuable tool in the struggle against religious extremism.

Military operations can also carry significant risks, however. The expenditure of trillions of dollars on military interventions, drone wars, foreign-imposed regime change, and special operations in various parts of the Muslim world inadvertently but unquestionably paved the way for state collapse and militia rule, fueled Islamist insurgencies, spawned refugee crises, and directly contributed to radicalization and sympathy for terrorists (Downes & Monten, 2013; Wade & Reiter, 2007). This has resulted in the deaths of thousands of servicemen and women and hundreds of thousands of innocent civilians. The war in Iraq, for example, opened a Pandora's Box of suppressed communal hostility that had been brewing for decades, creating a sense of angst among Sunnis, who believed they would have no place in the new Iraq. Shiite strongman Nouri al-Maliki pursued a punitive policy toward the minority Sunni community, including the use of brutal security forces. Iraq descended into a religious civil war between dispossessed Sunnis and long-repressed Shia. From this cauldron would eventually emerge the world's most ruthless terrorist organization, ISIS, whose ideology would inspire numerous attacks against European and American targets. In short, the application of conventional and nonconventional military power has frequently contributed to the rising tide of religious extremism.

The first two approaches to countering religious terrorism—homeland security and military campaigns—may have their place, but they do little to address the roots of religious extremism. Indeed, in some cases, they can exacerbate the problem. A third—and perhaps the most promising—approach to countering religious terrorism seeks to address the ideas underpinning religious terrorism by leveraging religion itself. For example, deradicalization and counter-radicalization programs aim to reverse and prevent the process of radicalization that leads some individuals to become terrorists in the first place, allowing them to become productive members of society (Rubin et al., 2011). Countries like Singapore have cooperated with religious groups to decrease the threat from extremism (Abdullah, 2013, 2016). Some counterterrorism programs have benefited greatly from the wisdom and experiences of former religious terrorists, who are in a unique position to challenge radical interpretations of religion. The examples of Maajid Nawaz of the Quilliam Foundation, Ismail Royer of the Religious Freedom Institute, and Zainab Al-Suwaij of the American Islamic Congress testify to the possibilities of using former extremists as intermediaries to counter terrorist impulses among the vulnerable populations. As noted earlier, evidence suggests that religious freedom, too, can offer an important antidote to terrorism. Religious liberty can empower rival liberal and moderate voices to challenge the theological claims made by religious militants who believe they represent the will of God. Through the protection of religious liberty, states can indirectly contest religious terrorist groups and naturally weaken the appeal of extremism at its root by amplifying its internal inconsistencies and challenging its mythology on theological grounds. In short, an emphasis on religious education and religious freedom might, paradoxically enough, offer the best strategy against religious terrorism.

Future Research

Much work is yet to be done on religious terrorism. The uniquely lethal threat arising from this discrete form of political violence calls for a greater understanding of its causes and consequences. Such insights will also be of much importance to policymakers who attempt to fashion effective counterterrorism policies. Here, I identify four potential avenues for future research.

First, more work needs to be done on religious terrorism in faith traditions outside of Islam. After the events of September 11, 2001, policymakers, journalists, and academics tended to focus on events in the Middle East and the relationship between Islam and violence when discussing terrorism. This has had the effect of reinforcing the perception among many in Western audiences that religious extremism pertains only to Islam (though it should be noted that the majority of religious terrorist groups in existence are indeed Islamic organizations). Yet, all of the world's major religions contain violent movements within them, and Muslims in general are not more likely to be involved in violent conflict than members of other faith traditions. "Saffron terrorism" carried out by Hindu extremists in India, for instance, has received scant scholarly attention. The same can be said of Central Africa's Christian-syncretistic terrorist traditions. Sikhism, Buddhism, and Judaism all have their own terrorist strains. More attention ought to be given to terrorism in these traditions, including its causes and consequences, and its implications for domestic and international peace and security. Future work in this area may strive to compare terrorism found in different religious traditions.

A second potential avenue for future research concerns how religious terrorism ends. While some analyses have addressed this topic from a more general standpoint (Cronin, 2011), further research is needed focusing on the cessation of religious terrorist violence. Past scholarship has found that religious terrorists tend to be more unconstrained in terms of their weapons and tactics and more expansive in their targets and goals than their secular counterparts. If religious terrorists are unique in these fundamental ways, then it stands to reason that the ways in which religious terrorist groups end might be different as well. It has been shown, for example, that terrorism with a religious impulse is less amenable to negotiations and more resilient in the face of police and counterterrorism operations—strategies that have been successful in ending many secular terrorist campaigns. Work in this vein also ought to look at the role that faith communities and religious education play in ending or reducing terrorism.

Third, since much of the work on religious terrorism takes the form of singular case studies, more theoretical work would be helpful in elucidating any structural similarities that give rise to this form of religious violence. Here, more quantitative work comparing country-level correlates of religious terrorism would be beneficial in advancing generalizable structural explanations for religious terrorism. Future work here also should examine the causes of international religious terrorism—why terrorist groups based in one country attack targets in another.

Fourth, future work on terrorism should attempt to disaggregate religious terrorism from the broader category of terrorism. Much of the quantitative work on terrorism, for example, does not attempt to disaggregate terrorism with respect to ideology, motivations, or tactics. The majority of these studies tend to lump terrorist groups together without considering the guiding ideologies of different organizations. As highlighted in this chapter, however, there are good reasons to disaggregate religious and secular terrorism. Religious terrorists look to their faith as a source of inspiration, legitimation, and worldview, resulting in a totally different incentive structure than exists for their secular counterparts. The belief that they have divine sanction to wage a spiritual war plausibly influences the nature and scope of the demands religious militants make and the violence they undertake. If religious and secular terrorists are different in important ways and constitute distinct forms of political violence, then it stands to reason that their causes and consequences might differ as well.

References

Abdullah, W.J. (2013). Religious representation in secular Singapore: A case study of MUIS and Pergas. *Asian Survey*, 53, 1182–1204.
Abdullah, W.J. (2016). Of co-optation and resistance: State-ulama dynamics in Singapore. *Journal of Church and State*, 58, 462–482.
Abdullah, W.J. (2017). Conflating Muslim "conservatism" with "extremism": Examining the "merry Christmas" saga in Singapore. *Journal of Muslim Minority Affairs*, 37, 344–356.
Abrahms, M. (2007). Why democracies make superior counterterrorists. *Security Studies*, 16, 223–253.
Appleby, S.R. (1999). *The ambivalence of the sacred: Religion, violence, and reconciliation*. Lanham, MD: Rowman & Littlefield Publishers.
Asad, T. (1993). *Genealogies of religion: Discipline and reasons of power in Christianity and Islam*. Baltimore, MD: Johns Hopkins University Press.
Asal, V., & Rethemeyer, R.K. (2008). The nature of the beast: Organizational structures and the lethality of terrorist attacks. *Journal of Politics*, 70, 437–449.
Atran, S. (2010). *Talking to the enemy: Faith, brotherhood, and the (un)making of terrorists*. New York: HarperCollins.
Berger, P. (1999). *The desecularization of the world: Resurgent religion and world politics*. Grand Rapids, MI: William B. Eerdmans.
Berman, E. (2009). *Radical, religious, and violent: The new economics of terrorism*. Cambridge, MA: MIT Press.
Bloom, M. (2007). *Dying to kill: The allure of suicide terror*. New York: Columbia University Press.
Casanova, J. (1994). *Public religions in the modern world*. Chicago, IL: University of Chicago Press.
Cavanaugh, W.T. (2009). *The myth of religious violence: Secular ideology and the roots of modern conflict*. New York: Oxford University Press.
Crenshaw, M. (1981). The causes of terrorism. *Comparative Politics*, 13, 379–399.
Cronin, A.K. (2011). *How terrorism ends: Understanding the decline and demise of terrorist campaigns*. Princeton, NJ: Princeton University Press.
Dawkins, R. (2001). Religion's misguided missiles. *The Guardian*. September 15.
Dawkins, R. (2006). *The god delusion*. Boston, MA: Houghton Mifflin Company.
de Soysa, I., & Nordås, R. (2007). Islam's bloody innards? Religion and political terror, 1980–2000. *International Studies Quarterly*, 51, 927–943.
Downes, A.B., & Monten, J. (2013). Forced to be free? Why foreign-imposed regime change rarely leads to democratization. *International Security*, 37, 90–131.
Esposito, J.L. (2003). *Unholy war: Terror in the name of Islam*. New York: Oxford University Press.
Farr, T.F. (2008). *World of faith and freedom: Why international religious liberty is vital to American national security*. New York: Oxford University Press.
Fine, J. (2008). Contrasting secular and religious terrorism. *Middle East Quarterly*, 15, 59–69.

Fox, J. (2002). *Ethnoreligious conflict in the late twentieth century: A general theory*. Lanham, MD: Lexington Books.

Fox, J. (2003). Do Muslims engage in more domestic conflict than other religious groups? *Civil Wars*, 6, 27–46.

Fox, J. (2004). *Religion, civilization, and civil war: 1945 through the new millennium*. Lanham, MD: Lexington Books.

Fox, J., & Sandler, S. (Eds.). (2004). *Bringing religion into international relations*. London: Palgrave Macmillan.

Gregg, H.S. (2016). Three theories of religious activism and violence: Social movements, fundamentalists, and apocalyptic warriors. *Terrorism and Political Violence*, 28, 338–360.

Grim, B.J., & Finke, R. (2011). *The price of freedom denied: Religious persecution and conflict in the twenty-first century*. New York: Cambridge University Press.

Gunning, J., & Jackson, R. (2011). What's so "religious" about "religious terrorism"? *Critical Studies on Terrorism*, 4, 369–388.

Hafez, M.M. (2003). *Why Muslims rebel: Repression and resistance in the Islamic world*. Boulder, CO: Lynne Rienner Publishers.

Harris, S. (2005). *The end of faith: Religion, terror, and the future of reason*. New York: W.W. Norton & Company.

Hassner, R.E. (2009). *War on sacred grounds*. Ithaca, NY: Cornell University Press.

Henne, P.S. (2012). The ancient fire: Religion and suicide terrorism. *Terrorism and Political Violence*, 24, 38–60.

Henne, P.S., Saiya, N., & Hand, A.W. (2020). Weapon of the strong? Government support for religion and majoritarian terrorism. *Journal of Conflict Resolution*. Available at: https://doi.org/10.1177/0022002720916854.

Hitchens, C. (2008). *God is not great: How religion poisons everything*. New York: Twelve Books.

Hoffman, B. (1995). "Holy terror": The implications of terrorism motivated by a religious imperative. *Studies in Conflict & Terrorism*, 18, 271–284.

Hoffman, B. (2006). *Inside terrorism*. New York: Columbia University Press.

Huntington, S.P. (1993). The clash of civilizations. *Foreign Affairs*, 72, 22–49.

Isaacs, M. (2016). Sacred violence or strategic faith? Disentangling the relationship between religion and violence in armed conflict. *Journal of Peace Research*, 53, 211–225.

Jones, S.G., & Libicki, M.C. (2008). *How terrorist groups end: Lessons for countering al Qa'ida*. Santa Monica, CA: Rand Corporation.

Juergensmeyer, M. (1993). *The new cold war? Religious nationalism confronts the secular state*. Berkeley, CA: University of California Press.

Juergensmeyer, M. (2003). *Terror in the mind of god: The global rise of religious violence*. Berkeley, CA: University of California Press.

Juergensmeyer, M. (2008). *Global rebellion: Religious challenges to the secular state, from Christian militias to Al Qaeda*. Berkeley, CA: University of California Press.

Kepel, G. (2002). *Jihad: The trail of political Islam*. London: I.B. Tauris.

Kimball, C. (2008). *When religion becomes evil*. San Francisco, CA: Harper.

Kydd, A.H., & Walter, B.F. (2006). The strategies of terrorism. *International Security*, 31, 49–80.

Laqueur, W. (1999). *The new terrorism: Fanaticism and the arms of mass destruction*. New York: Oxford University Press.

Lewis, B. (1990). The roots of Muslim rage. *The Atlantic*, September. Available at: www.theatlantic.com/magazine/archive/1990/09/the-roots-of-muslim-rage/304643/.
Lifton, R.J. (2000). *Destroying the world to save it: Aum Shinrikyo, apocalyptic violence, and the new global terrorism*. New York: Henry Holt.
Lincoln, B. (2006). *Holy terrors: Thinking about religion after September 11*. Chicago, IL: University of Chicago Press.
Magen, A. (2018). Fighting terrorism: The democracy advantage. *Journal of Democracy*, 29, 111–125.
Marty, M.E., & Appleby, R.S. (1993). *Fundamentalisms and the state: Remaking polities, economies, and militance*. Chicago, IL: University of Chicago Press.
Moghadam, A. (2009). *The globalization of martyrdom: Al Qaeda, Salafi jihad, and the diffusion of suicide attacks*. Baltimore, MD: Johns Hopkins University Press.
Nardin, T. (2001). Review: Terror in the mind of God: The global rise of religious violence. *Journal of Politics*, 63, 683–684.
Pape, R.A. (2005). *Dying to win: The strategic logic of suicide terrorism*. New York: Random House.
Petito, F., & Hatzopoulos, P. (2003). *Religion in international relations: The return from exile*. London: Palgrave Macmillan.
Philpott, D. (2007). Explaining the political ambivalence of religion. *American Political Science Review*, 101, 505–525.
Piazza, J.A. (2009). Is Islamist terrorism more dangerous? An empirical study of group ideology, organization, and goal structure. *Terrorism and Political Violence*, 21, 62–88.
Ranstorp, M. (1996). Terrorism in the name of religion. *Journal of International Affairs*, 50, 41–62.
Rapoport, D.C. (1984). Fear and trembling: Terrorism in three religious traditions. *American Political Science Review*, 78, 658–677.
Rapoport, D.C. (2004). The four waves of modern terrorism. In A. Cronin & J.M. Ludes (Eds.), *Attacking terrorism: Elements of a grand strategy*. Washington DC: Georgetown University Press, pp. 46–73.
Rubin, L., Gunaratna, R., & Jerard, J.A.R. (Eds.). (2011). *Terrorist rehabilitation and counter-radicalisation: New approaches to counter-terrorism*. London: Routledge.
Sageman, M. (2004). *Understanding terror networks*. Philadelphia, PA: University of Pennsylvania Press.
Saiya, N. (2015). The religious freedom peace. *International Journal of Human Rights*, 19, 369–382.
Saiya, N. (2017). Blasphemy and terrorism in the Muslim world. *Terrorism and Political Violence*, 29, 1087–1105.
Saiya, N. (2018). *Weapon of peace: How religious liberty combats terrorism*. New York: Cambridge University Press.
Saiya, N. (2019). Religion, state and terrorism: A global analysis. *Terrorism and Political Violence*, 31, 204–223.
Saiya, N., & Scime, A. (2015). Explaining religious terrorism: A data-mined analysis. *Conflict Management and Peace Science*, 32, 487–512.
Satana, N.S., Inman, M., & Birnir, J.K. (2013). Religion, government coalitions, and terrorism. *Terrorism and Political Violence*, 25, 29–52.
Sheehan, M. (2000). Terrorism: The current threat. February 10. Available at: www.brookings.edu/events/2000/0210terrorism.aspx.

Simon, S., & Benjamin, D. (2000). America and the new terrorism: An exchange. *Survival*, 42, 156–172.
Simon, S., & Benjamin, D. (2001). The terror. *Survival*, 43, 5–18.
Spencer, A. (2006). Questioning the concept of "new terrorism." *Peace, Conflict and Development*, 8, 1–33.
Stern, J. (2003). *Terror in the name of God.* New York: Ecco.
Svensson, I. (2007). Fighting with faith. *Journal of Conflict Resolution*, 51, 930–949.
Svensson, I., & Harding, E. (2011). How holy wars end: Exploring the termination patterns of conflicts with religious dimensions in Asia. *Terrorism and Political Violence*, 23, 133–149.
Thomas, S. (2005). *The global resurgence of religion and the transformation of international relations: The struggle for the soul of the twenty-first century.* London: Palgrave Macmillan.
Toft, M.D. (2007). Getting religion? The puzzling case of Islam and civil war. *International Security*, 31, 97–131.
Toft, M.D., & Shah, T.S. (2006). Why God is winning. *Foreign Policy*, 155, 38–43.
Toft, M.D., & Zhukov, Y.M. (2015). Islamists and nationalists: Rebel motivation and counterinsurgency in Russia's North Caucasus. *American Political Science Review*, 109, 222–238.
Toft, M.D., Philpott, D., & Shah, T.S. (2011). *God's century: Resurgent religion and global politics.* New York: W.W. Norton & Company.
Wade, S.J., & Reiter, D. (2007). Does democracy matter? Regime type and suicide terrorism. *Journal of Conflict Resolution*, 51, 329–348.
Wictorowicz, Q. (2006). Anatomy of the Salafi Movement. *Studies in Conflict and Terrorism*, 29, 207–239.

4

Explaining White Supremacy and Domestic Terrorism

Amanda Graham

The 1995 bombing of the Murrah Building in Oklahoma City; the 2016 Orlando Pulse nightclub shooting; the 2019 El Paso, Texas Walmart shooting; the 2018 Parkland, Florida high school shooting; the 2015 San Bernardino, California shooting; the 2009 Ft. Hood, Texas shooting; and the 2018 Pittsburgh, Pennsylvania Tree of Life synagogue shooting—these violent acts make up the US top seven deadliest instances of domestic terrorism (ADL, 2020b). Although a universal definition is absent, domestic terrorism, also termed "internal terrorism" (Engene, 2007), is defined by the research group RAND (2020a) as involving "violence against the civilian population or infrastructure of a nation—often but not always by citizens of that nation and often with the intent to intimidate, coerce, or influence national policy." Enders and Sandler (2006) alternatively define it as involving "only the host country so that the perpetrators, victims, financing, and logistical support are all homegrown. More important, domestic incidents generate implications for just the host country or its interests." However, under the USA PATRIOT Act (2001), the United States government defines it as:

> activities that—(A) involve acts dangerous to human life that are a violation of the criminal laws of the United States or of any State; (B) appear to be intended—(i) to intimidate or coerce a civilian population; (ii) to influence the policy of a government by intimidation or coercion; or (iii) to affect the conduct of a government by mass destruction, assassination,

or kidnapping; and (C) occur primarily within the territorial jurisdiction of the United States.

(18 U.S. Code §2331, 2018)

Looking across these definitions, the diversity of inclusion and exclusion principles used to define domestic terrorism are highly variable. Yet, simply stated, these violent acts are perpetrated against community members by their own countrymen and women.

However, domestic terrorism is not unique to the United States. The 2011 bombing and shooting attack in Norway (Oslo and on the island of Utøya), the 2015 Île-de-France shootings, and the 2020 shootings in Hanau, Germany may also fall under the definition of domestic terrorism (Hinnant & Ganley, 2015; Hinnant & Jordans, 2020; Lewis & Lyall, 2012). Furthermore, domestic terrorism is not a new type of terrorism. Rather, examples of this violence date back centuries (see, e.g., the Jacobins of the late 1700s; the Clerkenwell Outrage in 1867), even to 66 ad with the *Sicarii* movement (D'Alessio & Stolzenberg, 1990).

Yet, the motivations for this violence vary from political (both left- and right-wing), ideological, environmental, religious-based, economic, and more (Berlet & Vysotsky, 2006; Bjelopera, 2012; Harris, 1987; Piazza, 2017). Given this array of potential grounds for committing domestic terrorism, this chapter will specifically focus on those of White supremacy as a motive for domestic terrorism. As such, it is important to explicitly define what is meant by White supremacy. However, much like domestic terrorism, a universally shared definition of White supremacy is not present. For example, Crawford and colleagues (1994) define White supremacy as "an individual, group or action embodying the ideological notion of biological, genetic, intellectual or other inherent superiority of whites over other population groups" (p. A-8; quoted in Chin, 2013). Bjelopera (2012, p. 16) explains it more simply as an ideology that "purports that the white race ranks above all others." Furthermore, Adams and Roscigno (2005, p. 761) describe it as the belief in "the divinely sanctified supremacy of the white race and inherent inferiority of all other races, and the abrogation of white rights." Although on the surface these definitions share striking similarities, the underlying narratives that drive these beliefs provide divergence. Nonetheless, understanding this unique cause for violence has substantial implications, especially because White supremacy is the greatest terror threat, domestic or international, for the United States

(Cullen, 2019; Sands, 2020; Swan, 2020b). Thus, the remainder of this chapter focuses on the roots of White supremacist violence, White supremacist groups, research efforts in White supremacy and domestic terrorism, and future avenues of research on this matter.

Roots of White Supremacist Violence

White supremacy and white nationalism has existed from the founding of our country.
–Veteran national security prosecutor and Georgetown Law professor Mary McCord (quoted in Graff, 2020)

As denoted in the original 1787 version of the US Constitution, White supremacy, or at least the denigration of those who were enslaved (predominantly Blacks), was written into the foundation of the United States. For example, under Article I, Section 2, enslaved individuals were treated as three-fifths of a person for the purpose of taxation and, under Article IV, mandated the return of escaped slaves to the party who claimed them (U.S. Constitution, 1787a, 1787b). These aspects of the constitution would not be changed until 1865 and 1868, respectively. Consequently, formal groups dedicated to White supremacy would form following the Civil War, initially starting with the Ku Klux Klan (KKK) in 1865 in Pulaski, Tennessee (Barnes, 1996; History.com Editors, 2020; SPLC, n.d.a). This group donned the signature white robes and hoods and participated in violent attacks, including torture, intimidation, and lynching of Blacks, in an effort to restore White supremacy in the South (Barnes, 1996; History.com Editors, 2020; SPLC, n.d.a). In an attempt to suppress this violence, Congress passed multiple acts, including the Ku Klux Klan Act of 1871 (16 Stat. 140 (1870) and 17 Stat. 18 (1871); codified as amended at 42 U.S. Code §1981 et seq. (1994)), which created federal offenses for certain crimes, such as conspiring to deprive people the right to vote, hold office, serve as a juror, and have equal protection under the law (Barnes, 1996; Baysinger, 2006; History.com Editors, 2020).

In the 1920s, White supremacist violence saw a resurgence that targeted not only Blacks but also Jews and Catholics as well as foreigners and organized laborers (Barnes, 1996; History.com Editors, 2020; Skutsch, 2017; SPLC, n.d.a). In fact, at the time, this violence was often "all but openly endorsed by many government officials," with few offenders ever facing charges because "judges, politicians, and law enforcement officers were fellow Klansmen and loyal sympathizers" (Barnes, 1996, p. 1099). At this point, the KKK included over 4 million members in both Southern and Northern states, with some members even openly running for political offices (Chow, 2018; History.com Editors, 2020; Rothman, 2016; SPLC, n.d.a). However, the KKK would see a massive decline at the end of the 1920s, in part due to falling out of favor with both presidential candidates, but predominantly because of infighting, self-destructiveness, scandals, internal power struggles, and newspaper exposés (Chow, 2018; Rothman, 2016; SPLC, n.d.a).

The KKK and many other White supremacist organizations, such as the Aryan Nation, Posse Comitatus, and the Christian Identity movement, would see another resurgence in the 1950s, 1960s, and 1970s to oppose the civil rights movements (History.com Editors, 2020; Skutsch, 2017). Again, these groups used violence, such as bombings, beatings, assassinations, and lynchings, not only against Blacks but also Whites who supported the civil rights movement (History.com Editors, 2020; SPLC, n.d.a; Skutsch, 2017). As Barnes (1996) notes, "for many parts of the nation, particularly the South, the 1950s and '60s were decades of pure violence" (p. 1101). Two particularly violent attacks from this era of White supremacy were the 1963 Birmingham, Alabama bombing of the 16th Street Baptist Church, which killed four young Black girls, and the 1964 "Mississippi Burning" of three voter registration workers (SPLC, n.d.a; Winter, 2010).

As with the movement's membership in the 1920s, White supremacy groups of the 1950s through 1970s enjoyed membership of local officials and law enforcement (MacLean, 1995; Skutsch, 2017). These officials sought to build upon Whites' resentment of Blacks and other minorities by presenting the civil rights movement and underlying economic changes as a threat to Whites (Inwood, 2015). However, with the passage of the Civil Rights Act of 1964 and the Voting Rights Act of 1965, which further penalized "Klan-style intimidation" and broadened the Attorney General's power to enforce these laws, the support for the KKK and other White supremacy groups faded, and the groups splintered (Barnes, 1996, p. 1102; Skutsch, 2017).

Because these groups did not simply disappear, concern about White supremacist groups returned throughout the 1980s, 1990s, and 2000s (Chow, 2018; Graff, 2020). Instead, as McCord (quoted in Graff, 2020) states, they were "hidden under rocks and in caves for the last couple of decades." Nonetheless, the 1980s saw public demand for the US Department of Justice to address White supremacist violence in the form of a lawsuit filed by the National Anti-Klan Network against the US Department of Justice, which noted the failure of the government to prosecute those engaging in racially motivated violence (Barnes, 1996). Likewise, in the 1990s, White supremacy and White supremacist violence were brought to the public's attention with news stories such as the 60 Los Angeles County Sheriff's Deputies involved in a Neo-Nazi White supremacist gang known as the "Vikings" (McMillan & Sahagun, 1990; Tobar, 1991). Further concern regarding White supremacists, specifically the Christian Identity and Patriot movements, came from a change in strategy. Starting with the 1992 "Rocky Mountain Rendezvous in Estes Park, Colorado," these groups began to adopt the "Leaderless Resistance" strategy, which was inspired by William Pierce's 1978 *Turner Diaries*, to combat the improvements in law enforcement and military efforts to address White supremacy (Bjelopera, 2012; SPLC, 2000).

Throughout the remaining decades, White supremacy violence has ebbed and flowed with everything from the 1995 Oklahoma City bombing (Skutsch, 2017), the 2008 failed assassination attempt of then-President nominee Barack Obama (Lichtblau, 2008), the 2013 Sikh temple attack in Wisconsin (Skutsch, 2017), the 2015 Emanuel African Methodist Episcopal Church attack in Charleston, South Carolina (Skutsch, 2017), and the 2020 attempted kidnapping and assassination of Michigan Governor Gretchen Whitmer (Goudie et al., 2020). However, McCord notes that there has been a recent resurgence and openness to this ideology, in part because of "the 2016 campaign when there was so much high-level, open talk about 'anti-other'" (quoted in Graff, 2020). She continues, "It became acceptable among some to speak more openly and participate in visible, physical demonstrations and open marches" (McCord quoted in Graff, 2020). These marches have included the 2017 "Unite the Right" rally in Charlottesville, Virginia, which left one dead (ADL, 2019a), and the 2020 Patriot Front march in Washington, DC (Oppenheim, 2020).

Although membership has declined since its peak in the 1920s, a complete measure of the number of White supremacists in the United States has been complicated by (1) the advent of the Internet, and (2) the sheer number of different groups and subgroups of various White supremacists (e.g., neo-Nazis, neo-Confederates, alt-right, KKK, Christian Identity, skinheads) (Chow, 2018; Skutsch, 2017). Yet, these groups still use a host of similar symbols and iconography to denote their allegiances to the White supremacist movement. These symbols include the "double lightning bolts and swastikas" (Harris, 1987), the blood drop cross,

Celtic cross, and the confederate flag, and more recently, the iron cross, the Othala Rune, "1488" (a reference to David Lane's "14 words" and "Heil Hitler"), and the "OK" hand sign (ADL, n.d.).

Ideology

In short, the overarching ideological value of White supremacy is that "the white race ranks above all others" (Bjelopera, 2012, p. 16). However, the ideological roots for why this statement is believed to be true varies by group, as will be seen below. For example, some groups, such as Christian Identity, use religion as a backing to support their belief in "the divinely sanctified supremacy of the white race and inherent inferiority of all other races, and the abrogation of white rights" (Adams & Roscigno, 2005). Nonetheless, in examining a broad range of ideologies, Bowman-Grieve (2009) provides five key features, though there are more, of the White supremacist "worldview."

First and foremost, these individuals believe in "White 'pride,'" specifically related to preventing the extinction of the White race (Bowman-Grieve, 2009, p. 995). The centrality of this belief is most exemplified in the international White power movement's "14 words" credo by David Lane—"We must secure the existence of our people and a future for White children"—(Michael, 2009 p. 43). A more current and shorter rallying cry also derived from Lane's work states: "You will not replace us," referring to "replacement theory" or "white genocide" which posits that low birth rates of White children from White parents would lead to the "replacement" of Whites with non-Whites in society (ADL, 2017; Berger, 2016; Bowles, 2019). Aside from physical replacement by non-White community members, these individuals believe that the White population is losing its power and influence in society, leading to a need to engage in "defensive collective action" to retain and regain power (McVeigh, 1999, p. 1463). As such, along with a "call to arms" as a collective action (Adams & Roscigno, 2005, p. 762), for many of these groups, there is a call for "leaderless resistance" from underground cells or individuals to maintain the White race at any cost, including crime and violence (Bjelopera, 2012, p. 54).

Second, individuals in these groups hold a belief in the "Zionist Occupation Government" (ZOG; Bowman-Grieve, 2009, p. 995). Under this tenant, these individuals believe that there is a massive conspiracy in which Jews intend to make the White race extinct (Adams & Roscigno, 2005; Bjelopera, 2012; Bowman-Grieve, 2009). To accomplish this task, it is believed that Jews pursue powerful positions in government and the media to keep the White race ignorant of the immigration and multicultural policies set forth by the Jews (Adams & Roscigno, 2005; Bowman-Grieve, 2009). Eventually, they allege, these policies will lead to an end of the White race, but meanwhile keep the Jews "pure" so that they can have ultimate control over everyone (Adams & Roscigno, 2005; Bowman-Grieve, 2009, p. 995).

Third, there is a core principle, belief, and "condemnation of other races and of miscegenation" (Bowman-Grieve, 2009, p. 995). This principle aligns with the first principle in that it promotes the superiority of the White race, which is inward-looking. Still, it is also outward-looking by noting, "the inherent inferiority of all other races" (Adams & Roscigno, 2005, p. 761). These groups are usually staunchly opposed to immigration, with most recent concerns regarding Latino immigration along the US/Mexico border (Beirich et al., 2007; Schafer et al., 2014). In fact, there is great concern about immigration in these groups after it was announced that, by 2044, Whites would constitute a minority of the overall US population (Hogan et al., 2015). This distress has been exacerbated by White supremacist leaders claiming that Mexicans, possibly sponsored by the Mexican government, planned to "invade" and "conquer" the Southwestern US (Beirich et al., 2007; Glenn Spencer quoted in Campbell, 2015, p. 1089).

Likewise, these groups view Blacks stereotypically as morally inferior and as innately criminal, engaged in drug use, violent, lazy, and lustful of White women (Schafer et al., 2014). This last characteristic—lustfulness of White women—not only serves as a source of disdain because Blacks are viewed as inferior but also because interracial marriage (i.e., miscegenation) violates the first principle of White supremacy through the creation of non-White children (Bowles, 2019; *Loving v. Virginia*, 1967). In addition to hatred of Blacks, these groups also view Jews as "dishonest, untrustworthy, deceitful, and criminal" (Schafer et al. 2014, p. 180). However, in an analysis of online White supremacy group forums, Schafer and colleagues (2014) find "relatively little discussion of Jews (mentioned in only two accounts), despite the central role that anti-Semitism plays in much of the white supremacist discourse" (p. 189).

Fourth, the belief in an inevitable Racial Holy War (RAHOWA) serves as a core principle of White supremacist beliefs (Bjelopera, 2012; Bowman-Grieve, 2009). Coined by Klassen in 1986, RAHOWA is a "battle cry," which was used initially by the Creativity group, but has extended to other White supremacist groups because it applied for all Whites (p. 6). It alleges that there is only "space and survival on this Planet Earth" for Whites and that the "mud races" (i.e., non-Whites), and Jews are the lethal enemies that will bring about the extinction of Whites (ADL, 2020a; Klassen, 1986, p. 6). Therefore, Klassen (1985) calls for a "politically, militantly, financially, morally, and religiously" (p. 1) driven racial holy war as an "Ultimate and Only solution" to this threat (Klassen, 1987, p. 1). This belief in RAHOWA is especially salient because of the "unwavering identification of oppositional 'others' and a conspiratorial worldview" that is perpetuated by White supremacists (Adams & Roscigno, 2005, p. 772). Here, social problems are interpreted in racialized contexts, and "appropriate (and allegedly causally related) courses of action" are suggested (Adams & Roscigno, 2005, p. 772).

The fifth core White supremacist principle is "a belief in some variation of Revisionism" (Bowman-Grieve, 2009, p. 995). For example, Neo-Nazis and many other White supremacist groups hold Holocaust revisionist views (i.e., Holocaust denial), which "deny that the Nazis killed six million Jews … asserting that this is either a lie created for propaganda reasons or, at least, a gross exaggeration" (Burris et al., 2000, p. 219). Conversely, the Identity Christian Movement interprets the biblical text in a revisionist fashion that provides legitimacy to "murder targeting specifically identified victims" under the guise of "restoring their White God's law" (Sharpe, 2000, p. 619). These views, whether overtly racist or not, work to unify the White supremacist groups by supplying credibility for these beliefs (Burris et al., 2000).

Groups

Because of the often leaderless-ness occurring in White supremacy (Inwood, 2015), these groups and individuals are frequently referred to as "threats" instead of "groups" (Bjelopera, 2012). However, for simplicity, this chapter will use the term "group" to provide distinctions between sets of ideologies. Nonetheless, the individuals comprising these groups are often fluid/changing frequently and, at times, hold similar names but are drastically different (see, e.g., Aryan Nations-New Hampshire vs. Aryan Nations: Church of Jesus Christ Christian in Berlet & Vysotsky, 2006). Unlike international groups or threats, no official public listing of White supremacist or domestic extremist list exists, which may be due, in part, to concerns regarding First Amendment rights (Bjelopera, 2012).

Nonetheless, Berlet and Vysotsky (2006) provide a group "genealogy," describing the relations and interrelations of many of these groups' ideas and influences (see Berlet & Vysotsky, 2006, p. 18, figure 1). They present four different roots or "generalized influences" of groups being (1) conspiracy theories about Jews, (2) Greek and Roman mythology, (3) ethno-racial White supremacy, and (4) paganism, pantheism, and Odinism. From these roots, Berlet and Vysotsky (2006) build a typology to categorize White supremacist groups into three broad categories, (1) political, (2) religious, and (3) youth culture, to "allow the classification of white Supremacist groups by focusing on their activities and the source of their ideology," specifically to aid law enforcement (p. 19). Following this typology, the remainder of this section outlines several groups. For a complete list of groups based on this typology, see Berlet and Vysotsky's (2006, p. 46) "List of Groups by Category."

Political

Per Berlet and Vysotsky (2006), the majority of groups categorized under their "Political" typology are rooted in neo-fascist or neo-Nazi ideology. Specifically speaking about neo-Nazism—the "obsession with Adolph Hitler and Nazi Germany"—George Lincoln Rockwell is considered to be the Father of American neo-Nazism, publicly appearing in the late 1950s (Bjelopera, 2012, p. 16). His view of this ideology held that the term "White" included people from Southern and Eastern European descension lines, the denial of the Holocaust, and encouraged the tying of religion to the ideology (Bjelopera, 2012). However, Rockwell was assassinated by a follower in 1967 before reaching his ultimate goal of becoming president of the United States (Kaplan, 1995). At its core, the neo-Nazi movement uses religion to "establish an impression of historical continuity between a glorious Aryan past and the present" while also viewing social problems as a result of "racial and cultural degradation, both biologically and socially" (Adams & Roscigno, 2005, p. 772). In its current state, the movement lacks central leadership, a sense of unity, and tactical agreements with other groups, and suffers from fragmentation (Kaplan, 1995).

A closely related neo-Nazi group, the National Alliance, was founded in West Virginia by William Pierce, who believed in Cosmotheism and supported the "overthrow of the American political system" (Berlet & Vysotsky, 2006, p. 22; Burris et al., 2000). However, most National Alliance members disregard the religious aspect of this movement, instead focusing on Pierce's political motives, specifically attending to his book *The Turner Diaries*, which details a fictitious group of White supremacists who are preparing for, and engage in, racial war to bring about a "pure Aryan society" (Barnes, 1996; Burris et al., 2000, p. 223). This book has been said to have been written "for the sole purpose of teaching militant strategy—urging training in the use of military weaponry, bombings, assassinations, and guerrilla warfare," which has inspired multiple attacks, including the Oklahoma City bombing (Barnes, 1996, p. 1106; Bjelopera, 2012). Although this group was a leading neo-Nazi group in the 1990s, following the 2002 death of Pierce, the group has struggled with intra-group power and resource battles that have led to the group's declining influence (Berlet & Vysotsky, 2006; Freilich et al., 2009).

Given the decline of the National Alliance, along with the advent of the Internet, the National Socialist Movement (NSM) saw growth in the early 2000s (Bjelopera, 2012; Freilich et al., 2009). Only loosely tied to the neo-Nazi movement, the NSM provides members flexibility in participating in multiple White supremacist organizations while also "fighting for Race and Nation" (Berlet & Vysotsky, 2006, p. 24; Bjelopera, 2012).

One group that can be classified as either political or religious, depending on the sect, is the Ku Klux Klan, which was founded in Pulaski, Tennessee, following the Civil War (Baysinger, 2006; Berlet & Vysotsky, 2006). Originally founded as a nonpolitical organization aimed at amusing themselves and other community members, the group's members wore white-hooded costumes to represent "'the ghosts of the Confederate dead, who had arisen from their graves in order to wreak vengeance on an undesirable class' of people" (Wade, 1998, p. 35). When tied to religion, the KKK uses Christianity as a source of identity, claiming that "white Christian values" are under siege (Adams & Roscigno, 2005, p. 772). As such, the KKK seeks to rectify these attacks from the so-called "homosexual agenda" as well as disrupt any decreases in legislative power or any "perceived legal sanctions against whites (e.g., affirmative action)" (Adams & Roscigno, 2005, p. 772). Throughout its history, KKK members were called to use violence as part of the leaderless resistance movement to address these issues (Bowman-Grieve, 2009). As mentioned, following its initial post-Civil War surge, the KKK did subside until approximately the 1920s, when it was reinvigorated by the 1915 film, *Birth of a Nation*, which depicted Klansmen as heroic "saviors of a post-war South" (Baysinger, 2006; Clark, 2019). Although membership and leadership have ebbed and flowed throughout history, today, the largest KKK group, the Knights of the KKK, is headed by Don Black, a Klansman from Alabama (Burris et al., 2000). Additionally, the total membership of the KKK is estimated to be between 5,000 and 10,000 members, with most located in the South (History.com Editors, 2020; SPLC, n.d.a)

Religious

Individuals ascribing to the Christian Identity group believe that "Anglo-Saxons are the direct descendants of the Lost Tribes of Israel," who are considered God's chosen people (Berlet & Vysotsky, 2006; Bowman-Grieve, 2009, p. 991; Kaplan, 1995). Based on the "Two seeds doctrine," descendants of Adam are aligned with the White race and Israelites, whereas other races are descendants of Eve, Cain, and their seed-of-Lucifer-carrying offspring, including the Jews (Bowman-Grieve, 2009; Kaplan, 1995, p. 51; Sharpe, 2000). Based on this doctrine, the group's definition of "White" is narrower than other groups, being that of only White, Anglo-Saxon Protestants (Aho, 1990). In addition to this view of "White," Christian Identity groups are also associated with "(a) the theories of British Israelism; (b) a perversion of fundamentalist Christianity; (c) an antigovernment, paramilitary survivalist/conspiracy mentality based on a fear of the elimination of the White race; (d) a polygenist view of origins of humanity; and (e) the notion of White supremacy" (Bowman-Grieve, 2009; Sharpe, 2000, p. 606).

This group has been known for its use of violence, for example, legitimizing the "murder of doctors who perform abortions on White women" (Barnes, 1996; Sharpe, 2000, p. 617). Additionally, one of the more outspoken Identity members, Louis Beam, is acknowledged as the founder of the points system in which Identity members who wanted to be Aryan warriors could accumulate points through the assassination of "federal officials, civil rights leaders, Blacks, gays, and others ... as a symbol of honor" (Sharpe, 2000, p. 617; SPLC, 1998).

Although Christian Identity leadership has changed hands since its start in the 1940s, for example, Wesley Swift, William Potter Gale, and Richard G. Butler, Butler left the Christian Identity movement and started his own Aryan Nations group in the 1970s on a 20-acre plot of land in Idaho (Barnes, 1996; Berlet & Vysotsky, 2006). This site has been one of Christian Identity's "most visible institutional outposts," and has been associated with the Klansmen, neo-Nazis, and other White supremacist groups (Barnes, 1996; Berlet & Vysotsky, 2006, p. 28).

However, Zhou and colleagues (2005) note that "it's generally difficult to make clear separations between Christian Identity, neo-Nazi, and white supremacist groups" (p. 48; see also Burris et al., 2000). Since Butler's death in 2004, the Aryan Nations and Christian Identity movement, more broadly, have struggled internally over leadership and headquarters location, leading to a decline in these movements (Berlet & Vysotsky, 2006).

Another group categorized by Berlet and Vysotsky (2006) as religious is the Creativity Movement, formerly known as the World Church of the Creator (WCOTC) (Bjelopera, 2012). Founded in 1973 by Ben Klassen, this group's ideology centers on Klassen's writings: *Nature's Eternal Religion* (1973), *The White Man's Bible* (1981), and *Salubrious Living* (1982) (Berlet & Vysotsky, 2006; Bowman-Grieve, 2009). The Creativity Movement heavily focuses on the impending racial holy war (Berlet & Vysotsky, 2006). As a part of this group, members must memorize and repeat a sacred religious ritual five times per day, which states

> Based on the Eternal Laws of Nature, History, Logic and Common Sense, we Creators believe: WE BELIEVE that our Race is our Religion. WE BELIEVE that the White Race is Nature's Finest. WE BELIEVE that racial loyalty is the greatest of all honors, and racial treason is the worst of all crimes. WE BELIEVE that what is good for the White Race is the highest virtue, and what is bad for the White Race is the ultimate sin. WE BELIEVE that the one and only, true and evolutionary White Racial Religion—Creativity—is the only salvation for the White Race. To the fulfillment of these religious beliefs, we Creators forever pledge our Lives, our Sacred Honor, and our Religious Zeal.
> (The Creativity Movement, 2017)

Currently, the Creativity Movement's most extensive base is located in Illinois, but it also has over 40 chapters established across North America and is seeing "signs of revival under new leadership" (Bjelopera, 2012; Bowman-Grieve, 2009).

Aside from protestant religious affiliations, some White supremacist groups center on Norse mythology, specifically Odinism (Berlet & Vysotsky, 2006). Although not all who practice Odinism are White supremacists, those who are believe that it is the "true religion of the White northern Europeans" and, as such, the Norse gods of the Vikings are the true Aryan gods (Baysinger, 2006; Berlet & Vysotsky, 2006, p. 30). Furthermore, Odinists tend to hold conspiratorial views of historical events, racist feelings/opinions that merge with racial mysticism, and "consider forceful retaliation for past injustices by the dominant culture" (Baysinger, 2006, p. 11). Odinists also emphasize the oversimplification of complex information, particularly with the "revitalized tribal ideas of Vikings" (Baysinger, 2006, p. 11).

Youth Culture

The predominant youth-centric White supremacist group is the skinheads, whose origins begin in the United Kingdom in the 1960s, but did not take hold in the United States until the early 1980s (Bjelopera, 2012; SPLC, 2009). Considered the "foot soldiers of the right-wing movement" (Baysinger, 2006), the skinheads are known for their extreme violence, even targeting one another (Bjelopera, 2012). These youth are recruited by other organizations, such as the Aryan Nation, the KKK, and the Church of the Creator (Baysinger, 2006). Typically, these youth have a distinct appearance including "Levi jeans, red suspenders, Fred Perry shirts, and Doc Martens steel-toed boots" as well as tattoos with imagery such as Vikings, swastikas, and eagles (Baysinger, 2006, p. 14)

Conclusion

Although these groups are described distinctly above, they are often interrelated. In studying the social network of White supremacy groups online, Burris and colleagues (2000) find that, at least online, White supremacist groups are relatively decentralized and share many of the same doctrine and ideology (e.g., Christian Identity). Burris and colleagues (2000) are also quick to note that these groups are not intertwined with militia movements nor the mainstream Christian Right. Furthermore, these online White supremacist groups are "relatively isolated from mainstream conservatives and other extremist groups" (Burris et al., 2000, p. 215).

Nonetheless, this ideology of White supremacy is not unique to the United States. Instead, this ideology and its core tenants are present around the world (see, e.g., Cherkaoui & Dewan, 2019; DeLeeuw & Pridemore, 2018; Sánchez-Cuenca & de la Calle, 2009). For example, the 2019 attack on two mosques in Christchurch, New Zealand, was carried out based on White supremacist motives, per the attacker's manifesto (Cherkaoui & Dewan, 2019). Likewise, an analysis of attacks in the UK finds that most right-wing attacks have been associated with

White supremacy (DeLeeuw & Pridemore, 2018). Furthermore, Burris and colleague's (2000) analysis confirms that these groups are often internationally connected online, which, they argue, creates a "white supremacist 'cyber-community' that transcends regional and national boundaries" (p. 215).

Research on White Supremacy as a Motive for Domestic Terrorism

Research on White supremacy in the United States has generally focused on three key questions: (1) what are the avenues that lead people to join White supremacy groups? (2) what is the extent and prevalence of violence perpetrated by White supremacists? and (3) what leads people to desist from this violence and leave White supremacy behind? As such, the following sections provide the current evidence related to these questions.

Entry into White Supremacy

Two predominant lines of research surrounding entry into White supremacy involve (1) why people join these groups and (2) how people join these groups. Starting with the first—why people join—Simi and colleagues (2016) provide a three-factor risk model for involvement in extremism. First, they argue that individuals involved in White supremacy face early childhood risk factors, such as abuse, witnessing abuse, substance abuse by family members, family dysfunction or disruption, and victimization. These early experiences produce negative emotions, such as anger and depression. Second, Simi and colleagues (2016) argue these individuals have a "subsequent onset of adolescent conduct problems," including, but not limited to, drug and alcohol use and abuse, academic failure, truancy, and aggressive behavior (p. 8). Third, the individual is non-ideologically motivated to participate in extremist groups; instead participation is often based on circumstances (Simi et al., 2016). Such motivations, Simi and colleagues (2016) argue, could be social support, scapegoating, and even providing an outlet for the individual's aggression. As such, based on their analyses and model, "the importance of ideology primarily follows rather than precedes entry"—an essential revelation for addressing why people join these extremist groups (Simi et al., 2016, p. 15). These members initially sought out these groups to establish a "tough" reputation, seek physical shelter, receive mentorship, and express their anger and frustration (Simi et al., 2016). However, these researchers caution that this process is not necessarily linear, suggesting that these individuals do not necessarily need to have early childhood risk factors or adolescent conduct problems to engage with extremist groups.

Similarly, Bowman-Grieve's (2009) analysis of personal narratives on a White supremacist forum, Stormfront, finds that many individuals felt drawn into these groups based on personal experiences, perceptions of politics or the government, patriotism following the 9/11 terrorist attacks, White supremacist literature, and having children. Schafer and colleagues (2014) note similar frustrations in their analysis of Stormfront forums and another forum, World Church of the Creator, describing them as "seeds of discontent" that motivated these individuals (p. 180). Predominantly, they find that "exposure to minorities within various daily social environments," such as school, the workplace, and the military, produced distress and feelings of injustice (Schafer et al., 2014, p. 180). For example, Schafer and colleagues (2014) note that these individuals "notice differences in the way African Americans/Jews behaved and were treated by social systems" and how they were "slighted ... because of their status as a white" (p. 180). Likewise, these individuals were aggrieved, feeling that they were "expected to study non-white cultures [in school] while being made to feel guilty for their own heritage," a "behavioral double standard" in the workplace, and a "discontent if not outright astonishment that their black peers did not seem to take soldiering [in the military] as seriously as whites" (Schafer et al., 2014, pp. 181–183). It is these perceived grievances along with racial pride that act as a catalyst for their "awakening" (Bowman-Grieve, 2009; Schafer et al., 2014, p. 181).

The second line of research—how people join White supremacist groups—finds multiple avenues by which ideology is shared and groups are formed. First and foremost, the Internet is a robust resource for those exploring this ideology, inquiring about membership, and recruitment (Burris et al., 2000; McGarrity & Shivers, 2019; Simi & Futrell, 2006). Simply stated, this content is "easily found" through keyword searches, which produce results related to music, literature, symbolism, chatrooms, video games, parenting advice and strategies for "indoctrinating their children into the movement," crossword puzzles, coloring pages, live streams (e.g., Panzerfaust.com), racist books, videos, jewelry, and clothing (Simi & Futrell, 2006, pp. 128–129). Additionally, this material provides an avenue for "research" or self-initiated investigations (Schafer et al., 2014). A clear example of this online indoctrination of White supremacist values comes from the Christchurch shooter who, "in the manifesto he posted online prior to murdering 51 Muslim worshipers in Christchurch, New Zealand, the killer posed a question to himself: 'From where did you receive/research/develop your beliefs?' He answered thusly: 'The internet, of course. You will not find the truth anywhere else'" (quoted in Brooks, 2020).

Aside from ideological material, these websites provide an international "community" for like-minded individuals (Burris et al., 2000; Simi & Futrell, 2006). These communities offer new members an example of how to "maintain involvement and faith in the movement over time" as well as mentorship from veteran members (Simi & Futrell, 2006, p. 136). Likewise, this online community evokes a sense of solidarity through "expressions of fraternity and kinship, with terms like 'brother' and 'sister'" (Simi & Futrell, 2006, p. 134). Additionally, these online communities provide an outlet to express instances of stigma and ostracization, which will typically be met with "sympathy, support, and solutions" (Simi & Futrell, 2006, p. 133). Through these online activities, members may virtually participate, much like they do in the real world, but in an unconstrained place, allowing for the expression of their radical views, which is often encouraged and supported (Simi & Futrell, 2006).

Several websites serve as content providers and community spaces for White supremacy groups, such as 4chan, 8chan, Parler, Stormfront, The-Donald, the Daily Stormer, Twitter, and YouTube (Brooks, 2020; Graff, 2020; Zhou et al., 2005). Established in March of 1995 and operated by former Klansman, Don Black, Stormfront.org is considered the first domestic "hate site" for White supremacy and continues to play an integral role in White supremacy today (Bowman-Grieve, 2009; Burris et al., 2000; Zhou et al., 2005, p. 44). With a membership exceeding 159,000, this website "has its own radio hosting service, ... provides information on current events, press coverage, and also recently ran a scholarship competition where essays could be submitted for three cash prizes" (Bowman-Grieve, 2009, p. 996). The second primary website for these groups is the Daily Stormer, which provides similar content "under layers of humor that are designed to desensitize readers to grossly racist content and ease them into the world of hate" and is "mainly designed to target children," according to the site's operator Andrew Anglin (quoted in Hatewatch Staff, 2018).

Most recently, the social media site, Parler, has served as a Twitter-alternative for its over 2.8 million users who wish to engage in "free speech" in a place that will not censor their posts and discussion (Di Stefano et al., 2019; Lerman, 2020). However, this site has quickly become home to conspiracy theories, misinformation, antisemitism, Islamophobia, far-right content, and White supremacist content (Manavis, 2020; Saul, 2019; Sullivan, 2020). Regardless of which group an individual seeks to know more about or even join, these online sites provide them with content quickly and easily to "find the ideology that 'fits' the individual's temperament in a much shorter period of time" (Schafer et al., 2014, p. 188).

However, these online communities do not necessarily simply remain online. Wellman and Gulia (1999, p. 182) note that "people do not neatly divide their worlds into two discrete sets: people seen in person and people contacted online. Rather, many community ties connect offline as well as online." As such, these online communities also serve as a means for members to plan in-person meetings (Simi & Futrell, 2006). However, they also serve as a location to announce their lethal plans (e.g., three in one year, including the El Paso Walmart attack, on 8-chan) and live stream their attacks for online viewers (Barrett, 2019; Graff, 2020).

A second major source for recruitment into a White supremacy group comes from the prison setting. In this institutional setting that is highly racialized, many of those who are disaffected are receptive to the messaging of incarcerated White supremacists (Bjelopera, 2012; Brandon, 2009; Schafer et al., 2014). This radicalization takes the form of personal relationships between mentees and mentors engaging in "long periods of study and discussion, often led by the mentoring individual that set them on their current path" (Brandon, 2009; Schafer et al., 2014, p. 186). The prison setting poses a unique challenge in that White supremacy exists within those who are incarcerated and the officials who operate these facilities as well as a lack of decisive steps to address prison radicalization (e.g., separate extremists from the general population; Barnes, 1996; Brandon, 2009).

A third avenue for joining White supremacist groups is found in the relationships and networks of an individual—their family and friends (Schafer et al., 2014; Simi & Futrell 2009). Simi and Futrell (2009) describe instances in which parents may name their children or pets after symbols of their ideology, birthday parties are held with White power themes, homes are adorned with prominent White power symbols, and even house parties are themed around these symbols and ideologies. Furthermore, "congresses" or "conferences," as well as music festivals and concerts (e.g., Aryan Nations Congress, Christian Identity Conference, White Christian Heritage Festival, Hammerfest, and Nordi Fest), are held to bring like-minded individuals together (Simi & Futrell, 2009). In fact, despite the Internet's capability of sharing content for recruitment, Aho (1990) finds that a social contact (i.e., family, friend, co-worker, other acquaintance) was the primary influence for 70 percent of individuals interviewed. Schafer and colleagues (2014) dive deeper into these relationships, finding that not all family or peer relationships were positive (i.e., supportive of White supremacy or related ideology); some were negative (e.g., interracial relationships). Additionally, of those interviewed, despite being a source of racial beliefs and racial pride, many were dismayed by their family's lack of commitment to the cause based on the family's lack of active steps toward producing a "White and Proud" society (Schafer et al., 2014, p. 185). Central to the individual's "awakening" about race, Schafer and colleagues (2014) find, are the friends who are already active in the various White supremacist movements, who provided them with leaflets, newsletters, and even copies of *Mein Kampf.*

One unique vein of research on entry into White supremacy involves how women become incorporated into these groups. Blee's (1996) life history narratives of 34 women of varying leadership roles (i.e., known leaders, not publicly known leaders, rank-and-file), active in White supremacist groups from around the United States, provide three unique avenues for how these women describe their inception and involvement in these groups. First, Blee (1996) describes a "conversion" of these women from their "previous weak, distorted, ignorant, directionless, and naive self" to an "all-knowing, committed, impassioned" self, mainly hinging on a singular life event, such as the loss of a loved one or a near-death experience (pp. 689–690). However, Blee (1996) notes that these narratives are "best understood as *learned* narratives, retrospectively formatted by the political, ideological, and even stylistic conventions of racist group imagery" (p. 192). As such, this conversion process might best be described as "learning to become a racist" (Blee, 1996, p. 693).

The second set of narratives about involvement in White supremacist groups involved the "selective adoption" of ideologies or agendas (Blee, 1996, p. 693). For these women, some of the group's values were inconsistent with their own (e.g., support for adoption, homosexuality, and biracial marriages). These women argued that these groups were "too male-oriented [and] too sexist" with men only wanting these women to have White children (Blee, 1996, p. 694). However, by selectively adopting their ideology and agenda, these women were provided with the flexibility to participate in group activities without having to fully convert to the group's ideology (Blee, 1996).

The third and final set of narratives described by Blee (1996) encompass those who found themselves resigned to this ideology and agenda because they felt they were onerously burdened with "the truth" and a responsibility associated with it (p. 695). Many of these women did not want to actively acknowledge their activism in the movement, and those that did "tried not to be 'too active'" (Blee, 1996, p. 695). Instead, these women viewed themselves as victims of a world that unjustly characterized them as "haters," "sick," and "the problem of society" (Blee, 1996, p. 696). Ultimately, for women whose narrative was that of resignation, they were not enthused, empowered, or excited members of these groups, but hopeless and concerned for the safety of themselves and their children in a racialized world (Blee, 1996).

Overall, Blee's research (1996, 2005) provides evidence that women have a role in White supremacist groups, which often is the result of associating with members of these groups (e.g., friends, family, acquaintances), as opposed to seeking out participation in these groups. Furthermore, these women were educated, had resources and connections, had stakes at risk in conventional society, were not raised in abusive homes, and were not mentally ill (Blee, 2005).

Regardless of how individuals (men, women, or others) come to join these groups, Simi and colleagues (2017b; see also Simi et al., 2017a) argue, much like Blee (1996), that there is a "complete identity transformation" that "dominates everything from their thoughts, feelings, and relationships to their selection of television shows, music and even food they consume" with "rigid boundaries of 'us' and 'them' and various types of dehumanization."

Extent and Prevalence of Violence

Laden with the view that Whites are under attack, alongside their emphasis on masculinity, White supremacists differ from some other domestic terror groups in that they use violence as a means of expression (Gruenewald, 2011; Van McVey, 2008). For example, a group of neo-Nazis was alleged to have engaged in a "months-long campaign of harassment, intimidation, and fear against various Black churches, journalists, government officials, and universities—including by 'swatting'" (Graff, 2020; Olding, 2020). In contrast, other domestic terror groups use "paper terrorism" (i.e., liens, frivolous lawsuits, retaliatory filings), economic sabotage, web sabotage, cyberattacks, and even doxing instead of physical violence (Bjelopera, 2012). For White supremacist groups, this use of violence aligns with their belief in an impending racial holy war (Adams & Roscigno, 2005; Berlet & Vysotsky, 2006; Klassen, 1987). However, "similar to street gangs, not all White supremacists are violent" (Simi et al., 2016, p. 4).

Even so, analyses into this violence find that White supremacists committed 31.2 percent of the domestic terror incidents and 51.6 percent of the domestic terror fatalities between 1954 and 2000 (Hewitt, 2003). In raw numbers, over 530 people have been killed in the United States by this far-right extremism in more than 275 incidents, including over 47 law enforcement officers killed in the line of duty in 35 incidents, since 1990 (Freilich & Chermak, 2009). More recent analyses find that these same groups were responsible for 73 percent of domestic terror fatalities between 2009 and 2018, with fatalities in 2018 being the highest (50 deaths) since the Oklahoma City bombing in 1995 (ADL, 2019b; Bergengruen & Hennigan, 2019). Of concern, 62 percent of these groups' violent plots are successfully completed (Braniff, 2019). By comparison, Islamic terrorism accounts for 1.1 percent of incidents and 1.7 percent of fatalities in the US between 1954 and 2000 (Hewitt, 2003). Former senior Justice Department official for National Security and Georgetown University law professor, Mary McCord, notes that "In the U.S., more people are killed by far-right extremists than by those who are adherents to Islamist extremism" (quoted in MacFarquhar, 2020).

However, MacFarquhar (2020) warns that "There is no official source on the number of attacks carried out by white supremacists in the United States." Further complicating our understanding of White supremacist violence, the data and statistics that are available from "academic centers or nongovernmental organizations rarely match because of different methods, including various definitions of right-wing extremism" (MacFarquhar, 2020). These are known issues within the Federal Bureau of Investigation (FBI), which has not recently had a "receptive audience in the White House" to address the matter but a point that I will return to briefly (Bergengruen & Hennigan, 2019).

A review of these White supremacist homicides, compared to all other homicides, finds that these cases are six times more likely to have multiple offenders, three times as likely to target victims who are strangers, almost 35 times more likely to involve a White suspect, and over five times more likely to involve a male suspect (Gruenewald,

2011). Although the majority (76.2 percent) of White supremacist homicides were not related to profit, Gruenewald (2011) finds that nearly one in four are profit-related, suggesting that these groups may be versatile in their offending instead of merely "mission-" or ideology-driven offenders (p. 189). Likewise, analyses of White supremacist homicides find a majority tend to use firearms, followed by the use of knives, to commit their homicides (ADL, 2019b; Gruenewald, 2011). Additional analysis of White supremacists perpetrating homicide finds that, since 2011, at least one in three were inspired by, professed reverence for, or showed an interest in the tactics of individuals who perpetrated similar attacks (Brooks, 2020; Cai & Landon, 2019).

Nonetheless, Harris (1987) notes that this violence is "cyclical in nature. Activities occur because of certain issues; when the issues fade or the terrorists are arrested, the activities will generally subside. But different issues will arise and different terrorists will come forth to commit new acts" (p. 13). Although Harris makes this assertion in the late 1980s, in the current political context, the concern of White supremacist domestic terror is palpable. Cohen, a former counter-terrorism coordinator at the Department of Homeland Security, notes that "political leaders are playing with fire when they promote white supremacist talking points such as exaggerated claims of the security threat immigrants present and their supposed drain on public resources, to stoke their supporters" (quoted in Ortiz, 2020). Cohen goes on to state that "By mainstreaming those ideological beliefs for the purposes of inspiring their political base, they have also inspired disaffected, violence-prone individuals to conduct attacks" (quoted in Ortiz, 2020). This is most recently evidenced in the October 2020 arrest of over a dozen White supremacist-affiliated individuals charged in connection with the attempted kidnapping of Michigan Governor Gretchen Whitmer, the plotting of attacks on law enforcement, and plotting to overthrow the government, which was intended to start a race-based civil war (Romo, 2020; Zapotosky et al., 2020). In seeming dismay, Daryl Johnson, a former senior analyst at the Department of Homeland Security (DHS), notes, "I'm afraid we've reached a tipping point where we're in for this kind of violence for a long time" (Bergengruen & Hennigan, 2019).

Desistance

Although less studied than entry into White supremacy, desistance from White supremacy ideology has multiple theoretical views. On the one hand, theorists argue that holders of this ideology are seen as "once a hater, always a hater," leaving little room for individuals to change their views and beliefs (Simi et al., 2017b). However, Simi and colleagues (2017b) argue that "there may be shreds of truth in this statement in that any kind of powerful identity will leave traces on the remainder of a person's life," but they also note that the "persistence of hate is not inevitable."

Instead, Simi and colleagues (2017a) equate desistance from White supremacy ideology to managing addiction. Much like treatments used for addiction, such as cognitive-behavioral therapy (CBT), these individuals use "extensive self-talk strategies" to "suppress manifestations of a self they no longer embrace" (Simi et al., 2017b; see also Simi et al., 2017a).

Preventing White Supremacist Violence

Efforts to prevent or control White supremacist violence can be relegated into two broad domains—(1) criminal law enforcement efforts and (2) civil litigation efforts.

Criminal Law Enforcement

At the federal level, the FBI has recently attempted to bolster its efforts to address domestic terrorism by creating the Domestic Terrorism–Hate Crimes Fusion Cell in 2019 (MacFarquhar, 2020). Its mission is to help "ensure seamless information sharing across divisions and [augment] investigative resources to combat the domestic terrorism threat" (McGarrity & Shivers, 2019). To further advance efforts to combat domestic terrorism, specifically White supremacist violence, the FBI has internally moved White supremacist terror groups to the same level as international terror groups, such as Al-Qaeda and ISIS, to attempt to focus on this potential threat (Graff, 2020). However, even with the addition of the Fusion Cell and an internal emphasis on White supremacist domestic terrorist groups, only 20 percent of the FBI's counterterrorism field agents are focused on domestic terror investigations (Bergengruen & Hennigan, 2019).

Thus, federal law enforcement efforts are heavily enhanced through cooperation with and reliance upon the state, local, tribal, and territorial law enforcement partners (McGarrity & Shivers, 2019). Formal partnerships, such as Regional Information Sharing Systems and Joint

Terrorism Task Forces, aid in collecting and disseminating intelligence as well as threat assessments between law enforcement agencies to disrupt domestic terror efforts (Bodrero, 1999; McGarrity & Shivers, 2019).

Even with these partnerships, addressing domestic terrorism through law enforcement is especially challenging because domestic terrorism is not a federal crime (Bergengruen & Hennigan, 2019). Instead, there are 57 specific acts the federal government define as crimes of terrorism, including violence at an international airport, using a weapon of mass destruction, hostage-taking, destruction of energy facilities, or attacking federal officials; none of these 57 acts specifically reference domestic terror, although 51 of these acts may be applied to domestic terrorism cases (MacFarquhar, 2020; 18 U.S. Code §2339A, 2009). Nonetheless, this absence of federal domestic terrorism laws limits prosecutors to using federal hate-crime laws or other miscellaneous laws, such as conspiracy statutes and RICO (the Racketeering Influenced and Corrupt Organization Act), to charge suspects (Bergengruen & Hennigan, 2019; MacFarquhar, 2020). When invoked, these hate-crime laws have been applied unevenly, with a Mexican American individual being the only individual prosecuted for White supremacy speech online as of 2009, suggesting a racialized notion of protected speech (Daniels, 2009).

Recognizing these limitations, there has been a push to codify domestic terrorism as a federal crime, with Brian O'Hare, president of the FBI Agents, stating, "Acts of violence intended to intimidate civilian populations or to influence or affect government policy should be prosecuted as domestic terrorism regardless of the ideology behind them" (quoted in Bergengruen & Hennigan, 2019). But, there are some with reservations about such a law potentially infringing upon the First Amendment rights of Americans (MacFarquhar, 2020).

Regardless of the legal codes used against perpetrators of domestic terror, law enforcement officers at all levels have been called to be prepared to address this violence, should it occur in their jurisdiction (Bodrero, 1999). Therefore, multiple governmental and public agencies, such as the Anti-Defamation League (ADL) or the Southern Poverty Law Center (SPLC), provide training programs on domestic terrorism, such as the Department of Justice's (DOJ) State and Local Anti-terrorism Training (SLATT) and courses in "Domestic Terrorism" and "Special-interest/Anarchist groups" (Chermak et al., 2009). Still, the number of international terrorism training programs for law enforcement officers vastly outnumber those of domestic terror training, suggesting a more significant concern in law enforcement agencies for preparing for international threats (Chermak et al., 2009).

Conversely, this lack of domestic terror training for law enforcement may reflect the relative ease in identifying and infiltrating far-right extremists' efforts to engage in terrorism (as opposed to international terrorists) because these domestic extremist groups hold a "public persona, dress, and participation in open, extremist activities (such as gun shows, racist music festivals, and other racist gatherings) [that] make such groups vulnerable to undercover infiltration" (Chermak et al., 2009, p. 1317). Hamm (2005) argues that law enforcement officers contact these individuals through typical criminal investigative techniques, in part, because of the crime they commit and their inability to silence members who have converted to law enforcement informants.

McGarrell et al. (2007) step back from this labeling debate (i.e., domestic vs. international terrorism), arguing that the focus should be on the ideology of the offender. They ask a more direct question: "Was the perpetrator of the incident at issue a supporter of the domestic far-right when the crime was committed?" (quoted in Chermak et al., 2009). In focusing on the offender's ideology instead of their "group," law enforcement can dismiss the subtle differences between and within these groups, which, as described above, can become quite complex, and instead focus on the harm these individuals seek to undertake.

Be this as it may, the Trump administration's approach toward addressing White supremacist violence or even domestic terrorism has continued to diverge from past administrations (Graff, 2020; Swan, 2020a). Early in his presidency, the DHS's Domestic Terror Intelligence Unit tasked with focusing on domestic violent extremism was disbanded (Swan, 2019) and cut grant funding to previously awarded groups who aimed to combat White supremacy and neo-Nazism (Bergengruen & Hennigan, 2019; Zanona, 2017). In addition, the Justice Department's categorization of domestic terrorism was reorganized, which has made it more challenging to track and measure attacks because they are often misclassified (Bergengruen & Hennigan, 2019).

Civil Litigation Strategies

Based on some of the challenges in addressing White supremacy via law enforcement, groups such as the SPLC and the ADL have opted to use civil litigation strategies to bankrupt and dismantle White supremacist groups (Daniels, 2009; Garland & Simi, 2011). By treating White supremacist groups as organizations, civil litigation provides for the use of "vicarious liability" to hold these groups accountable for their members, which has led to successful cases bringing in millions of dollars (Garland & Simi, 2011). This methodology was pioneered by the SPLC, who has been "monitoring extremist white supremacist activity throughout the United States" since 1981 (Daniels, 2009, p. 173).

Additionally, the SPLC has used civil law to pressure online platforms to stop funding and earning commission from hate groups (Brooks, 2020). For example, the SPLC found that "at least 69 hate groups were using PayPal" and at least another "54 white power bands were [selling music on iTunes] earning 70 cents for each downloaded song" (Brooks, 2020). Additional sites identified by the SPLC for providing an online avenue for hate groups to collect funding or support were YouTube, Facebook, Google, and Reddit (Brooks, 2020). As part of this campaign to end online support and financing of these hate groups, in October of 2018, the SPLC and other civil rights groups provided technology companies with recommended policies for prevention and removal of these groups and their content from their platforms.

Before the SPLC's efforts, the United States had attempted to implement a law mandating the use of "filtering" software to remove or restrict content, such as pornography, on public computers (Daniels, 2009). But this law did not pass, in part, due to the software's woeful inadequacies for addressing White supremacy content online (Daniels, 2009). Likewise, online portals, such as AOL and Google, have tried unsuccessfully to use "terms of service" agreements to limit content (Daniels, 2009). Even private citizens, such as Harvard's Law School Librarian, David Goldman, have attempted to address White supremacy online—in Goldman's case, starting the website "Hatewatch" in 1995 to track White supremacy online (Daniels, 2009).

However, using civil litigation as a strategy does have its critiques. Garland and Simi (2011) worry that the efforts to bankrupt and disrupt groups with civil lawsuits might lead to feelings of injustice, victimization, martyrdom, and even a strengthened collective identity for these groups. They are also quick to note that the use of online platforms to spread their ideology is relatively inexpensive, which means that even heavy financial losses in civil litigation may lead to only marginal reductions in the use of the Internet by these groups and their leaders (Garland & Simi, 2011). More recently, online platforms, such as Twitter, have attempted to use algorithms to remove content, only to run into the challenge that some of the content of Republican politicians, and even the President, would be flagged as objectionable (Cox & Koebler, 2019).

Challenges and Recommendations

One of the critical challenges in combating White supremacy and domestic terrorism is the infiltration of these members into military and law enforcement bodies. In fact, in October of 2006, the FBI's Counterterrorism Division labeled the infiltration of White supremacists in law enforcement as "a threat" not only for communities but also for law enforcement officers, elected officials, and protected persons (FBI Counterterrorism Division, 2006, p. 3). But this infiltration of White supremacists in law enforcement is not new; instead, it dates back to the period immediately following the Civil War (Barnes, 1996).

A resurgence of ties between law enforcement and White supremacy occurred during the civil rights era (Barnes, 1996), and again following the 2004 speech from Tom Metzger, a former California grand dragon of the Knights of the Klu Klux Klan and founder of the White Aryan Resistance (Chin, 2013). Metzger called for his audience to advance the White cause, stating "We have to infiltrate! Infiltrate the military! Infiltrate your local governments! Infiltrate your school board! Infiltrate law enforcement!" (quoted in SPLC, n.d.b; also quoted in Chin, 2013, pp. 44–45). It appears this call was heeded; a 2010 FBI National Gang Intelligence Center report notes this threat of infiltration by White supremacists or their friends, family, and associates, specifically in civilian law enforcement positions.

The dangers posed by this infiltration are widespread. This line of employment provides "training, weapons, and authority" (Chin, 2013, p. 31), which empowers these individuals and leaves them "heavily armed, exceedingly dangerous, and engaged in active preparation for [a] race war" (Barnes, 1996, p. 1087). Because these officers are both authorized and trained to use violence, Barnes (1996) speculates that these White supremacist-affiliated officers seek to "perpetrate [violence] under color of law" (p. 1090). These concerns are bolstered by audio recordings of a White supremacist leader, Rinaldo Nazzaro, who specifically sought out military and law enforcement members to "… be in a position where [they are] ready, [they are] prepared enough, ready enough that [they] can take advantage of whatever chaos, power vacuum, that might emerge" when a race war begins (quoted in Hjelmgaard, 2020).

As such, racial and ethnic minority community members face violence not only when engaging with private individuals but also public officials, specifically law enforcement, associated with White supremacy (Barnes, 1996). Looking through the lens of procedural justice, this potential for violence at the hands of law enforcement officers, who are associated with White supremacy, leads to the degradation of police–community relationships and trust, which is ultimately harmful to law enforcement (FBI, 2006; see also Tyler, 2004). Conversely, people of color also face the possibility of under-policing by these officers affiliated with White supremacist groups (FBI, 2006). These officers may fail to act to protect community members and/or fail to serve communities equitably, which again undermine the police–community relationship through promoting resentment and distrust (FBI, 2006).

Relatedly, the infiltration of White supremacy in law enforcement has the potential to compromise law enforcement investigations through the thwarting of investigations and the collection and exploitation of intelligence (Chin, 2013; FBI, 2006). As such, law enforcement officers themselves are at risk of harm when this intelligence, particularly when related to investigations of White supremacist groups, is collected and shared among White supremacist groups (FBI, 2006; National Gang Intelligence Center, 2010).

Aside from violence, these officers are placed in roles that provide them, among other opportunities, access to falsify crime reports, to cover up officer misconduct, to improperly collect and inventory evidence, and to identify and interview witnesses and suspects (Barnes, 1996). In each of these opportunities, an officer affiliated with White supremacy may use their power and ideology to undermine justice, particularly for people of color (Barnes, 1996). Yet, it is surprising that there is no exhaustive investigation into the extent to which unmonitored police discretion, mismanagement of department resources, and police officers' code of silence specifically influence the progress and process of the criminal justice system and its actors as they address racially motivated crimes (Barnes, 1996).

But, these physical and nonphysical dangers are not mere hypotheticals. As Barnes (1996) states, "[the] nation's law enforcement agencies ... have acted in reckless disregard, if not official complicity, of the epidemic of hate-crime activity" (p. 1081). For example, in 1985, Kentucky officers of a Klan-cop group were suspected of firebombing the home of a Black family in a mostly White neighborhood (Barnes, 1996). Similarly, a Houston officer engaged in a series of fatal incidents including killing two Black men, fatally shooting an off-duty Black security guard in the back six times who was stopped for not wearing his seatbelt, and beating two Hispanic men, before being fired in 1990 for excessive force amidst civil rights complaints (Bardwell, 1993).

In yet another display of police-initiated White supremacist violence, a group of 22 Los Angeles County Sheriffs' deputies, linked to a neo-Nazi group, were accused of 43 incidents in one Latino community, including shootings, brutality, terrorism, and excessive force (McMillan & Sahagun, 1990). In 2009, a Fruitland Park, Florida officer was allowed to resign after discovering he handed out fliers supporting the Klan as part of Klan recruitment efforts (Eckinger & Sentinel Staff Writer, 2009). More recently, in 2018, a police chief, who was recorded by his officers engaging in several racist rants, was charged with a federal hate crime as a result of an alleged assault of an African American juvenile who was arrested (Rose, 2018). Furthermore, a Lafayette, Indiana officer, who was still in training, was fired for his participation in an online neo-Nazi message board, claiming that he was "exposed to the vile 'culture' of the African and learned that everything [he] had been taught on race had been a flimsy fabrication which was not supported by real world evidence" (quoted in Chen, 2020; Panzerleiter, 2016).

Although this Lafayette officer only engaged in a neo-Nazi online message board, legal opinions note that, despite First Amendment rights, the government has the right to encroach upon personal liberty when there is a compelling, "legitimate and vital state interest" (*Gibson v. Florida Legislative Investigation Commission*, 1963). In the case of law enforcement officers, the state grants these officers positions of power and trust to uphold the law and provide protection for all community members, which may be antithetical to the views of White supremacists, thus leading to their termination (Barnes, 1996). However, this termination is often at the discretion of the police leaders, which may result in inaction (Barnes, 1996), retaliation for officers who provide information about their fellow officer's engagement in White supremacy or race-related violence (see, e.g., *Neubauer v. City of McAllen*, 1985; *United States v. City of Buffalo*, 1978), or retaliation against non-law enforcement officers who report these improprieties (see, e.g., *Rode v. Dellarciprete*, 1988).

Despite these challenges, an argument has been made for zero-tolerance for White supremacy and White supremacists in law enforcement (Chin, 2013), as well as specialized rules that would preclude White supremacists from serving in public service positions (e.g., law enforcement and military personnel, judges, firefighters, correctional worker; Barnes, 1996). More broadly, scholars have made several recommendations that may be used to address domestic terrorism. For instance, Braniff (2019) contends that the federal government should pass the Domestic Terrorism DATA Act, which would improve transparency by requiring the FBI, DOJ, and DHS to provide yearly reports on varying facets of domestic and international terrorism as well as fund $1 million in terrorism research (Domestic Terrorism DATA Act, H.R. 3106, 2019). Relatedly, Braniff (2019) argues that the US Department of Homeland Security's Office of Targeted Violence and Terrorism Prevention should be augmented in a way that replicates the successful program being run in Colorado, as evidenced in their over 40 interventions. To address domestic terrorism at the local level, Chermak and colleagues (2009) push for "a carefully constructed training curriculum on far-right extremism ... [that] focus[es] on driving violations, traffic stops, and successfully managing potentially violent situations, such as serving an arrest warrant at a far rightist's home" (p. 1318).

However, not all recommendations involve the criminal justice system as an intervention to address domestic terrorism. Instead, a public health approach to this matter could invest in programs that promote community resilience, address at-risk individuals, and foster the rehabilitation and reintegration of former members of domestic threat groups (Braniff, 2019). Nonetheless, these recommendations serve as potential avenues for addressing domestic terrorism beyond the current means.

Future Avenues of Research on White Supremacy and Domestic Terrorism

Researchers interested in studying White supremacist violence and domestic terrorism have multiple data sources they may be able to turn to. For example, the National Consortium for the Study of Terrorism and Responses to Terrorism (START) hosts several databases, such as LaFree and Dugan's (2007) Global Terrorism Database (GTD), which includes domestic and international terror events from around the world from 1970 to 2018 (LaFree et al., 2006). However, this database uses a broad definition of terrorism, may include media bias or misinformation, and may lack specific information for incidents (LaFree et al., 2006). START also hosts the Terrorism and Extremist Violence in the United States (TEVUS) Database and portal, which provides researchers with access to incident-, individual-, group-, and crime-related data dating back to 1970 (START, 2018c). Likewise, START hosts the Profiles of Individual Radicalization in the United States (PIRUS) database, which provides de-identified data on over 2,200 violent and nonviolent extremists between 1948 and 2018 (START, 2018b). Relatedly, the Bias Incidents and Actors Study (BIAS) data provide individual-level data on violent and nonviolent actors who are motivated by a form of hate within the United States (Bowie, 2020). A more specific database housed by START, the Chemical and Biological Non-State Actor Database (CABNSAD), explores individuals and motives for those in pursuit of chemical and biological agents (Braniff, 2019). The Extremist Crime Database (Freilich & Chermak, 2009; see also Gruenewald et al., 2009), housed in START and part of the TEVUS database, focuses on perpetrators, victims, events, and groups involved in extremist crimes (START, 2018a).

Data outside START include the International Terrorism: Attributes of Terrorist Events (ITERATE), which contains more than 150 analytic variables for over 12,000 international terror incidents, in quantitative and qualitative form, dating between 1968 and current (Mickolus et al., 2009), and the RAND Database of Worldwide Terrorism Incidents (RDWTI) dataset, which contains domestic incidents from 1998 to 2009 as well as international terrorist incidents from 1968 to 2009 (RAND, 2020b). However, these databases are only a handful of the total potential data sources for studying domestic terrorism. Bowie's (2020) inventory of datasets, as well as terrorism-related academic journals (e.g., *Perspectives on Terrorism*; *Journal of Homeland Security and Emergency Management*; *Critical Studies on Terrorism*; *Journal of Policing, Intelligence and Counter Terrorism*; *Terrorism and Political Violence*), may provide even more information for scholars in this area.

However, even with these data sources, the current critiques of this literature point to a need for more research in this area. Particularly, frustrations have arisen from a highly variable definition of domestic terrorism, leading some to call this term "utterly unhelpful" (McCord quoted in Graff, 2020). Differing methods for enumerating this violence and definitions of White supremacists have led to difficulties when attempting to assess the seriousness of the problem, including the number of attacks perpetrated by White supremacists (MacFarquhar, 2020; Ritchie et al., 2019). Additionally, with the advent of the Internet, the distinction between domestic and foreign terrorism has become a bit blurred (Wray, quoted in Graff, 2020). One avenue for future work would be to develop a cohesive and standardized definition of White supremacy and White supremacist groups so that data collection may be more uniform and comparable.

Relatedly, as mentioned, several of the cited data sources have their limitations, which preclude robust data collection and analysis. Therefore, future researchers should establish a robust data collection tool and archive for domestic and foreign terrorism that distinguishes between and among domestic terror groups, such as White supremacist groups.

To address prevention and desistance from participation in White supremacy, researchers should also follow in the footsteps of Simi and colleagues, as well as Blee, to capture rich narratives about the current factors that draw people into these groups as well as how and why they leave. These narratives may provide a sequence or script (see Cornish, 1994) for participation and withdrawal from such groups that may point to avenues for intervention for those currently in groups, or early intervention for those who are at risk. Relatedly, researchers may seek to heed the advice of Bonilla-Silva's 2019 American Sociological Association presidential address by exploring the racialized emotions tied to group entry and participation as well as the construction of ingroups and outgroups (see Jardina, 2020) that persist in White supremacy.

For researchers exploring the effectiveness of prevention efforts, Chermak and colleagues (2009) point to a dearth of research on the development of training for law enforcement specifically focused on White supremacy and domestic terrorism. What information do local law enforcement officers need to know, or what skills do officers need to have to combat domestic terrorism at the local level effectively? What courses of action do they have to address White supremacy within their ranks? And, is the current training effective at what it is intended to do?

In the same vein, researchers could also empirically explore the current effectiveness of civil litigation on White supremacy violence. Although this strategy is limited because the Internet provides a low-cost means of distributing materials and recruitment, it may be worth investigating the efficacy that groups such as the American Civil Liberties Union (ACLU) have used.

Ultimately, the study of White supremacy and domestic terrorism is likely to persist (Bergengruen & Hennigan, 2019). Given that the interrelation of race and class has become more salient in not only American society but also sociological research, Inwood (2015) observes, "when one undertakes an academic and political project, ... it becomes all too clear that the complexity of the political economy is held together by and through white supremacy" (Inwood, 2015, p. 420). Thus, as with the previous rises and declines that we have seen in the history of White supremacist groups and White supremacist violence, so too will the research about White supremacy ebb and flow, but likely never cease to exist.

References

16 Stat. 140 (1870).
17 Stat. 18 (1871).
18 U.S. Code §2331 (2018).
18 U.S. Code §2339A (2009).
42 U.S. Code §1981 et seq. (1994).
Adams, J., & Roscigno, V.J. (2005). White supremacists, oppositional culture and the World Wide Web. *Social Forces*, 84(2), 759–778.
ADL (Anti-Defamation League). (2017). White supremacists adopt new slogan: "You will not replace us." June 9. Available at: www.adl.org/blog/white-supremacists-adopt-new-slogan-you-will-not-replace-us.
ADL. (2019a). Two years ago, they marched in Charlottesville. Where are they now? August 8 [blog post]. Available at: www.adl.org/blog/two-years-ago-they-marched-in-charlottesville-where-are-they-now.
ADL. (2019b). Right-wing extremism linked to every 2018 extremist murder in the U.S., ADL finds. January 23 [press release]. New York.
ADL. (2020a). *Defining extremism. A glossary of white supremacist terms, movements and philosophies.* Available at: www.adl.org/education/resources/glossary-terms/defining-extremism-white-supremacy
ADL. (2020b). *Murder and extremism.* Available at: www.adl.org/media/14107/download
ADL. (n.d.). *Hate on Display(™) Hate symbols database.* Available at: December 7, 2020 from www.adl.org/hate-symbols. Accessed December 7, 2020.
Aho, J.A. (1990). *The politics of righteousness: Idaho Christian Patriotism.* Seattle, WA: University of Washington Press.
Bardwell, S.K. (1993). Tschirhart leaves law enforcement. *Houston Chronicle*, June 25, A30, p. 30.
Barnes, R.D. (1996). Blue by day and white by (k)night: Regulating the political affiliations of law enforcement and military personnel. *Iowa Law Review*, 81, 1079–1172.
Barrett, B. (2019). The wrong way to talk about a shooter's manifesto. *Wired*, August 4. Available at: www.wired.com/story/wrong-way-talk-about-shooter-manifesto/.
Baysinger, T.G. (2006). Right-wing group characteristics and ideology. *Homeland Security Affairs*, 2(2), 1–19.
Beirich, H., Bramblett, M., Freeman, A., Griggs, A., Smith, J., & Wood, L. (2007). Number of hate groups up 5 percent from last year. *Intelligence Report*, Spring. Available at: www.splcenter.org/fighting-hate/intelligence-report/2007/number-hate-groups-5-percent-last-year
Bergengruen, V., & Hennigan, W.J. (2019). "We are being eaten from within." Why America is losing the battle against White nationalist terrorism. *Time*, August

8. Available at: https://time.com/5647304/white-nationalist-terrorism-united-states/.
Berger, J.M. (2016). Alt history. *The Atlantic*, September. Available at: www.theatlantic.com/politics/archive/2016/09/how-the-turner-diaries-changed-white-nationalism/500039/.
Berlet, C., & Vysotsky, S. (2006). Overview of US white supremacist groups. *Journal of Political and Military Sociology*, 34(1), 11.
Bjelopera, J.P. (2012). *The domestic terrorist threat: Background and issues for Congress*. Washington, DC: Congressional Research Service.
Blee, K.M. (1996). Becoming a racist: Women in contemporary Ku Klux Klan and neo-Nazi groups. *Gender & Society*, 10(6), 680–702.
Blee, K.M. (2005). Women and organized racial terrorism in the United States. *Studies in Conflict & Terrorism*, 28(5), 421–433.
Bodrero, D.D. (1999). Confronting terrorism on the state and local level. *FBI Law Enforcement Bulletin*, 68(March), 11–18.
Bonilla-Silva, E. (2019). Feeling race: Theorizing the racial economy of emotions. *American Sociological Review*, 84(1), 1–25.
Bowie, N.G. (2020). A new inventory of 30 terrorism databases and data sets. *Perspectives on Terrorism*, 14(1), 54–66.
Bowles, N. (2019). "Replacement theory," a racist, sexist doctrine, spreads in far-right circles. *The New York Times*, March 18. Available at: www.nytimes.com/2019/03/18/technology/replacement-theory.html.
Bowman-Grieve, L. (2009). Exploring "Stormfront": A virtual community of the radical right. *Studies in Conflict & Terrorism*, 32(11), 989–1007.
Brandon, J. (2009). The danger of prison radicalization in the west. *CTC Sentinel*, 2(12), 1–5.
Braniff, W. (2019). *Homeland Security and Government Affairs Committee "Countering domestic terrorism: Examining the evolving threat."* September 25. Washington, DC: United States Senate. Available at: https://go.umd.edu/wLT.
Brooks, L. (2020). SPLC Testifies before Congress on financing of domestic terrorism. *Southern Poverty Law Center*, January 15. Available at: www.splcenter.org/news/2020/01/15/splc-testifies-congress-financing-domestic-terrorism.
Burris, V., Smith, E., & Strahm, A. (2000). White supremacist networks on the internet. *Sociological Focus*, 33(2), 215–235.
Cai, W., & Landon, S. (2019). Attacks by white extremists are growing. So are their connections. *The New York Times*, April 9. Available at: www.nytimes.com/interactive/2019/04/03/world/white-extremistterrorism-christchurch.html.
Campbell, K.M. (2015). A dry hate: White supremacy and anti-immigrant rhetoric in the humanitarian crisis on the US–Mexico border. *West Virginia Law Review*, 117(3), 1081–1129.
Chen, R. (2020). Former Lafayette police officer fired for white supremacist posts. *The Exponent*, October 17. Available at: www.purdueexponent.org/city_state/article_70467080-10b5-11eb-a15e-4302551602be.html.
Cherkaoui, T., & Dewan, K. (2019). *War on terror 2.0: The rise of white supremacy terrorism*. Washington, DC: TRT World Research Centre.
Chermak, S.M., Freilich, J.D., & Shemtob, Z. (2009). Law enforcement training and the domestic far right. *Criminal Justice and Behavior*, 36(12), 1305–1322.

Chin, W.Y. (2013). Law and order and white power: White supremacist infiltration of law enforcement and the need to eliminate racism in the ranks. *Journal of Law & Social Deviance*, 6, 30–98.

Chow, K. (2018). What the ebbs and flows of the KKK can tell us about white supremacy today. *NPR*, December 8. Available at: www.npr.org/sections/codeswitch/2018/12/08/671999530/what-the-ebbs-and-flows-of-the-kkk-can-tell-us-about-white-supremacy-today.

Clark, A. (2019). How "The birth of a nation" revived the Ku Klux Klan. *History.com*, July 29. Available at: www.history.com/news/kkk-birth-of-a-nation-film.

Cornish, D.B. (1994). The procedural analysis of offending and its relevance for situational prevention. *Crime Prevention Studies*, 3, 151–196.

Cox, J., & Koebler, J. (2019). Why won't Twitter treat white supremacy like ISIS? Because it would mean banning some Republican politicians too. *Vice*, April 25, Available at: www.vice.com/en/article/a3xgq5/why-wont-twitter-treat-white-supremacy-like-isis-because-it-would-mean-banning-some-republican-politicians-too.

Crawford, R., Gardiner, S.L., Mozzochi, J., & Taylor, R.L. (1994). *The Northwest imperative: Documenting a decade of hate.* Portland, OR: Coalition for Human Dignity.

Cullen, T.T. (2019). Opinion: The grave threats of white supremacy and the far-right extremism. *The New York Times*, February 22. Available at: www.nytimes.com/2019/02/22/opinion/christopher-hasson-extremism.html.

D'Alessio, S.J., & Stolzenberg, L. (1990). Sicarii and the rise of terrorism. *Studies in Conflict & Terrorism*, 13(4–5), 329–335.

Daniels, J. (2009). Combatting global white supremacy in the digital era. In J. Daniels (Ed.), *Cyber racism: White supremacy online and the new attack on civil rights.* Lanham, MD: Rowman & Littlefield.

DeLeeuw, J.G., & Pridemore, W.A. (2018). The threat from within: A conjunctive analysis of domestic terrorism incidents in the United States, United Kingdom, and Ireland. *Perspectives on Terrorism*, 12(4), 26–54.

Di Stefano, M., Spence, A., & Mac, R. (2019). Pro-Trump activists are boosting a Twitter app used by banned personalities and it appears to have already stalled. *Buzzfeed*, February 12. Available at: www.buzzfeed.com/markdistefano/pro-trump-activists-are-boosting-a-twitter-app-for-banned.

Domestic Terrorism DATA Act, H.R. 3106, 116th Congress. (2019).

Eckinger, H., & Sentinel Staff Writer (2009). Fruitland Park cop linked to Klan quits. *Orlando Sentinel*, February 7. Available at: www.orlandosentinel.com/news/os-xpm-2009-02-07-kkkcop07-story.html.

Enders, W., & Sandler, T. (2006). Distribution of transnational terrorism among countries by income class and geography after 9/11. *International Studies Quarterly*, 50(2), 367–393.

Engene, J.O. (2007). Five decades of terrorism in Europe: The TWEED dataset. *Journal of Peace Research*, 44(1), 109–121.

FBI (Federal Bureau of Investigation) Counterterrorism Division. (2006). *White supremacist infiltration of law enforcement.* Washington, DC: Federal Bureau of Investigation. Available at: https://cpb-us-e1.wpmucdn.com/blogs.uoregon.edu/dist/9/13250/files/2017/11/doc-26-white-supremacist-infiltration-1-110a4e4.pdf

Freilich, J.D., & Chermak, S.M. (2009). Preventing deadly encounters between law enforcement and American far-rightists. *Crime Prevention Studies*, 25(1), 141–172.

Freilich, J.D., Chermak, S.M., & Caspi, D. (2009). Critical events in the life trajectories of domestic extremist white supremacist groups: A case study analysis of four violent organizations. *Criminology & Public Policy*, 8(3), 497–530.

Garland, B., & Simi, P. (2011). A critique of using civil litigation to suppress white supremacist violence. *Criminal Justice Review*, 36(4), 498–512.

Gibson v. Florida Legislative Investigation Commission. (1963). 372 U.S. 539, 544–546.

Goudie, C., Markoff, B., Tressel, C., & Weidner, R. (2020). Disturbing new details in alleged plot to kidnap Michigan Governor Gretchen Whitmer. November 18. Available at: https://abc7chicago.com/michigan-governor-gretchen-whitmer-kidnapping-plot-militia/8079861/.

Graff, G.M. (2020). 25 years after Oklahoma City, domestic terrorism is on the rise. *Wired*, April 19. Available at: www.wired.com/story/oklahoma-city-bombing-christopher-wray/.

Gruenewald, J. (2011). A comparative examination of homicides perpetrated by far-right extremists. *Homicide Studies*, 15(2), 177–203.

Gruenewald, J., Freilich, J.D., & Chermak, S.M. (2009). An overview of the domestic far-right and its criminal activities. In B. Perry (Ed.), *Hate crimes: Hate crime offenders*. Westport, CT: Praeger.

Hamm, M.S. (2005). *Final Report: Crimes Committed by Terrorist Groups: Theory, Research, and Prevention*. Washington, DC: National Institute of Justice, Office of Justice Programs, U.S. Department of Justice.

Harris, J.W. (1987). Domestic terrorism in the 1980s. *FBI Law Enforcement Bulletin*, 56(10), 5–13.

Hatewatch Staff. (2018). Andrew Anglin brags about "indoctrinating" children into Nazi ideology. *Hatewatch*, January 18. Available at: www.splcenter.org/hatewatch/2018/01/18/andrew-anglin-brags-about-indoctrinating-children-nazi-ideology.

Hewitt, C. (2003). *Understanding terrorism in America: From the Klan to al Qaeda*. London/New York: Routledge.

Hinnant, L., & Ganley, E. (2015). French security forces kill gunmen to end terror rampage; 20 dead in 3 days of violence. *StarTribune*, January 10. Available at: www.startribune.com/world/288018961.html.

Hinnant, L., & Jordans, F. (2020). Paranoia, racism: German killer drew on conspiracy tropes. *Associated Press*, February 20. Available at: https://apnews.com/article/22f46b2de06ebe04c59e0e9bff87850e.

History.com Editors. (2020). *Ku Klux Klan*. November 2. Available at: www.history.com/topics/reconstruction/ku-klux-klan. Accessed December 5, 2020.

Hjelmgaard, K. (2020). Secret audio recordings detail how white supremacists seek recruits from military, police. *USA Today*, October 15. Available at: www.usatoday.com/story/news/2020/10/15/splc-releases-audio-how-neo-nazi-group-recruits-military-police/3661460001/.

Hogan, H., Ortman, J.M., & Colby, S.L. (2015). Projecting diversity: The methods, results, assumptions and limitations of the US census bureau's population projections. *West Virginia Law Review*, 117, 1047–1079.

Inwood, J.F. (2015). Neoliberal racism: The "Southern Strategy" and the expanding geographies of white supremacy. *Social & Cultural Geography*, 16(4), 407–423.

Jardina, A. (2020). In-group love and out-group hate: White racial attitudes in contemporary US elections. *Political Behavior*. Advance online at https://doi.org/10.1007/s11109-020-09600-x.

Kaplan, J. (1995). Right wing violence in North America. *Terrorism and Political Violence*, 7(1), 44–95.
Klassen, B. (1985). Comparative religions—Part V—Greek Orthodox. *Racial Loyalty*, 28(September), 1–2.
Klassen, B. (1986). RAHOWA! Recognize your enemies! *Racial Loyalty*, 36(June), 1–7.
Klassen, B. (1987). *RAHOWA! This planet is all ours*. Creativity Book Publisher. Available at: www.jrbooksonline.com/PDF_Books/rahowa.pdf.
LaFree, G., & Dugan, L. (2007). Introducing the global terrorism database. *Terrorism and Political Violence*, 19(2), 181–204.
LaFree, G., Dugan, L., Fogg, H.V., & Scott, J. (2006). *Building a global terrorism database*. Washington, DC: U.S. Department of Justice.
Lerman, R. (2020). The conservative alternative to Twitter wants to be a place for free speech for all. It turns out, rules still apply. *Washington Post*, July 15. Available at: www.washingtonpost.com/technology/2020/07/15/parler-conservative-twitter-alternative/.
Lewis, M., & Lyall, S. (2012). Norway mass killer gets the maximum: 21 years. *The New York Times*, August 25. Available at: www.nytimes.com/2012/08/25/world/europe/anders-behring-breivik-murder-trial.html.
Lichtblau, E. (2008). Arrests in plan to kill Obama and Black schoolchildren. *The New York Times*, October 27. Available at: www.nytimes.com/2008/10/28/us/politics/28plot.html.
Loving v. Virginia. (1967). 388 U.S. 1.
MacFarquhar, N. (2020). As domestic terrorists outpace jihadists, new U.S. law is debated. *The New York Times*, February 25. Available at: https://nyti.ms/37RZDys.
MacLean, N. (1995). *Behind the mask of chivalry: The making of the second Ku Klux Klan*. Oxford University Press, USA.
Manavis, S. (2020). What is parler? Inside the pro-Trump "unbiased" platform. *The New Statesman*, June 23. Available at: www.newstatesman.com/science-tech/social-media/2020/06/parler-trump-platform-katie-hopkins-social-media-twitter-alt-right.
McGarrell, E.F., Freilich, J.D., & Chermak, S. (2007). Intelligence-led policing as a framework for responding to terrorism. *Journal of Contemporary Criminal Justice*, 23(2), 142–158.
McGarrity, M., & Shivers, C. (2019). Confronting white supremacy. Statement Before the House Oversight and Reform Committee, Subcommittee on Civil Rights and Civil Liberties, Washington, DC. Available at: www.fbi.gov/news/testimony/confronting-white-supremacy.
McMillan, P., & Sahagun, L. (1990). Lynwood deputies' reported gang-style activity investigated. *L.A. Times*, December 4. Available at: www.latimes.com/archives/la-xpm-1990-12-04-me-5733-story.html.
McVeigh, R. (1999). Structural incentives for conservative mobilization: Power devaluation and the rise of the Ku Klux Klan, 1915–1925. *Social Forces*, 77(4), 1461–1496.
Michael, G. (2009). David Lane and the fourteen words. *Totalitarian Movements and Political Religions*, 10(1), 43–61.
Mickolus, E.F., Sandler, T., Murdock, J.M., & Flemming, P.A. (2009). *International terrorism: Attributes of terrorist events 1968–2009*. Dunn Loring, VA: Vinyard Software.

National Gang Intelligence Center. (2010). Gangs infiltrating law enforcement and correction agencies intelligence report. Washington, DC: Federal Bureau of Investigation. Available at: https://info.publicintelligence.net/NGIC-GangInfiltration.pdf.

Neubauer v. City of McAllen. (1985). 766 F.2d 1567, 1569.

Olding, R. (2020). FBI rounds up five alleged new-Nazis tied to murderous Atomwaffen Division. *The Daily Beast*, February 26. Available at: www.thedailybeast.com/alleged-ex-atomwaffen-division-leader-john-cameron-denton-arrested-charged-with-swatting.

Oppenheim, M. (2020). Masked neo-Nazi white supremacists march in Washington DC. *Independent*, February 9. Available at: www.independent.co.uk/news/world/americas/white-supremacists-neo-nazis-patriot-front-march-washington-dc-marc-a9325906.html.

Ortiz, J.L. (2020). An invasion of propaganda: Experts warn that white supremacist messages are seeping into the mainstream. *USA Today*, February 14. Available at: www.usatoday.com/story/news/nation/2020/02/14/white-supremacy-propaganda-increasing-mainstream-violence/4755150002/.

Panzerleiter. (2016). *Iron March Exposed*. September 1 [blog post]. Available at: www.ironmarch.exposed/post/34570.

Piazza, J.A. (2017). The determinants of domestic right-wing terrorism in the USA: Economic grievance, societal change and political resentment. *Conflict Management and Peace Science*, 34(1), 52–80.

RAND. (2020a). *Domestic terrorism*. Available at: www.rand.org/topics/domestic-terrorism.html.

RAND. (2020b). *RAND database of worldwide terrorism incidents*. Available at: www.rand.org/nsrd/projects/terrorism-incidents.html.

Ritchie, H., Hasell, J., Appel, C., & Roser, M. (2019). Terrorism. *Our World in Data*, November. Available at: https://ourworldindata.org/terrorism.

Rode v. Dellarciprete. (1988). 845 F.2d 1195, 1198.

Romo, V. (2020). Michigan AG says white supremacist groups behind plot to kidnap Gov. Whitmer. *NPR*, October 8. Available at: www.npr.org/sections/live-updates-protests-for-racial-justice/2020/10/08/921923955/michigan-ag-says-white-supremacist-groups-behind-plot-to-kidnap-gov-whitmer.

Rose, L. (2018). This is the first police officer charged with a federal hate crime in at least 10 years. *CNN Politics*, December 21. Available at: www.cnn.com/2018/12/21/politics/first-police-officer-charged-with-hate-crime-in-years/index.html.

Rothman, J. (2016). When bigotry paraded through the streets. *The Atlantic*, December 4. Available at: www.theatlantic.com/politics/archive/2016/12/second-klan/509468/.

Sánchez-Cuenca, I., & De la Calle, L. (2009). Domestic terrorism: The hidden side of political violence. *Annual Review of Political Science*, 12, 31–49.

Sands, G. (2020). White supremacists remain deadliest US terror threat, Homeland Security report says. *CNN Politics*, October 6. Available at: www.cnn.com/2020/10/06/politics/white-supremacists-anarchists-dhs-homeland-threat-assessment/index.html.

Saul, I. (2019). This Twitter alternative was supposed to be nicer, but bigots love it already. *Forward*, July 18. Available at: https://forward.com/news/national/427705/parler-news-white-supremacist-islamophobia-laura-loomer/.

Schafer, J.A., Mullins, C.W., & Box, S. (2014). Awakenings: The emergence of white supremacist ideologies. *Deviant Behavior*, 35(3), 173–196.

Sharpe, T.T. (2000). The identity Christian movement: Ideology of domestic terrorism. *Journal of Black Studies*, 30(4), 604–623.
Simi, P., & Futrell, R. (2006). Cyberculture and the endurance of white power activism. *Journal of Political and Military Sociology*, 34(1), 115–142.
Simi, P., & Futrell, R. (2009). Negotiating white power activist stigma. *Social Problems*, 56(1), 89–110.
Simi, P., Blee, K., DeMichele, M., & Windisch, S. (2017a). Addicted to hate: Identity residual among former white supremacists. *American Sociological Review*, 82(6), 1167–1187.
Simi, P., Blee, K., DeMichele, M., & Windisch, S. (2017b). White supremacy can be addictive, and leaving it behind can be like kicking a drug habit. *USApp—American Politics and Policy Blog*. October 17 [blog post]. Available at: https://blogs.lse.ac.uk/usappblog/2017/10/10/white-supremacy-can-be-addictive-and-leaving-it-behind-can-be-like-kicking-a-drug-habit/.
Simi, P., Sporer, K., & Bubolz, B.F. (2016). Narratives of childhood adversity and adolescent misconduct as precursors to violent extremism: A life-course criminological approach. *Journal of Research in Crime and Delinquency*, 53(4), 536–563.
Skutsch, C. (2017). The history of white supremacy in America. *Rolling Stone*, August 17. Available at: www.rollingstone.com/politics/politics-features/the-history-of-white-supremacy-in-america-205171/.
SPLC (Southern Poverty Law Center). (1998). Profiles of Christian Identity Movement leaders. *Intelligence Report*, March 15. Available at: www.splcenter.org/fighting-hate/intelligence-report/1998/profiles-christian-identity-movement-leaders.
SPLC. (2000). A retrospective of hate incidents and groups in the 1900s. *Intelligence Report*, March 15. Available at: www.splcenter.org/fighting-hate/intelligence-report/2000/retrospective-hate-incidents-and-groups-1900s.
SPLC. (2009). Skinheads in America: Racists on the rampage. *Intelligence Report*. Available at: www.splcenter.org/sites/default/files/d6_legacy_files/downloads/publication/Skinhead_Report.pdf.
SPLC. (n.d.a). *Ku Klux Klan*. Available at: www.splcenter.org/fighting-hate/extremist-files/ideology/ku-klux-klan. Accessed December 5, 2020.
SPLC. (n.d.b). *Tom Metzger*. Available at: www.splcenter.org/fighting-hate/extremist-files/individual/tom-metzger. Accessed November 16, 2020.
START (The National Consortium for the Study of Terrorism and Responses to Terrorism). (2018a). Extremist crime database related projects. Available at: www.start.umd.edu/research-projects/extremist-crime-database-related-projects. Accessed December 2, 2020.
START. (2018b). Profiles of Individual Radicalization in the United Status (PIRUS). Available at: www.start.umd.edu/data-tools/profiles-individual-radicalization-united-states-pirus. Accessed December 12, 2020.
START. (2018c). TEVUS Portal. Available at: www.start.umd.edu/tevus-portal. Accessed December 12, 2020.
Sullivan, M. (2020). I joined Parler, the right-wing echo changer's new favorite alt-Twitter. *Fast Company*, June 27. Available at: www.fastcompany.com/90522049/i-joined-parler-the-right-wing-echo-chambers-new-favorite-alt-twitter.
Swan, B. (2019). Homeland Security disbands domestic terror intelligence unit. *Daily Beast*, April 2. Available at: www.thedailybeast.com/homeland-security-disbands-domestic-terror-intelligence-unit.

Swan, B.W. (2020a). They tried to get Trump to care about right-wing terrorism. He ignored them. *Politico*, August 26. Available at: www.politico.com/news/2020/08/26/trump-domestic-extemism-homeland-security-401926.

Swan, B.W. (2020b). DHS draft document: White supremacists are greatest terror threat. *Politico*, August 4. Available at: www.politico.com/news/2020/09/04/white-supremacists-terror-threat-dhs-409236.

The Creativity Movement. (2017). The five fundamental beliefs of Creativity. Available at: https://creativitymovement.net/creativity/five-fundamental-beliefs/.

Tobar, H. (1991). Deputies in "Neo-Nazi" gang judge found: Sheriff's Department: Many Lynwood officers have engaged in racially motivated violence against Blacks and Latinos, jurist said. *Los Angeles Times*, October 12. Available at: www.latimes.com/archives/la-xpm-1991-10-12-me-107-story.html.

Tyler, T.R. (2004). Enhancing police legitimacy. *The Annals of the American Academy of Political and Social Science*, 593(1), 84–99.

United States v. City of Buffalo. (1978). 457 F. Supp. 612.

Uniting and Strengthening America by Providing Appropriate Tools Required to Intercept and Obstruct Terrorism (USA PATRIOT ACT) Act of 2001. H.R. 3162, 107th Congress (2001).

U.S. Constitution. art. I, §2. (1787a).

U.S. Constitution. art. IV. (1787b).

Van McVey, S. (2008). Race, gender, and the contemporary white supremacy movement: The intersection of "isms" and organized racist groups. (Master's thesis). Wayne State University.

Wade, W.C. (1998). *The fiery cross: The Ku Klux Klan in America*. New York: Oxford University Press.

Wellman, B., & Gulia, M. (1999). Virtual communities as communities: Net surfers don't ride alone. In M.A. Smith & P. Kollock (Eds.), *Networks in the global village. Communities in cyberspace*. London: Routledge, pp. 167–194.

Winter, A. (2010). American terror: From Oklahoma City to 9/11 and after. In B. Brecher, M. Devenney, & A. Winter (Eds.), *Discourses and practices of terrorism: Interrogating terror*. Oxon: Routledge, Critical Terrorism Studies, pp. 156–176.

Zanona, M. (2017). Trump cuts funds to fight anti-right wing violence. *The Hill*, August 14. Available at: https://thehill.com/policy/national-security/346552-trump-cut-funds-to-fight-anti-right-wing-violence.

Zapotosky, M., Barrett, D., & Hauslohner, A. (2020). FBI charges six who it says plotted to kidnap Michigan Gov. Gretchen Whitmer, as seven more who wanted to ignite civil war face state charges. *Washington Post*, October 8. Available at: www.washingtonpost.com/national-security/michigan-governor-kidnap-plot/2020/10/08/0032e206-0980-11eb-9be6-cf25fb429f1a_story.html.

Zhou, Y., Reid, E., Qin, J., Chen, H., & Lai, G. (2005). US domestic extremist groups on the web: Link and content analysis. *IEEE Intelligent Systems*, 20(5), 44–51.

Part II

Being a Terrorist

5

Gender and Terrorism

Kathy Laster and Edna Erez*

Most commentators agree that the defining elements of terrorism include (a) the intentional use of violence (b) against noncombatant targets (c) to create fear (d) by virtue of the widest possible publicity coverage for the group, cause, or individual (e) in the pursuit of political, religious, or ideological objectives (Laster & Erez, 2015, p. 85). All definitions of terrorism, though, are inevitably value-laden and highly contested. As Yasser Arafat famously quipped, "one man's terrorist is another man's Freedom Fighter" (Laqueur, 1987, pp. 7, 302).

However it is defined, terrorism—and especially the so-called "fourth wave" or "new terrorism" (Weinberg & Eubank, 2011), which has such grave and devastating consequences—is properly analyzed as crime (Erez, 2006; Rosenfeld, 2002).

It is tempting to characterize terrorism as unique because it is ideological or cause-driven. However, it is now recognized that nonpolitically motivated crime can also be goal-directed (Curry, 2011; Felson, 1993; Rosenfeld, 2002).

Terrorism's publicity hunger is also said to be a distinguishing feature. But not all criminals want to "fly under the radar"—extortionists, for instance, rely upon their ruthless reputation through publicity about their violent acts. Organized crime, and even youth gangs, also engage in instrumental and symbolic violence to communicate and send a message (La Spina et al., 2014; Santino, 2019).

---

* We are deeply grateful to Ryan Kornhauser for his research efforts, editorial support and unfailing goodwill in assisting us with this chapter. The paper is much stronger because of his expert support.

The lines between terrorism and other forms of crime though are becoming blurred. Criminal groups engage in political activities, while terrorist groups engage in profit-seeking crime to fund their activities, such as white-collar crime, narcotics, or fraud (Lowe, 2006; Makarenko, 2004, pp. 133–135; Perri & Brody, 2011; Wannenburg, 2003). And, while ideologically driven terror organizations are sometimes considered the antithesis of organized crime, there is in fact a clear crossover between the two (Ballina, 2011).

But the most compelling reason for analyzing terrorism as crime is that this allows us to apply criminological theory to our understanding of the phenomenon. There is now a growing body of literature which explains terrorism through "traditional" criminological theory (e.g., Agnew, 2010; LaFree et al., 2009; Perry & Hasisi, 2015). In this chapter we suggest that Gender Theory is one of the sharpest theoretical and practical tools we have at our disposal.

We begin by briefly outlining some core elements of Gender Theory as both a framework and a method. Using 9/11 as a case study, we explain how hegemonic masculinity, rather than "mere maleness," lies at the heart of terrorism and the responses to it. Next, we show how the increasing involvement of women in all aspects of terrorism defies criminological orthodoxy—or the "pink thread" running through criminological theory—predicated on the maleness of crime, especially violent crime. We use the abrupt and culture-defying inclusion of women by Middle-Eastern terrorist organizations to demonstrate how terrorist organizations exploit stereotypes about women to advance their strategic objectives. Gender stereotypes, we go on to show, also underscore media reporting about women terrorists as well as the social science exploration of the motives of men and women terrorists. Despite efforts to portray some women terrorists as the pawns of men, we suggest that women actually fare worse as perpetrators, victims, and citizens. We conclude that a gender lens is not only critical to an understanding of terrorism but is simultaneously a proving ground for criminological theory more generally.

Gender Theory and Method in Brief

Gender is not the same as biological sex. Being born a "male" or "female" denotes biological differences, but Gender Theory is based on the idea that it is the social meaning that attaches to "being a man" or "being a woman" that shapes identity. The answer to the first inevitable question when a baby is born—"Is it a boy or a girl?"—immediately creates expectations that follow that baby as it goes through life.

Accordingly, the focus of Gender Theory is on how, sometimes consciously but mostly imperceptibly, in a given time and place, gender identity shapes the nature and experience of the social world for individuals, groups, and social systems (West & Zimmerman, 1987). A gender lens challenges the assumed "naturalness" of "maleness" and "femaleness" (see generally, in the context of crime, Zatz & Gough, 2014).

Gender Theory views the social world as constructed around categories, often simple binaries, the most obvious of which are the performative roles of "being a man" or "being a woman" (Butler, 1988; West & Zimmerman, 1987). Gender Theory exposes how aspects of gender (and intersectional identity: see Crenshaw, 1991) constitute the basis of social ordering and inequality: "gender differences ... provide the tacit rationale for differing fates of women and men within the social order" (West & Zimmerman, 1987, p. 142). Some traits or characteristics, like maleness (and whiteness), are valued while others, like femaleness (and brownness or blackness) are subordinated and subjugated.[1]

The best way to understand and test a theory's usefulness is to apply it to a particular social problem. Below, we outline a more recent branch of Gender Theory—"masculinity theory"—and show how it can be used to view the most dramatic episode of New Terrorism, the 9/11 attacks on New York.

Masculinity as Challenge and Threat

Masculinity theory holds that "normative masculinity" (Connell, 2005) is a social ideal which sets the bar impossibly high for what it is to be "a real man" in a given time and place. "Normative masculinity" is the ideal to which men strive "by doing maleness" (West & Zimmerman, 1987).

According to James Messerschmitt's theory of "hegemonic masculinity," the checklist varies according to the setting (Connell & Messerschmidt, 2005). For example, powerful men will "do masculinity" differently from powerless men. Successfully running your own company, or street gang, are both, in different cultural contexts, signifiers of masculinity.

Masculinity theory suggests that men "do crime" in order "to do masculinity" when other pathways or resources are unavailable to them (Messerschmidt, 1993, p. 85). In political environments where the regular means of attaining masculinity status is denied, contested, or out of reach, terrorism becomes the crime of choice for some men. Managing a "successful" terrorist organization is a marker of having "made it" in the masculinity stakes among certain (sub-)cultures. Being a suicide bomber is extreme risk-taking and so demonstrates one of masculinity's key traits—courage. But so too is leading, or participating in, a powerful and coordinated response to terrorism, such as the "War on Terror."

Below we use a case study of 9/11 based on the participant observer research undertaken by Heinz Steinert (2003), and other contemporaneous empirical work by Laster and Steinert (2002), to model how masculinity theory frames the 9/11 attack as well as the response to it.[2]

9/11: A Masculinity Moment

The destruction of the World Trade Center on 9/11 is now part of the world's store of historically significant acts, but, more particularly, images. The dramatic collapse of the Twin Towers, among one of the tallest buildings in the world, is the stuff of a Boy's Own Adventure, or nowadays, a particularly graphic blockbuster movie or video game. It was the association with culture industry destruction imagery that made the initial reaction to the hit one of disbelief: "it's like a movie"; "it's surreal."

Creating strong and threatening public images is precisely what terrorists deal in. Had the aim "just" been to create chaos and devastation in New York City, planting a limited number of bombs in the subway system would have done the job more effectively and been easier to achieve. But the goal was a spectacular global media opportunity. The image of those small planes bringing down the twin (phallic symbol?) buildings was a masculinist fantasy and, as it turned out, a military and political coup.

For Mohamed Atta and the other attackers, the stakes were high but so were the potential rewards, including serious recognition. They and their spokesman, Osama bin Laden, suddenly became significant players on the world stage. Like all terrorist groups, they had neither the means of domination nor the legitimacy to be granted any such status, but their actions allowed them to behave as if they were on an equal footing with the President of the United States.

For a particular target audience, this larger-than-life symbolic act was designed to prove this band of warriors' ingenuity, resolution, and courage—well satisfying the requirements of normative masculinity.

Al-Qaeda thrust itself to the top of the terrorist league ladder. Its newly acquired status swelled its ranks with volunteers and money flowed into its coffers.

But the attributes of hegemonic masculinity are contested. New Yorkers, unsurprisingly, saw the attack as "anti-masculinity." For example, the public intellectual, Susan Sontag, in her opinion piece about 9/11, was forced to retract her apparent "linguistic slip" in describing the suicide bombers as "brave young men." As with the Japanese attack on Pearl Harbor, that attribute of masculinity is confined to soldiers who "legitimately" go into combat after a formal declaration of war. In the context of a superpower which relies on de jure forms of domination, attack by stealth is the opposite of masculinity—it is cowardly.

The true brave men of the day, according to New Yorkers, were unequivocally the first responders: the archetypal masculinist heroes of firemen and "New York's finest," the police department, who risked their lives in the rescue efforts. George W. Bush, possibly making up for his (cowardly?) absence from the fray on the days following the fateful attack, had himself photographed with his arms draped over brave firefighters—vicarious masculinity.

The public response to the appeal for the families of fire fighters who lost their lives was overwhelming. Too much so. Funds raised later became an embarrassment because it would make wealthy the families of the relatively small numbers of firefighters who lost their lives.

Later, too, there was a different kind of embarrassment about the statue erected to the fire fighters. The statue depicted visible minorities as firefighters, which, the union complained, distorted the demographics of this brave, and largely White, occupational group. The obfuscation of class was also evident in the obituaries published by *The New York Times* about those killed in the attacks. The focus was on the cleaners and "ordinary people" who had lost their lives, whereas the reality was that more than 1,500 of New York's financial elite lost their lives. The obfuscation about class has a masculinist point—the white-collar warrior class of New York City on which the city's power depends could not be made to look weak and vulnerable. Hence, their identity as "family" and "community" folk became the focus of the stories about them. The New York Stock exchange opened the day after the attack to prove that it was indeed, "the Toughest City on Earth."

Class is irrelevant in death—we do not mourn any more or less for the rich than the poor. But the need to construct heroes out of masculinist stereotypes demonstrates the power of such categories.

Real Men Retaliate

The almost immediate popular consensus was that 9/11 was

> a monumental and singular tragedy, unparalleled and unprecedented, an act of war, against all of the USA, perhaps even Western civilization as we know it, by Muslim terrorists, primitive and violent, intolerant and women hating, who despise us and our way of life, who will stop at nothing to impose their religious beliefs on the whole world. But the US will "triumph" militarily, economically, politically and emotionally. The cowardly act of these barbarians cannot, the slogans boldly proclaimed, "defeat our spirit."
>
> (Laster & Steinert, 2002, p. 1)

In contemporaneous interviews in public places and in the media, the expectation was that a retaliatory strike was imminent. A few nights after 9/11 for example, even TV commentators wondered whether CNN's green night images of Kabul were actually US cruise missile hits. Retaliation was, in some quarters, deemed essential. One working-class informant articulated the then ubiquitous taken-for-granted masculinist logic,

> but we must hit, even ... if we don't hit we look, we're cowards, it's like me slapping you in your face, you're a man, I'm a man, and you're not doing that, then me slapping you again, so if I can get away with it the first time and no retaliation I'd know you're scared, so I'd do it again.
>
> (Steinert, 2003, p. 658)

Translating public sentiments into action is the grist of populist politics. George W. Bush, until 9/11 a figure of public ridicule, responded in a familiar masculinist way by declaring a "War on Terror." The discourse of "Wars" on Drugs, Poverty, and Crime is a regular feature of US political rhetoric and so shapes its actions (Lakoff & Johnson, 2003 [1980]). In responding to 9/11, the President was hardly going to shy away from the real thing. And so it was.

In 9/11 the "maleness" of New Terrorism was not discussed, it was just assumed. Terrorism was violent crime on a devastating scale and so, of course, "male." That perception had to change as women increasingly entered the frame as active, and effective, combatants.

Women in Terrorism: The Pink Thread of Criminological Theory

Criminological orthodoxy has long-maintained that there is a difference in the gender ratio of crime as well as in types of crimes committed by men and women (e.g., Brown, 1986; Daly & Chesney-Lind, 1988). Theorists, old and new, agree that men are more criminal, and are far more likely to be the perpetrators of violent, including lethal, crimes. The crimes of women—"women's crimes"—were a category distinct from "crimes" generally, both in etiology and form (e.g., Gilfus, 1993).

As Tariq and Sjoberg (2021) explain, many early studies of women's crime:

> highlighted not only different reasons that women had to engage in criminal activity than the assumed baseline reasons men did, but also different crimes women could be expected to commit compared to the baseline crimes men could be expected to commit. Most theories of who commits crimes and how they come to do so are based on the assumption that the offenders are male; theories of women's crimes often separate them from (men's) normal or expected crimes.

The propensity of males to commit crime, especially violent crime, is thus the thread that links the preoccupations of the early misogynist criminological fathers such as Ferraro and Lombroso and, in more recent times, Pollack's 1960s view of good women as conforming to gender expectations, and Adler's "sisters in crime" thesis of the 1970s which (incorrectly) associated the Women's Liberation Movement to an apparent spike in female offending rates (Laster, 1989).

A major contribution of feminist criminology was to emphasize women's inequality and so their lack of opportunity to engage in (male) crimes. Women were therefore more likely to commit crimes arising from their specific needs and circumstances such as social security fraud, shoplifting, prostitution, or poisoning. Other feminist theorists focused on the "social control" of women, which made them less likely to commit crimes (e.g., Heidensohn, 1985).

Mirroring the consistent pattern of gender blindness in the study of crime (Naffine, 2016), women's long-standing involvement in terrorism was initially either erased or discounted.

Yet, as scholarship has amply demonstrated, women have always been involved in the seemingly "male" business of terrorism (Weinberg

& Eubank, 2011). And contrary to the usual crimes of women, terrorism is no minor offence, but rather a violent and socially central crime.

There is an extensive roll call of women terrorists historically. It was a woman, Fanny Kaplan, who almost assassinated Lenin in 1918; German's major postwar revolutionary terrorism groups were heavily composed of women; and women have played major roles in the Chechen conflict (Weinberg & Eubank, 2011, pp. 23, 29, 35–36). Women have also featured prominently in more recent times in specific areas of conflict, including the successful assassination of Indian Prime Minister Rajiv Ghandi in 1991 by Thenmozhi Rajaratnam as she purported to garland him with flowers. In some contexts, women have also been leaders of terrorist organizations, like Ulricka Meinhoff in the Bader-Meinhof terrorist group in Germany in the 1970s (Weinberg & Eubank, 2011; Bloom, 2011a).

But, it has been women's increasing involvement in the front line of New Terrorism—in part driven by the democratizing effect of technology (Erez & Laster, 2020) and the tactical and strategic advantages of using women (Berko & Erez, 2007; Bloom, 2011a)—most notably as suicide bombers, that has suddenly thrust women into the terrorism (and theoretical) limelight (Bloom, 2011a; Erez & Laster, 2020; Laster & Erez, 2015).

In 2000, the estimate was that 20–30 percent of international terrorist acts were carried out by women (Harmon, 2000; Nacos, 2005). In Pape's (2005) study of 462 suicide bombers between 1980 and 2003, women constituted 50 percent of the actors among Kurds, Chechens, and Tamil Tigers. A more recent account of terrorism in Africa suggests that between 2011 and 2018, the Nigerian-based radical Islamist group Boko Haram has used hundreds of women and girls in this capacity, well in excess of the number of men sacrificed in this way (Markovic, 2019). And Cook and Vale (2018) estimated that up to 25 percent of foreign Islamic State affiliates in the theaters of conflict and up to 21 percent of returnees were women and minors.

While not true in every conflict zone, women now probably comprise the majority of suicide bombers in some geopolitical hotspots and almost certainly discharge a host of major and minor roles in most terrorist organizations. Women aid and abet terrorism in significant ways by, for instance, carrying arms, ammunitions, or supplies, or providing emotional and other support (Bakker, 2006; Bloom, 2007, p. 97; Bloom, 2011b) and are increasingly key propagandists on the Internet, recruiting supporters to the cause (Bloom, 2013; von Knop, 2008). The significance of women's "supporting role" in terrorism is probably still not accorded due weight, in the same way that women's roles more generally have traditionally been discounted or marginalized. The literature continues to analyze women's agency in discharging such support roles in terrorism through a patriarchal lens (Bloom & Lokmanoglu, 2020).

Theoretically and practically, though, we cannot afford to ignore the role of women as twenty-first-century terrorism's able and willing helpers and, increasingly, as effective front-line combatants. This trend flies in the face of assumptions about women as more peaceable, and rattles criminological theory which has long been preoccupied with the maleness of crime.

As Tariq and Sjoberg (2021) observe:

> If a theory of why crime occurs does not account for the behavior of those understood to be women, then at least one of two things is the case: either women commit crimes for reasons different than men do and/or the theories are wrong overall.

This observation holds true for studies of terrorism. A Gender Theory perspective demands that we examine this apparent anomaly which should then cause us to recast our understanding of terrorism, as well as the gender blinkers of criminological theory itself.

We contend that criminological theory's fundamental gender question, including that of feminist criminology, needs to be recast. Rather than asking, "How is it that men commit violent crime?" or "How is it that women commit less and different crimes than men," a gender lens reformulates the question as, "In a given time and place, what is the significance and impact of the presence (or absence) of women (or men) from the commission of a particular crime?—in this case, the socially central crime of terrorism."

To begin to answer this reformulated question, we consider a case study of a defining moment in twenty-first-century terrorism—the radical about-face by some terrorist organizations which abandoned their strict ideological ban on women from the front line to active recruitment of them as combatants (Laster & Erez, 2015).

Letting Women In: A Case Study of Terrorism as a Strategic Enterprise

While women have always been actively involved in terrorist organizations in particular theaters of conflict, observing moments of change—or the conscious decision to "let women in" at a particular time and place—is always theoretically illuminating (Laster & Douglas, 1995).

In the Middle East, many terrorist organizations, including Hamas, initially prohibited the involvement of women. However, quite abruptly, it reversed this position (Berko & Erez, 2007). Al-Qaeda and other extremist groups demonstrated a similar change of heart and started to actively recruit women into their ranks.

Allowing women into combat roles violates a core tenet of patriarchy. In strongly masculinist cultures, such as in much of the Middle East, the battlefield remained the exclusive preserve of men who, as a defining feature of masculinity, are obliged to protect and defend their womenfolk (Gan et al., 2019; Hasso, 2005).

Correspondingly, significant constraints are placed on women's freedom and autonomy in these cultures in order to protect them, especially their virtue and purity (e.g., Baxter, 2007; Hasan, 2005). In highly gender-segregated cultures, the prescribed role for women is as wives and mothers who manage the private sphere (e.g., Gan et al., 2019; Hasso, 2005; Tamimi, 2017). Through rule and custom, women largely remain confined to home and family, rendering their involvement in terrorist activism both ideologically and logistically difficult.

Initially promulgating this orthodox ideological position, Palestine Liberation Organization leader Yasser Arafat maintained that the Palestinian woman's womb was "the best weapon of the Palestinian people" (Berko & Erez, 2008, p. 161). Similarly, for Al-Qaeda, the key responsibility of women was to bear and nurture their sons and inculcate in them the ideological values of national/organizational liberation (von Knop, 2008).

But, by 2003—a year after Palestine's first female suicide bomber, Wafa Idris, killed herself and two Israelis (Naaman, 2007)—Yasser Arafat had done a U-turn, proclaiming instead that Palestinian women would become "my army of roses that will cross Israeli tanks" (Kimmerling, 2003; Victor, 2004). Following suit, Hamas created a unit of women to fight Israel, and Islamic Jihad, another fundamentalist terrorist organization, reversed its "no women" rule and threatened "to flood Israel with female suicide bombers" (Huberman, 2007).

The most frequent explanation for this cultural and gender somersault is pragmatism—the escalation of armed conflict, coupled with a shortage of males to fight Israel (Erez & Berko, 2008). Like recourse to terrorism itself, the deployment of women is often seen as a sign of military desperation—there is no choice but to use women in the front line.

There is, though, a less savory practical reason for enlisting women into active combat: the lives of women are deemed to be more expendable. Modern technology means that a suicide bomber does not need great physical strength or prolonged training to detonate a bomb. Amateurs and "walk-ins" are quite sufficient to get the job done (Hoffman, 2002). Men are more valuable and need to be freed up to assume more complex, and sustainable, roles in terrorist organizations. The pragmatism and adaptability of patriarchy should never be underestimated (Erez & Laster, 2020).

Some commentators explain this about-face as evidence of the impact of colonialism which undermines masculinist ideology and emasculates men. According to these scholars, long-term Israeli oppression has had the effect of feminizing and Orientalizing men so that they feel helpless and inadequate in the face of a powerful West (Holt, 2010; Shalhoub-Kevorkian, 2003). There is evidence that women engaged in terrorism appreciate the import of men abrogating their exclusive preserve to them. Masculinity taunts, for example, are regularly used to mobilize men into terrorist activism (Hasso, 2005, p. 37). In one martyrdom video, for example, a young 18-year-old Palestinian woman shames her comrades by asserting, "I am going to fight instead of the sleeping Arab armies who are watching Palestinian girls fighting alone" (Bloom, 2007, p. 99).

A Gender Theory perspective, however, exposes that terrorist leadership appreciates that involving women in the front line is a more effective means of achieving their strategic objectives. Contrary to popular assumptions about terrorism as "irrational" and "dysfunctional," it is now conceded that many terrorist organizations are run as high-level organizations, requiring the organizational skills of a project manager or CEO. Effective management of human resources is integral to the running of a strategic enterprise (Hoffman, 2002). Accordingly, terrorist organizations deftly exploit gender stereotypes about women in target societies to maximize their power, profile, and impact (Laster & Erez, 2015).

The Tactical Advantages of Gender Stereotypes

The principal goal of terrorism is, as the term implies, to instill "terror," or to psychologically intimidate, the target population. The most effective means of securing this outcome is through indiscriminate attacks which cause the highest possible number of fatalities and casualties.

In one grisly empirical study, women terrorist actions were found to be significantly more "successful" than those by men, measured using strike rate and the number of victims killed and injured as the criteria (O'Rourke, 2009). A more recent study using data from the Global Terrorism Database and the Suicide Attack Database could not establish that attacks by women suicide bombers were more lethal than those perpetrated by men, but the data did show that women were no less effective than their male counterparts (Fullmer et al., 2019).

Women's "success" in meeting this core objective of terrorism depends upon the target group's deeply entrenched stereotypes about women generally, and Arab women in particular. The Organization for Security and Co-operation in Europe's Women and Terrorist Radicalization: Final Report, for example, concluded that women were "often seen as passive, victims, helpless, subordinate and maternal ... As a result, women are neither considered to be potential terrorists, nor perceived to be as dangerous as their male counterparts" (Organization for Security and Co-operation in Europe, 2013, p. 3). Women therefore attract far less security attention than men (Cunningham, 2007) since cultural and gender sensitivities make security forces less inclined to suspect women, or to subject women to intrusive security controls, including body searches.

As a consequence, women combatants have a powerful advantage: the element of surprise (Cook, 2005). Women can, for example, easily and inconspicuously frequent heavily populated target areas, such as hospitals, schools, and marketplaces, obscuring their violent intentions by apparently going about "normal" activities for women such as shopping or family outings. They can also conceal explosives under conservative, loose-fitting clothing, pretend to be pregnant and wear maternity clothes, or alternatively distract security forces with immodest clothing (Berko & Erez, 2007; Bloom, 2011b).

But the objective of twenty-first-century terrorism is not merely to inflict "terror" through maximum harm, but also to secure maximum media coverage. Here, too, women combatants have proven to be a boon.

The Media Message

Terrorism can be understood as media-generated crime with the express intent of communicating its message of destruction as widely as possible (Matusitz, 2013). As terrorism scholar, Walter Laqueur, put it, "The media are a terrorist's best friend. The terrorist's act by itself is nothing. Publicity is all" (Laqueur, 2016, p. 98). Or, as one Islamic State defector candidly admitted, "The media people are more important than the soldiers" (Miller & Mekhennet, 2015). The now almost instantaneous global reporting of terrorist attacks has the desired ripple effect of spreading fear as widely as possible (Hearne, 2009; Nacos, 2005).

A woman suicide bomber is almost certain to attract mass media interest. According to one estimate, media reporting of acts committed by women terrorists outnumber the coverage of similar acts of men by 8 to 1 (Bloom, 2007). Terrorism is culture industry-adapted crime (Laster & Steinert, 2002) and media thrives on dramatic stories which pander to the public's fascination with women who commit extreme, violent acts (Nacos, 2005; Naylor, 1994). There is even a prurient interest in the bodies of women terrorists (Brunner, 2005).

The target population comes to feel permanently unsafe—anyone can be attacked, anywhere, at any time, by anyone, even by women and children. The heightened sense of anxiety and disruption of normal life squarely meets the strategic intent of terrorism. Media coverage of women who blow themselves up also communicates the uncompromising political will and ruthlessness of a terrorist organization.

The response to seemingly incomprehensible violence, especially by women, is to demand an explanation. Cowed populations want to know what could possibly motivate "these crazy terrorists" to commit such "incomprehensible" acts of savagery. Media and social science rush to oblige. But, as we show below, their answers are grounded in, and generally reinforce, gender and other stereotypes.

What Makes Terrorists Tick? Gendering Motivation

The media "continuously construct and reconstruct social problems, crises, enemies, and leaders and so create a succession of threats and assurances" (Edelman, 1988, p. 1).

During periods of armed conflict, the media manages to convey the "reality" of the threat while simultaneously seeking to provide reassurance to the populace. The easiest way of achieving these contradictory objectives is through recourse to traditional stereotypes; war needs the "dichotomy of friends and foes, of perpetrators and victims, of those who act and those who suffer" (Klaus & Kassel, 2005, p. 336).

Kathryn Brown's (2011) content analysis of the media representation of Muriel Degauque, the first European female suicide bomber in Iraq in 2011, for example, found that the media story quickly became one of an otherwise "normal" "caring" White Belgian woman who "misguidedly" converted to Islam, was radicalized by her extremist Brown Moroccan husband, and was duped or coerced by him into "blowing herself up." The fact that this narrative was patently wrong in critical respects—Degauque, for instance, converted to Islam before meeting her husband—was ignored. The story needed to fit into the accepted gender, race and, especially, Islamophobic frame.

For media theorists, Western media generally subscribes to the thesis that women suicide bombers who transgress accepted womanly roles are victims of patriarchy (Naaman, 2007, p. 943). The other reassuring trope is that these are hapless women who commit violent crime for understandable, if not excusable, personal reasons. The fact that Palestinian Wafa Idris claimed to have undertaken her suicide mission because she could not have children and so there was no point in her living (Naaman, 2007) made her actions fit within an acceptable gendered frame.

Feminist scholars have highlighted the consistent bifurcation of women into either heroes or hapless victims (e.g., Marway, 2011; Nacos, 2005). Women suicide bombers might be "extraordinary," but their motives can be accommodated within the conventional expectations of the "weaker sex," who are easily preyed upon by manipulative men acting in the name of a perverse ideology and misogynist religion.

Mental illness is often a handy explanation and readily applied to women ("they must be mad") to account for seemingly inexplicable behavior. Research, however, has now definitively established that suicide bombers generally do not suffer from mental illness, nor do they have any particular personality disorders (e.g., Horgan, 2014; Post, 2009). This finding applies equally to male and female suicide bombers (see review by Jacques & Taylor, 2009) although mental illness is typically more likely to be ascribed to women who commit crimes of all kinds (Zedner, 1991).

The other option is for female behavior at the extremes to be demonized—women terrorists for instance are considered either oversexed (Sjoberg & Gentry, 2007) or "unsexed" monster women. Naaman (2007, p. 942), for example, describes how the imagery of Wafa Idris and Ayat al-Akgras (another early Palestinian female suicide bomber) created an "unbridgeable gap whereby the Western viewer cannot reconcile the image of the young beautiful woman with her fundamentalist, terrorist dark side," the result of which was not only demonization of both the women but of the societies which socialized them.

Media reporting on women terrorists demonstrates "a dominant, even hegemonic, construction of femininity, one which subordinates women's actions and motives to men, places them on the margins of politics and demonizes exceptions" (Brown, 2011, p. 708). In her analysis of media reporting of Chechen terrorism, for instance, West (2005, p. 8) observes:

> Whereas women are "black widows," men are "terrorists." Whereas women are victims, men are brutalizers. Whereas women are apolitical, men are political. Whereas women are instruments, men are actors. In the end, this is a war between men.

But while it is in the media's interest to pander to, and feed, popular stereotypes and prejudices, similar reductionism and stereotyping has also permeated much scholarly research about motive.

Social Science's Motives

Establishing the "motive" for anti-social behavior is the Holy Grail for social scientists and policymakers. Discerning the motives underlying terrorist activism holds out the promise of devising effective interventions to counter violent extremism (Radlauer, 2006). Inevitably, though, studies seeking to establish the motivation of terrorists continue to grapple with the problems of essentialism and agency, which still beset much criminological theory.

Ascertaining "motive" for any kind of behavior remains methodologically fraught (Katz, 1988, 1991) and even more so in the case of terrorism (Erez & Laster, 2020). Suicide bombers are, for obvious reasons, unavailable to be interrogated. Piecing together information gleaned from informants such as family, friends, and neighbors is tainted by post facto sense-making, with built-in gender assumptions. Interviewing "failed" suicide bombers is problematic because inmates adapt to prison culture (Hamm, 2018; Horgan, 2012). Time erodes memory, but, more importantly, retrospective rationalizations recast past actions for a host of reasons including legal considerations, as well as the need to impress peers, political organizations, and family members (Hamm, 2018; Horgan, 2012). In Erez and Laster's (2020) study, for instance, some terrorists became "born again" Muslims while others purported to cast off their former allegiances.

Despite serious methodological issues, there is surprising scholarly consensus about the apparent self-evident motivations of men. "Ideology" and "politics" are deemed to be men's subjectively rational, if predatory, choices. Looking at women terrorist's motives is altogether a more complicated exercise. As Gentry and Sjoberg (2016, p. 145) warn,

> Media, scholarly, and policy world reactions to women's participation in violence classified as terrorism is to treat women's terrorism "as not terrorism but women's terrorism," and women terrorists are at once characterized as aberrant, personally motivated, and beyond the agency of the female perpetrator.

Women terrorists are generally considered to be driven by their emotions—a key feature of "the feminine" contrasted with the assumed rationality of "the masculine" (Naffine, 2016). Research that compares men's and women's motivations concludes that men are more likely to be motivated by religious or nationalistic concerns than women (Jacques & Taylor, 2008).

The language used by subjects, though, may itself be a reflection of gendered identity. The rhetoric of political intent, for instance, comes more easily to a man schooled in such beliefs and, in certain contexts, talking in these terms may be a more acceptable way of "doing maleness." Speckhard (2008) for instance finds that the motivation for female suicide bombers inside conflict zones is probably a variant of a broader category of "community outrage" that includes trauma, revenge, and nationalism. In non-conflict zones, women terrorists experience feelings of alienation, marginalization, and negative self-identity as well as solidarity with those living in conflict zones. In short, she suggests that there is not all that much separating female from male motivation, even though men and women might rationalize their involvement in different terms.

Feminist researchers have developed sophisticated methods such as "life course" interviewing (e.g., Devault, 1990) to discern the layered and interconnected factors that shape a subject's experiences. Using such methods, Bloom (2011a, 2011b) developed a widely used typology of four (plus one) overlapping motives to account for why women engage in terrorist activism—revenge (at the loss of significant others or other political grievances), redemption (women volunteer or are volunteered to perpetrate suicide bombings to erase moral blemishes, commonly resulting from actual or suspected sexual contacts outside marriage that tarnishes "family honor"), respect (admiration from others for their honorable contribution to the cause), and relationships (with men who are involved in terrorism). Other researchers have similarly documented that women's reasons for joining terrorist groups appear to be more personal, including avenging another's death, recruitment pressure, marginalization by society, and "serving as pawns in a man's game" (Simon & Tranel, 2011).

There are indeed some tragic stories about women suicide bombers: the burned and disfigured woman injured in a kitchen accident and so pushed by her parents into becoming a suicide bomber to prevent her becoming a drain on the family; or the women suspected of adultery who agree to become suicide bombers to salvage their and, more significantly, their family's honor (Berko & Erez, 2008). And there are also ample accounts of sexual exploitation by handlers of innocent young women who had had little experience of the world outside their sheltered upbringing (Berko & Erez, 2008).

Equally, there are clear examples of overt agency. For instance, some women terrorists, who are atypical in that they do not conform to gendered expectations, initiate their own involvement, even insisting on deployment despite initial refusals by terrorist organizations to use them (Berko & Erez, 2008; Bloom, 2011a, 2011b).

Gender theorists are caught in a double-bind. Gender analysis starts from the premise that social life is inevitably unequal. Women's life chances are reduced because of their gender and other intersectional factors. Placing too much store on women's individual choices, though, may overstate agency at the expense of structure (Giddens, 1984; Sewell, 1992). On the other hand, seeing women merely as "pawns" or victims ignores the quite deliberate, gender-defying choices made by some women who engage in terrorism (Bloom & Lokmanoglu, 2020).

There is probably not much to be gained from insisting too vigorously on a purist pursuit of agency. As a number of feminists have warned, the level of actual violence against women in deeply patriarchal societies means that structural victimization and agency inevitably coexist (e.g., Serendip Studio, 2012), and, in certain contexts, it is impossible to isolate choice or agency from the wider context in which women's individual decisions are made (MacKinnon, 1987).

Intersectionality theory goes even further and eschews reducing motives along gender lines altogether. A terrorist, whether man or woman, is many things at once. Their actions should not be isolated and explained independently of race, ethnicity, class, sexual orientation, and other realities of their lived experience (Harris, 1990, p. 585; Laster & Raman, 1997), because the differences *within* gender are often just as great, if not greater, than those between them.

The theoretical solution may be to apply "generalizable" theories which are broad enough to capture the complexity and diversity of individual motivations while acknowledging the contextual factors shaping individual circumstances and thus motive.

Perry and Hasisi (2015), for instance, utilize *rational choice theory* to explain the actions of suicide bombers, describing the religious, personal, and social rewards that suicide bombers expect to attain, based on a case study of failed suicide bomber Umar Farouk Abdul Mutallab (who attempted to detonate a bomb over Detroit in 2009). The authors argue that suicide bombing is generally not motivated by altruism, but rather a result of rational situational choices, based on evaluating the costs and anticipated benefits of one's actions (Perry & Hasisi, 2015, p. 72). The theory can fit both male and female motivation for terrorism. Similarly, Erez and Laster (2020) propose a version of "bounded rationality," which recognizes that individuals make decisions from a position of imperfect knowledge and under conditions of uncertainty. In the anthropological sense, "rationality" is thus embedded in the inconsistencies and paradoxes built into all cultures (Kuznar, 2007). Both these approaches recognize that local conflicts and circumstances remain the critical motivator for participation in terrorism for both men and women (Ali, 2006).

In the next section we demonstrate how, in an unequal world, gender analysis captures the unequal consequences of terrorism for women, individually and collectively.

Terrorism's Unequal Consequences: Women as Perpetrators, Victims, and Citizens

Gender Theory accepts that the powerful maintain their privileged position through systematic structural inequality. This process does not necessarily require overt forms of domination but is mostly achieved through deep (and socially accepted) ideological beliefs about "how things are," "how things work," and, of course, "what men and women are like." But all archetypes and stereotypes have consequences. Below, we consider how the net result of stereotyping is that women end up worse off as perpetrators, victims, and citizens.

Worse for Women Perpetrators

Women who choose to engage in terrorist activism face a gendered double-bind: their contribution to violent political struggle contradicts gender norms of femininity and womanhood under patriarchy (Ali, 2006). Women combatants are accordingly judged more harshly and experience more adverse outcomes as a consequence of their involvement than their male counterparts (Erez & Laster, 2020).

However strong the political rhetoric in particular global hotspots, the evidence is that terrorism activism, especially martyrdom by women, is not generally condoned in these societies (Speckhard & Akhmedova, 2006). There are exceptions of course, with some women suicide bombers, like Wafa Idris, being embraced as a revered martyr and female terrorist role model. However, most women suicide bombers suffer the worst possible fate and often die in obscurity because their involvement is deliberately not revealed to avoid family and community censure or because their participation would detract from the deeds of men (Ali, 2006; Erez & Berko, 2008; see also Davis, 2013).

For women combatants who fail in their mission, the outcomes are also usually less favorable than for men who are caught. The "mitigating factor" for a woman combatant who can prove she has been manipulated or coerced by a man may reduce the length of her sentence (Erez & Berko, 2008). But the so-called "chivalry" in the sentencing of women offenders is not always borne out, with some women made an example of because of their gender-defying behavior. For instance, a Chechen woman, an opportunistic terrorist recruit who changed her mind and gave herself up to Moscow police, nevertheless received the maximum penalty of 20 years' imprisonment as general (and gendered) deterrence (Bloom, 2007, p. 96). Women who transgress are typically dealt with more harshly than men because their gender-defying behavior means they are deemed to be "monsters" (Laster, 1994; see also Sjoberg & Gentry, 2007).

Women also tend to receive more limited rehabilitation and reintegration support. This puts women at a potentially greater risk of recidivism and re-radicalization, and may undermine their successful reintegration into society (United Nations Counter-Terrorism Committee Executive Directorate, 2019, p. 17).

The jail time served by women also disproportionately undermines their life chances. Time for women, as one Palestinian woman in an Israeli prison for security violations explained, is a form of indirect discrimination.

> For a woman the prison is more difficult than for a man. It is dependent on the sentence ... A woman thinks of her future, if she will get out or not. A man, if he sits 10 year or 15 years, when he is released he can build his life ... A woman is not like a man. It is important how old she is because it is difficult for her to build her life and look at the future if she older than 30.
>
> (Berko & Erez, 2007, p. 508)

That is even assuming that she would be in a position to marry and have children. For women in patriarchal cultures, spending time in jail outside the control of the family tarnishes their virtue beyond repair. As one Palestinian leader observed, a "woman who winds up in prison, her status is inferior. She is not ideal woman ... I don't think anyone would want to marry such a woman" (Berko, 2012, p. 7).

By contrast, for a male terrorist being jailed is a badge of honor and they are accorded prestige inside the prison, receive financial support, and upon release are offered a high-status marriage and even leadership positions in the terrorist organization.

Worse for Women as Victims

Empirically, women and children, directly and indirectly, are disproportionately affected by various aspects of terrorism (see e.g., United Nations Office on Drugs and Crime, 2020). This is hardly surprising as terrorist organizations consciously exploit "soft targets" such as markets, schools, hospitals, and transport hubs.

The increased surveillance of the places which women typically frequent makes them not only less safe, but counterterrorism measures make it more problematic for women to navigate their daily lives. And since women are now regarded as potential threats, in world hotspots intrusive surveillance, including body searches, has now become commonplace.

At the macro or political level, one saving grace of the stereotype of the West needing to save women from oppressive regimes, was that women were generally regarded as victims. But now that women are identified as part of the terrorist threat, they are no longer deemed worthy of sympathy and support. There is not the same squeamishness about collateral damage to bystander populations such as women and children. The harshness toward women is also evident in the punitive treatment of the wives, and especially the children, of terrorists left in refugee camps who seek to return to their countries of origin (United Nations Counter-Terrorism Committee Executive Directorate, 2019).

More broadly, there is also evidence that women typically live with greater levels of fear about terrorism generally. Dillon et al.'s (2019) analysis of the World Values Survey about Fear of Crime/Worry about terrorism, for instance, found that gender was a significant variable. In 22 of the 54 nations surveyed, women reported greater worry about terrorism, with men having higher levels of fear in only four of the nations surveyed (with no significant differences between the genders in 28 countries).

Even if women do not become actual victims of terrorism they have cause for concern. The gender card has been played to great effect to undermine the rights of women as citizens—even, and especially, in countries that allegedly eschew gender discrimination.

Worse for Women as Citizens

In banding together to fight terrorism, the West's stereotype is that Muslim terrorists are, as Kathryn Brown summarizes, members of a backward, barbaric, inferior, and the violent "Other" which must be defeated at all costs (Brown, 2011, p. 706). This kind of thinking lies at the heart of the "War on Terror" and sets the scene for an apparently inevitable, "Clash of Civilizations" (Huntington, 1993; Parfitt & Egorova, 2003). All-out global conflict is a very high price to pay, by women and men alike, for such racial and religious prejudices.

In Western democracies, paternalistic outrage at women's subordination under Fundamentalist regimes has served as a key justification for military and other counterterrorism measures. A number of feminist commentators link American military intervention in the Middle East to the discourse about the "just war" required to rescue Muslim women from both the oppression of their religion and their menfolk (Deylami, 2013). The "enlightened" West, the discourse holds, has a moral obligation to liberate Brown women from Brown men. In a radio address of November 2001, the then First Lady Laura Bush declared that "The

War on Terror" was also a fight for the "rights and dignity of women," including their rights to education, employment, and health care (Laster & Erez, 2015, p. 95).

Paradoxically, and almost imperceptibly, one effect of this moral outrage has been to undermine the demands for greater gender equality in Western democracies themselves. Laster and Erez argue that in the United States, the "War on Terror" is linked to what feminists have dubbed the "War on Women" domestically—the aggressive right-wing political campaign to roll back women's equality (Laster & Erez, 2015, p. 94), especially women's hard-won reproductive rights (Finlay, 2006; Flanders, 2004).

Then President George W. Bush, for example, explicitly linked the "evil" of abortion rights to terrorism. On the 29th anniversary of *Roe v. Wade* in 2002, which he declared as National Sanctity of Human Life Day, President Bush juxtaposed the Right-to-Life political agenda with opposition to terrorism: "On September 11, we saw clearly that evil exists in this world, and that it does not value life ... Now we are engaged in a fight against evil and tyranny to preserve and protect life" (Viner, 2002).[3]

Feminists challenging the prevailing view that the principal threat to women's emancipation is Fundamentalist adherents of Islam are discredited (Mohideen, 2008) and feminist critics of domestic policy are routinely belittled with variants of the relativist taunt, "You should be grateful that you are not a woman in Afghanistan" (see, e.g., Meinecke, 2013).

Women's involvement in terrorism has had adverse consequences for women's rights, including in Western democracies themselves.

Conclusion: Gender Theory Work/s

We have shown how Gender Theory casts a different light on terrorism and our responses to it. It is, for instance, possible to see terrorism as a way of "doing masculinity." This includes "using" women strategically as front-line combatants. Capitalizing on the gender stereotypes prevalent in target societies helps terrorist organizations to realize their twin objective of maximum harm and maximum publicity. Media reporting about women terrorists often reinforces these self-same stereotypes about women as the perennial pawns of men or, alternatively, as "unnatural," women. Similarly, stereotyping and essentializing of men and women's behavior also underscores much social science exploration of the motivation for involvement in terrorism. But as we have shown, women terrorists, just like their male counterparts, exercise agency, although this itself needs to be understood in a gendered context. A gender lens reveals that inequality lies at the core of the different experiences of women and men, including the harsher consequences of terrorism for women as perpetrators, victims, and citizens.

Behavior at the extremes is theory's best proving ground. Inevitably, though, it sends us back to the theoretical drawing board. Applying Gender Theory to terrorism reveals gaps and shortcomings in our understanding. Terrorism, for instance, challenges traditional criminological theory, including Feminist theory, which shares the same assumption about the "maleness" of crime, particularly violent crime. As we have seen, though, this violent and socially central crime is committed by women as well as men. This is true historically, but also increasingly in some global hotspots. Mirroring the gender blindness of traditional criminology, the importance of women acting behind the scenes as facilitators of terrorism has also been underestimated.

Gender Theory, including feminist criminology, is still challenged when accounting for two critical issues in terrorism research and policy—the "why" or the motivation for terrorism, as well as "what" we do about it. For instance, the social control strand of Feminist theory has difficulty accounting for why some women defy their gender socialization and engage in such extreme behavior. Likewise, we still do not have convincing accounts of how it is that most men, who are subjected to the same masculinist pressure to engage in, or at least support, violent extremism in particular geopolitical hotspots, nevertheless manage to desist.

Intersectionality theory's critique that the binary category of "gender" is too crude to be the basis of analysis does not resolve the problem. Identity is fluid and contradictory, and complicated by the overlapping dimensions of race, class, ethnicity, sexuality and, in the context of New Terrorism, religion (Burgess-Proctor, 2006). Unraveling the various strands of the social construction of identities comes into its own as "thick description" of individual behavior but is less helpful as a basis for wider policy intervention.

Gender Theory and intersectionality are strongest when used as a method, or lens. Other theories, appropriately informed by a gender perspective, probably have more grunt as a basis for intervention at both the micro and macro levels.

For instance, General Strain Theory (GST) focuses on how negative treatment (including stereotyping) by others can lead to anti-social (typically delinquent) behavior (Agnew, 1992, 2001; Agnew et al., 2002). GST takes the emotions of offenders seriously in holding that strain or stress can produce actions grounded in anger, frustration, depression, and despair. Individuals then seek to overcome these negative emotions by forming relationships and engaging in anti-social behavior, such as delinquency, to help readdress these feelings of inadequacy. Agnew (2010) applies GST to terrorism, presenting a theory by which terrorism is more likely when people experience "collective strains" that are high in magnitude, affect civilians, are unjust, and are inflicted by more powerful "others."

On the other side of the emotions equation, Jack Katz's theory of the "seduction of crime" (1988) recognizes that criminal behavior is just as often grounded in positive emotions. For instance, the search for excitement, or even relief from boredom, are often drivers of anti-social behavior for both men and women. In Erez and Laster's empirical study of Palestinian women engaged in terrorist activism, for example, a number of the women admitted that escaping the confines of family and home was a thrill. Interacting with men, taking off the veil and wearing Western clothing was exhilarating. There were psychological rewards too—a feeling that they were "different" or "unique," because they were contributing to the national cause: "I did something that is manly. There are hardly any women who are doing what I have done" (Erez & Laster, 2020, p. 451).

At least implicitly, these theoretic approaches probably already underscore some forms of Countering Violent Extremism (CVE) interventions. But a gender lens also cautions against adopting a "one-size-fits-all" approach, which sees women terrorists as miniature males (Yon & Milton, 2019). Male and female terrorists are diverse, and counter-radicalization efforts must take these variations into consideration (Schmidt, 2020; Yon & Milton, 2019) including, at the very least, their quite different gendered social circumstances. Otherwise, there is a real risk that CVE measures will, rather than empower women, inadvertently reinforce gender stereotypes (Phelan, 2020).

At the macro level of "why" and "what we do" about terrorism, one promising line of recent research fits squarely within the Gender Theory frame. There is now growing support for a strong correlation between greater levels of gender equality, and lower levels of terrorism and conflict in a given society (Harris & Milton, 2016). The empirical evidence for the "gender equality–peace thesis" across multiple countries over several decades indicates that variables such as increasing female rights, higher levels of female labor force participation (e.g., Berrebi & Ostwald, 2016) and enhanced educational opportunities for women (e.g., Salman, 2015) are all associated with lower levels of terrorism and conflict generally, whereas hostile attitudes toward women and support for violence against women are factors strongly associated with support for violent extremism (Johnston & True, 2019). Such findings reinforce Gender Theory's focus on structural inequality as a key driver in the subordination of groups defined by their "Otherness" (e.g., Collins, 1990).

In criminology, feminist theory is only a short few decades old and Gender Theory is even more recent. The strength of the gender approach is that it is now almost impossible to imagine how we could study crime generally, and terrorism in particular, without taking account of gender as a key variable. Perhaps the greatest strength of a gender lens, though, is that it is a litmus test for all theories trying to account for such a socially central and devastating crime as terrorism.

Notes

1 While this chapter focuses largely on gender, such roles are now regarded as only one aspect of fluid "intersectional" identities where gender, ethnicity, race, class, sexuality, and age overlap and play out in different ways for individuals and social systems (Laster & Raman, 1997). Any analysis must also layer the complex assumptions about multiple aspects of identity, particularly in the case of terrorism, religion, and race.
2 The viewpoint of this case study is in the tradition of "critical theory." We fully appreciate that 9/11 was a horrific crime which did untold damage. Our analysis does not seek to dissolve "truth" into an extreme form of relativism through mirror-in-mirror reflections of endless "diversity." Nevertheless, the gender dimension of both the act and the response to it cannot be ignored.
3 Barbara Finlay (2006) documents the suppression of political, economic, and scientific knowledge by the George W. Bush Administration about birth control as well as the systematic denial of women's health and social rights, including attempts to weaken Title IX, the 1972 law that sought to guarantee women and girls equitable treatment by educational institutions.

References

Agnew, R. (1992). Foundation for a general strain theory of crime and delinquency. *Criminology*, 30(1), 47–87.

Agnew, R. (2001). Building on the foundation of general strain theory: Specifying the types of strain most likely to lead to crime and delinquency. *Journal of Research in Crime and Delinquency*, 38(4), 319–361.

Agnew, R. (2010). A general strain theory of terrorism. *Theoretical Criminology*, 14(2), 131–153.

Agnew, R., Brezina, T., Wright, J.P., & Cullen, F.T. (2002). Strain, personality traits, and delinquency: Extending general strain theory. *Criminology*, 40(1), 43–71.

Ali, F. (2006). Rocking the cradle to rocking the world: The role of Muslim female fighters. *Journal of International Women's Studies*, 8(1), 21–35.

Bakker, E. (2006). *Jihadi terrorists in Europe: Their characteristics and the circumstances in which they joined the jihad: An exploratory study*. Clingendael, Netherlands: Netherlands Institute of International Relations.

Ballina, S. (2011). The crime–terror continuum revisited: A model for the study of hybrid criminal organisations. *Journal of Policing, Intelligence and Counter Terrorism*, 6(2), 121–136.

Baxter, D. (2007). Honor thy sister: Selfhood, gender, and agency in Palestinian culture. *Anthropological Quarterly*, 80(3), 737–775.

Berko, A. (2012). *The smarter bomb: Women and children as suicide bombers*. Lanham, MD: Rowman & Littlefield.

Berko, A., & Erez, E. (2007). Gender, Palestinian women, and terrorism: Women's liberation or oppression? *Studies in Conflict & Terrorism*, 30(6), 493–519.

Berko, A., & Erez, E. (2008). Martyrs or murderers? Victimizers or victims? The voices of would be Palestinian female suicide bombers. In C. Ness (Ed.), *In the name of the cause: Female militancy and terrorism in context*. Abingdon: Taylor and Francis, pp. 146–166.

Berrebi, C., & Ostwald, J. (2016). Terrorism and the labor force: Evidence of an effect on female labor force participation and the labor gender gap. *Journal of Conflict Resolution*, 60(1), 32–60.

Bloom, M. (2007). Female suicide bombers: A global trend. *Daedalus*, 136(1), 94–102.

Bloom, M. (2011a). *Bombshells: The many faces of women terrorists*. Ontario, Canada: Penguin Press.

Bloom, M. (2011b). Bombshells: Women and terror. *Gender Issues*, 28, 1–21.

Bloom, M. (2013). In defense of honor: Women and terrorist recruitment on the internet. *Journal of Postcolonial Cultures and Societies*, 4(1), 150–173.

Bloom, M., & Lokmanoglu, A. (2020). From pawns to knights: The changing role of women's agency in terrorism? *Studies in Conflict & Terrorism* (forthcoming in print).

Brown, B. (1986). Women and crime: The dark figures of criminology. *Economy and Society*, 15(3), 355–402.

Brown, K.E. (2011). Muriel's wedding: News media representations of Europe's first female suicide terrorist. *European Journal of Cultural Studies*, 14(6), 705–726.

Brunner, C. (2005). Female suicide bombers—Male suicide bombing? Looking for gender in reporting the suicide bombings of the Israeli–Palestinian conflict. *Global Society*, 19(1), 29–48.

Burgess-Proctor, A. (2006). Intersections of race, class, gender, and crime: Future directions for feminist criminology. *Feminist Criminology*, 1(1), 27–47.

Butler, J. (1988). Performative acts and gender constitution: An essay in phenomenology and feminist theory. *Theatre Journal*, 40(4), 519–531.

Collins, P.H. (1990). *Black feminist thought: Knowledge, consciousness, and the politics of empowerment*. New York: Routledge.

Connell, R.W. (2005). *Masculinities* (2nd Edn.). Sydney, Australia: Allen & Unwin.

Connell, R.W., & Messerschmidt, J.W. (2005). Hegemonic masculinity: Rethinking the concept. *Gender & Society*, 19(6), 829–859.

Cook, D. (2005). Women fighting in jihad? *Studies in Conflict & Terrorism*, 28(5), 375–384.

Cook, J., & Vale, G. (2018). *From Daesh to "diaspora": Tracing the women and minors of Islamic State*. London: International Centre for the Study of Radicalisation.

Crenshaw, K. (1991). Mapping the margins: Intersectionality, identity politics, and violence against women of color. *Stanford Law Review*, 43(6), 1241–1299.

Cunningham, K.J. (2007). Countering female terrorism. *Studies in Conflict & Terrorism*, 30(2), 113–129.

Curry, G. (2011). Gangs, crime, and terrorism. In B. Forst, J. Greene, & J. Lynch (Eds.), *Criminologists on terrorism and homeland security*. Cambridge: Cambridge University Press, pp. 97–112.

Daly, H., & Chesney-Lind, M. (1988). Feminism and criminology. *Justice Quarterly*, 5(4), 497–538.

Davis, J. (2013). Evolution of the global Jihad: Female suicide bombers in Iraq. Studies in Conflict & Terrorism, 36, 279–201.

Devault, M.L. (1990). Talking and listening from women's standpoint: Feminist strategies for interviewing and analysis. *Social Problems*, 37(1), 96–116.

Deylami, S.S. (2013). Saving the enemy: Female suicide bombers and the making of American empire. *International Feminist Journal of Politics*, 15(2), 177–194.

Dillon, L., Hayes, B.E., Freilich, J.D., &. Chermak, S.M. (2019). Gender differences in worry about a terrorist attack: A cross-national examination of individual- and national-level factors, *Women & Criminal Justice*, 29(4–5), 221–241.

Edelman, M. (1988). *Constructing the political spectacle*. Chicago, IL: University of Chicago Press.

Erez, E. (2006). Protracted war, terrorism and mass victimization: Exploring victimological/criminological theories and concepts in addressing terrorism in Israel. In U. Ewald & K. Turković (Eds.), *Large-scale victimisation as a potential source of terrorist activities: Regaining security in post-conflict societies*. Amsterdam, Netherlands: ISO Press, pp. 89–102.

Erez, E., & Berko, A. (2008). Palestinian women in terrorism: Protectors or protected? *Journal of National Defense Studies*, 6, 83–110.

Erez, E., & Laster, K. (2020). Palestinian women in terrorism: A double-edged sword? *International Journal of Offender Therapy and Comparative Criminology*, 64(5), 443–469.

Felson, R. (1993). Predatory and dispute-related violence: A social interactionist approach. In R. Clarke & M. Felson (Eds.), *Advances in criminological theory, Vol. 5*. New York: Routledge, pp. 189–235.

Finlay, B. (2006). *George W. Bush and the war on women: Turning back the clock on progress*. New York: Zed Books.

Flanders, L. (2004). *The W effect: Bush's war on women*. New York: Feminist Press at the City University of New York.

Fullmer, N., Mizrahi, S.L., & Tomsich, E. (2019). The lethality of female suicide bombers. *Women & Criminal Justice*, 29(4–5), 266–282.

Gan, R., Neo, L.S., Chin J., & Khader, M. (2019). Change is the only constant: The evolving role of women in the Islamic State in Iraq and Syria (ISIS). *Women & Criminal Justice*, 29(4–5), 204–220.

Gentry, C., & Sjoberg, L. (2016). Female terrorism and militancy. In J. Richard (Ed.), *Handbook of critical terrorism studies*. Abingdon: Routledge, pp. 145–155.

Giddens, A. (1984). *The constitution of society: Outline of the theory of structuration*. Berkeley, CA: University of California Press.

Gilfus, M.E. (1993). From victims to survivors to offenders: Women's routes of entry and immersion into street crime. *Women & Criminal Justice*, 4(1), 63–89.

Hamm, M.S. (2018). Using prison ethnography in terrorism research. In S. Rice & M. Maltz (Eds.), *Doing ethnography in criminology: Discovery through fieldwork*. Cham, Switzerland: Springer, pp. 195–202.

Harmon, C.C. (2000). *Terrorism today*. London: Frank Cass.

Harris, A.P. (1990). Race and essentialism in feminist legal theory. *Stanford Law Review*, 42, 581–616.

Harris, C., & Milton, D.J. (2016). Is standing for women a stand against terrorism? Exploring the connection between women's rights and terrorism. *Journal of Human Rights*, 15(1), 60–78.

Hasan, M. (2005). Growing up Palestinian. In E. Fuchs (Ed.), *Israeli women's studies: A reader*. New Brunswick, NJ: Rutgers University Press, pp. 181–190.

Hasso, F.H. (2005). Discursive and political deployments by/of the 2002 Palestinian women suicide bombers/martyrs. *Feminist Review*, 81, 23–51.

Hearne, E.B. (2009). *Participants, enablers, and preventers: The roles of women in terrorism*. Research paper presented at the British International Studies Association, Leicester, UK.

Heidensohn, F. (1985). *Women and crime*. London: Macmillan.

Hoffman, B. (2002). Rethinking terrorism and counterterrorism since 9/11. *Studies in Conflict and Terrorism*, 25(5), 303–316.

Holt, M. (2010). Challenging preconceptions: Women and Islamic resistance. In M. Pace (Ed.), *Europe, the USA and political Islam: Strategies for engagement*. London: Palgrave, pp. 79–101.

Horgan, J. (2014). *The psychology of terrorism* (2nd Edn.). New York: Routledge.

Horgan, J.G. (2012). Interviewing the terrorists: Reflections on fieldwork and implications for psychological research. *Behavioral Sciences of Terrorism and Political Aggression*, 4(3), 195–211.

Huberman, H. (2007). We will use suicide bombers against the IDF invasion. *Israel National News*, May 20. Available at: www.inn.co.il/News/Flash.aspx/185204 (in Hebrew).

Huntington, S.P. (1993). The clash of civilizations? *Foreign Affairs*, 72(3), 22–49.

Jacques, K., & Taylor, P.J. (2008). Male and female suicide bombers: Different sexes, different reasons? *Studies in Conflict & Terrorism*, 31(4), 304–326.

Jacques, K., & Taylor, P.J. (2009). Female terrorism: A review. *Terrorism and Political Violence*, 21(3), 499–515.

Johnston, M., & True, J. (2019). *Misogyny & violent extremism: Implications for preventing violent extremism*. Melbourne: Monash University. Available at: https://asiapacific.unwomen.org/en/digital-library/publications/2019/10/misogyny-violent-extremism.

Katz, J. (1988). *Seductions of crime: Moral and sensual attractions in doing evil*. New York: Basic Books.

Katz, J. (1991). The motivation of the persistent robber. *Crime and Justice*, 14, 277–306.

Kimmerling, B. (2003). Sacred Rage. *The Nation*, November 26. Available at: www.thenation.com/article/archive/sacred-rage/.
Klaus, E., & Kassel, S. (2005). The veil as a means of legitimization: An analysis of the interconnectedness of gender, media and war. *Journalism*, 6(3), 335–355.
Kuznar, L. (2007). Rationality wars and the war on terror: Explaining terrorism and social unrest. *American Anthropologist*, 109(2), 318–329.
LaFree, G., Dugan, L., & Korte, R. (2009). The impact of British counterterrorist strategies on political violence in Northern Ireland. *Criminology*, 47(1), 17–45.
Lakoff, G., & Johnson, M. (2003). *Metaphors we live by*. Chicago, IL: University of Chicago Press. (Original work published 1980).
Laqueur, W. (1987). *The age of terrorism*. Boston, MA: Little, Brown.
Laqueur, W. (2016). *The political psychology of appeasement: Finlandization and other unpopular essays*. New Brunswick, NJ: Routledge.
La Spina, A., Giovanni, F., Punzo, V., & Scaglione, A. (2014). *How mafia works: An analysis of the extortion racket system*. Paper presented at the ECPR General Conference, Glasgow, 3–6 September 2014.
Laster, K. (1989). Infanticide: A litmus test for feminist criminological theory. *Australian & New Zealand Journal of Criminology*, 22(3), 151–166.
Laster, K. (1994). Arbitrary chivalry: Women and capital punishment in Victoria, Australia 1842–1967. *Women & Criminal Justice*, 6(1), 67–95.
Laster, K., & Douglas, R. (1995). Feminized justice: The impact of women decision makers in the lower courts in Australia. *Justice Quarterly*, 12(1), 177–205.
Laster, K., & Erez, E. (2015). Sisters in terrorism? Exploding stereotypes. *Women & Criminal Justice*, 25, 83–99.
Laster, K., & Raman, P. (1997). Law for one and one for all? An intersectional legal subject. In N. Naffine & R.J. Owens (Eds.), *Sexing the subject of law*. Auckland, New Zealand: Sweet & Maxwell, pp. 193–212.
Laster, K., & Steinert, H. (2002,). Unspeakable Sept 11: Taboos and cliches. *Eurozine* March 5. Available at: www.eurozine.com/unspeakable-sept-11-taboos-and-clichi%C2%BDs/.
Lowe, P. (2006). Counterfeiting: Links to organised crime and terrorist funding. *Journal of Financial Crime*, 13(2), 255–257.
MacKinnon, C.A. (1987). *Feminism unmodified: Discourses on life and law*. Cambridge, MA: Harvard University Press.
Makarenko, T. (2004). The crime-terror continuum: Tracing the interplay between transnational organised crime and terrorism. *Global Crime*, 6(1), 129–145.
Markovic, V. (2019). Suicide squad: Boko Haram's use of the female suicide bomber. *Women & Criminal Justice*, 29(4–5), 283–302.
Marway, H. (2011). Scandalous subwomen and sublime superwomen: Exploring portrayals of female suicide bombers' agency. *Journal of Global Ethics*, 7(3), 221–240.
Matusitz, J. (2013). *Terrorism and communication: A critical introduction*. Los Angeles, CA: Sage.
Meinecke, E. (2013). The real war on women. *Townhall Magazine*, February 13. Available at: http://townhall.com/tipsheet/elisabethmeinecke/2013/02/13/the-real-war-on-women-n1510094.
Messerschmidt, J.W. (1993). *Masculinities and crime: Critique and reconceptualization of theory*. Lanham, MD: Rowman & Littlefield.
Miller, G., & Mekhennet, S. (2015). Inside the surreal world of the Islamic State's propaganda machine. *Washington Post*, November 20. Available

at: www.washingtonpost.com/world/national-security/inside-the-islamic-states-propaganda-machine/2015/11/20/051e997a-8ce6-11e5-acff-673ae92ddd2b_story.html?utm_term=.e92f675db9a2/.
Mohideen, R. (2008). The "war on women" belies the "war on terror." *Women in Action*, 1, 13–16.
Naaman, D. (2007). Brides of Palestine/angels of death: Media, gender, and performance in the case of the Palestinian female suicide bombers. *Signs*, 32(4), 933–955.
Nacos, B.L. (2005). The portrayal of female terrorists in the media: Similar framing patterns in the news coverage of women in politics and in terrorism. *Studies in Conflict & Terrorism*, 28(5), 435–451.
Naffine, N. (2016). *Female crime: The construction of women in criminology*. New York: Routledge.
Naylor, B. (1994). Fair trial or free press: Legal responses to media reports of criminal trials. *Cambridge Law Journal*, 53(3), 492–501.
Organization for Security and Co-operation in Europe. (2013). Women and terrorist radicalization: Final report. Vienna, Austria: Organization for Security and Co-operation in Europe.
O'Rourke, L.A. (2009). What's special about female suicide terrorism? *Security Studies*, 18(4), 681–718.
Pape, R. (2005). *Dying to win: The strategic logic of suicide terrorism*. New York: Random House.
Parfitt, T., & Egorova, Y. (Eds.). (2003). *Jews, Muslims and mass media: Mediating the "other."* London: Routledge.
Perri, F., & Brody, R. (2011). The dark triad: Organised crime, terror and fraud. *Journal of Money Laundering Control*, 14(1), 44–59.
Perry, S., & Hasisi, B. (2015). Rational choice rewards and the jihadist suicide bomber. *Terrorism and Political Violence*, 27(1), 53–80.
Phelan, A. (2020). Special issue introduction for terrorism, gender and women: Toward an integrated research agenda. *Studies in Conflict & Terrorism* (forthcoming in print).
Post, J. (2009). *The mind of the terrorist: The psychology of terrorism from the IRA to al-Qaeda*. New York: Palgrave Macmillan.
Radlauer, D. (2006). Rational choice deterrence and Israeli counter-terrorism. In S. Mehrotra, D.D. Zeng, H. Chen, B. Thuraisingham, & F.Y. Wang (Eds.), *Intelligence and security informatics. ISI 2006. Lecture notes in Computer Science, Vol. 3975*. Berlin, Heidelberg: Springer, pp. 609–614.
Rosenfeld, R. (2002). Why criminologists should study terrorism. *The Criminologist*, 27(6), 1, 3–4.
Salman, A. (2015). Green houses for terrorism: Measuring the impact of gender equality attitudes and outcomes as deterrents of terrorism. *International Journal of Comparative and Applied Criminal Justice*, 39(4), 281–306.
Santino, U. (2019). Violence and mafia: Symbol and project. In M. Massari & V. Martone (Eds.), *Mafia violence: Political, symbolic, and economic forms of violence in Camorra clans*. New York: Routledge.
Schmidt, R. (2020). Duped: Examining gender stereotypes in disengagement and deradicalization practices. *Studies in Conflict & Terrorism* (forthcoming in print).

Serendip Studio. (2012). Feminism and female suicide bombers: Feminism for female suicide bombers and the imagined community. Available at: https://serendipstudio.org/exchange/node/12028.
Sewell, W.H. (1992). A theory of structure: Duality, agency, and transformation. *American Journal of Sociology*, 98(1), 1–29.
Shalhoub-Kevorkian, N. (2003). Liberating voices: The political implications of Palestinian mothers narrating their loss. *Women's Studies International Forum*, 26(5), 391–407.
Simon, R., & Tranel, A. (2011). Women terrorists. In B. Forst, J. Greene, & J. Lynch (Eds.), *Cambridge studies in criminology: Criminologists on terrorism and homeland security*. Cambridge: Cambridge University Press, pp. 113–126.
Sjoberg, L., & Gentry, C.E. (2007). *Mothers, monsters, whores: Women's violence in global politics*. New York: Zed Books.
Speckhard, A. (2008). The emergence of female suicide terrorists. *Studies in Conflict & Terrorism*, 31(11), 995–1023.
Speckhard, A., & Akhmedova, K. (2006). Black widows: The Chechen female suicide terrorists. In Y. Schweitzer (Ed.), *Female Suicide Terrorists*. Tel Aviv, Israel: Jaffe Center for Strategic Studies, pp. 63–80.
Steinert, H. (2003). Unspeakable September 11th: Taken-for-granted assumptions, selective reality construction and populist politics. *International Journal of Urban and Regional Research*, 27(3), 651–665.
Tamimi, T.T. (2017). Violence against women in Palestine and mediocre accountability. *Legal Issues*, 5(1), 75–100.
Tariq, I., & Sjoberg, L. (2021). Women and violent extremism: Concepts and theories. Oxford research encyclopedia of criminology. Available at: https://oxfordre.com/criminology/view/10.1093/acrefore/9780190264079.001.0001/acrefore-9780190264079-e-683.
United Nations Counter-Terrorism Committee Executive Directorate. (2019). Gender dimensions of the response to returning foreign terrorist fighters: Research perspectives. Available at: www.un.org/sc/ctc/wp-content/uploads/2019/02/Feb_2019_CTED_Trends_Report.pdf.
United Nations Office on Drugs and Crime. (2020). Mainstreaming gender in terrorism prevention. Available at: www.unodc.org/documents/Gender/Thematic_Gender_Briefs_English/Terrorism_brief_23_03_2020.pdf.
Victor, B. (2004). *Army of roses: Inside the world of Palestinian women suicide bombers*. London: Constable and Robinson.
Viner, K. (2002). Feminism as imperialism. *The Guardian*, September 21. Available at: www.theguardian.com/world/2002/sep/21/gender.usa.
von Knop, K. (2008). The multifaceted roles of women inside Al-Qaeda. *Journal of National Defense Studies*, 6, 139–162.
Wannenburg, G. (2003). Links between organised crime and Al-Qaeda. *South African Journal of International Affairs*, 10(2), 77–90.
Weinberg, L., & Eubank, W. (2011). Women's involvement in terrorism. *Gender Issues*, 28(1), 22–49.
West, C., & Zimmerman, D. (1987). Doing gender. *Gender and Society*, 1(2), 125–151.

West, J. (2005). Feminist IR and the case of the "Black Widows": Reproducing gendered divisions. *Innovations*, 5(2), 1–16.

Yon, R., & Milton, D. (2019). Simply small men? Examining differences between females and males radicalized in the United States. *Women & Criminal Justice*, 29(4–5), 188–203.

Zatz, M., & Gough, H. (2014). Gendered theory and gendered practice. In G. Bruinsma & D. Weisburd (Eds.), *Encyclopedia of criminology and criminal justice*. New York: Springer, pp. 1876–1883.

Zedner, L. (1991). Women, crime, and penal responses: A historical account. *Crime and Justice*, 14, 307–362.

6

Terrorist Target Selection

Max Abrahms and Joseph Mroszczyk

Terrorism is typically defined as attacks by non-state actors against civilian targets for a political goal (Abrahms, 2006; Schmid et al., 1984). But this common definition belies important differences in the actual attack patterns of what we call terrorist organizations. In practice, they exhibit wide variation in their target selection. Take a look at the State Department's official list of Foreign Terrorist Organizations. Although groups such as the Armed Islamic Group mainly struck civilians in Algeria, the Mujahedin-e Khalq has mainly struck military and other government personnel in Iran. Not only is there variation in the targeting choices between militant groups but also within them over time (Abrahms, 2018). Al-Qaeda, for example, became notorious for blowing up the World Trade Center towers on September 11, 2001. Leading up to his death in May 2011, however, its founder Osama bin Laden came to eschew such mass casualty civilian attacks, especially against Muslims (Abrahms, 2012). How do we account for such variation in attack preferences? And what, if anything, drives terrorist targeting strategy?

The answer to this question has profound implications for terrorism scholars and counterterrorism practitioners. Intellectually, scholars would better understand the internal thought process of terrorists, particularly why they are liable to strike some targets over others. From a practical perspective, counterterrorism effectiveness will improve to the extent to which security practitioners are able to anticipate, preempt, deter, and prevent terrorist operations (Perry et al., 2016). Clearly, knowing which targets terrorists will attack and why is critical for those tasked with defending them. If law enforcement, intelligence, and other security agencies grasp how terrorist groups formulate targeting decisions, they can identify potential targets of interest, enhance security measures around those targets, and ultimately reduce future attacks (Bier, 2007). Ideally, theories on terrorist targeting can inform and thus enhance counterterrorism responses.

Yet the literature on terrorist targeting remains contested. Several methodological limitations impede clarity on this issue of terrorist targeting. Since the September 11, 2001 attacks, the quality of terrorism research has progressed unevenly. Although the creation of new datasets supplies researchers with fine-grained information to study which targets around the world terrorists have struck, the motivations behind their targeting decisions are more elusive. This makes sense because researchers can observe and thus code the physical consequences of terrorist attacks but nonetheless lack direct access into the minds of the perpetrators. The Global Terrorism Database at the University of Maryland, for example, has data on the precise targets of many thousands of attacks since 1970 all over the world but can at best note the official ideologies of perpetrators to explain their motives. Indeed, the question of terrorist motives remains unresolved in the academic community (Abrahms, 2008). Even with direct access to deliberations or minutes from meetings among terrorist leadership cadre, scholars and practitioners must infer the thoughts of terrorists from their behavior, decipher patterns, and attempt to deduce meaning.

Terrorist leaders often espouse a targeting preference in their propaganda messaging, but fail to act on it. A recent content analysis of the most lethal terrorist groups in the world reveals that their online propaganda videos are an unreliable predictor of the actual targets that they tend to attack (Abrahms et al., 2017). Bin Laden, for example, railed against Israel even though his group steered clear of the Jewish state (*Bin Laden's Warning*, 2001). Similarly, Islamic State has long expressed interest in its propaganda messaging to attack Rome and Vatican City, but has not committed mass casualty attacks there (Moore, 2017). This disconnect between the threat and behavior of the group may be due to specific counterterrorism measures taken (Bonino & Beccaro, 2019). But it may also be due to luck or a lack of organizational investment in attacking this country. Indeed, a flurry of recent studies highlights how terrorist leaders lie for instrumental reasons, particularly to gain potential supporters (Abrahms, 2020; Abrahms & Conrad, 2017; Brown, 2020; Hoffman, 1997, 2010; Kearns et al., 2014). The lack of clarity about terrorist targeting preferences is compounded by missing data on attack attempts. For obvious reasons, terrorism datasets suffer from a selection issue in which they are more likely to include operationally successful attacks than thwarted ones. This omission of failed attempts skews understanding of terrorist targeting preferences.

Scholars have identified several theoretical lenses to explain terrorist targeting choices notwithstanding the aforementioned methodological limitations. This chapter develops three paradigms in particular to elucidate terrorist targeting. First, we explore terrorist targeting choices from an ideological lens. This section presents the view that ideological beliefs drive terrorist target selection and highlights conceptual weaknesses with this lens. Second, we examine terrorist targeting choices from the vantage of the dominant paradigm in political science known as the Strategic Model of Terrorism. As its name denotes, the Strategic Model posits that terrorists select targets strategically to maximize the odds of political success (Abrahms, 2008; Crenshaw, 1988, 1990; McCormick, 2003). This section underlines how civilian attacks theoretically advance the political goals of terrorist groups but then presents a growing body of countervailing empirical work suggesting that such indiscriminate violence may actually be politically costly to the perpetrators. Third, we account with organizational theory for this paradox of why militant groups may engage in terrorist attacks against civilians despite the negative political return. Specifically, we show how conflict scholars are increasingly employing the principal–agent framework to explain the apparent puzzle of civilian attacks given their potential political costs. Below, we develop these lenses sequentially, underscore their relevance for terrorist targeting, and then explore the counterterrorism implications.

The Ideological Lens

Why do militants attack certain targets over others? The most common explanation hinges on the ideological orientation of the perpetrators (e.g., Ahmed, 2018). Unlike gangs and other criminal entities, terrorist groups must possess a presumed ideology. Kruglanski (2006, p. 272) defines ideology as "a coordinated set of convictions about how things are versus how they ought to be from the standpoint of a group, or a category of people." Terrorist groups are intertwined with their respective ideologies, making it nearly impossible to separate from their behavior. More specifically, the ideology of a terrorist group is thought to inform how it perceives its victims, uses violence, and calculates potential costs and benefits associated with the use of force. Drake (1998) is often credited as the first scholar to elaborate on how the ideological orientation of a group establishes boundaries for its use of violence. He maintained that "terrorists' targeting choices are crucially affected by their ideology and that ideological differences lead to differences in the targeting patterns of terrorist groups." Without full acknowledgment of, and appreciation for, a terrorist group's ideological beliefs, its targeting may appear "mindless or indiscriminate" (Drake, 1998, p. 78).

This emphasis on ideology appears to have considerable explanatory power in helping to account for terrorist target selection. In his statistical analysis of terrorist attacks in Western Europe from 1965 to 2005, Wright (2013) finds that ideology played a crucial role in the targeting choices. Similarly, Becker (2014) finds in his study of lone wolf attackers in the United States that their targeting choices closely aligned with their stated ideology. Asal and Rethemeyer (2008, p. 246) emphasize that ideology can restrict aggrieved groups to nonviolent tactics, as "ideology can, depending on the [ideological] frame, also encourage organizations to avoid killing." For this reason, leftist ideologies are associated with lower levels of lethal violence. Scholars often cite radical environmental and animal rights groups as examples of leftist terrorist organizations that refrain from lethal violence in their targeting strategy. Ackerman (2003), for example, details how the Earth Liberation Front (ELF) has eschewed human targets because harming people violates its ecological philosophy of sparing animals, especially sentient ones. Although this nonviolent characteristic of ELF's ideology is a central tenet of the group, ideologies have been known to mutate over time and assume more violent tendencies (Ackerman, 2003, p. 145).

Terrorist groups motivated by more extreme ideologies tend to engage in more extreme attacks (Kruglanski, 2006) though this is not always the case (Abrahms, 2013). In the 1990s, researchers identified a "new" type of terrorism characterized by increased civilian targeting in the name of religion (Lesser et al., 1999). The belief quickly spread that religiously motivated extremists—especially ones driven by radical interpretations of Islam—are responsible for the uptick in indiscriminate violence. A growing body of empirical research indicates that Islamist terrorist groups are indeed more prone than other types of terrorist groups to engage in mass casualty violence against civilians (e.g., Enders & Sandler, 2000; Juergensmeyer, 2005; Piazza, 2009; Wiktorowicz & Kaltner, 2003). Scholars have tried to explain the relationship between religiously motivated terrorists and elevated fatalities especially against civilians. Hoffman (1995, p. 272) says that for a religious terrorist, "Violence first and foremost is a sacramental act or divine duty executed in direct response to some theological demand or imperative." Religiously inspired terrorists perceive themselves as part of a transcendental struggle in which there are no constraints on the use of violence. Religiously motivated terrorists justify and legitimize indiscriminate violence as the most expedient way to achieve their goals whereas secular-oriented terrorists may view such violence as immoral and counterproductive. Similarly, Juergensmeyer (1997, p. 19) believes that the violence is often part of the "religious mission" regardless of the political outcome. Benjamin and Simon (2002, p. 420) echo this perspective, arguing that with religiously motivated violence "killing becomes an end in itself, rather than one instrument arrayed among nonlethal instruments in a bargaining process." More recently, empirical research has confirmed that religiously inspired terrorist groups are indeed more lethal, particularly toward civilians. Both Moghadam (2008) and Henne (2012), for example, find that suicide attacks carried out by jihadists tend to kill more people than when perpetrators are guided by other ideologies. Other scholars (e.g., Piazza, 2009) have demonstrated that the association between Islam and terrorism is correlated but not causal, driven by other confounds such as organizational structure.

Despite the popular and scholarly appeal of the ideological lens, it is open to criticism. Even when terrorist groups appear to share a similar ideology, their targeting strategies can differ drastically and even lead to an organizational schism. In July 2005, Al-Qaeda leader Ayman al-Zawahiri wrote to Abu Mus'ab al-Zarqawi, then the leader of the Iraqi affiliate, to express his disagreement with its practice of targeting Shia Muslims. Al-Zawahiri wrote:

> ... many of your Muslim admirers amongst the common folk are wondering about your attacks on the Shia. The sharpness of this questioning increases when the attacks are on one of their mosques ... My opinion is that this matter won't be acceptable to the Muslim populace however much you have tried to explain it, and aversion to this will continue.

Zawahiri also called into question Al-Qaeda in Iraq's practice of broadcasting graphic videos of hostage executions. He warned Zarqawi that the Muslim population "will never find [these videos] palatable," and that they only expose the group to more questions and doubts from potential supporters (Al-Zawahiri, 2005). This dispute on targeting strategies culminated in a break on February 2014 between Al-Qaeda and the Islamic State (Zelin, 2014). Both Zarqawi and Islamic State leaders expressed their intentions to target Muslims deemed as "apostates" or infidels and expanded the definition of what types of behavior should be considered *takfiri* (Wood, 2015). This split between Islamic State and Al-Qaeda, which is partially attributable to differences in targeting strategy, led to ideological infighting and fissures among other jihadi groups around the world as members debated the nature of their own terrorist campaigns and what constituted legitimate targets for their cause (Kassim, 2018, p. 6).

A disagreement over targeting philosophy also contributed to the 2016 split of the Nigerian terrorist group Boko Haram. Two factions coalesced around leaders that espoused different interpretations of jihadi ideology and ultimately different targeting strategies. Boko Haram pledged allegiance to Islamic State in 2015 under the leadership of Abubakar Shekau. His brand of extremism was characterized by barbaric violence, even for a terrorist group. Shekau frequently directed the group to indiscriminately target Sunni Muslims with brutal attacks in places such as markets and mosques, often using child suicide bombers. Islamic State leaders in Iraq and Syria apparently disapproved of this targeting strategy, and appointed a new leader for the group, Abu Musab al-Barnawi, who indicated that he would direct the group to focus its targeting more narrowly on Nigerian Christians. Shekau, however, did not recognize the appointment of al-Barnawi as the new leader. Both factions claimed that the other had strayed from a pure form of their shared faith (Trofimov, 2016). This case illustrates how even though a group may appear to have a uniform ideology, differences in targeting strategy can be substantial and even prove irreconcilable, leading to division.

Another problem with the ideological lens is that ideologies can be polysemic, that is, interpreted in multiple ways, leading to underspecified predictions about target selection. Indeed, the definition of ideology itself is contested. As Ackerman and Burnham (2019, p. 2) note,

> If scholars have entirely dissimilar notions of what an ideology is, the operationalization of the concept in data collection and analysis will differ, and it is little wonder that they reach different conclusions about the relevance or impact of ideology in the context of terrorism.

Ideological explanations can also suffer from tautology, where perpetrators are seen as acting on behalf of a particular ideology retroactively, depending on the target struck. Finally, ideological explanations often suffer from a unit of analysis problem. Is the relevant unit the official goals of the terrorist group or stated preferences of its members? Do they vary among them? And how can researchers truly know the role of ideology in what makes terrorists tick (Chenoweth et al., 2009)? In sum, the ideological lens offers a promising perspective for understanding terrorist target selection, albeit one with limitations.

The Strategic Lens

More than any other scholar, Pape (2003, 2005) has contested the idea that ideology—particularly radical Islamist thinking—can explain terrorist attacks. More specifically, Pape asserts that suicide attacks are adopted by aggrieved groups not due to their religious ideology, but because they are effective at coercing governments into making concessions. According to Pape, aggrieved groups turn to suicide terrorism simply because the tactic works politically. Pape is thus a proponent of an intellectual tradition called the Strategic Model of Terrorism. Numerous studies have summarized and applied versions of this model (e.g., Abrahms, 2008; Crenshaw, 1988, 1990; McCormick, 2003). Abrahms (2008) outlines three key assumptions of the Strategic Model: (1) Terrorists have consistent political preferences that drive their behavior; (2) Terrorists carefully consider available options based on the relative payoffs; and (3) Terrorists use violence against civilians when the expected political outcome is superior to available tactical alternatives. This school of thought is steeped in the rational actor model. As Crenshaw (1981, p. 385) puts it, "terrorism depend[s] on rational political choice." By rational, scholars typically mean that terrorist leaders observe the successes and failures of past approaches. And based on their track record, terrorists try to optimize their goals given their constraints (Dugan et al., 2005; Pape, 2003). The Strategic Model has been utilized to describe a variety of terrorist dynamics from the use of suicide tactics (Mroszczyk, 2019; Pape, 2003; Perry & Hasisi, 2015;) to terrorist propaganda videos (Abrahms et al., 2017) and airline hijackings (Dugan et al., 2005).

Proponents of the Strategic Model invariably regard terrorism as a "communication strategy" in which targets are struck to convey important information about the perpetrators (Matusitz, 2013; Pape,

2005; Weimann, 1987). Attacking targets—particularly high-profile ones such as the 1972 Olympic Games in Munich—ensures that the outrage of terrorists cannot be ignored (Hoffman, 2006). Weaker than the government, people turn to terrorism to amplify their political grievances. As the leader of the Tamil Tigers put it: "The Tamil people have been expressing their grievances ... for more than three decades. Their voices went unheard like cries in the wilderness" (Richardson, 2007, p. 50). The head of the United Red Army, an obscure offshoot of the Japanese Red Army, shared a similar strategic rationale: "There is no other way for us. Violent actions ... are shocking. We want to shock people everywhere ... It is our way of communicating with the people" (McKnight, 1974, p. 168). Osama bin Laden and his deputy Ayman al-Zawahiri likewise described September 11 as a "message with no words" which is "the only language understood by the West" (Abrahms, 2005).

According to the Strategic Model, terrorists attack various targets not only to attract attention, but to signal capability if their political demands remain unmet (Abrahms, 2013). As Schelling (1966, p. 3) explained in other contexts, terrorist violence conveys the "power to hurt" if concessions are not forthcoming. In comparison with terrorism, moderate tactics such as labor strikes, consumer boycotts, and sit-ins require little physical capability in terms of agility, stamina, or strength (Chenoweth & Lawrence, 2010, p. 54). Nor do nonviolent methods require arms, ammunition, explosives, or training to master them. Reliance on nonviolence therefore does not settle a crucial question under anarchy of whether the challenger poses a legitimate physical threat, whereas terrorism leaves no doubt that he is capable of making the target pay (DeNardo, 1985, p. 36). Terrorism is a "weapon of the weak," but only in the sense that its practitioners are non-state actors and therefore less capable than their government foes. Indeed, historically the strongest terrorist groups have killed the most civilians, such as Al-Qaeda, Al Shabaab, Boko Haram, Islamic State, the Shining Path, and the Taliban (Abrahms, 2018). Conversely, other aggrieved groups aspire to use terrorism, but are too weak to sustain attacks (Horowitz, 2010).

The Strategic Model therefore predicts that the violence will help non-state actors to coerce government compliance, especially as the level of pain rises. Kydd and Walter (2006, pp. 59–60) maintain, "The greater the costs a terrorist organization is able to inflict, the more credible its threat to inflict future costs, and the more likely the target is to grant concessions." Pape (2003, p. 345) likewise contends that terrorists aiming to exact concessions will try to kill as many people as possible because the apparent risk of future pain "maximizes the coercive leverage." He states, terrorism succeeds by creating "mounting civilian costs to overwhelm the target state's interest in the issue in dispute and so to cause it to concede the terrorists' political demands" (Pape, 2005, p. 30). Hoffman and McCormick (2004, p. 250) also draw on the Strategic Model, predicting that terrorists will gain "leverage at the bargaining table" in proportion to their lethality.

Despite its theoretical appeal, the Strategic Model lacks a strong empirical basis. Evidence is mounting that the likelihood of a terrorist group achieving its political objectives depends heavily upon the targets attacked. Compared to selective violence against military and other government targets, indiscriminate violence against civilian targets is ineffective, even counterproductive for aggrieved groups to achieve their political goals (Abrahms, 2011). Contrary to the dominant paradigm, numerous studies have found that militant groups seldom achieve their political goals with terrorism and that the civilian attacks actually tend to backfire. In other words, the latest wave of scholarship suggests that terrorism is not only a strategy of political losers, but also a losing political strategy. The preponderance of empirical evidence indicates that selective violence against military targets is typically more politically effective than indiscriminate violence against civilian targets (Abrahms, 2006). Specifically, civilian attacks carry substantial downside risks by strengthening the resolve of target countries (Abrahms, 2006; Berrebi & Klor, 2008; Chowanietz, 2010; Getmansky & Zeitzoff, 2014), eroding their confidence in negotiations (Abrahms, 2013; Kydd & Walter, 2002), lowering the odds of government concessions (Abrahms, 2012; Abrahms & Gottfried, 2016; Fortna, 2015; Gaibulloev & Sandler, 2009; Getmansky & Sinmazdemir, 2018); eroding popular support for the group (English, 2016; Muro, 2018; Stanton, 2016), and expediting its demise (Abrahms, 2018; Cronin, 2009; Lahoud, 2012). Interestingly, studies on national militaries likewise find that they, too, tend to fare better politically by eschewing civilian targets (Downes, 2007; Horowitz & Reiter, 2001; Kocher et al., 2011). Together, such empirical findings challenge the external validity of the Strategic Model and suggest that alternative paradigms may have superior explanatory power in accounting for why militant groups engage in terrorism by committing attacks on civilian targets, given the political risks. Like the ideological lens, the Strategic Model of Terrorism thus offers an intriguing perspective to comprehend terrorist target selection, albeit one with non-trivial limitations.

The Organizational Lens

Increasingly, scholars regard terrorist attacks against civilians not as strategic behavior issued from the top of the militant group, but as costly behavior committed by those at the bottom against the wishes of the leadership (Abrahms & Potter, 2015). Of course, not all militant leaders oppose terrorism. Notorious leaders such as Antar Zouabri of the Armed Islamic Group (GIA) in Algeria, Abu Musab al-Zarqawi of Al-Qaeda in Iraq (AQI), and Islamic State's (ISIS) Abu Bakr al-Baghdadi never understood the perils of civilian attacks. Yet the leaders of numerous militant groups throughout history have instructed their foot soldiers to refrain from civilian attacks due to the political risks. The leaders of the Kenyan Land and Freedom Army prohibited fighters from attacking noncombatants because indiscriminate bloodshed was seen as an impediment to ending colonial rule (Kariuki, 1975). Sinn Fein was known to assail Provisional Irish Republican Army operatives when they attacked civilians because of the political fallout (Smith, 1995). Fuerzas Armadas Revolucionarias de Colombia (Revolutionary Armed Forces of Colombia—FARC) leaders have likewise "repudiated and condemned" fighters for their "lack of foresight" in harming bystanders (Navarro, 2014). Murat Karayilan, leader of the Kurdistan Workers' Party (PKK), directed his forces to hit "military targets" but to "not harm civilians" (Mavioglu, 2010). Historically, many terrorist group leaders have even issued apologies when their operatives contravened their instructions by killing civilians, such as the leaders of the Afghan Taliban, Colombian National Liberation Army, Lebanese Hezbollah and Abdullah Azzam Brigades, the Nepalese Communist Party, and the Irish Republican Army (IRA) ("Nepalese Rebels Apologize," 2005; "Rebel Leader Apologizes," 1999).

Only a naive observer would accept every utterance of terrorist leaders' at face value; of course, terrorist leaders have been found to dissemble (Kearns et al., 2014). Nonetheless, there is credible evidence that the pronouncements against civilian targeting are often in earnest in the sense that they accurately reflect the leadership's preferences. Historical cases abound in which the leaders, even of extreme Islamist terrorist groups, have been found to make identical targeting appeals in private correspondences with other members. As CNN's national security analyst, Peter Bergen notes, "We know from the documents recovered at the bin Laden compound in Abbottabad by U.S. Navy SEALS in May 2011 [that] al Qaeda's leaders were often writing to each other privately and also to groups they are associated with about the need to minimize civilian (Muslim) casualties and often wrote about the damage to the al Qaeda brand that killing civilians had achieved by al Qaeda operations in Iraq" (Basil & Shoichet, 2013). Specifically, internal records reveal that bin Laden urged the mujahidin "to prevent explosions and using methods that kill generally indiscriminately in Muslim mosques or similar, general gathering places, such as markets, streets, playgrounds ..." because such civilian attacks have backfired politically in the past (Basil & Shoichet, 2013). Similarly, documents seized from the Communist Party of India-Maoist (CPI-Maoist) leadership in 2015 expressed disappointment for an attack that killed the Indian leader Mahendra Karma because it also resulted in "unintentional killings of the innocent" (Ghatwai, 2015).

Additionally, terrorist leaders often demonstrate the sincerity of their opposition to civilian targeting by engaging in "costly signaling." Terrorist leaders frequently punish subordinates when they disobey their targeting instruction by attacking civilians. The Northern Command disbanded in 1989 the Fermanagh unit of the IRA for flouting its instructions by engaging in sectarian violence against the Protestant population (Bell, 1997, p. 610). PKK leaders handed out a 24-year prison sentence in 2010 to a small cell of fighters for ignoring their targeting commands by attacking civilians in Turkey's Batman province ("Report: PKK Punished," 2010). Leaders of the New People's Army in the Philippines dealt a variety of "disciplinary actions" to wayward rebels in 2012 and 2014 for incidents against civilians ("Philippine Rebels Apologize," 2014). Al-Nusra Front leaders in 2015 brought several members to trial before an Islamic court for defying their attack guidelines by killing 20 Druze villagers in Idlib, Syria ("Syria's al-Qaeda Affiliate," 2015). Similarly, in 2016 four operatives of Tehrik-e-Taliban (the Pakistani Taliban) launched an assault on Bacha Khan University's campus in northern Pakistan, killing a number of students and teachers. A spokesman for the Tehrik-e-Taliban central leadership threatened to take the organizers of the attack to a Shariah court, saying the group "condemns this un-Islamic act in strongest terms and disassociates itself from this entirely" (Walsh et al., 2016). The punishment is sometimes moderate, such as when Ayman al-Zawahiri merely wrote a harsh rebuke to Abu Musab al-Zarqawi for his indiscriminate violence in Iraq or when other leaders of his Al-Qaeda affiliate scolded a Ramadi cell for perpetrating a similar offense against the population in defiance of Al-Qaeda Central's instructions ("Instructions to Abu-Usamah," n.d.).

How do we explain such violence given the response of the leaders? In the parlance of economics, civilian attacks may reflect a principal–agent problem where the leaders are the principals and the operatives are the agents. Principal–agent theory emphasizes a recurrent disconnect between the preferences of leaders and the behavior of subordinates, which often runs counter to the mission of the organization (Hawkins et al., 2006). Agency problems happen because prospective members have an incentive to misrepresent their qualifications and pursue private agendas upon joining (Gould, 2006). When applied to terrorist groups, the principal–agent framework suggests that operatives will sometimes act in defiance of leadership preferences, including in their targeting choices.

Within most terrorist groups, there are many reasons to suspect that a member's position in the organizational hierarchy is inversely related to his incentives for striking civilians (Abrahms & Potter, 2015). The leaders are usually the oldest members, with the most exposure to asymmetric campaigns. Foot soldiers, by contrast, are typically the newest recruits with the least combat experience (Sageman, 2004). Leaders are hence more likely to appreciate the political risks of harming civilians and to therefore oppose such targeting practices. The lowest members of terrorist groups also suffer the most severe resource constraints, incentivizing them to strike softer targets, whereas leaders are freer to access organizational resources to launch comparatively sophisticated attacks against hardened targets. The lowest-level members also may stand to gain the most personally from civilian targeting. Prior research suggests that the rank-and-file sometimes harms civilians to gain status among their peers, whereas leaders already command respect owing to their superior stature in the hierarchy (Humphreys & Weinstein, 2006). Moreover, fighters are more likely to be emotionally driven than their leaders and to lash out against the population for nonstrategic reasons. This is because the former has often lost close friends on the frontline whereas the latter is more likely to be based far away from the battlefield. Finally, some research indicates that terrorist leaders are simply "smarter" than operatives when it comes to mapping the relationship between tactical choice and political outcome (Shapiro, 2013).

Sundry empirical evidence indicates that civilian attacks are often the result of principal–agent problems, contrary to leadership preferences. Studies show, for example, that killing the leader of militant groups changes their target selection. Groups are significantly more likely to redirect their attacks from military to civilian targets in the immediate aftermath of an operationally successful leadership decapitation, when lower-level members are calling the shots (Abrahms & Mierau, 2017; Reeder & Smith, 2019; Rigterink, 2018). Indeed, leadership deficits in militant groups are positively associated with civilian attacks. All else equal, groups are more likely to engage in civilian targeting when they are organizationally diffuse rather than hierarchically structured as well as when operatives travel further away from the leader to commit attacks (Abrahms & Potter, 2015). The leaders of militant groups are also significantly less likely to claim organizational credit when operatives strike civilian targets rather than military ones in order to limit the political costs (Abrahms & Conrad, 2017; Kearns, 2019). Conversely, leaders are significantly more likely to feature in their propaganda videos of attacks committed by their operatives on military targets as opposed to civilian ones (Abrahms et al., 2017). Together, such theoretical and empirical evidence indicates that civilian attacks may be due to lower-level members calling the shots in defiance of leadership targeting preferences.

Conclusion

Clearly, additional research is needed to understand terrorist targeting. In this chapter, we explored three main lenses—ideological, strategic, and organizational—and reviewed some of the strengths and limitations of each in terms of their ability to account for variation in terrorist targeting strategies. These are not purely theoretical or academic differences. Indeed, each approach has profound implications for the methods and strategies that security agencies use to combat the terrorism threat.

Security officials and policymakers have recognized the importance of ideology in the counterterrorism mission for some time. The US government's *National Strategy for Counterterrorism* (2018) repeatedly highlights the role of ideology in counterterrorism. In the opening letter to that document, President Donald Trump vowed that the US would "combat the violent, extreme, and twisted ideologies that purport to justify the murder of innocent victims." The document notes that

"To defeat radical Islamist terrorism, we must also speak out forcefully against a hateful ideology that provides the breeding ground for violence and terrorism" (2018, p. 2). Discrediting extremist ideologies can be achieved with information operations campaigns, public diplomacy, and other covert and overt actions designed to reduce the allure and influence of extremist ideologies. This effort to harm recruitment, by its nature, is non-kinetic; it involves skilled information and influence campaigns rather than guns, missiles, and bombs to defeat terrorist groups by undercutting the ideologies upon which the groups are built. An important example is the Center for Strategic Counterterrorism Communications (CSCC) at the US Department of State, which President Barack Obama created in 2011. The mission of the CSCC was to coordinate messaging against extremist groups and to counter terrorist group propaganda and misinformation. The organization also worked to amplify religious leaders, Muslim academics, and other voices that would have credibility among target audiences (Schmitt, 2015).[1] In these ways, counterterrorism practitioners have sought to leverage their understanding of terrorists to combat them by taking aim at their ideological appeal.

If terrorist groups are viewed instead as strategically motivated, an entirely different approach to counterterrorism would be required. Terrorist groups that weigh the costs and benefits associated with different courses of action may be swayed based upon a calculation of estimated net benefit. A counterterrorism approach aligned with this lens must then emphasize the need to either increase the costs to a terrorist group or reduce the benefits of certain terrorist targeting efforts. Costs can be imposed on a group by strong responses to an attack, which can include military strikes against the terrorist group's compounds, swift action to arrest group members, and other covert and overt actions designed to dismantle and cripple the group. Hardening potential targets could also serve as a deterrent. A hardened target could increase the costs associated with conducting an attack due to either increased risk of failure or additional training and funding needed to carry out a successful attack against the target. Conversely, reducing the benefits to a group can also affect the strategic calculus of a terrorist group. Terrorist groups seek media attention and political influence, but a society that demonstrates resiliency to terrorist targeting efforts can signal to a terrorist group that there are few benefits to gain. Speckhard (2011, p. 15–2) contends that "A population that is resilient in the face of terrorism and remains steadfast and cohesive in the face of attacks on the civilian population refusing to be moved by fear into political concessions is one of the most overlooked and perhaps best tools in the fight against terrorism." The Strategic Model of Terrorism, though increasingly contested in the academic literature (Abrahms, 2008; Abrahms and Potter, 2015), remains an important perspective for counterterrorism, assuming terrorist perpetrators are rational actors who carefully weigh the benefits of terrorism relative to alternative actions.

With an organizational lens to explain terrorist targeting, counterterrorism officials may utilize strategic communications and information operations methods to draw attention to attacks targeting civilians in an effort to sow discord between terrorist group leaders and their operatives. Communications efforts following a terrorist attack can shape the perception and implications of the attack. Government officials must compete against the narrative of terrorist groups to shape the meaning of the attack among target audiences (Reed & Ingram, 2019). Representing a group as disorganized, undisciplined, and lacking strategic direction can erode moral authority of the group's leadership among its members and also potential recruits. Further, broadcasting the toll that attacks have taken on a civilian population can discredit the group among the population, and can encourage the government to take more hardline counterterrorism measures against the group. An example is when the CSCC disseminated on the Internet to jihadi recruits an image of a young man crying at a coffin with the message, "How can slaughtering the innocent be the right path?" The government propaganda warned: "Think again, turn away" (Schmitt, 2015). Drawing upon the organizational lens, the information operation tried to combat terrorism by exploiting divisions in membership support for the violence, especially against civilians, which can attract opprobrium even among extremists (Wheatley & McCauley, 2008).

Future research should continue to investigate the decision-making process by which terrorists decide to strike some targets but not others. A clearer understanding of these dynamics, including how they may differ among groups, is critical to inform counterterrorism policies. Despite the methodological challenges, scholars must continue to enhance understanding of terrorist targeting decisions by collecting data, developing theories, testing them, and establishing scope conditions to add explanatory power. In all likelihood, the lenses are all relevant but must be properly synthesized for maximal counterterrorism application.

Note

1 The CSCC was subsequently replaced by the Global Engagement Center in 2016 (Toosi, 2017).

References

Abrahms, M. (2005). Al Qaeda's miscommunication war: The terrorism paradox. *Terrorism and Political Violence*, 17, 529–549.
Abrahms, M. (2006). Why terrorism does not work. *International Security*, 31, 42–78.
Abrahms, M. (2008). What terrorists really want: Terrorist motives and counter-terrorism strategy. *International Security*, 32, 78–105.
Abrahms, M. (2011). Does terrorism really work? Evolution in the conventional wisdom since 9/11. *Defence and Peace Economics*, 22, 583–594.
Abrahms, M. (2012). The political effectiveness of terrorism revisited. *Comparative Political Studies*, 45, 366–393.
Abrahms, M. (2013). The credibility paradox: Violence as a double-edged sword in international politics. *International Studies Quarterly*, 57, 660–671.
Abrahms, M. (2018). Correspondence: Ideological extremism in armed conflict. *International Security*, 43, 186–190.
Abrahms, M. (2020). Denying to win: How image-savvy militant leaders respond when operatives harm civilians. *Journal of Strategic Studies*, 43, 47–73.
Abrahms, M., & Conrad, J. (2017). The strategic logic of credit claiming: A new theory for anonymous attacks. *Security Studies*, 26, 279–304.
Abrahms, M., & Gottfried, M.S. (2016). Does terrorism pay? An empirical analysis. *Terrorism and Political Violence*, 28, 72–89.
Abrahms, M., & Mierau, J. (2017). Leadership matters: The effects of targeted killings on militant group tactics. *Terrorism and Political Violence*, 29, 1–22.
Abrahms, M., & Potter, P.B.K. (2015). Explaining terrorism: Leadership deficits and militant group tactics. *International Organization*, 69, 311–342.
Abrahms, M., Beauchamp, N., & Mroszczyk, J. (2017). What terrorist leaders want: A content analysis of terrorist propaganda videos. *Studies in Conflict and Terrorism*, 40, 899–916.
Ackerman, G.A. (2003). Beyond arson? A threat assessment of the Earth Liberation Front. *Terrorism and Political Violence*, 15, 143–170.
Ackerman, G.A., & Burnham, M. (2019). Towards a definition of terrorist ideology. *Terrorism and Political Violence*, 1–30.
Ahmed, R. (2018). Terrorist ideologies and target selection. *Journal of Applied Security Research*, 13, 376–390.
Al-Zawahiri, A. (2005). *Zawahiri's letter to Zarqawi*. West Point, NY: Combating Terrorism Center. Available at: https://ctc.usma.edu/harmony-program/zawahiris-letter-to-zarqawi-original-language-2/.
Asal, V., & Rethemeyer, R.K. (2008). The nature of the beast: Organizational structures and the lethality of terrorist attacks. *Journal of Politics*, 70, 437–449.
Basil, Y., & Shoichet, C.E. (2013). Al Qaeda: We're sorry about Yemen hospital attack. *CNN*, December 22. Available at: www.cnn.com/2013/12/22/world/meast/yemen-al-qaeda-apology/index.html.

Becker, M. (2014). Explaining lone wolf target selection in the United States. *Studies in Conflict & Terrorism*, 37, 959–978.
Bell, J.B. (1997). *The secret army: The IRA*. New York: Transaction Publishers.
Benjamin, D., & Simon, S. (2002). *The age of sacred terror: Radical Islam's war against America*. New York: Random House.
Berrebi, C., & Klor, E.F. (2008). Are voters sensitive to terrorism? Direct evidence from the Israeli electorate. *American Political Science Review*, 102, 279–301.
Bier, V. (2007). Choosing what to protect. *Risk Analysis*, 27, 607–620.
Bin Laden's warning. (2001). *BBC*, October 7, full text. Available at: http://news.bbc.co.uk/2/hi/south_asia/1585636.stm.
Bonino, S., & Beccaro, A. (2019). Why has Italy avoided jihadist terrorist attacks? Our research helps explain. *The Washington Post Monkey Cage*, December 24. Available at: www.washingtonpost.com/politics/2019/12/24/why-has-italy-avoided-jihadist-terrorist-attacks-our-research-helps-explain/.
Brown, J.M. (2020). Notes to the underground: Credit claiming and organizing in the Earth Liberation Front. *Terrorism and Political Violence*, 32, 237–256.
Chenoweth, E., & Lawrence, A. (2010). Mobilization and resistance: A framework for analysis. In E. Chenoweth & A. Lawrence (Eds.), *Rethinking violence: States and non-state actors in conflict*. Cambridge, MA: MIT Press.
Chenoweth, E., Miller, N., McClellan, E., Frisch, H., Staniland, P., & Abrahms, M. (2009). What makes terrorists tick. *International Security*, 33, 180–202.
Chowanietz, C. (2010). Rallying around the flag or railing against the government? Political parties' reactions to terrorist acts. *Party Politics*, 17, 673–698.
Crenshaw, M. (1981). The causes of terrorism. *Comparative Politics*, 13, 379–399.
Crenshaw, M. (1988). Theories of terrorism: Instrumental and organizational approaches. In D. Rapoport (Ed.), *Inside Terrorist Organizations*. New York: Columbia University Press, pp. 13–31.
Crenshaw, M. (1990). The logic of terrorism: Terrorist behavior as a product of strategic choice. In W. Reich (Ed.), *Origins of terrorism: Psychologies, ideologies, theologies, states of mind*. New York: Colombia University Press, pp. 7–24.
Cronin, A.K. (2009). *How terrorism ends: Understanding the decline and demise of terrorist campaigns*. Princeton, NJ: Princeton University Press.
DeNardo, J. (1985). *Power in numbers: The political strategy of protest and rebellion*. Princeton, NJ: Princeton University Press.
Downes, A.B. (2007). Draining the sea by filling the graves: Investigating the effectiveness of indiscriminate violence as a counterinsurgency strategy. *Civil Wars*, 9, 420–444.
Drake, C.J. (1998). The role of ideology in terrorists' target selection. *Terrorism and Political Violence*, 10, 53–85.
Dugan, L., LaFree, G., & Piquero, A.R. (2005). Testing a rational choice model of airline hijackings. *Criminology*, 43, 1031–1065.
Enders, W., & Sandler, T. (2000). Is transnational terrorism becoming more threatening? A time-series investigation. *Journal of Conflict Resolution*, 44, 307–332.
English, R. (2016). *Does terrorism work? A history*. Oxford: Oxford University Press.
Fortna, V.P. (2015). Do terrorists win? Rebels' use of terrorism and civil war outcomes. *International Organization*, 69, 519–556.
Gaibulloev, K., & Sandler, T. (2009). The impact of terrorism and conflicts on growth in Asia. *Economics & Politics*, 21, 359–383.

Getmansky, A., & Sinmazdemir, T. (2018). Settling on violence: Expansion of Israeli outposts in the West Bank in response to terrorism. *Studies in Conflict & Terrorism*, 41, 241–259.

Getmansky, A., & Zeitzoff, T. (2014). Terrorism and voting: The effect of rocket threat on voting in Israeli elections. *American Political Science Review*, 108, 588–604.

Ghatwai, M. (2015). Naxal attack: CPI (Maoist) leadership regrets killing congress leaders. *The Indian Express*, May 31. Available at: http://indianexpress.com/article/india/indiaothers/2013-naxal-attack-cpi-maoist-leadership-regrets-killing-congress-leaders/.

Gould, E.R. (2006). Delegating IMF conditionality: Understanding variations in control and conformity. In D.G. Hawkins, D.A. Lake, D.L. Nielson, & M.J. Tierney (Eds.), *Delegation and agency in international organizations*. Cambridge: Cambridge University Press.

Hawkins, D.G., Lake, D.A., Nielson, D.L., & Tierney, M.J. (Eds.). (2006). *Delegation and agency in international organizations*. Cambridge: Cambridge University Press.

Henne, P.S. (2012). The ancient fire: Religion and suicide terrorism. *Terrorism and Political Violence*, 24, 38–60.

Hoffman, A. (2010). Voice and silence: Why groups take credit for acts of terror. *Journal of Peace Research*, 46, 1–22.

Hoffman, B. (1995). "Holy terror": The implications of terrorism motivated by a religious imperative. *Studies in Conflict and Terrorism*, 18, 271–284.

Hoffman, B. (1997). Why terrorists don't claim credit. *Terrorism and Political Violence*, 9, 1–6.

Hoffman, B. (2006). *Inside terrorism*. New York: Columbia University Press.

Hoffman, B., & McCormick, G.H. (2004). Terrorism, signaling, and suicide attack. *Studies in Conflict & Terrorism*, 27, 243–281.

Horowitz, M., & Reiter, D. (2001). When does aerial bombing work? Quantitative empirical tests, 1917–1999. *Journal of Conflict Resolution*, 45, 147–173.

Horowitz, M.C. (2010). Nonstate actors and the diffusion of innovations: The case of suicide terrorism. *International Organization*, 64, 33–64.

Humphreys, M., & Weinstein, J.M. (2006). Handling and manhandling civilians in civil war. *American Political Science Review*, 100, 429–447.

Instructions to Abu-Usamah. (n.d.). *Harmony documents*. West Point, NY: Combating Terrorism Center. Available at: www.ctc.usma.edu/harmony-program/.

Juergensmeyer, M. (1997). Terror mandated by God. *Terrorism and Political Violence*, 9, 16–23.

Juergensmeyer, M. (2005). *Terror in the mind of God: The global rise of religious violence*. Berkeley, CA: University of California Press.

Kariuki, J.M. (1975). *Mau Mau detainee: The account by a Kenyan African of his experience in detention camps*. Nairobi, Kenya: Oxford University Press.

Kassim, A. (2018). Boko Haram's internal civil war: Stealth takfir and jihad as recipes for schism. In A. Kassim (Ed.), *Boko Haram beyond the headlines: Analyses of Africa's enduring insurgency*. West Point, NY: Combating Terrorism Center. Available at: www.ctc.usma.edu/wp-content/uploads/2018/05/Boko-Haram-Beyond-the-Headlines_Chapter-1.pdf.

Kearns, E.M. (2019). When to take credit for terrorism? A cross-national examination of claims and attributions. *Terrorism and Political Violence*, 1–30.

Kearns, E.M., Conlon, B., & Young, J.K. (2014). Lying about terrorism. *Studies in Conflict & Terrorism*, 37, 422–439.

Kocher, M.A., Pepinsky, T.B., & Kalyvas, S.N. (2011). Aerial bombing and counterinsurgency in the Vietnam War. *American Journal of Political Science*, 55, 201–218.

Kruglanski, A. (2006). Inside the terrorist mind: The relevance of ideology. *Estudios de Psicología*, 27, 271–277.

Kydd, A.H., & Walter, B.F. (2002). Sabotaging the peace: The politics of extremist violence. *International Organization*, 56, 263–296.

Kydd, A.H., & Walter, B.F. (2006). The strategies of terrorism. *International Security*, 31, 49–80.

Lahoud, N. (2012). *Beware of imitators: Al-Qa'ida through the lens of its confidential secretary*. West Point, NY: Combating Terrorism Center.

Lesser, I.O., Hoffman, B., Arquilla, J., Ronfeldt, D., Zanini, M., & Jenkins, B.M. (1999). *Countering the new terrorism*. Santa Monica, CA: RAND Corporation. Available at: www.rand.org/pubs/monograph_reports/MR989.html.

Matusitz, J. (2013). *Terrorism & communication: A critical introduction*. Los Angeles, CA: Sage.

Mavioglu, E. (2010). Civilians in Turkey off target list, PKK boss says. *Hurriyet Daily News*, October 28.

McCormick, G.H. (2003). Terrorist decision making. *Annual Review of Political Science*, 6, 473–507.

McKnight, G. (1974). *The mind of the terrorist*. London: Michael Joseph.

Moghadam, A. (2008). *The globalization of martyrdom: Al Qaeda, Salafi Jihad, and the diffusion of suicide attacks*. Baltimore, MD: Johns Hopkins University Press.

Moore, J. (2017). Pope's Swiss guards say "only matter of time" before ISIS attacks Rome, Vatican. *Newsweek*, August 25. Available at: www.newsweek.com/popes-swiss-guards-say-only-matter-time-isis-attacks-rome-vatican-655025.

Mroszczyk, J. (2019). To die or to kill? An analysis of suicide attack lethality. *Terrorism and Political Violence*, 31, 346–366.

Muro, D. (Ed.). (2018). *When Does Terrorism Work?* New York: Routledge.

National Strategy for Counterterrorism of the United States of America. (2018). The White House. October. Available at: www.whitehouse.gov/wp-content/uploads/2018/10/NSCT.pdf.

Navarro, A. (2014). Divisions erupt as Columbia rebels criticize their own. *AFP*. January 24.

Nepalese rebels apologize for deadly bombing of civilian bus. (2005). *USA Today*, June 7. Available at: http://usatoday30.usatoday.com/news/world/2005-06-07-nepal-rebels_x.htm.

Pape, R. (2003). The strategic logic of suicide terrorism. *The American Political Science Review*, 97, 343–361.

Pape, R. (2005). *Dying to win: The strategic logic of suicide terrorism*. New York: Random House.

Perry, S., & Hasisi, B. (2015). Rational choice rewards and the jihadist suicide bomber. *Terrorism and Political Violence*, 27, 53–80.

Perry, S., Newman, R., Graeme, R., & Clarke, R.V. (2016). The situational prevention of terrorism: An evaluation of the Israeli West Bank barrier. *Journal of Quantitative Criminology*, 33, 727–751.

Philippine rebels apologize for attack on medics. (2014). *UCA News.* March 7. Available at: www.ucanews.com/news/philippine-rebels-apologize-for-attack-on-medics/70446.

Piazza, J.A. (2009). Is Islamist terrorism more dangerous? An empirical study of group ideology, organization, and goal structure. *Terrorism and Political Violence*, 21, 62–88.

Rebel leader apologizes for Columbian church kidnapping (1999). *CNN.* June 7. Available at: www.cnn.com/WORLD/americas/9906/07/colombia/.

Reed, A., & Ingram, H.J. (2019). Towards a framework for post-terrorist incident communications strategies. *International Centre for Counter-Terrorism*. August 20. Available at: https://icct.nl/publication/towards-a-framework-for-post-terrorist-incident-communications-strategies/.

Reeder, B.W., & Smith, J.R. (2019). US strikes in Somalia and targeted civilian killings by al-Shabaab: An empirical investigation. *Foreign Policy Analysis*, 15, 589–603.

Report: PKK punished those behind Batman blasts. (2010). Today's Zaman, December 2.

Richardson, L. (2007). *What terrorists want: Understanding the enemy, containing the threat.* New York: Random House.

Rigterink, A.S. (2018). The wane of command. OxCarre Research Paper 218.

Sageman, M. (2004). *Understanding terror networks.* Philadelphia, PA: University of Pennsylvania Press.

Schelling, T.C. (1966). *Arms and influence.* New Haven, CT: Yale University Press.

Schmid, A.P., Jongman, A.J., Stohl, M., & Horowitz, I.L. (1984). *Political terrorism: A new guide to actors and authors, data bases, and literature.* New Brunswick, NJ: Transaction Publishers.

Schmitt, E. (2015). U.S. intensifies effort to blunt ISIS' message. *The New York Times*, February 16. Available at: www.nytimes.com/2015/02/17/world/middleeast/us-intensifies-effort-to-blunt-isis-message.html.

Shapiro, J.N. (2013). *The terrorist's dilemma: Managing violent covert organizations* Princeton, NJ: Princeton University Press.

Smith, M.L.R. (1995). *Fighting for Ireland? The military strategy of the Irish Republican Movement.* New York: Routledge.

Speckhard, A. (2011). Modeling psycho-social resilience to terrorism. In A. Speckhard (Ed.), *Psychosocial, organizational and cultural aspects of terrorism*, NATO, pp. 15.1–15.9, Available at: https://apps.dtic.mil/dtic/tr/fulltext/u2/a555076.pdf.

Stanton, J.A. (2016). *Violence and restraint in civil war: Civilian targeting in the shadow of international law.* Cambridge: Cambridge University Press.

Syria's al-Qaeda affiliate says it regrets killing of Druze. (2015). *Times of Israel*, June 13. Available at: www.timesofisrael.com/syrias-al-qaeda-affiliate-says-it-regrets-killing-of-druze/.

Toosi, N. (2017). Tillerson spurns $80 million to counter ISIS, Russian propaganda. *Politico*, August 2. Available at: www.politico.com/story/2017/08/02/tillerson-isis-russia-propaganda-241218.

Trofimov, Y. (2016). Behind Boko Haram's split: A leader too radical for Islamic State. *The Wall Street Journal*, September 15. Available at: www.wsj.com/articles/behind-boko-haram-s-split-a-leader-too-radical-for-islamic-state-1473931827.

Walsh, D., Mehsud, I.T., & Khan, I. (2016). Taliban attack at Bacha Khan University in Pakistan renews fears. *The New York Times*, January 20. Available at: www.nytimes.com/2016/01/21/world/asia/bacha-khan-university-attack-charsadda.html.

Weimann, G. (1987). Media events: The case of international terrorism. *Journal of Broadcasting & Electronic Media*, 31, 21–39.

Wheatley, J., & McCauley, C. (2008). Losing your audience: Desistance from terrorism in Egypt after Luxor. *Dynamics of Asymmetric Conflict*, 3 , 250–268.

Wiktorowicz, Q., & Kaltner, J. (2003). Killing in the name of Islam: Al-Qaeda's justification for September 11. *Middle East Policy*, 10, 76–92.

Wood, G. (2015). What ISIS really wants. *The Atlantic*, March. Available at: www.theatlantic.com/magazine/archive/2015/03/what-isis-really-wants/384980/.

Wright, A.L. (2013). *Terrorism, ideology, and target selection*. The Pearson Institute. Available at: https://thepearsoninstitute.org/sites/default/files/2017-02/9.%20Wright_Terrorism%2C%20ideology.pdf.

Zelin, A.Y. (2014, February 4). *Al-Qaeda disaffiliates with the Islamic State of Iraq and al-Sham*. The Washington Institute. Available at: www.washingtoninstitute.org/policy-analysis/view/al-qaeda-disaffiliates-with-the-islamic-state-of-iraq-and-al-sham.

7

Explaining Suicide Bombings

Susanne Martin

Suicide bombings are among the deadliest tactics of twenty-first-century warfare. Thus far, this century's conflicts have been fought primarily by non-state militants and states engaging in counterterrorism and counterinsurgency. Militant groups include insurgents seeking to overthrow and replace regimes and, in some cases, reimagining nations and states. Their adversaries include the states they seek to replace and other non-state actors vying for power within the same domains. Insurgent groups use guerrilla tactics and terrorism (Boot, 2013; Martin & Weinberg, 2016), though violence is not their only tool (Laqueur, 1996; Weinberg, 1991). Even while the most formidable among militant groups have the capacity to challenge states, they cannot defeat them militarily. Non-state actors are weak by comparison to states, and the groups relying solely on terrorism are among the weakest.

Explosives are among militant groups' most destructive tools, and they can be especially destructive in the hands of suicide attackers. Suicide bombers serve as "smart" weapons for the subset of militant groups employing them. Suicide bombers can do what militants' other weapons cannot. Suicide bombers carry explosives, making them part of the weapon. They can approach targets, alter paths, and change plans, determining when and where to attack for maximum effect (e.g., Ganor, n.d.). Their explosions are powerful, even more so when heavy explosive loads are carried in vehicles. While producing bombs requires a level of expertise, transporting them typically does not. The success of suicide bombings, however, may depend on attackers' willingness.

For the groups employing suicide bombers, they are expendable and replaceable. Some groups aim their bombers at harder targets, such as government and military infrastructures, in acts that may be described as guerrilla warfare or terrorism. Many of the same groups use suicide bombers in attacks on softer civilian targets in acts of terrorism.

It is not surprising that attacks by suicide bombers draw considerable interest. They have proven to be deadlier, on average, than non-suicide attacks (Pape, 2005; Pedahzur, 2005). The bombers' willingness to die gives the impression that they cannot be deterred. As a tactic of warfare, suicide bombers allow relatively weak insurgents to raise the costs of conflict for states and their militaries. Suicide bombings create widespread fear in attacks aimed at civilians, no less when they target places of presumed safety and relative peace.

Suicide bombings stun, in part, because their attackers seem to be willing to kill themselves while killing others. They roam among their targets prior to detonating their explosives. The fear they create derives in part from their ability to catch their victims off guard, as well as from their ability to raise alerts and create uncertainty in public spaces.

For the groups using them, the appeal of suicide bombings exceeds their destructive capacity. They impart "an enormous psychological effect," capturing widespread attention in the process (Schweitzer, 2007, p. 671). The attention given to suicide bombings as a tactic of terrorism and warfare has had much to do with interests in understanding why groups use these types of attacks, why individuals participate in them, the conditions under which these individuals and groups are more likely to originate and operate, and where and when they are most likely to strike. There is also quite a bit of interest in how suicide bombers and the groups that employ them can be stopped.

The discussion that follows engages these topics through a focus on why some groups use suicide bombings while others do not and why groups may stop. The discussion begins with an explanation of suicide bombings as a tactic of militancy, which has increased and spread since the 1980s. The discussion continues with consideration of suicide tactics as a group phenomenon, which relates to group strategy. The discussion includes explanations for why some groups use suicide bombings and what they may expect to gain from doing so. The discussion also includes explanations for why some groups abstain from using suicide bombings, and how suicide bombings have been effectively countered in the past and how they may be countered in the future, and to what effect. A central argument, which the discussion reinforces, is the difficulty associated with effectively countering suicide bombings as a tactic of violent political groups.

Defining Concepts

Suicide bombings are a type of suicide attack in which the mode of attack and manner of death involves explosive detonation. Suicide bombings fit a narrow definition of suicide attacks, which requires the death of the perpetrator as a prerequisite for the success of a mission (Moghadam, 2006). For an attack to be a suicide bombing, the attacker must detonate the explosives they carry. They must be willing to die and be expecting to die (Moghadam, 2006). In the rare cases in which they survive their missions, the likely reasons include malfunctioning explosives or capture prior to detonation. Because suicide bombings almost always result in the deaths of the attackers, and because there are few other modes of attack that do, most suicide attacks by non-state actors have been suicide bombings.

Not all bombings that appear to be suicide bombings are. There are cases in which a person carries explosives, which are remotely detonated, as well as cases in which individuals are forced to carry explosives. These individuals may be better understood as unwitting accomplices or victims (Moghadam, 2006). The reality, however, is that cases of forced participation and remote detonation are unlikely to be distinguishable from cases of voluntary participation.

Some suicide bombings are terrorist attacks, but many are not. Militants have used suicide bombings as a tactic of guerrilla warfare and terrorism. Targets have included governments, militaries, law enforcement, and civilians, among others. Some suicide bombings occur in contexts of war; others occur in times and places of relative peace.

The attacks on September 11, 2001, are examples of suicide attacks, though they may not be suicide bombings. Whereas suicide bombings require constructing, transporting, and detonating bombs, the terrorists used airplanes as weapons in the attacks on September 11 (9/11), 2001. The explosions produced on 9/11 were more destructive and deadlier than even the most powerful conventional bombs used by terrorists. There are, however, effective means of countering threats to air travel. It is more difficult to counter the use of smaller explosive devices on the ground. Suicide bombers' explosive capacity may be lower by comparison to the attacks on 9/11, but their attacks are far more numerous.

Most suicide bombings are the work of militant groups. Militant groups are non-state actors that use violence to achieve their goals. Insurgents, terrorists, and guerrilla fighters are examples of militants, and the groups to which they belong are militant groups. The militant groups of interest in most discussions of suicide bombings are politically motivated. In other words, they are violent political groups.

Spread of Suicide Bombings

Non-state militants began using suicide bombings in guerrilla and terrorist attacks in the early 1980s, midway through Lebanon's 15-year sectarian civil war. The earliest attacks involved vehicle bombings. Much of the credit for popularizing the use of vehicle bombings has gone to Hezbollah (e.g., Pedahzur, 2005), the militant group established at this time with support from Iran (e.g., Wiegand, 2009). Their methods included equipping suicide bombers with explosive-laden vehicles, which drivers would transport and propel into their desired targets. Numbers of suicide bombings increased after apparent successes (Pape, 2005). The introduction of suicide bombings in Lebanon preceded the withdrawal of American and French peacekeepers and coincided with the movement of Israel's military to a smaller security zone along the countries' shared border. Hezbollah is credited with facilitating the spread of suicide bombings to other groups, including those operating in other parts of the world as well as some operating in neighboring Israel and the Palestinian territories (Crenshaw, 2007; Pedahzur, 2005).

Groups such as Sri Lanka's Liberation Tigers of Tamil Eelam (LTTE) adopted suicide bombing tactics while also introducing new means of concealing and transporting their explosives. Among these were suicide belts and suicide vests (Hoffman, 2006; Hopgood, 2005; Pedahzur, 2005). Portable suicide bombs allowed attackers to carry smaller explosive loads by foot. The bombers would not require roadways; instead, they could enter buildings and mingle with crowds. Palestinian groups used vehicle bombers and suicide vests in Israel and the Palestinian territories. Several Palestinian suicide bombings targeted Israel's public transportation, with bombers riding busses alongside their victims.

Most of the early targets of suicide bombings were states and their militaries. This was the case in the 1980s in Lebanon, and it remained the case in the 1990s and early 2000s in Sri Lanka. The LTTE reportedly sought to avoid the "terrorist" label, especially after 9/11 (Cronin,

2006). Suicide bombings in both states took place during civil wars. Civilians were more frequent targets of suicide bombings in Israel and the Palestinian territories in the early 1990s. The onset of suicide bombings by Palestinian militants coincided with the negotiation and implementation of peace accords in Oslo, Norway, at the end of, and following, the first Palestinian intifada. Most of the Palestinians' early suicide bombings occurred in a context of relative peace. Suicide bombings became more frequent during the second Palestinian intifada, which began in the early 2000s. Israeli deaths came closer to matching Palestinian deaths during this time (e.g., Schweitzer, 2007). Suicide bombings spread from Lebanon, Sri Lanka, and the Palestinian territories to more groups and more contexts (Crenshaw, 2007; Pape, 2005).

The number of suicide bombings and the deaths and destruction associated with these attacks increased manyfold after the suicide attacks on 9/11 and the initiation of the Global War on Terrorism (e.g., Global Terrorism Database, 2020). It may seem ironic that terrorism increased in response to these counterterrorism efforts, though it is not surprising that increases in violence correspond to invasions, regime changes, power struggles, and new sources of insecurity. The initial multinational counterterrorism effort was aimed at removing a specific terrorist threat in the forms of the group behind the 9/11 attacks and that group's supporters. A more ambitious goal would involve addressing terrorists' use of weak or failed states as places from which to operate.

The 2003 invasion of Iraq contributed further to insecurity and added to the pool of potential insurgents. Iraq, Afghanistan, Pakistan, Nigeria, and Syria, places lacking prior experience with suicide bombings, became the new "hotspots" of these attacks, with the frequencies of suicide bombings in these countries far surpassing their numbers in previous decades in Lebanon, Sri Lanka, Israel-Palestine, and elsewhere (e.g., Global Terrorism Database, 2020). Another irony, perhaps, is that the former innovators of suicide bombings, Lebanon's Hezbollah, later became the targets of the attacks it helped to spread.

Explaining Suicide Bombings

It is important to understand suicide bombings as a group phenomenon. Groups plan and orchestrate suicide bombings. They use these bombings strategically as a tool to help them achieve their goals. Understanding the increase in, and spread of, suicide bombings in the twenty-first century requires a focus on the groups that use or do not use these tactics and the contexts in which they operate. Group-level explanations tend to draw attention to groups' strategies, organizational capacities, and ideologies. Groups will use suicide bombings if they expect to benefit from doing so and if they have the resources or capacity to adopt and employ these tactics (Horowitz, 2010). A group's strategy is constrained by the contexts in which it operates as well as by its resources and capabilities. A group's objectives may change over time, as may their leadership and favored tactics. Successes and failures inform changes. Other factors include technological developments, or the introduction of new modes of attack. Suicide bombings may be more popular, or more advantageous, under some conditions than under others (e.g., Bloom, 2004). Moreover, suicide bombings may be viewed more favorably by some groups some of the time while being avoided by other groups at all times.

Suicide bombings are one tactic among many available to militant groups, though they are not militants' only tactic nor the most frequently used tactic (e.g., Gupta, 2005; Hafez, 2006). Suicide bombings represent an innovation in terrorism and guerrilla warfare. Once adopted, groups may continue using suicide bombings so long as they expect to gain, or at least lose less, with these tactics.

Individuals may be amenable to participating in suicide bombings, but they rarely work independently of groups. In most cases, it is groups that plan and orchestrate suicide bombings. Even while there are examples of lone suicide bombers, they are unlikely to be responsible for large numbers of bombings. Individual militants generally lack the expertise required to construct bombs or plan and carry out bombings on their own. They would not have much opportunity to become suicide bombers were there not groups willing to employ them in these roles. Moreover, an individual suicide bomber could carry out one suicide bombing, one time. Groups can carry out multiple suicide bombings, and the groups survive to enjoy whatever benefits may accrue to them for doing so. The individuals used as suicide bombers are not central actors in the militant groups employing them. While groups tend to select capable attackers (Bueno de Mesquita, 2005), their suicide bombers are expendable. They are employed as single-use weapons.

Studies of individual suicide bombers provide some insights relevant to explaining suicide bombings. Observations of patterns among suicide bombers, such as an increasing involvement of women and children or evidence of kidnapping or coercion of attackers, are useful for understanding groups' strategies, resources, and support. Evidence that groups mistreat or force people to carry out suicide bombings suggests limitations in groups' appeals and inconsistencies between ideologies and operations (e.g., Lankford, 2011). The presence of willing volunteers and support for suicide bombings is better explained by context than by individual motivations. Groups may be more willing to use suicide bombings in places where there is a ready supply of potential volunteers or recruits and where the groups will retain support despite their use of suicide tactics.

Most suicide bombings occur, and most attackers operate, in contexts characterized by insecurity and instability. Many of the groups using suicide bombings operate in weak or failed states, where there is prolonged unrest, violent conflict, or civil war. These conditions are not determinative of suicide bombings, however. While most suicide bombings are concentrated in a smaller number of the states where these conditions are present, there are many places with similar conditions that have little or no exposure to suicide bombings. Moreover, there are also groups operating under these conditions, in places with ongoing conflicts, that do not use suicide bombings, as well as times in which the groups that do use suicide bombings cease doing so, at least temporarily.

Smaller numbers of suicide attacks, including suicide bombings, have occurred in stable and otherwise peaceful environments. One explanation for these cases is that the groups operating in one place have orchestrated attacks or inspired attackers residing elsewhere. If they operate independently, however, those inspired by, or claiming ideological affiliation with, distant groups are unlikely to have the capacity to carry out suicide bombings. For this, they may rely on connections to militant groups with relevant experience (Horowitz, 2010). Alternatively, they may rely on the weapons available to them, including guns, knives, or automobiles (e.g., Kurzman, 2011).

The groups that use suicide bombings share some attributes and objectives. They tend to be insurgents, seeking to change or replace existing regimes. Suicide bombings are not a tool for groups working in concert with states or their institutions. They tend not to be oriented toward cooperation, compromise, or democracy. The groups employing suicide bombings also tend to have resources, including sources of support, a weapons infrastructure, and a pool of volunteers or victims to coerce into carrying out their attacks. Some of the groups that have used suicide bombings have been nationalists, with primarily local objectives. Lebanon's Hezbollah, Turkey's Kurdistan Workers' Party, and the various Palestinian militant groups are among these. Some of these are Islamists, others are secular. Other groups are more globally oriented, including al Qaeda, the Islamic State group, and their numerous affiliates. Despite the growing appeal of some fundamentalist religious ideologies, the ideologies of many of the groups using suicide bombings in the second decade of the twenty-first century lack widespread appeal within their larger religious communities, as do the violent tactics they use (Kurzman, 2011).

If militants are strategic and capable, they will continue to innovate. They will adapt to changing circumstances and adopt new modes of attack when new tactics may help them achieve their objectives. For the groups that adopt suicide bombing tactics, these modes of attack become part of their tactical repertoire. Suicide bombings require resources to develop new expertise. Groups may cease suicide bombings for a period—such as when a conflict ends, when the parties to conflict join nonviolent political processes, when suicide tactics lose popularity or are replaced by new tactics, or when the desired targets of bombings become too difficult to reach—yet they will return to these tactics so long as they remain available and are viewed as advantageous by decision makers.

Why Militant Groups Use Suicide Bombings

If militant groups are strategic actors, they will prioritize their objectives and the tactics they deem most likely to help them achieve these objectives. They will use suicide bombings when they expect these tactics to be advantageous and avoid them if they expect the costs to exceed the benefits. This determination will depend on the context in which they operate, their resources, and their goals.

One of the reasons that militants use suicide bombings is their tactical advantages. Because they are the smart bombs of the militarily weak actors, suicide bombers allow militant groups to reach their harder targets, and to do so with greater accuracy than they could otherwise. Bombers can select the timing and placement of attacks to maximize their impacts and impose higher costs on their adversaries. Suicide vehicle bombers can propel their vehicles through some types of barriers prior to detonating their explosives, and they can carry a sufficient load of explosives to devastate their targets, even from a small distance. Because of this, and because their weapons are explosives, suicide bombings kill more people, on average, and cause more damage than other types of attacks.

Suicide bombings offer militant groups another tactical advantage. The groups employing suicide bombers do not expect them to survive their attacks; hence, they do not require escape plans. If anonymity is desired, it may also be beneficial that successful suicide bombers leave little to identify themselves. This is also true if the bombers were peripheral to the group employing them, meaning there would be little to connect them to a group even if their identities were known. There are many examples of suicide bombers who remain unidentified and perpetrator groups that do not take credit for attacks (e.g., Global Terrorism Database, 2020). Many suicide bombings in Iraq are unclaimed, perhaps because those responsible stood to gain from the disruption caused by these attacks but also would stand to lose if they took credit (Hafez, 2006). The groups could avoid some of the repercussions associated with claiming unpopular attacks, perhaps even more so when the attackers they used were foreign fighters employed to target local Iraqis (Hafez, 2006).

Suicide bombings also offer strategic advantages. Militant groups use suicide bombings to help them achieve some of their shorter-term or intermediate objectives, though not necessarily their ultimate objectives. They use suicide bombings destructively to impose high costs and gain attention, which are shorter-term objectives. Suicide bombings draw attention by their scale of destruction, their capacity to raise death tolls, and the surprise and fear often associated with their attacks. These effects, along with the bombers' self-detonation, make suicide bombings, "by their very nature, 'media prone'" (Schweitzer, 2007, p. 671).

Militants use suicide bombings for other strategic purposes. These include signaling resolve, outbidding, and spoiling a peace process. Militant groups may use suicide bombings to signal resolve to their adversaries and commitment to their supporters (Kydd & Walter, 2006). Gaining attention through violence paints militant groups as formidable opponents, capable of raising the costs of war while remaining elusive and difficult to defeat. Suicide bombings also draw attention because the bombers appear to be undeterrable, willing to sacrifice themselves to kill others. Militant groups may use suicide bombings to help gain support at the expense of competing groups. As part of a strategy of outbidding, militant groups may use increasing violence to distinguish themselves from their competitors (Bloom, 2004; Kydd & Walter, 2006). Violence carried out in peacetime or during peace negotiations shows that those negotiating the peace do not have a monopoly in terms of the use of force or control over the violence and are therefore not reliable representatives of the larger community (Kydd & Walter, 2002, 2006). Increasing violence contributes to instability and raises questions regarding the likelihood or sustainability of peace agreements (Bloom, 2005).

Militant groups also use suicide bombings to achieve bigger goals, even though they may not be able to achieve their ultimate objectives. Militants can use violence, including suicide bombings, to destabilize a regime or pressure a state into making policy changes (Pape, 2005). Suicide bombings may contribute to instability by demonstrating a state's weakness in protecting itself and its populations. Militants in Iraq have used suicide bombings to destabilize Iraq's new regime (Hafez, 2006).

Suicide bombings can also impose high costs, lending them efficacy in wars of attrition (Kydd & Walter, 2006). In some cases, suicide bombings may be sufficiently costly to spark a change in foreign policies. Between 1983 and 1984, militants used suicide bombings against American, French, and Israeli targets, purportedly to influence their policies regarding intervention in Lebanon (Pape, 2005).

Militant groups use a combination of tactics in efforts to achieve their ultimate objectives, though they seldom succeed. Some of Iraq's militants aimed to establish a new secular Iraqi state while others sought to include Iraqi territory and people in a new Islamist caliphate (Hafez, 2006). Even though suicide bombings contributed to instability in the country, neither set of militants is likely to achieve its desired outcome. Palestinian militants have sought to establish a Palestinian state, though the various militant groups clash in their views regarding Palestinian governance and borders. Suicide bombings helped spoil the peace and create instability, but suicide bombings were also catalysts for Israel's reoccupation of the West Bank as well as the construction of walls, fences, and other barriers to movement for Palestinians. The groups that used suicide bombings against foreign militaries and diplomatic installations in Lebanon were fighting for local dominance, though attacking, and encouraging the withdrawal of, foreign forces may have served some of their interests. Many of the same groups that used suicide bombings now participate in Lebanon's power-sharing arrangement, which represents a compromise solution. Prior to the attacks on September 11, 2001, al-Qaeda directed suicide bomb strikes at US embassies in Kenya and Tanzania in 1998 and the *USS Cole* in Yemeni waters in 2000. Al Qaeda's attacks were likely aimed at influencing American foreign policy (Abrahms, 2006). Despite the devastation wrought by al Qaeda, it is not obvious that al Qaeda realized the outcome it sought (Abrahms, 2006). Despite these shortcomings, suicide bombings have been part of a strategy used by militant groups to achieve short-term and intermediate objectives.

Why Militant Groups Abstain from Suicide Bombings

Many militant groups do not use suicide bombings. They engage in violence, yet they do so through other means. The reasons for this vary, though they relate to groups' strategies, capacities, and the contexts in which they operate.

Suicide terrorism can be costly for groups (Pape, 2005). The groups that use suicide bombings risk losing support, including popular support from those they claim to represent. They also risk losing the support of other backers and passive support from those who may otherwise sympathize with their cause. These losses may be particularly problematic for those groups that claim to represent the interests of a community, as well as for those that rely on external contributions to fund their operations. Lost popular support corresponds with lost legitimacy and lost influence. Lost financing, in the absence of alternative sources, corresponds with decreased ability to continue a violent resistance, as well as decreased ability to meet the other needs of local supporters. Such losses are likely to interfere with a group's ability to achieve its objectives.

Groups' strategies reflect their objectives, which relate to ideology and views regarding how their objectives may be achieved. Suicide bombings are inconsistent with some strategies. Militant groups preferring to work within an existing system are less likely to use suicide bombings than those seeking to replace that system (Hafez, 2006). Shi'a militants in post-invasion Iraq, for instance, abstained from using suicide bombings while some of their secular Sunni counterparts and Islamist groups did not abstain (Hafez, 2006). The groups that did not use suicide bombings also distinguished themselves with this choice (Hafez, 2006).

Another issue associated with strategy is group capacity. There are suggestions that some militant groups are unlikely ever to use suicide bombing tactics because they lack the capacity to adopt new modes of attack (Horowitz, 2010). By this logic, some groups are less equipped to innovate than others. They may be unable to invest in or develop new weapons technologies. They may not have a sufficient base of support to succeed with otherwise unpopular tactics. This understanding of groups' limited capabilities finds support in questions regarding how members of an Islamist group in Sri Lanka could have coordinated and carried out multiple suicide bombings on Easter Sunday 2019 without support from a more capable entity, such as the Islamic State group (Amarasingam, 2019). Groups also may lack an interest in changing tactics, perhaps because of the institutionalization of the group's established *modus operandi* or, alternatively, because of associations between tactics and the groups or types of groups using them. By this logic, only some types of groups would use suicide bombings, and carrying out suicide bombings places groups in this category. A decision not to use suicide bombings may relate to perceptions of these tactics as foreign or unjustifiable as well as counterproductive. The Provisional Irish Republican Army officially disarmed the month after the July 7, 2005, al-Qaeda-linked suicide bombers targeted London's transportation system.

Context also factors into strategic considerations. The costs of carrying out suicide bombings may be higher in stronger, more stable states than in weaker, war-torn, or failed states. Some states have sufficient capacity to effectively counter militant groups. In these contexts, suicide bombings, and suicide attacks in general, provoke strong state responses. This does not mean that there is no terrorism in strong, stable states, or that suicide bombings do not occur; rather, it means that violence is more likely to involve isolated acts, perpetrated primarily by extremists who lack widespread appeal. The militant groups using suicide bombings can find more room to operate in contexts characterized by state weakness, lawlessness, and warfare, where they can organize and terrorize without facing immediate repercussions.

There is also a potential cultural element associated with context, though such an effect may not be independent of other factors relating to state strength and capacity. The costs of carrying out suicide bombings would be higher for groups whose supporters would not support the use of such tactics. This lack of support may have something to do with culture, though it likely has more to do with popular expectations regarding security, political and economic stability, and institutionalized alternatives for nonviolent political action, as well as in the ways in which these factors may influence culture. In addition, political groups with any level of popular support will be more likely to work within legitimate, nonviolent institutions where these alternatives exist. If institutions are legitimate, then those engaging in violence against, or seeking to work outside, them tend to have limited support.

Stopping Suicide Bombings

There are many responses to suicide bombings. There are also significant limitations in the applications of these responses to halting suicide bombings. One approach to countering political violence, and potentially suicide bombings, involves encouraging participation in nonviolent forms of conflict resolution. Many militant groups maintain varying commitments to violent and nonviolent forms of political action. Some groups use violent and nonviolent tactics simultaneously, and some eventually abandon violence. One expectation is that groups will eventually give up violent tactics, or at least use violence less frequently, as they become more committed to nonviolent activities. As groups shift their limited resources toward nonviolent politics and privilege nonviolent roles within the organization, there are fewer resources to direct toward violent activities. With successes, inclusion in nonviolent political processes may contribute to moderation in terms of tactics as well as objectives. There have been successes bringing terrorist groups into legitimate party politics. Over time, the Provisional Irish Republican Army abandoned militancy in favor of party politics, with its political wing, Sinn Fein, becoming the dominant part of the organization even before the group officially disarmed (e.g., Neumann, 2005).

One problem with encouraging nonviolent political opportunities as a means of countering suicide bombings is that this logic may not apply to the subset of militant groups that carry out suicide bombings. Another problem is that it may not work. Groups using suicide bombings may not be welcome bargaining partners. Aiming suicide bombings at civilians may discredit a group as a potential negotiating partner and preclude opportunities to participate in nonviolent political forums, such as elections, peace negotiations, or governance. Participation practically requires groups to cease violence, including suicide bombings. In addition, groups using suicide bombings may not be willing participants in nonviolent politics. This means that, unlike militant groups that have not used suicide tactics or those that have ceased these attacks, the groups that use suicide bombings may not have the same opportunities, or the same incentives, to abandon them.

Another counterterrorism effort involves making it more difficult to carry out suicide bombings. One method involves hardening potential targets. This means adding security, such as barriers to entry and surveillance of potential threats, in attempts to prevent attackers from reaching high-value targets and to deter those who otherwise may try to do so.

There are many problems with relying on the hardening of targets to stop suicide bombings. Hardening a target does not necessarily prevent attacks on it. Suicide bombers have the capacity to approach, even if they cannot enter, their targets. For example, attackers may not gain entry to a military base, embassy, or police station, but suicide bombers may approach these targets with sufficient explosive power to wreak havoc from outside. Similarly, there are effective measures in place to prevent individuals from carrying bombs onto airplanes, but there are fewer measures in place to prevent bombers from approaching or entering airports, where the first layers of security tend to be located.

In some ways, suicide bombings are a reaction to militant groups' goals of attacking harder targets. Attacks on fortified targets, and especially those with armed guards, are likely to become suicide missions even when the weapons being used are not explosives. This is true of attacks involving militants operating in proximity to their targets, not to those waging attacks from a distance, which is something militants have less capacity to do. From a strategic perspective, militants' attacks on armed targets may be more effective—more likely to succeed—if they approach with explosives and without provoking a preemptive strike from their target.

Another problem is that there are too many potential targets, and most are difficult to protect. Hardening some targets will not prevent attacks on softer, unarmed targets. Suicide bombers often aim attacks at civilians, which are more vulnerable and difficult to protect. As with attacks on harder targets, suicide bombers can approach civilian targets, even hiding among them. Suicide bombers can maximize the fear they instill in places where their targets feel "safe" and in places where they gather in large numbers. Places where people roam freely, such as public spaces and businesses, are more numerous and more difficult to protect than government or military installations. If militant groups' goals are served by deploying high casualty and highly destructive attacks, they can achieve these effects whether they direct attacks at softer, civilian targets or harder, military or state targets. Moreover, in peacetime, it may be that attacks on softer targets spark the most fear and gain the most attention.

Another approach to countering suicide bombings involves identifying and stopping the militants responsible for directing and carrying out attacks. The problem with this approach is that there are many potential perpetrators, and they are difficult to identify. Suicide bombers tend to be peripheral to the groups employing them (e.g., Sabri & Schulze, 2020). As such they may not draw attention as members of militant groups. It is also difficult to identify in advance the smaller number of lone suicide bombers who act independently of a group or organization.

Yet another approach to countering suicide bombings involves reducing the numbers of volunteers. The idea is that having fewer willing bombers will lead to fewer bombings. As with other approaches, this is not without problems. One issue is that there are very few suicide bombings overall, meaning there is limited demand for attackers. Groups need not recruit large numbers of volunteers to carry out their deadliest attacks. A second issue is that many of the groups do not rely on volunteers for suicide bombings. Some use force or coercion to fill these roles (Lankford, 2014; Nnam et al., 2018). In some cases, they use children, who are less discriminating and less capable of thinking critically about their options or the repercussions of their acts (e.g., Gutierrez-Sanin, 2010). There are also cases of remote detonation, where "attackers" are unaware of their missions. Examples are plentiful. The Taliban has kidnapped children to send on suicide missions, including children as young as four years of age (Bezhan & Furogh, 2017). Boko Haram and the Islamic State group use women and children in suicide bombings, including many who are presumed to be forced into these roles (Pinheiro, 2015; *United Nations News*, n.d.). Many, perhaps an overwhelming majority, of suicide bombers in Pakistan are children (Lakhani, 2010). The Tamil Tigers raised their own young militants, in some cases in group-run orphanages (Singer, 2006). There are also reports of drugs being used to make attackers more compliant (Nnam et al., 2018). Whether attackers are willing, compromised, or forced may not be obvious to observers of their attacks. A third issue relates to the appeal of suicide missions. Changes that make it more difficult for suicide bombers to succeed in their missions may contribute to a reduction in the numbers of willing attackers (Bueno de Mesquita, 2005). The temporary celebrity of a martyrdom mission, such as those that have been celebrated in the Palestinian territories, would be diminished by a failed attack.

Encouraging transitions to nonviolent politics, hardening targets, and reducing volunteering or support for suicide bombings appear to be potential, if imperfect, means of countering suicide bombings. Even if they could be implemented effectively, however, these approaches cannot sufficiently explain why a group ceases carrying out suicide bombings.

An End to Suicide Bombings?

Despite limitations in the application of counterterrorism efforts, there are cases in which suicide bombings have ended, at least temporarily. Three examples stand out. In each of the cases, suicide bombings decreased or ceased. In two cases, Israel and the Palestinian territories and Lebanon, the militant groups switched to new violent and nonviolent tactics. In the third case, Sri Lanka, the militant group was defeated, ceasing operations altogether. All three cases also coincided with an end to wider-scale warfare.

In the case of Israel, the spate of suicide bombings largely ended following effective counterterrorism and counterinsurgency efforts without the defeat of the groups employing them. In Sri Lanka, suicide bombings ended because the group responsible for these attacks was defeated. In Lebanon, suicide bombings ended with the end of the civil war and the initiation of power-sharing governance.

Israel countered suicide bombings by raising the costs and diminishing the potential gains of these tactics. The agreement negotiated at Oslo had failed to produce peace and had, in many ways, allowed Palestinian groups to arm and train stronger militant groups (Levin, 2018). Stopping suicide bombings required more than hardening targets, identifying potential attackers, and dissuading volunteers. Israel reentered the West Bank during Operation Defensive Shield (ODS), a counterinsurgency and counterterrorism effort initiated during the second intifada. ODS facilitated the reoccupation of the territory. Israel cleared West Bank cities of militants and weapons. These efforts alone would not explain the long-term decline in suicide bombings, however. Militants could build new weapons caches and mobilize new supporters. Success in stopping suicide bombings required creating circumstances under which these militant groups would no longer be able to reach their desired targets, where suicide bombings would no longer have their desired effects, where the costs of carrying out suicide bombings would exceed any potential gains, and where militants—not those who carry out suicide bombings, but those who plan and facilitate these activities and generally benefit from them—would fear identification and incarceration. Success required improvements in human intelligence, something Israel achieved with its reoccupation of the West Bank.

Israel was able to stop large numbers of Palestinian suicide bombings by mid-2006 (Byman, 2012; Global Terrorism Database, 2020). The success followed from a combination of efforts. Israel had previously constructed physical barriers, which have had the effect of separating Palestinian and Israeli communities. The Gaza Strip has been isolated behind increasingly impervious barriers since 1994. The fortifications achieved the goal of stopping suicide bombers in the Gaza Strip from entering Israel, while Israel's withdrawal from the Gaza Strip eliminated targets within the territory. This was only one front, however, as suicide bombers emerged from the West Bank and suicide bombings increased during the second intifada.

Construction of another set of barriers began in 2002, midway through the second intifada. With these barriers, the West Bank became divided within itself and separated from Israel. The arrangements of the barriers and borders in the West Bank were more complicated than they were in the Gaza Strip. West Bank communities were separated from each other and from Israeli settlements and Israel, while the Israeli settlements scattered throughout the West Bank maintained access to Israel.

Along with barriers between communities, Israel instituted roadblocks and checkpoints within the West Bank. Roadblocks and checkpoints were used in response to intelligence regarding potential or impending threats (Kaplan et al., 2005). They hindered the movement of people and could be installed strategically and defensively. In addition to allowing Israeli security forces to identify and detain passersby, they had the added effect of facilitating surveillance. As a result, militants suffered interruptions in the flow of people, weapons, and communications alongside an increasing likelihood of detection not only of potential bombers but also of other members of militant groups, including those who would potentially plan or coordinate suicide bombing attacks (Byman, 2012).

In short, these efforts made it more difficult for militant groups to carry out their operations, while simultaneously raising the stakes of travel for any purpose for those who could be suspected of involvement in militancy and may fear detention. Unable to travel far from home, militant leaders' "situational awareness," their understanding of the situation outside their neighborhoods, also waned (Byman, 2012, p. 833). Simultaneously, Israel's intelligence and awareness of militants' activities grew. Where checkpoints and roadblocks could fail, the fences and walls provided another layer of security.

Israel may not have succeeded in stopping most of these suicide bombings had it not also reoccupied the West Bank and regained access to human intelligence (e.g., Perliger & Pedahzur, 2006). Israel had previously partly withdrawn from the West Bank as part of the agreement to facilitate Palestinian autonomy, but it had not removed settlements in the West Bank as it had from the Gaza Strip. Israel's withdrawal from West Bank cities and Palestinian autonomy in policing and security had cost the state access to the types of human intelligence that had previously facilitated effective counterterrorism efforts. Israel had maintained visual and signal intelligence capabilities, yet these were insufficient without information about what was happening on the ground (Perliger & Pedahzur, 2006). With reoccupation, Israel began rebuilding these resources, which could be used alongside visual and signal intelligence to identify threats, inform the placement of roadblocks, and guide the focus of searches at checkpoints and along barriers.

Although the effect was not immediate, nor fully effective, numbers of suicide bombings decreased overall. The number of suicide bombings and related deaths in Israel and the Palestinian territories peaked in 2002, while the numbers of "thwarted" suicide attacks peaked in 2003 (Byman, 2012, p. 838). Militants planning attacks were more likely to be detected and stopped; it became more difficult for militant groups to arm and dispatch suicide bombers from, and within, the West Bank; and the bombers were less likely to reach Israeli targets, regardless of whether these targets were within or outside the West Bank. In addition, militants were more likely to be identified and detained, meaning the costs of engaging in militancy rose significantly, even for those who planned to survive to enjoy the benefits of their resistance. The measures made it more difficult to carry out suicide bombings in Israel's civilian centers.

The Israeli case is interesting for several reasons. It appears that Israel found a way to stop many suicide bombings. Israel accomplished this without defeating the Palestinian militant groups that carried out these attacks. Instead, Israel's use of barriers within the West Bank have contained the territory's main militant actors and their suicide bombers, similar to how bombers from Gaza and the militant groups employing them had been hindered by barriers on those borders (Byman, 2012). Instead of sending suicide bombers, Hamas and Palestinian Islamic Jihad, operating primarily out of Gaza, rely more heavily on rockets directed over the barriers separating Gazans from Israel. Their newer tactic of terrorism comes with the sounds of rockets flying and exploding. Their attacks have been more frequent, though less deadly, than the suicide bombings that preceded them. Former militants in the West Bank no longer operate outside Israel's view. In addition, with the end of the second intifada in 2005, and after the short-lived attempt at democracy in 2006, the Palestine Liberation Organization (PLO) seems to be occupied more with governance, including internal policing. Even while the groups that once carried out many suicide bombings survive and their resistance continues, they carry on with far fewer suicide bombings (e.g., Global Terrorism Database, 2020).

In the case of Israel, one could argue that the end of the second intifada partially explains the reduction in suicide bombings independent of other efforts. The problem with this argument is that there are militant groups in the Palestinian territories that have used suicide bombings during peacetime, as competitors to the PLO. Were this option not blocked, these groups likely would continue to do so from the West Bank. This may have been even more likely after Hamas's failure to consolidate power over the Palestinian Authority (PA), despite their victory in the Palestinian national elections in 2006. Much of the explanation for the decrease in suicide bombings lies in Israel's effective blockade of the West Bank, including the creation of barriers and checkpoints, which prevented many suicide bombers from reaching their targets, alongside renewed access to human intelligence, which allowed Israel to anticipate and respond to potential threats.

While it stands as one example of stopping suicide bombings, what was accomplished in Israel and the Palestinian territories is unlikely to be replicable in other cases. This is a unique case situated within a small geographic area. Furthermore, Israel's counter-efforts have not stopped all suicide bombings, nor have they resolved the conditions under which people may support the use of these tactics. Israel's efforts, including its barriers and reoccupation, have coincided with increasing numbers of terrorist attacks, though of a less deadly form (e.g., Global Terrorism Database, 2020). Moreover, these measures and their seeming successes have come at a high cost to Israel and a high cost to the Palestinian communities.

It is clearer in the case of Lebanon that the end to suicide bombings was related to the end of the civil war and changes in the conditions under which the groups and their supporters resided. As in the Palestinian territories, the groups that carried out Lebanon's suicide bombings survived the war. They also found new roles in the postwar power-sharing regime. Lebanon offers an example in which the decrease in suicide bombings coincided with changes in tactics and expectations on the parts of militant groups. Similar to how suicide bombings are more likely associated with attempts to damage a political system than with attempts to work within it (e.g., Hafez, 2006), a willingness to participate in governance, form political parties, engage in peace talks, or abandon violence demonstrates a commitment to peaceful conflict resolution. In addition, working within a political system requires investments in a distinct set of tools and skills, which serve to privilege a group's nonviolent elements.

What amounted to a temporary end to suicide bombings in Lebanon coincided with the introduction of new power-sharing institutions that reserved positions in government for representatives from the previously warring confessional groups. Hezbollah, which was known for its use of suicide bombings during the war (e.g., Pape, 2005; Pedahzur, 2005), was one such representative. Hezbollah is an Islamist group that fought on the side of Lebanon's Shi'a community with support from Iran's Islamist (Shi'a) Republic and, later, Syria's Shi'a-led government (e.g., Wiegand, 2009). Hezbollah's political wing won a place in Lebanon's new government as a representative of the Shi'a community. Amal, Hezbollah's former competitor for the support of the Shi'a community, and the Syrian Social Nationalist Party, which also carried out suicide bombings in Lebanon, also found positions in the new government. Hezbollah did not abandon violence or disarm after its political wing became a legitimate political party. In fact, the group's militant capabilities have continued to rival those of Lebanon's state (e.g., Wiegand, 2009), and the group continued to engage in bombings and other attacks in Lebanon and elsewhere after the civil war ended in 1990. Many of these attacks were aimed at other militants and Israel rather than at Lebanon or its civilians. Hezbollah also provides services to people residing in the parts of Lebanon where the group is dominant and where the Lebanese state is weak (e.g., Azani, 2013; Wiegand, 2009).

Suicide bombings ceased for more than five years in Lebanon as the country emerged from the civil war. However, the end of suicide bombings in Lebanon was not permanent. Hezbollah was credited with at least two suicide bombings in the late 1990s, even while the group's party participated in governance. Within a few years, new militant groups began carrying out suicide bombings in Lebanon. The perpetrators included al-Qaeda affiliates and the Islamic State group operating primarily out of neighboring Syria, in the context of Syria's civil war. Hezbollah, a participant in this war on the side of Syria's incumbent regime, has been a target of these attacks (e.g., Global Terrorism Database, 2020).

While some Islamist political parties can be dissuaded from violence and brought into nonviolent political processes (McCants, 2011), many others are unlikely to view a transition to shared governance, such as the one undertaken by Hezbollah, as an option, much less as an appealing one. The Islamic State group and other Islamist groups who claim to share violent versions of Salafist ideologies and global ambitions will be unwilling to work within the parliamentary institutions of the states they wish to replace (McCants, 2011). Such participation would be incompatible with their ideologies and objectives and would give legitimacy to the same entities they view as illegitimate.

The end of suicide bombings in Sri Lanka was longer-lasting than in Lebanon and the reason seems to be a combination of the end of the country's civil war and the defeat of the remaining Tamil insurgents. The era of LTTE-orchestrated suicide bombings ended in 2009 with the defeat of the organization, the end of the civil war, and the death of the group's charismatic leader. In the LTTE's case, neither the group's leader nor his family, including his minor children, survived. The LTTE had already outlived, or eliminated, its competitors for Tamil support (Kaarthikeyan, 2006), and the group was responsible for, or at least was credited with, carrying out Sri Lanka's civil war-era suicide bombings (e.g., Global Terrorism Database, 2020).

There were reasons to anticipate suicide bombings could have continued even after the LTTE's defeat. There are cases in which groups, even once defeated, reappear in weakened forms. These remnants tend to lack support and resources, however, and they tend to find the conditions less favorable to a return to wider-scale violence. Adding to this, one group's defeat does not necessarily mean an end to violence or, as in the case of Sri Lanka's violence, an end to suicide bombings. It simply means that the defeated group ceases contributing to the violence.

Suicide bombings returned to Sri Lanka ten years after the LTTE's defeat. The perpetrators of the coordinated suicide bombings on Easter 2019 were part of a relatively young local Islamist group, National Tawheed Jamaat, which claimed inspiration from the Islamic State group (Amarasingam, 2019). Sri Lanka had no experience with Islamist suicide terrorism prior to the Easter attack, nor did the group have experience with suicide bombings. The group likely received operational support from the Islamic State group (United States Department of State, 2020). The group's leader, who had reportedly become increasingly radicalized over the years preceding the bombing, was one of the team of eight Sri Lankan suicide bombers (Amarasingam, 2019). One may expect that the group will die with the leader. One may also expect that the Islamic State group's interest in spreading to the Indian Subcontinent leaves them open to other collaborations (United States Department of State, 2020).

Changing Perceptions and New Tactics

There are other potential explanations for ends to the use of suicide bombings, including changes in popular support for these tactics and the introduction of new, perhaps more effective tactics. The first of these depends on militant groups' concerns regarding public opinion and their reliance on, or expectations of, support. As such, some groups' strategies would be influenced more than others by changes in support for their violent tactics. Perhaps the more important question is how changes such as these could or would come about, and whether they could be orchestrated or would depend more on changes in the conditions under which support is found. If groups using suicide bombings find support as a byproduct of the popularity of their ideologies and the narratives they use to legitimize their violence, then one can imagine that challenges to these ideologies may contribute to changes in tactics. There is already evidence that suicide bombings are not popular tactics, including in many of the places where suicide bombings are used most frequently (Pew Research Center, 2013). There is also evidence that suicide bombers are generally in short supply (Kurzman, 2011). The use of children in suicide bombings, some of them kidnapped and many of them very young, provides further support for this assertion (Horgan et al., 2017; Nnam et al., 2018; Singer, 2010; Vale, 2018). Another issue is whether people reside in places where they have the autonomy or opportunities to oppose the violence used by militant groups with control over the territories in which they reside.

The identification of new or "better" tactics is of particular interest as it relates to groups' strategies. New tactics may replace old ones in cases in which militants view them as more effective or more likely to help them achieve their goals. Suicide bombings may remain part of a group's repertoire alongside new tactics. One issue is whether the new tactics will be used in place of suicide bombings or alongside them.

There are precedents for expectations that strategies and tactics will change. If suicide bombings are the "emblematic deed" of this most recent wave of terrorism (Rapoport, 2012; Weinberg, 2007), it is possible to imagine that a future "deed" will eventually replace or supplement suicide bombings, much as suicide bombings replaced the skyjackings of a previous generation of terrorists (Rapoport, 2012). At the same time, even with the introduction of new tactics, suicide bombings may become less common or less frequent, but they will not necessarily cease altogether. Skyjackings ended not because suicide bombings began, but because of improvements in security around air travel. These changes made it much more difficult to carry out skyjackings with attackers who planned to survive their missions. They did not prevent the attacks on September 11, 2001, however, where the attackers expected to die. Counterterrorism efforts aimed at stopping suicide bombings differ from those employed against threats to air travel. Air travel is far more limited and more easily policed than other types of transportation or other spaces where people gather. Suicide bombers do not rely on a single mode of transportation, and they are able to hide among their many potential targets.

Even while suicide bombings have not always been the preferred tactic or the most frequently used tactic of terrorists and insurgents, they have been used to gain considerable attention from media and target audiences, to spread fear and raise the costs of conflicts. Militant groups' new tactics will likely be violent, but they may not be as deadly as suicide bombings. In addition, militant groups may not require as much attention from independent media, and they may not benefit from carrying out the deadliest types of attacks. Control over media output has allowed some groups to create their own theater. Militants need not carry out dramatic attacks with high numbers of deaths to gain attention when they can draw attention through other means.

The Islamic State group and its organizational predecessors, al Qaeda in Iraq and the Islamic State of Iraq, are credited with carrying out large numbers of suicide bombings, and they are suspected of participating in many more (e.g., Hafez, 2006). They are also known for attempting to establish a state and a more conventional fighting force, though not one that would eschew terrorism or suicide attacks. More to the point, they are known for producing their own media, some of which takes the form of propaganda videos glorifying the group's executions, beheadings, and immolations. Their violence has a gruesome quality, and it is produced for mass viewing (e.g., Horgan et al., 2017). Some of the group's videos even showcase children in the role of executioner (Vale, 2018). With these tools, the Islamic State does not need suicide bombings or high numbers of deaths to gain media attention. Despite this, they have continued to use and support suicide bombing attacks.

For militant groups to stop using suicide bombings, there would need to be a reason to cease that goes beyond the introduction of new tactics. In the case of replacing suicide bombings, it may matter whether the new tools are violent or nonviolent. Suicide bombings would not work well alongside participation in nonviolent activities, such as peace negotiations or governance. At the same time, many of the groups using suicide bombings in the twenty-first century draw inspiration from, or claim affiliation with, the al Qaeda or Islamic State groups, which are coincidentally less likely to compromise or work with states to secure some of their objectives (e.g., McCants, 2011). These movements have proven difficult to defeat, in part because of the ways in which they are organized and the appeal, even if limited, of their ideologies (e.g., Kenney, 2003; Kurzman, 2011).

None of these potential changes, including changes in popular support, the introduction of new tactics, or the defeat of global terrorist networks, would result in an end to suicide bombings by individual actors (though, as discussed, individual attackers have not been, and are unlikely to become, the most prolific suicide bombers). Moreover, the end of a group or the end of a conflict will not prevent the use of suicide bombing tactics by other groups or in other conflicts.

References

Abrahms, M. (2006). Al Qaeda's scorecard: A progress report on al Qaeda's objectives. *Studies in Conflict and Terrorism*, 29(5), 509–529.

Amarasingam, A. (2019). Terrorism on the teardrop island: Understanding the Easter 2019 attacks in Sri Lanka. *CTC Sentinel*, 12(5), 1–10. Available at : https://ctc.usma.edu/terrorism-teardrop-island-understanding-easter-2019-attacks-sri-lanka/.

Azani, E. (2013). The hybrid terrorist organization: Hezbollah as a case study. *Studies in Conflict and Terrorism*, 36(11), 899–916.

Bezhan, F., & Furogh, S. (2017). Afghan police: Children kidnapped to be suicide bombers for Taliban. *Radio Free Europe Radio Liberty*, July 10. Available at: www.rferl.org/a/afghan-police-children-kidnapped-by-taliban-to-be-suicide-bombers/28606744.html.

Bloom, M. (2005 [1968]). *Dying to kill: The allure of suicide terror*. New York: Columbia University Press.

Bloom, M.M. (2004). Palestinian suicide bombing: Public support, market share, and outbidding. *Political Science Quarterly*, 119(1), 61–88.

Boot, M. (2013 [1968]). *Invisible armies: An epic history of guerrilla warfare from ancient times to the present*. New York: Liveright Publishing.

Bueno de Mesquita, E. (2005). The quality of terror. *American Journal of Political Science*, 49(3), 515–530.
Byman, D. (2012). Curious victory: Explaining Israel's suppression of the second intifada. *Terrorism and Political Violence*, 24(5), 825–852.
Crenshaw, M. (2007). Explaining suicide terrorism: A review essay. *Security Studies*, 16(1), 133–162.
Cronin, A.K. (2006). How al-qaida ends: The decline and demise of terrorist groups. *International Security*, 31(1), 7–48.
Ganor, B. (n.d.). The rationality of the Islamic radical suicide attack phenomenon. In *Countering Suicide Terrorism*. Herzliya, Israel: IDC Herzliya, Institute for Counter-Terrorism, ICT, pp. 5–11.
Global Terrorism Database (GTD). (2020). National Consortium for the Study of Terrorism and Responses to Terrorism (START). Available at: www.start.umd.edu/gtd/access/.
Gupta, D. (2005). Exploring roots of terrorism. In T. Bjørgo (Ed.), *Root causes of terrorism: Myths, reality and ways forward*. New York: Routledge, pp. 16–32.
Gutierrez-Sanin, F. (2010). Organizing minors: The case of Colombia. In S. Gates & S. Reichs (Eds.), *Child soldiers in the age of fractured states*. Pittsburgh, PA: University of Pittsburgh Press, pp. 121–140.
Hafez, M.M. (2006). Suicide terrorism in Iraq: A preliminary assessment of the quantitative data and documentary evidence. *Studies in Conflict and Terrorism*, 29(6), 591–619.
Hoffman, B. (2006). *Inside Terrorism*. New York: Columbia University Press.
Hopgood, S. (2005). Tamil Tigers, 1987–2002. In D. Gambetta (Ed.), *Making Sense of Suicide Missions*. New York: Oxford University Press, pp. 43–76.
Horgan, J.G., Taylor, M., Bloom, M., & Winter, C. (2017). From cubs to lions: A six stage model of child socialization into the Islamic State. *Studies in Conflict and Terrorism*, 40(7), 645–664.
Horowitz, M.C. (2010). Nonstate actors and the diffusion of innovations: The case of suicide terrorism. *International Organization*, 64(1), 33–64.
Kaarthikeyan, S.D.R. (2006). The root causes of terrorism? A case study of the Tamil insurgency and the LTTE. In T. Bjørgo (Ed.), *Root causes of terrorism: Myths, reality, and ways forward*. New York: Routledge, pp. 131–140.
Kaplan, E.H., Mintz, A., Mishal, S., & Samban, C. (2005). What happened to suicide bombings in Israel? Insights from a terror stock model. *Studies in Conflict and Terrorism*, 28(3), 225–235.
Kenney, M. (2003). From Pablo to Osama: Counter-terrorism lessons from the war on drugs. *Survival (London)*, 45(3), 187–206.
Kurzman, C. (2011). Why is it so hard to find a suicide bomber these days? *Foreign Policy*, 188, 58–64. Available at: https://foreignpolicy.com/2011/08/15/why-is-it-so-hard-to-find-a-suicide-bomber-these-days/.
Kydd, A., & Walter, B.F. (2002). Sabotaging the peace: The politics of extremist violence. *International Organization*, 56(2), 263–296.
Kydd, A.H., & Walter, B.F. (2006). The strategies of terrorism. *International Security*, 31(1), 49–80.
Lakhani, K. (2010). Indoctrinating children: The making of Pakistan's suicide bombers. *CTC Sentinel*, 3(6), 11–13. Available at: https://ctc.usma.edu/indoctrinating-children-the-making-of-pakistans-suicide-bombers/.
Lankford, A. (2011). Could suicide terrorists actually be suicidal? *Studies in Conflict and Terrorism*, 34(4), 337–366.

Lankford, A. (2014). A suicide-based typology of suicide terrorists: Conventional, coerced, escapist and indirect. *Security Journal*, 27(1), 80–96.

Laqueur, W. (1996). Postmodern terrorism. Foreign Affairs (New York, N.Y.), 75(5), 24–36.

Levin, J. (2018). Exploring Palestinian weapon proliferation during the Oslo Peace Process. *The Middle East Journal*, 72(1), 48–65.

Martin, S., & Weinberg, L. (2016). *The role of terrorism in twenty-first-century warfare*. Manchester: Manchester University Press.

McCants, W. (2011). Al Qaeda's challenge: The jihadists' war with Islamist democrats. *Foreign Affairs*, 90(5), 20–32.

Moghadam, A. (2006). Defining suicide terrorism. In A. Pedahzur (Ed.), *Root causes of suicide terrorism: The globalization of martyrdom*. London: Routledge, pp. 1–19.

Neumann, P.R. (2005). The bullet and the ballot box: The case of the IRA 1. *Journal of Strategic Studies*, 28(6), 941–975.

Nnam, M.U., Arua, M.C., & Otu, M.S. (2018). The use of women and children in suicide bombing by the Boko Haram terrorist group in Nigeria. *Aggression and Violent Behavior*, 42, 35–42.

Pape, R.A. (2005 [1960]). *Dying to win: The strategic logic of suicide terrorism*. New York: Random House.

Pedahzur, A. (2005). *Suicide terrorism*. Malden, MA: Polity.

Perliger, A., & Pedahzur, A. (2006). Coping with suicide attacks: Lessons from Israel. *Public Money & Management*, 26(5), 281–286.

Pew Research Center (2013). The world's Muslims: Religion, politics and society. April 30. Available at: www.pewforum.org/2013/04/30/the-worlds-muslims-religion-politics-society-overview/#extremism-widely-rejected.

Pinheiro, C. (2015). The role of child soldiers in a multigenerational movement. *CTC Sentinel*, 8(2), 11–13. Available at : https://ctc.usma.edu/wp-content/uploads/2015/02/CTCSentinel-Vol8Issue26.pdf.

Rapoport, D.C. (2012). The four waves of modern terrorism. In J. Horgan & K. Braddock (Eds.), *Terrorism studies: A reader*. New York: Routledge, pp. 41–60.

Sabri, A., & Schulze, G.G. (2020). Are suicide terrorists different from "regular militants"? *Public Choice*, 1–27. Available at: https://doi.org/10.1007/s11127-020-00817-2.

Schweitzer, Y. (2007). Palestinian Istishhadia: A developing instrument. *Studies in Conflict and Terrorism*, 30(8), 667–689.

Singer, P.W. (2006). *Children at war*. Berkeley, CA: University of California Press.

Singer, P.W. (2010). The enablers of war: Causal factors behind the child soldier phenomenon. In S. Gates & S. Reich (Eds.), *Child soldiers in the age of fractured states*. Pittsburgh, PA: University of Pittsburgh Press, pp. 93–107.

United Nations News (n.d.). Girls groomed for suicide missions fight back against the extremists of Lake Chad. Available at: www.un.org/africarenewal/news/girls-groomed-suicide-missions-fight-back-against-extremists-lake-chad.

United States Department of State (2020). Country Reports on Terrorism 2019. June 24. Available at: www.state.gov/reports/country-reports-on-terrorism-2019/.

Vale, G. (2018). *Cubs in the lions' den: Indoctrination and recruitment of children within Islamic State territory*. London: International Centre for the Study of Radicalisation, ICSR. Available at: https://icsr.info/wp-content/uploads/2018/07/ICSR-Report-Cubs-in-the-Lions%E2%80%99-Den-Indoctrination-and-Recruitment-of-Children-Within-Islamic-State-Territory.pdf.

Weinberg, L. (1991). Turning to terror: The conditions under which political parties turn to terrorist activities. *Comparative Politics*, 23(4), 423–438.

Weinberg, L. (2007). Observations on the future of terrorism. In J.O. Ellis III (Ed.), *Terrorism: What's coming, the mutating threat*. Oklahoma City, OK: Memorial Institute for the Prevention of Terrorism, p. 41.

Wiegand, K.E. (2009). Reformation of a terrorist group: Hezbollah as a Lebanese political party. *Studies in Conflict and Terrorism*, 32(8), 669–680.

8

Code of the Terrorist

Murat Haner, Michael L. Benson, and Francis T. Cullen

The Turkish government and media sources have often depicted the Kurdistan Workers' Party—known worldwide by the acronym PKK—as a tool of foreign powers designed to destroy the economic, political, and territorial integrity of Turkey through terrorist methods (Akyol, 2016; Eyrice, 2013; Gunter, 2000). The PKK has been criticized for being a regional subcontractor that serves the interests of Europe and the United States and has been held responsible for many criminal acts, including but not limited to extortion, human trafficking, narcotics trading, money laundering, and arms smuggling (Altun, 2016; Beriker-Atiyas, 1997; Cline, 2004; Eyrice, 2013; International Crisis Group, 2012; Laciner, 2008; Romano, 2006).

Beyond accusations of receiving external Western patronage and engaging in criminal activities, the government-controlled mainstream media has also portrayed PKK members as vicious, cold-blooded killers who have committed violent acts in an indiscriminate way. The PKK has been accused of targeting innocent people with its bloody attacks and systematically carrying out civilian massacres by murdering children, women, the elderly, and other civilians (*Agence France-Presse*, 2015; Ben-Meir, 2017a; Feridun & Sezgin, 2008; Kaplan, 2017). Abdullah Ocalan, the leader of the PKK commonly referred to as "Apo," has been the focal point of this campaign. The Turkish media and nationalist indoctrination have presented Apo as a Stalin-like, murderous terrorist, who has a huge ego and who is so ruthless that he even ordered the killings of his own friends to consolidate his power in the group (Bacik & Coskun, 2011; Cline, 2004; Gunter, 2000; Haner, 2018; Worth, 2016).

Due to these media representations, the Turkish public has come to believe that the PKK is a bunch of bandits, terrorists, child kidnappers, drug dealers, and baby killers. On any given day, it is commonplace to see news headlines such as: "PKK Continues to Target Civilians" (*Daily Sabah*, 2017), "Children Driven to Death by the PKK" (*Atinabe*, 2017), "PKK Bombs Hospitals" (*Hurriyet Daily News*, 2015), "Civilians Killed in PKK Attack" (*Yeni Safak News*, 2017), "PKK Terrorists Open Fire Targeting Civilians" (*TRT World*, 2017a), "PKK Kills Innocent Children" (Ozkaya, 2016), "PKK Camps Exposed as Rape and Torture Centers" (Arslan, 2017), "PKK Is a Bloody Terrorist Organization" (*A News*, 2017), "PKK Murdered Thousands of Children, Women, and Teachers" (*TRT World*, 2017b), and "PKK Is a Project of the British Deep State" (Yahya, 2017).

In contrast to this social construction of the PKK, the organization's use of violence is, in fact, governed by a code that can be called "the code of the terrorist" (Haner, 2018; Yackley, 2015). This phrase has a conceptual link to, but differs from, the "code of the street" articulated by Elijah Anderson (1999) in his classic ethnography. In brief, Anderson's code is defined by five features (see also Brezina et al., 2004; Swartz, 2010). First, it is an informal set of norms that governs behavior in public spaces, mainly located in inner-city neighborhoods. Second, the key goal is for individuals to attain and maintain respect. Third, affronts to an individual's respect mandate interpersonal violence. Fourth, using Swidler's (1986) distinction, the code often functions as "culture in action"—as a "took kit" that is accessed situationally. In particular, youths from so-called decent families "code switch," adhering to prosocial values in private settings and violent values in public settings. Fifth, the code of the street is an adaptation to concentrated disadvantage and the alienation from conventional society this inspires (see also Sampson & Bean, 2006).

As will be revealed ahead, the code of the terrorist differs on these dimensions. The code is a prescribed set of norms that governs behavior in public and private spaces; the key goal is to advance the emancipation of the PKK; violence is used to serve organizational interests; the code functions as a "culture as values," with members expected to learn and adhere to cultural mandates; and the code of the terrorist is based in an organization seeking ethnic liberation. Still, the two codes are similar in a crucial way: The violence committed in their names is not random but tends to occur according to certain rules that are widely known and given allegiance by the members of a social group (Anderson, 1999; Haner, 2018).

For Anderson (1999), inner-city youths are not "the other"—inherently pathological, cold-blooded super-predators beyond moral redemption (see Dilulio, 1995). Instead, their violence is regulated by shared beliefs about respect and self-protection that arise from the deprivations of contemporary urban life. In a similar way, critical terrorism studies alert us to the media's tendency to "psychologize, and to reduce structural and political problems to those of individual pathologies and personal problems" (Stohl, 2008, p. 7). In particular, Stohl identifies as a popular myth the idea "that all terrorists are madmen" and should be viewed as "evildoers." He continues that "rarely are actions of insurgent terrorists presented as part of an ongoing political struggle, related to any particular goals or presented as reasonable or even meaningful" (2008, p. 7). Members of the PKK are far from "madmen," and their violence is guided by a code, not perpetrated impulsively.

Understanding the code of the terrorist is important because it reveals that the PKK's violence typically is not indiscriminate and wantonly ruthless, but it is used as a political instrument aimed at achieving basic human rights for the Kurdish minority in Turkey. The code of the terrorist thus is replete with insights on how PKK terrorist violence might be ended—a possibility excluded by the current official social construction of PKK resistance by the Turkish state and the media it controls. It is this possibility that the present inquiry into the code of the terrorist seeks to address. Critical terrorist studies advocates refer to this approach as a commitment to "emancipation" or a commitment "to addressing the conditions that can be seen to impel actors to resort to terrorist tactics" (Jackson, 2010, p. 5).

The Rise of the PKK

The PKK is a political organization that uses terrorism to enhance its goal of securing cultural and political freedom for the Kurdish population in Turkey. It was founded on Marxist–Leninist principles and identified itself with the PLO and IRA (Haner, 2018). Over the years, the ultimate goal of the PKK has shifted from establishing an independent Kurdish state, to an autonomous Kurdistan, and finally to existence within a truly democratic Turkey under which the Kurds would have equal citizenship status with Turks (Çandar, 2012; Eyrice, 2013; Philips, 2017).

Throughout the 1970s, Apo and his followers raised awareness of existing social inequalities through political activism (Ben-Meir, 2017b). In fact, between the 1970s and the early 1980s, thousands of Kurds joined leftist groups to seek out their cultural, national, and linguistic rights (de Bellaigue, 2009). However, the 1980 military coup in Turkey destroyed the possibility of any kind of nonviolent legal expression of Kurdish demands through political means. Under the new regime, political groups were outlawed, their leading figures were arrested, and all kinds of political activities, including peaceful demonstrations, were prohibited throughout the country (Entessar, 1992; McDowall, 2000).

The policies implemented during this period disrupted the social patterns of daily life and eventually traumatized Kurdish society (Bacik & Coskun, 2011). The Kurds were forced to attend schools that taught only in Turkish and were asked to use Turkish in their private and public circles (Haner, 2018; Romano, 2006). The use of the words "Kurd" and "Kurdistan" had been prohibited, and Kurdish families were forced to give Turkish names to their children (Ergil, 2000; Worth, 2016). Thousands of Kurds were arrested under the pretext of establishing social order in the country (Romano, 2006). Kurdish politicians were stripped of their parliamentary immunity and jailed as terrorists (Worth, 2016). The journalists and academics who became advocates of Kurdish rights faced prosecution, dismissal, and harassment on the grounds of promoting a culture of terrorism (Haner, 2018). Several politically active Kurds and Kurdish intelligentsia were murdered by unknown perpetrators to intimidate the Kurdish people from challenging the monolithic nature of Turkey's political culture—a single nation, a single language, and centralized power (Aydinli & Ozcan, 2011; Ergil, 2000).

This climate of fear and frustration—the unwarranted violence applied by the security forces, the suppression of the public expression of Kurdish identity, the denial of diversity, and the blockage of political means to secure cultural rights—generated widespread discontent among the Kurds and radicalized many of them into PKK (Ergil, 2000; Haner, 2018; Romano, 2006). The PKK promised to reverse these unjust practices under a Marxist and Kurdish nationalist program (Worth, 2016). According to the group, violence and military retaliation then became the only means for the Kurds to make their voices heard (Izady, 1992). Thousands of Kurds found the PKK's message appealing and joined the group (Beriker-Atiyas, 1997; Gunter, 2000).

Since 1984, tens of thousands of people (on both sides) have lost their lives; Kurdish villages have been destroyed, millions of people have been displaced, and other severe human rights violations have occurred (Bacik & Coskun, 2011; Çandar, 2012). Turkish armed struggle has not produced any significant results as the PKK remained in existence and Kurds continued to join the organization. Yet the Turkish authorities have continued to perceive the extension of cultural rights to the Kurds as a concession to terrorism and to insist that military operations will continue until the very last Kurdish rebel is killed (Ben-Meir, 2017a; Beriker-Atiyas, 1997).

The violence and suppression against the Kurds have been hidden from the Turkish public view by media censorship and military curfews (Worth, 2016). There has been no mention of Turkish tanks encircling Kurdish cities, of Kurdish civilian casualties (including the images of dead children lying on streets), and of the Kurds being forcibly evicted from their hometowns (Marcus, 2009; Romano, 2006, Worth, 2016). On the contrary, the frequent footage of Turkish soldiers' funerals on television with images of families grieving the loss of sons killed fighting the PKK, and the portrayal of the PKK as cold-blooded baby killers have deepened the ethnic polarization between the Turks and the Kurds (White, 2000; *Yesilgazete*, 2012).

Little in Turkey today suggests that this situation is likely to change. In fact, there is now a renewed conflict that is very similar to what occurred in the 1990s—unaccounted murders, repression, denial of identity, declaration of state of emergency, curfews, and forced migration (Haner, 2018). As the conflict between the Turkish government and the PKK persists, more Kurds will be recruited and will engage in terrorist attacks. The code of the terrorist thus promises to guide the PKK's terrorist activities into the foreseeable future.

The PKK's Ideology and the Use of Violence

Terrorist, separatist, insurrectionist, and nationalist groups vary in the ideologies they adopt, their commitments to them, and in their use of violence. Ideologies constrain goals and strategies that groups pursue and hence play an important role in the functioning of armed groups, such as the PKK (Sanín & Wood, 2014). Established in 1978, the PKK first defined itself as a Marxist–Leninist national movement with the goal of creating a classless society for the Kurdish people through the formation of a new state (Haner, 2018; Manafy, 2005). It was originally modeled after the national liberation movements that had seized state power and transformed political and economic realities over the course of the twentieth century in countries as diverse as China, Mexico, Algeria, and Vietnam (Jongerden, 2017; Yarkın, 2015). But after the challenges faced by socialism as a political system toward the end of the twentieth century—especially the collapse starting in 1989 of eastern European governments and the Soviet Union (Geoghegan, 2003; Nuti, 2018; Romano, 2006; Wallerstein, 1986)—the PKK had to adapt to new political realities. Thus, beginning in the 1990s, it moved away from the goal of seceding from Turkey and establishing a Kurdish state. This change is captured in the words of the member of the PKK (identified ahead) interviewed for this project:

> In 1995, while the Turkish government was trying to crack down on the emerging Kurdish groups, the PKK wisely undertook to relinquish its Marxist-Leninist ideology to soothe its relations with Western democracies. The leaders of the party argued that the PKK's leftist ideology was reinforcing its image as a terrorist organization, rather than an insurgent movement that was trying to protect its people. Thus, to attract the support of European countries and the United States, the party administration removed the hammer and sickle symbols from the flag of the PKK.
>
> Although, up until 1993 we consistently wanted to establish an independent Kurdistan, our people were too intermingled throughout Turkey. Now, we only wanted to live in peace with the Turkish people, with rights equal to theirs.

In its place, the PKK redefined its main goal as creating a democratic society that would be non-sexist and non-exploitative in the Kurdish region. This new "Ecological Democratic Confederalist Society" would in theory conduct its affairs with limited political autonomy from Turkey (Jongerden, 2017; Yarkın, 2015). As we describe below, the individual upon whom the current study is based joined the PKK in 1992 as it was beginning to move away from Marxism–Leninism, and he stayed until 2011.

Although the goals of the PKK have changed since the 1970s, the movement still maintains its guerrilla forces, and it still uses violence against Turkish targets. However, it is broadly accepted that the PKK has for the most part not engaged in mass violence against civilians. One reason that the PKK has avoided the indiscriminate use of violence is because doing so would run the risk of being counterproductive in the sense that random violence would not conform with the group's ideology and could potentially harm the PKK's ability to gather and to socialize recruits effectively, a task that all resistance movements must accomplish (Sanín & Wood, 2014). From the beginning, the PKK has defined itself in opposition to the Turkish government and the Turkish military, not the Turkish people, and it has recruited members by appealing to their desire for cultural and political autonomy from Turkey. This appeal was couched at first in the ideological terminology of Marxism and Leninism and emphasized the creation of a socialist state. Now the PKK advocates the creation of an autonomous, egalitarian, and non-exploitative society based on radical democracy (De Jong, 2016; Jongerden, 2017; Yarkın, 2015). These are attractive and noble goals that are worth fighting for, and they provide recruits with a sense of purpose that extends beyond their own personal preferences and goals. Unlike some other movements that recruit individuals by offering short-term material benefits, such as drugs or money or access to sexual slaves, and that have a difficult time controlling their use of violence (Weinstein, 2006), the PKK offers recruits a new identity. It also goes to great lengths to socialize recruits into the normative commitments that accompany this identity (Haner, 2018).

As a result of his early training in Marxism–Leninism, Apo has written extensively regarding the goals of the PKK and the strategies and the mindset that it will take to accomplish those goals (De Jong, 2016). He has consistently expressed the idea that the use of violence must always be justified in terms of its relation to the group's long-term objectives. In addition, as interpreted by Apo, the notion of equality among all peoples is a fundamental tenet of Marxism–Leninism as a political philosophy and ideology, and Apo has repeatedly championed the rights of women through the dismantling of traditional forms of patriarchy in Kurdish society (Bengio, 2016; Celebi, 2010; Düzgün, 2016). While this ideology does not prohibit violence against those who would oppress freedom-seekers, such as political and military authorities, it proscribes the indiscriminate use of violence against ordinary civilians, who are, by definition, not oppressors. When violence against civilians, such as Village Guards and schoolteachers, is deemed necessary, they are targeted because they are seen as either threats to the legitimacy of the PKK's claim to represent the Kurds as a people or because they are seen as collaborating with Turkish security forces (Masullo & O'Connor, 2017). Targeting of civilians, in other words, is purposive and not indiscriminate. These considerations provide a context for understanding the code of the terrorists described below.

Finally, similar to some other armed insurgencies—such as the FMLN (The Farabundo Martí National Liberation Front) in El Salvador, the EZLN (Zapatista Army of National Liberation of Mexico) in Mexico, the NRA (Ugandan National Resistance Army) in Uganda, and the Shining Path of Peru—the PKK is a highly disciplined group (Kampwirth, 2002; Luciak, 2001; Mason, 1992; Reif, 1986; Thomas & Wood, 2018; Viterna, 2013). As Weinstein (2006) outlined in his seminal work, *Inside Rebellion*, movements that emerge in resource-poor environments need the support of local populations to survive. Accordingly, these organizations recruit highly disciplined and committed individuals; develop cooperative relationships with noncombatants; cultivate respect among civilians, and exhibit restraint in the use of indiscriminate violence by developing meaningful control structures (Weinstein, 2006). Similarly, by recruiting individuals who are committed to its ideology and holding them up to high disciplinary standards, the PKK maintains its members to be selective and restrained in their use of violence against civilians because doing otherwise could jeopardize its access to vital resources (e.g., preexisting networks, ethic identities, and cultural ties) that are necessary for the group's survival (Weinstein, 2006). Further, this degree of organization is salient because it allows the PKK to inculcate its ideology—and its code of conduct—systematically and typically effectively.

Methods

Data

The data for this study come from a series of recorded interviews that were conducted with an incarcerated member of the PKK, who had served as an active combatant in the organization for 18 years. Over a four-month period from January 13 to May 8, 2015, this individual was interviewed by the first author in a Turkish prison located in the city of Diyarbakir. The interviews were usually five days a week for about seven hours a day. Because of his long tenure, leadership role, and diverse experiences, the subject—known as "Deniz"—was able to shed considerable light on the ideology, policies, practices, and day-to-day activities of the PKK. Born in 1973, Deniz is the third eldest son of a peasant Kurdish family. During nearly two decades in the PKK, he participated in operations across four countries—Turkey, Iraq, Syria, and Iran—holding different ranks and positions. Over time, he gradually rose from the lowest level to near the top of the PKK in terms of the strategic and tactical military operations conducted by the organization.

The primary goal of the interviews was to construct a life history of a terrorist that would shed light on how one comes to join the PKK, what one does while a member, and what one's life is like after leaving the organization. Thus, the interviews were open-ended but guided by a focus on four domains: (1) growing up, (2) becoming a terrorist, (3) being a terrorist, and (4) life in prison and after. The interviewer posed questions in each of these areas but also let Deniz raise and explore issues of his own choosing. Although our main goal was to record Deniz's life history, we also wanted to take advantage of this unique opportunity to learn as much as possible about all aspects of the PKK from a veteran insider. Although not a social scientist, his observations based on his extensive experiences can be seen as an "ethnography" of the PKK.

In describing his life history, Deniz discussed at length the people with whom he interacted while he was in the PKK, how the organization was structured and operated, and how missions were planned and carried out. These discussions naturally opened up opportunities for the interviewer to ask Deniz questions about his own personal involvement with violence as well as about the use of violence in general by the PKK. These segments of the interviews form the basis for the present investigation and for our description of the code of the terrorist. Unless otherwise indicated, all block quotes presented in the text are from Deniz.

Whether to conceal or disclose the identity of our subject was an issue that we struggled with. Our original intent was to conceal his name, as this has long been standard practice in academic studies. For example, "Stanley" was a pseudonym invented by Clifford Shaw for the jack-roller he interviewed (Snodgrass, 1982). However, our interviewee wanted his true identity revealed, in spite of our trepidations about doing so in a society where retaliation against a family member would not be out of the ordinary. Fortunately, it was the PKK's practice to assign a new name to all its operatives, presumably to mask their true identities if captured. Our subject had been given the pseudonym of "Deniz Koçer" upon joining the PKK, and that is the name that we use in this report, but it is not the subject's real name.

Validity

Since the emergence of American criminology in the Chicago School, life histories have been employed in criminological research.

Life histories have the advantage of providing rich qualitative insights, especially on topics where gaining data are difficult, and have become classics in the field (see, e.g., Chambliss, 1990; Shaw, 1930; Steffensmeier, 1986; Sutherland, 1937). Still, because these data come from a single source, questions of validity naturally arise; after all, any interview raises the question of whether the subject is telling the truth or recalling events accurately. Although our findings will merit replication, three considerations increase our confidence in the information conveyed by Deniz in his life history.

First, Deniz had no discernable reasons to misrepresent his accounts. He had strong human subject protections. Turkey has been in the process of accession to the EU. Any state that wishes to be a member of the EU has to undertake and promote the common values of the Member States. Therefore, as a Turkish prisoner, Deniz was afforded access to lawyers whose duty it was to protect inmates' human rights. More specifically, the Institutional Review Board (IRB) protocol for this project was based on that used for studies with terrorists conducted at two other universities and was carefully vetted and approved by the first author's home institution. Deniz also was serving a life sentence so that his participation in the study could not affect his sentence in any way. Finally, despite his long-standing membership in the PKK, at the time of the interview, Deniz had limited sympathy for the organization. In a decision that led to his incarceration, Deniz had left the PKK under acrimonious terms for personal reasons and because he felt that he had been betrayed by some of his former colleagues. Thus, he had little incentive to portray the PKK in favorable terms.

Second, Deniz understood that his life history would be the basis for scholarly writings and thus that it was important that he provide information in detail and as accurately as possible if the project was to be of value. As noted, the interview format—virtually unlimited time to think, convey information, and revisit topics—was conducive to his explaining events and features of the PKK with care. After the interviews ended in May 2015, they were transcribed, resulting in more than 2,000 pages of dialogue. The transcribed interviews were returned to Deniz; he was asked to read and approve them for accuracy, which he did.

Third, to the extent possible, efforts were made to cross-check the information that Deniz provided. During the period when the data were being collected, the first author was a member of the counterterrorism department of the Turkish National Police, and in that position, he had access to official documents—court records, intelligence reports, and criminal justice records—that could be used to corroborate Deniz's accounts. His descriptions of important events and missions matched the data kept by the Turkish authorities to a remarkable degree. Indeed, Deniz not only accurately estimated the date and time of events that occurred several years in the past but also often correctly remembered the number of casualties on both sides. Further, using the resources of the Turkish National Police, the first author was able to contact two former PKK members that were mentioned by Deniz in the interviews who agreed to read the life history (arranged in the form of a 750-page story) for inaccuracy or exaggeration. Both confirmed that Deniz's story accurately portrayed what life was like in the PKK. In addition, the present manuscript was reviewed by both a former and a current member of the PKK who also confirmed that it accurately portrays the norms and codes that govern the use of violence by the PKK.

The Code of Ethics in the PKK

Terrorism is such a complex phenomenon that little consensus exists on what the term actually means or on which groups can be described as terrorists (Gibbs, 2012; Gupta, 2008; Horgan, 2003; Richardson, 2006; Silke, 2003). Despite this complexity, the terms "terrorism" and "terrorist" typically carry a negative connotation because they involve the use of deliberate and random violence primarily against noncombatants (Rapoport, 2012; Stern, 2003). Especially in the era of 9/11, people across the globe are at risk of terrorist attacks, whether from planes flown into buildings, trucks driven into pedestrians, assault weapons spraying bullets into a crowd, bombs left on subways, or knife-wielding perpetrators stabbing unsuspecting lone victims. These events are not daily occurrences, but they occur with sufficient frequency and with such stunning lethality that they constitute a realistic threat to the well-being of societies.

The unpredictable and treacherous nature of terrorist violence distinguishes it from violence in war where combatants embrace the constitutive role of morality and ethics in structuring the conduct of their soldiers (Sucharov, 2005). In fact, in today's world, the actions of several military forces are restricted by the *just cause* and the *just conduct* principles (e.g., the Geneva Convention). That is, soldiers must bind themselves to certain rules of conduct to guide their application of violence, such as under what circumstances the violence can be used and what types of violence/force can be legitimately employed against the enemy (Crawford, 2003; Gordon, 2006).

Similarly, the use of violence by the PKK is highly regulated by definitive codes. PKK members have to act in a highly normative and structured way because there is a code for every aspect of their conduct, including the use of violence. For example, there are codes for the use of violence, for punishing members' transgressions, and for the treatment of captured enemies. There is a code that controls how to respond to the violence of others. There is a code that governs the selection of targets to be destroyed. There is a code defining where and when armed actions should be taken. Moreover, there is a code that distinguishes between the moral and immoral behaviors of actors during a fight (Haner, 2018).

These codes are embedded in every PKK members' lives so that everyone—regardless of their rank and order within the group—needs to know, understand, and abide by them. Even though these codes are not published anywhere as a whole document or posted on the group's official website, PKK members' instruction on combat ethics is accomplished through three methods. First, every PKK member has to go through a continuous training program to learn these ethical principles and guidelines. The code is reinforced throughout a member's career by reviewing all aspects of the fight through a discussion and scenario-based teaching method. Second, leaders of all units have to set an example for their soldiers and support the code under any circumstances. Deniz indicated that, without the support of the commanders, it would be impossible to establish a uniform code of ethics for the PKK members. Third, to ensure that the codes are followed appropriately, the PKK enforces a system of sanctions to punish violations. Enforcement is essential to the successful implementation of the code, and like other professions, the PKK does not tolerate those who consistently violate the code of ethics and all violations are dealt with swiftly (Haner, 2018).

Thus, contrary to the common perception that the violence of terrorists is always indiscriminate and abides by no rules, the terrorism of the PKK is bound by certain rules. PKK members cannot just go out and kill someone randomly. They are not religious extremists such as the Islamic State (ISIS), under which the use of violence against defenseless people—women, children, and the old—is encouraged and considered as acceptable conduct. Contrary to many other terrorist groups, the PKK works like a military organization. Its members are guided by ethical principles and rules of conducts to protect their organizational values, to orient their day-to-day activities, to prevent unnecessary suffering, and to safeguard certain fundamental human rights of those who are involved in conflicts.

Elements of the Code

The following sections will describe the code of ethics in the PKK, which is divided into four elements: (1) legitimate and forbidden targets, (2) the principles of rules of engagement (tactics and the techniques), (3) enemy captives and detainees, and (4) private property and protected places. Later, the discussion will turn to how the PKK enforces the code.

It is important to note that, as with all the other military units, the PKK is not immune to the violation of rules. Simply having rules of conduct does not guarantee that all members of the PKK actually follow the code all of the time, especially since the actual combat environment is physically and emotionally turbulent. For example, at several points in the interviews, Deniz related how in certain situations the death of comrades can create an overpowering rage and how this rage then pushed them to violate the code of ethics or made them reluctant to report an atrocity committed by their peers.

> The passion for revenge was something that we guerillas had to be extremely careful. In some missions, we lost comrades we had known for years with whom we had eaten our meals, and with whom we shared memories. In such circumstances, our eyes would be completely blinded, and we desired to kill anyone related to the enemy, regardless of their gender or age. Those were the times we lost our rational thinking and sought nothing but revenge.

Thus, even though the PKK members understand and accept the rules of conduct in the comfort of the training environment—away from the strain of actual conflict—they may, like soldiers everywhere, suffer from lapses in character when tested by the extremes of fighting. Despite this reality, Deniz indicated that considering the large number of guerillas who serve in the organization across the Middle East, relatively few commit atrocities during missions.

Legitimate and Forbidden Targets

The PKK training curriculum classifies persons at a battlefield into two categories, combatants and noncombatants, to differentiate between legitimate targets (perpetrator of grievances) and forbidden targets (non-involved third parties).

Combatants

Combatants are defined as those who engage in hostilities including enemy soldiers, groups (or volunteers) helping the enemy (e.g., Kurdish peasants who enroll in the village protection system), and any other groups that take up arms against the PKK (e.g., Al-Qaeda, Islamic State). The PKK guerillas are allowed to use their weapons and force to attack anyone considered as combatant. They are thus legitimate targets.

However, missions against enemy combatants are considered unethical and strictly forbidden during a ceasefire or an armistice. During the cessation of hostilities (for an agreed limited time or within a limited area), missions that were already planned have to be cancelled. The PKK considers military engagement with enemy forces as dishonest during an armistice and allows the guerillas to resume fighting only after proper notification of the enemy forces.

One type of legitimate target that is unique to Kurdish conflict with Turkey is the Kurdish "rangers." The rangers, also known as "village protection guards," are armed and trained by the Turkish state to fight against the PKK in rural areas. Since the 1990s, the status of the rangers has changed over time from enemy combatants to noncombatants (or vice versa) based on their attitudes toward the PKK. Initially, the PKK did not take any military action against the rangers because the peasants registered into this village protection system out of necessity. The state of emergency and war in the countryside had limited their ability to earn a livelihood. The peasants were not allowed to graze their animals or go to the highlands to tend their fields unless they clearly showed their support to the Turkish state. Additionally, they were being forcefully relocated to other parts of the nation if they refused to serve as rangers.

However, after the mid-1990s, the PKK began to consider rangers as legitimate targets for three main reasons. First, it became almost impossible for guerillas to pass through the rangers in order to reach and attack security forces because the Turkish soldiers often camped inside (or nearby) the ranger villages. Second, to collect reward money (bounty) from the state, the rangers started to patrol the rural areas to report the activities of the guerillas to the Turkish security forces. The bounty hunting not only restricted the freedom of movement of the guerillas but also physically exhausted them, as they had to constantly move to new locations to avoid being detected by the rangers. Third, the rangers were aware of the PKK's policy not to target any Kurdish group no matter what they did. This immunity from retaliation encouraged them to use deadly force against the guerillas in hopes of being awarded large sums of money and other material rewards by the Turkish state.

Despite this status change (from noncombatants to combatants), the PKK still made efforts to reduce the deadliness of its violence by giving rangers and their villages the opportunity to disarm to avoid being attacked (Masullo & O'Connor, 2017). Even though the PKK targeted villages selectively and even though it attempted to minimize the damage to the villages that were attacked, the leaders of the PKK soon realized that the attacks were counterproductive because the collateral damage (deaths and injuries inflicted on unintended targets) had harmed the reputation of the group and turned both domestic and foreign public opinion against the PKK. Thus, to prevent noncombatant casualties and to protect its status in the international arena, the PKK outlawed the attacks and implemented a policy of reconciliation with the Kurdish rangers. A deal was struck in which the rangers were allowed to continue their service for the Turkish state "on paper" in return for providing strategic information to the PKK about the plans, tactics, and whereabouts of the security forces. Today, the rangers are not considered as enemy combatants unless they pose a clear threat to the guerillas. Deniz described how it happened.

> The completed action was now a horror for the other ranger villages to suffer. We had never taken any action against rangers until that time. We had never disproven the popular theory that the guerila would never kill their own people. Now, everyone knew we would execute missions against soldiers and rangers, if we so chose.
>
> Then, the headquarters learned that we had killed the women, children, and elderly. Immediately they sent a written order to the region. Such a mission was never to happen again, no matter what.

Noncombatants

Noncombatants include anyone who does not actively partake in the fight, such as doctors, nurses, teachers, politicians, bureaucrats, social workers, farmers, storekeepers, children, and the aged and the infirm. Noncombatants also include prisoners of war. The conduct of war ethics—also known as the "restrictive principle"—requires the PKK members to refrain from the deliberate targeting of the people listed above.

The PKK views as the real source of their oppression the governmental authorities who do not recognize the democratic rights of the Kurdish people and members of the military forces and the police who enforce Turkish cultural and political hegemony. Attacking anyone not taking up arms in the fight is thus regarded as unjust and is prohibited by the code. Accordingly, the political or ideological curriculum developed by the PKK for its guerillas does not encourage animosity toward civilians or more broadly toward the Turkish ethnic identity. In fact, PKK members have to enroll in a class called the "Democratic Republic" in which they are taught that the Turks and Kurds will eventually live together and the argument of separation from Turkey is beside the point. The Democratic Republic class is part of a training curriculum that all forces in the PKK receive. As Deniz observed:

> In all his orders and trainings, Apo always underscored the fact that, "We do not fight with the Turkish public. Ours is not a fight against the Turkish people. It is against the government and the system. There is no such thing as taking the civilians as captives or hurting a bureaucrat or a deputy. We can't solve the problem by acting from the desire for revenge and killing innocent people. On the contrary, if we used such a method, we would lose the validity of our own struggle. So, although it is right that we fight for our own people, we should never include innocent people in this war."

Related to this principle, the PKK also views indiscriminate attacks as unjust because noncombatants may be killed. Guerillas are only allowed to attack legitimate military targets. By contrast, they must make efforts to ensure that noncombatants are distinguished so as to limit the mission's collateral damage—especially civilians' injury or loss of life.

Finally, the restrictive principle also forbids the targeting of noncombatants even when it is required for the successful completion of the mission. For example, attacking enemy combatants who are traveling on public transportation, or shopping at open-air markets and malls, where civilians are also present, is not legitimate. Thus, the killing of civilians, even when it is integral to the completion of the mission, is not allowed and is subject to punishment. If civilians or noncombatants could possibly be hurt because of a mission, the mission should be performed with great care so as to avoid collateral damage. Still, in the past, civilians lost their lives occasionally as an unintended consequence of guerilla missions. As a result, the restrictive principle was updated over the years and now states that most missions should be aborted if they cannot be accomplished without risking the lives of noncombatants.

The PKK forbids attacks on noncombatants because such acts often serve to increase the level of hostility between the parties of the conflict and weaken the influence of the moderate forces on both sides who advocate for a peaceful settlement. Accordingly, PKK leaders argue that adherence to such standards (e.g., not targeting civilians) can facilitate the reestablishment of peaceful relations after the conflict ends. Further, the PKK has an obligation to act within international law to protect its status because international support for its constituency depends on the extent to which ethical guidelines are actually observed. In today's world, not only the legitimacy of their use of revolutionary violence, but also adherence to ethical standards, are important for sustaining continued international and popular support. Therefore, the PKK imposes certain obligations on its guerillas (e.g., avoiding injuring civilians) since ethical lapses can make the front-page news and diminish public trust in the PKK.

The Rules of Engagement

The PKK limits its armed activities to self-defense and for retaliatory purposes. However, both of these armed activities need to follow a strict guideline that details the conditions of engaging enemy forces, the kind and degree of violence that can be used, and the ways to fight justly in a battle. These rules, commonly known as the "rules of engagement" (or restraints on the use of force), are composed of three main principles: (1) necessity, (2) distinction, and (3) proportionality and de-escalation.

Necessity

The "necessity principle" dictates that there needs to be a just cause for attacking enemy forces. The PKK describes just cause as the existence of a hostile act or intent. The guerillas have the right to engage with the force necessary to stop the threat when one of these conditions exists. Different levels of force can be used incrementally to secure the enemy's submission or to destroy the enemy threat.

The incremental use of force is important because the group has to consider the domestic and international political repercussions of its military engagements. In the past, the more members of the enemy security forces that were killed, the more successful the guerillas would be considered. However, this calculus changed because the PKK is now enmeshed in world politics. It cannot risk its relations and legitimacy with world powers by carrying out predatory or proactive attacks that are seen as excessive (e.g., a needless massacre). Thus, the guerillas are only allowed to use violence strategically to achieve specific goals, such as neutralizing attacks (self-defense) or exacting a measure of retribution (retaliation).

For example, the guerillas are not allowed to attack garrisons if the soldiers stationed in there have pledged not to attack them. Turkey has a large collection of military bases located in distant rural areas in which thousands of troops are permanently stationed. Originally, the idea of having this many garrisons resulted from the Turkish government's perceived need to assert control in the countryside—to hem in and contain the PKK's supposed domination in the region. However, the cost of garrisoning the region was high because the PKK simply undertook hit-and-run attacks whenever it wished to inflict damage on these hundreds of isolated police stations and military posts across this region. Thus, these military installations actually decreased the security of the soldiers, as they made for vulnerable and thus attractive targets for the guerillas. Soldiers who were already experiencing the strain of distant deployment and family separation did not want to take the risk of death by engaging with guerillas. Deniz indicated that, especially during the late 1990s, as soon as they noticed the presence of the guerillas in their areas, soldiers would contact the guerillas. The soldiers would inform them that they would not interfere with the guerrillas' infiltrating into Turkey as long as the soldiers' stations were not targeted. According to Deniz, both groups were weary of fighting, and that is why they reached an informal agreement to ignore each other.

> While we were patrolling within our territory in 1994, a Turkish military post commander contacted us via radio. "Fellas, do not cross into my area, and I promise I will not carry out missions against you in the

countryside. Do whatever you want in other areas. I do not care!" One of our guerilla commanders replied to him, "Okay, we will not! We will never lay siege to your post, no matter how many soldiers you have there, as long as you do not carry out any mission against us!" The military commander accepted our terms. Even back then, the soldiers were sick of fighting and losing their friends, just as we guerillas were.

The fighting near the border posts were really just a sham. We had scratched the soldiers' back, and they had scratched ours. This still goes on in the region.

Not all the military stations were like this, of course, but the stations on the plains held the attitude that, "If you do not interfere in our business, we won't interfere in yours."

Beyond self-defense, PKK members are also authorized to use force during retaliatory missions ordered by their commanders. These guerilla tactics include assault, ambush, raid, infiltration, siege, forestallment, mining, and assassination. Two factors, however, must be considered before an attack can be initiated. First, actions against the enemy must not violate the code of ethics. For example, in an assassination mission, targeting an important figure in the military is allowed, but the assassination of a civilian or a political figure is strictly prohibited. Another example would be launching an unlawful reprisal attack (e.g., a chemical response to a chemical attack, or killing Turkish civilians if Turkish soldiers attack Kurdish civilians).

Second, the military engagement should be postponed if it poses a serious risk to the lives of the guerillas in the unit. The unit commander must initially make a feasibility analysis by acting on the best available information (e.g., analysis of the intelligence, the number of soldiers to be destroyed, whether there is a support group that would come to the help of the soldiers, possible escape routes after the attack). Then, the commander must make a recommendation to the chain of command for the use of deadly force, showing that the attack can be accomplished without a heavy loss. While the commander in the field makes the ultimate decision regarding the use of force, this leader would risk discipline (even prosecution) if the governing rules of engagement were violated and the engagement goes awry.

The soldiers were stupidly walking in a group, and only 10 to 15 meters away from us—a convenient target. We easily could have killed them all. It was our ignorance of not knowing where we were that prevented us from taking this opportunity. If we had shot them, where would we run? Where could we hide? We could not take the chance.

We could see hundreds of soldiers patrolling the field. Some of the comrades became angry with me, saying, "Comrade Deniz, why on earth are we not killing those soldiers while they walk right across from us like sitting ducks?" From this reaction, you could see that they were clearly inexperienced. They did not consider the possible consequences of such an abrupt attack on the soldiers. In a sense, they were right; the soldiers were walking one behind the other, without leaving any space for security. Just three of us could easily have killed them all with Kalashnikovs. However, it would be dangerous for us later, because there were hundreds of other soldiers in the field, and eventually they would kill us all in the end.

Related to this second rule, the guerillas are not allowed to carry out an attack while sequestered in their winter camp or, in the fall season, when preparations for the camp are undertaken. During this time, the PKK establishes living quarters for active guerillas in the countryside that are located in bunkers constructed underground and in caves. Armed initiatives are prohibited because any contact with the enemy during this period would alert them to the presence of the PKK in the area and lead them to conduct searches to detect and destroy camp locations. Thus, the guerrillas would absolutely avoid any contact in the fall.

Soldiers often carried out missions trying to detect our bunkers and even sometimes walked just above us. We could hear their voices, but they were unaware of our presence. If we had wanted to, we could kill them all without losing a single guerilla. However, our actions would reveal our bunker location to the security forces, so, no matter what happened, we would do nothing but wait quietly until winter was over.

Distinction

Positive identification of the enemy combatants is required prior to any engagement because, as noted, the PKK uses a discriminate attack strategy—combatants are distinguished from noncombatants. Thus, the guerillas must be reasonably certain that the proposed target is a legitimate enemy target before using deadly force. If the guerillas are not sufficiently confident that the target is the source of the threat, they are required to cancel it and inform their commander for a decision.

Our scouting showed that there were no civilians left inside the village. This would make our raid much easier, because we would not have to worry about the risk of killing civilians by mistake.

As soon as our mission began, I heard the screams of women coming from one of the houses in the village. I immediately contacted the other guerillas on the radio and said, "Do not attack this house, there are probably civilians hiding inside."

However, guerillas have the right to engage directly, and without discrimination, if they are ambushed by enemy combatants who are intermixed among civilians. This situation is difficult because the counterattack can cause incidental loss of civilian life, injury to civilians, and damage to civilian objects. But if the enemy is using a village and/or civilians as cover and concealment, they make them a legitimate target for the guerillas.

... it was sometimes difficult to fight in the countryside without killing innocent people, for reasons that were out of our control. For example, we would sometimes be put under heavy fire from a house in a village. Someone would be shooting at us from the door or the windows of the house. We would not know who else might be inside the house, but in order to protect ourselves in those situations, we would use a rocket-propelled grenade to destroy the house. However, we never had a clear conscience about whoever else might have been in that house. There was no way of finding out if there had been women, children, or elderly people hiding in there, therefore, it was morally difficult for us to attack an enclosed target.

Proportionality and De-escalation

The use of force must be not only necessary but also proportional. This rule protects enemy combatants from superfluous injury and useless suffering. That is, the nature and the extent of the harm to enemy fighters must not exceed what is required to counter the threat and it should be in proportion to the mission they are assigned.

In the midst of a hostile act, the guerillas can use their weapons and force sufficient to respond decisively to counter the threat, so as to ensure the continued safety of the PKK forces. They can proportionally use whatever means necessary, including deadly force, when they have positively identified a hostile act against them. For example, if the guerillas have been attacked by a group of people who are hiding in a village, they have the right to destroy the target by firing on the enemy attackers. If the attackers are intermixed among civilian peasants as a cover and concealment, the guerillas still have the right to protect themselves by force, but the force should be reasonable in nature, duration, and scope. They should fire with due regard for the safety of innocent bystanders, should fire no more rounds than necessary, and should stop firing as soon as the situation de-escalates. If the threat is neutralized, the enemy should be given the opportunity to withdraw or surrender, based on all the facts known to the commander at that time. Pointless extermination (or unnecessary suffering) is not allowed if the enemy has already submitted or stopped being a threat.

> When their reinforcements didn't arrive and they had no way to replenish their ammunition, both the rangers and the soldiers fled down the route of escape that we intentionally opened for them. We let them all escape.
> We left an exit open. We knew the soldiers were going to see it and leave the area without making any further stand against us. The soldiers in the station knew very well that they wouldn't receive any reinforcements at this time of night.

Similarly, for retaliatory missions, force can be used to execute a mission, but only to the extent required. The decisions and actions should minimize unnecessary suffering to the enemy. That is, the guerillas have to take special efforts not to cause destruction beyond the requirement of the assigned mission.

> At 11:00 p.m., we raided the station. We killed nine of the soldiers and sustained no losses. We withdrew from the battlefield at about one in the morning. Our mission had been to disable the station, not to kill every soldier.

Enemy Captives/Detainees

Besides having regulations that govern the rules of engagement with the enemy, the PKK has specific rules that offer fundamental rights to surrendered, wounded, sick, and captured enemy, regardless of their prior conduct. According to these rules, all persons that are detained or captured on the battlefield should be treated humanely. They cannot be subject to mistreatment, such as deprivation, abuse, starvation, and physical or psychological torture. It is prohibited to kill enemy combatants if they can be taken out of action through capture. That is, if capturing is an effective possibility (e.g., if it does not endanger the lives of the guerillas), then killing an enemy fighter is considered unnecessary and prohibited by the code of ethics.

Additionally, guerillas are not allowed to use force against wounded enemy soldiers that are already unable to fight. Thus, when an individual becomes *hors de combat* (out of action due to an injury), he or she becomes immune from any kind of attack. Only a strictly necessary amount of force—such as to weaken the wounded enemies' resistance to surrender and keep them under control—can be used to capture them. But once they are taken as captives, the wounded should be treated properly.

> Even in the military trainings, the instructors were emphasizing that we were to be merciful to the enemy. It was impressed upon us that an injured enemy would never be hurt no further, but rather be taken captive and be treated.

Further, enemy soldiers should be allowed to surrender when they clearly express an intention to do so. Those who surrender should never be attacked or killed, because they are considered noncombatants once they stop showing signs of threat. However, they can be made prisoners so that they cannot attack the guerillas again and can then be used as a bargaining chip in exchange for incarcerated PKK members. Similar to the enemy captives in war, the surrendered enemy combatants should be treated with dignity and respect. However, both the captives and the surrendered forfeit their status if they engage in a hostile act (e.g., attempt to escape) while under the custody of the guerillas. In such a case, the guerillas have the right to take countermeasures—including lethal force if there is no other way to prevent them from escaping—until the perpetrator is pacified.

It should be noted that the PKK has not been successful in prisoner exchange with the Turkish authorities who refuse to negotiate. Despite this reality, the group continues to detain and hold enemy soldiers and host them in their camps to show the conditions in which the guerillas are living and working. Later, these enemy combatants are released as a propaganda tool—in the hopes of gaining the sympathy of the Turkish public.

> It made us look very good if we released our prisoners even if the Turkish Government did not accede at all to our demands to negotiate.

A ceremony was held for delivery of our Turkish hostages back to their families. The Turkish families were grateful for this act by the PKK.

Finally, the guerillas are not allowed to detain female enemy combatants or civilians under any circumstances due to the risk of sexual accusations. Even if they surrender, the women have to be freed in a safe location, rather than taken as captives to the PKK camps. In the past, the guerillas were blamed for the rape and sexual abuse of women captives, which seriously tarnished the reputation of the organization and worsened the group's relations with its supporters. Therefore, the risk that women captives would be sexually molested—or would be portrayed in this way—prompted the PKK to discontinue holding females as prisoners of war.

Private Property and Protected Places

The guerillas are required to treat civilian property with respect and dignity. They are not allowed to terrorize civilians by ravaging their property or forcing them to move and resettle to other locations. They are not allowed to fire into civilian homes, buildings, or any other property unless it represents a security threat for the guerillas (e.g., if the enemy forces are using civilian populated areas or buildings for military purposes).

Additionally, guerillas have no right to seize civilians' belongings, including vehicles, food, animals, crops, and other valuable items unless they pay the equivalent value of the items to the owner. Under extreme circumstances (such as the shortage of food or medical items), with the permission of their company commander, the guerillas are entitled to seize items from peasants by providing a receipt to the owner, indicating that the monetary value of the items would be paid later. The PKK has strict punishment for the violation of this code because the survival of the PKK depends on the support of the villagers. The guerillas often are given access to provisions such as food, drink, and medical items through the villagers who support the PKK. Further, they sometimes need to stay and hide in peasants' houses when they patrol the countryside. Thus, any kind of behavior that would damage this relationship with the peasants is subject to punishment.

But it was occasionally reported in the Turkish media that the organization forcibly confiscated the property of innocent villagers and held them for ransom. This is nothing but a lie. For example, in the winter of 1994, we needed a heater for our winter camp. We found such a stove in one of the summerhouses, and we left twice as much money as was the value of the stove. We never had an attitude to usurp the property of the people, although I cannot vouch for everyone in this regard, because not every human being is as scrupulous. Some got what they needed from villagers and paid no money in return. But I am telling you, the overall perspective of the organization was one of honesty and fairness. If the organization heads heard something like that, you would get direct criticism or punishment, and you would be accused of being a thief.

For example, if you were walking along during the day, or entered into a field at night, and saw tomatoes, watermelons, or other things and took them without the owner's consent, the organization would directly accuse you of theft. An investigation would be ordered, and some compensation would be paid to the family.

It should be noted, however, that the PKK has allowed its guerilas to confiscate the belongings of shepherds who spy for the Turkish authorities. Even though they would not engage in any hostilities against the guerillas, the shepherds would carry out reconnaissance missions for the security forces about the activities and locations of the guerillas under the guise of animal grazing. Thus, the guerillas are entitled to put the shepherds out of action by capturing them and confiscating their animals.

In addition to civilian property, some buildings and structures are not considered valid targets by the PKK's code of ethics. Known as "protected places," these structures include some historical, cultural, medical, and religious sites (such as mosques, churches, hospitals (also ambulances), schools, museums, monuments) or parts of the enemy's infrastructure (such as dams, tunnels, bridges, and public works). Striking these structures is forbidden. However, if the enemy forces are using these structures to stage an attack against PKK units, then they become valid military targets. For example, if enemy forces are staging an attack from a hospital or school, the guerillas have the right to fire on these structures. When engaging these sites, the goal should be to disable and disrupt the enemy soldiers, rather than their complete destruction. Any damage to these properties during the engagement with the enemy must be reported to headquarters because these situations may undermine the reputation of the PKK.

Finally, the PKK's code of ethics prohibits the confiscation of enemy combatants' belongings during natural disasters. For example, it is unethical to collect the weapons and ammunition of enemy soldiers who died in a traffic accident. Similarly, the PKK does not allow the plunder of military posts that had been hit by avalanches.

> When we reached the first village, the villagers told us there was a Turkish military outpost located very close to the village. It had been hit by an avalanche, and around 40 Turkish soldiers had been buried and killed. The villagers suggested that we could collect all their weapons and ammunition. The experienced ones among us criticized this offer harshly. "A natural disaster happened, and it would be against the morals of the organization to profit from the spoils in such a situation."

Enforcement of the Code

The PKK seeks to safeguard the code by enforcing compliance with its mandates in three ways: (1) training, (2) by setting the leaders as exemplary role models, and (3) by enforcement. First, the topics around combat ethics are incorporated into the guerilla training curriculum. Again, for PKK operatives, training is constant and includes not only military exercises but also classroom-like courses that reinforce the PKK's organizational ideology and procedures. In this regard, each guerilla must know and obey the rules discussed above, virtually "word for word." However, the reason for the existence of each rule is explained with real-world examples so guerillas would not question them. Thus, there is no imposition without clear understanding of the logic behind each rule.

> The trainings on ethics were very significant in shaping our thoughts. At first, many of us had joined the organization out of passion and emotion alone. Most militants were acting purely from the bloodlust of "When do we get our weapons? When do I get my revenge?" The experienced ones knew they had to first convince us to understand the aim and purpose of the organization. Only in this way, would all of our actions align with the organization's goal.

Additionally, as the code is regarded as a living document (that is, the PKK assesses and makes improvements to the code as necessary), the guerillas are required to refresh their knowledge of the rules year-round through various training activities.

Second, the leaders of all units must set an example and support the compliance of the code as much as possible. If the commanders do not follow the rules, it could set a precedent that allows low-ranking guerillas to be similarly neglectful, and that would risk attenuating the core values that form the foundation of the organization. Thus, the PKK not only does not tolerate the violation of the codes by high-ranking guerillas, but it also subjects them to heavier punishments compared to foot soldiers. Commanders with decades of experience can be dismissed from their positions and lowered to the rank of a regular guerila, even after a simple violation of the code.

Third, and most importantly, the code is enforced by an organizational commitment to zero-tolerance of violations. The PKK has a system of reporting bad conduct, having trials, and sanctioning those who are convicted. As Deniz related, even though the guerrillas pledge to be loyal to the code of conduct, the continuous struggle for physical survival, the natural stirring of emotions such as vengeance and anger, and the unremitting reality of death and violence would sometimes overcome ethical training:

> There was left only the women, children, and elderly people in the village. The commander ordered our comrades to put the rest of the people into a line to be executed by firing squad.
>
> Although it was contrary to the rules of guerrillas, we broke our own code when PKK forces killed 33 Turkish soldiers. These soldiers were unarmed and defenseless ...
>
> The youngest guerila of us all was martyred in this ambush. His head was severed from his body, his organs were removed, and his feet were pulverized. We were enraged. We ambushed these rangers and killed them all. One of the men next to me said, "Comrade, if you let me, I want to bash the body of this asshole into pieces, just like he did with the body of our friend." We were all highly emotional. I told him, "Go and do whatever you want to him but don't touch the corpses of the others." He first cut off the nose and the ears of the ranger. Then he beheaded him.
>
> His emotions caused him to react in a way that ruined the purpose of the mission. Some civilians had run and hid inside a house during the battle. He set the house on fire, though he was fully aware that there were women, children, and old people inside.
>
> While the mission plan could have been applied in traditional ways, this comrade was cruel in his execution of it. ... the guerillas, under his command, frog-marched this group of 16 rangers and soldiers and executed them by firing squad. But even this atrocity was insufficient for the commander, he ordered his guerrillas to throw the corpses in the van and light the van on fire.

Regardless of the rationale for engaging in these kinds of acts, there is prosecution for such misconduct. All rules and associated penalties are clearly defined, and the guerillas are continually reminded about them. For example, killing of an unarmed enemy combatant (when killing is unnecessary to achieve a military end) can result in a penalty of up to six years' suspension from the organization. Suspension of membership from the organization is the most severe sanction for a guerrilla because a member with a suspension can neither participate in the meetings nor provide opinion in organizational matters. From Deniz's own words, "Though they are allowed to stay among us, they are ostracized, and considered to not exist." If the person repeats the same offense for a second time, he/she is dismissed from the group.

The PKK encourages social control by employing a violation-reporting (self-regulation) and evaluation system. By providing the guerillas with these options to report the noncompliance issues, the PKK maintains the enforcement of the code and helps its members to remain within the ethical boundaries. Under the self-regulation system, everyone, regardless of their rank and position, has a responsibility to report the actual or suspected violation of the code through the chain of command or through other appropriate investigative branches. Similarly, guerillas have a duty to prevent criminal acts before they occur. Orders that violate the code of conduct are not supposed to be followed, and appropriate PKK authorities are required to be immediately notified.

The guerillas can disclose violations by sending a report to the appropriate authority. The report should include specific information about the description of the alleged violation, the sequence of the events and the consequences of the violation, the intention of the accused (whether it was accidental, intentional, or unknown), affected subjects, and any communication between the complainant and the person in alleged violation of the rules. If more than one guerilla committed the same violation, separate reports should be submitted for each case.

The complainant has to provide contact information for the headquarters to review the tip or the complaint. However, the headquarters is responsible for safeguarding the complainant's confidentiality. As another safeguard of the security of the reporting system, reports can only be opened by the office to which they are sent. No other office of the organization can open a report, even if it is mistakenly delivered to them. Violation of this rule requires the dismissal of the person from the PKK.

The investigative branch reviews the complaints and contacts necessary parties for additional information to determine whether an investigation into the matter is warranted. If the claims are substantiated, then a committee would be charged, and a trial date is set for the involved parties. The defendant can be held under custody or set free until the trial date, based on the scale of the misconduct. Before the trial, the investigation committee informs the accused about the charges. The trials are conducted in front of other guerillas, where the defendant is required to stand on a stage. The accusations are read in front of the entire group, and then the defendant is given a chance to respond to the critiques that have been leveled. Based on the judgment, the accused can be acquitted or found guilty. All decisions are open to appeal. Thus, the defendant can ask for a retrial if he or she believes that there was a miscarriage of justice.

Further, the PKK uses an evaluation system for assessing each military mission. Following a mission, the guerillas have to evaluate the pros and cons of the engagement. Each guerilla is expected to provide a verbal statement to questions such as whether the mission was performed as planned and whether any kind of violations occurred. A decision is then made regarding the appropriate response to those who violated the codes. All the officers and commanders are assessed during these platforms. If the group does not approve of the performance, war tactics, or the behaviors of a guerilla during the mission, it can immediately elect to dismiss that person. Although those at the rank of company commander or above cannot be dismissed from their duties by this process, operatives are required to report any of their violations of the code to authorities at PKK headquarters who are empowered to sanction PKK leaders.

Conclusion: Terrorism, Violence, and the PKK

Violence is not only an objective reality but also can be socially constructed in diverse ways that have disparate policy implication. As juvenile urban violence spiked in the 1990s, John Dilulio (1995) depicted wayward youths as "super-predators." As he observed, "We're talking about kids who have absolutely no respect for human life and no sense of the future" (p. 23). He later described them as suffering from "moral poverty" and lamented that the only solution for most of these lost souls was long-term incarceration (Bennett et al., 1996). By contrast (Elijah Anderson, 1999) years on the streets of Philadelphia yielded a very different understanding. Violence was not rooted in individual pathology but shaped by an emergent culture—which he called the "code of the street"—that dictated the circumstances under which violent acts occurred. Equally important, cultural endorsement of violence did not arise out of thin air but was produced by a history of racial oppression and contemporary disadvantage that robbed the conventional order of its legitimacy. For Anderson (1999, p. 325) the policy solution was not to provide more prison cells but to provide more jobs—to "reestablish a viable mainstream economy."

Although a very different topic, how terrorism is understood—a product of wanton, undeterrable pathology versus a response to oppression governed by a code—has significant policy ramification. Thus, terrorists are often described as cold-blooded mindless murderers who use violence against innocent victims with no regard for the pain and suffering that they cause or for the collateral consequences of their actions. For the opponents of a terrorist organization, this rhetorical strategy makes good sense as it objectifies and dehumanizes the group's members and thus excuses the use of severe and indiscriminate violence against them. This narrative certainly holds in regard to the Turkish government's portrayal of the PKK and the government's reaction to the organization and its supporters. Portraying the PKK as brutally and indiscriminately violent is a means by which the government can thwart peace talks and suppress Kurdish demands for cultural and political autonomy. By describing PKK violence as being directed against innocent and defenseless Turks, the government has created an enduring sense of grievance against the PKK and Kurds in general, making the idea of forgiveness unthinkable. Portraying violence by the PKK as random, the government creates the impression that the organization is run by irrational people who will never negotiate in good faith. Hence, the only way to deal with the PKK is to fight violence with violence.

The plight of the PKK in Turkey, however, has grown even more precarious following the unsuccessful coup attempt in 2016 against President Recep Tayyip Erdogan. In the aftermath of this event, the Erdogan government moved to consolidate control and assume authoritarian power. The administration has engaged in a systematic crackdown that has led to extensive human rights violations and to the imprisonment of security and justice personnel, members of the professional classes, and anyone suspected of being an opponent of the regime. During this period, the Kurdish minority has been scapegoated and defined as politically dangerous. Several democratically elected Kurdish lawmakers were arrested, Kurdish mayors were removed from their offices, tens of thousands of teachers working in Kurdish regions were suspended from their instructional activities, and dozens of Kurdish media outlets were shut down for what Erdogan called the spreading of terrorist propaganda (Yeginsu & Timur, 2016). More steps have been taken to exterminate the PKK. Hard-line militarist rhetoric from Turkish leaders is now commonly reported in the media—as these statements illustrate: "The military operations against the PKK will continue until the very last rebel is killed" (Ben-Meir, 2017b), "Sooner or later, we will have our vengeance. This blood will not be left on the ground, no matter what the price, what the cost" (*Al Jazeera*, 2016).

It is doubtful, though, that this goal will be reached. This sort of state-sanctioned repressive violence risks evoking an oppositional response from those it targets, leading not to reduced terrorism but to a cycle of violence. This outcome is especially likely when the use of state violence occurs—as has been the case with the Turkish government's attempt to repress the PKK and stifle its demands—over a lengthy period of time and its effects are widespread (see Mason & Krane, 1989). In fact, Mason (1989) argues that the threat and actuality of violence by the state is what really drives noncombatants to join revolutionary resistance groups, not the promise of reward or the appeal of an ideology. Although we agree with Mason that state-sponsored terrorism, which certainly has been practiced against the Kurds, can be an important motivating factor for individuals to join the PKK, the PKK's ideology is nevertheless also a drawcard.

Importantly, the Turkish government's portrayal of the PKK does not match reality—according to the former member and leader of the organization interviewed here, and according to other researchers—in that the PKK does not use violence indiscriminately (Masullo & O'Connor, 2017). Rather, the PKK's use of violence is governed by a code comprising a set of rules, rules that the organization enforces through both formal and informal mechanisms. Its use of violence is organizationally guided, politically purposeful, restrained, and responsive to Turkish oppression. In other words, as a court in Brussels recently ruled, it is misleading to describe the PKK as a terrorist organization. It is more accurately conceptualized as a party to a civil war with Turkey (*Flanders News.Be*, 2017). Other commentators have gone further and noted that the PKK has evolved into a vital ally in the West's fight against radical Islam (Levy, 2014).

Not all "terrorist" groups are the same—an obvious reality but one that is often overlooked. As noted, the PKK has secular roots in liberation ideology. Unlike ISIS and similar Islamic-rooted organizations, it is not conducting a jihad or attempting to inflict death and injury on Western nations, whether soldiers in the Middle East or in their home nations. The PKK's intent is to be viewed as "freedom fighters" who use violence purposively and not in ways that would erode support from Western nations, especially in Europe.

Even so, the PKK is often categorized as a terrorist organization by Western observers not only because of misinformation spread by Turkish authorities but also because Western observers hold to what Masullo and O'Connor (2017) term an "ontological individualism" in which individual involvement in a specific act is what determines culpability. From this perspective, any individual who does not personally take up arms against the PKK is by definition an "innocent civilian" and if that person's death is caused by the PKK, either intentionally or as a result of collateral damage, he or she automatically is seen as the victim of a terrorist act committed by terrorists. However, this view of the PKK and its actions ignores the sociocultural context in which the PKK operates. In rural Kurdistan, the fundamental societal unit of analysis has historically been the tribe rather than the individual. Culpability for acts committed by one person historically has been generalized to the members of his or her tribe. Although this historical tradition is weakening (Masullo & O'Connor, 2017), it still plays a role in how the PKK selects targets and carries out its operations. As Masullo and O'Connor (2017) argue, the PKK sometimes engages in collective targeting in which groups of individuals, some of whom may be "innocent" from the perspective of Western observers, are the targets of extreme violence. These killings, however, are not indiscriminate. Rather, they are seen by the PKK as steps that are necessary, even if regrettable, for self-preservation and to pursue the larger goals of cultural and political autonomy for Kurds.

In this context, the goal in this chapter has been to describe the code that governs the PKK's use of violence in its conflict with Turkey so that the PKK's actions can be better understood. As with any code of conduct, there will be, of course, occasional deviations and lapses in observance, but, as noted above, the PKK has established policies and procedures to minimize such events and to correct them when they happen. For the most part, violence by the PKK is purposeful, restrained, and used only when necessary to respond to Turkish oppression. To characterize the PKK's use of violence as indiscriminate is to simply misunderstand what they are doing and why they are doing it and this sort of misunderstanding inevitably undermines any chance at peace. Prospects for a peaceful solution to the conflict between Turkey and the Kurds will be improved only when Turkey accepts that the PKK is not a terrorist organization populated by bloodthirsty and irrational radicals. Rather, it is a political organization pursuing political aims that should be settled at the negotiating table and not on the battlefield.

References

A News (2017). PKK, bloody terrorist organization, admits its own collapse. *A News*, November 1. Available at: www.anews.com.tr/turkey/2017/11/01/pkk-bloody-terrorist-organization-admits-its-own-collapse.

Agence France-Presse (2015). Erdogan vows Turkey will attack PKK "to last terrorist." *The Jordan Times*, August 11. Available at: www.jordantimes.com/news/region/erdogan-vows-turkey-will-attack-pkk-last-terrorist%E2%80%99.

Akyol, M. (2016). Something worse on the Kurdish front. *Hurriyet Daily News*, May 4. Available at: www.hurriyetdailynews.com/opinion/mustafa-akyol/something-worse-on-the-kurdish-front-98682.

Al Jazeera. (2016). Istanbul: Armed group TAK claims deadly attack. *Al Jazeera*, December 11. Available at: www.aljazeera.com/news/2016/12/istanbul-armed-group-tak-claims-deadly-attack-161211132135392.html.

Altun, F. (2016). What is the relationship between US and the PKK? *Foundation for Political, Economic, and Social Research (SETA)*, August 19. Available at: www.setav.org/en/what-is-the-relationship-between-us-and-the-pkk/.

Anderson, E. (1999). *The code of the street: Decency, violence, and the moral life of the inner city.* New York: W.W. Norton.

Arslan, S. (2017). PKK camps exposed as rape and torture centers by female militants. *The Daily Sabah*, February 1. Available at: www.dailysabah.com/war-on-terror/2017/02/01/pkk-camps-exposed-as-rape-and-torture-centers-by-female-militants.

Atinabe. (2017). Children driven to death by the PKK. *The Turkish Embassy in Athens*, June 27. Available at: https://atinabe.blogspot.com/2017/06/children-driven-to-death-by-pkk.html.

Aydinli, E., & Ozcan, N.A. (2011). The conflict resolution and counterterrorism dilemma: Turkey faces its Kurdish question. *Terrorism and Political Violence*, 23, 438–457.

Bacik, G., & Coskun, B.B. (2011). The PKK problem: Explaining Turkey's failure to develop a political solution. *Studies in Conflict & Terrorism*, 34, 248–265.

Ben-Meir, A. (2017a). Turkey and the PKK: Mutual violence is not the answer. *The Huffington Post*. Available at: www.huffingtonpost.com/alon-benmeir/turkey-and-the-pkk-mutual_b_12141604.html.

Ben-Meir, A. (2017b). The Kurds under Erdogan's tyrannical governance. *The Huffington Post*, July 5. Available at: www.huffingtonpost.com/entry/the-kurds-under-erdogans-tyrannical-governance_us_595cef79e4b0c85b96c66561.

Bengio, O. (2016). Game changers: Kurdish women in peace and war. *The Middle East Journal*, 70, 30–46.

Bennett, W.J., Dilulio Jr., J.J., & Walters, J.P. (1996). *Body count: Moral poverty and how to win America's war against crime and drugs.* New York: Simon & Schuster.

Beriker-Atiyas, N. (1997). The Kurdish conflict in Turkey: Issues, parties and prospects. *Security Dialogue,* 28, 439–452.

Brezina, T., Agnew, R., Cullen, F.T., & Wright, J.P. (2004). The code of the street: A quantitative assessment of Elijah Anderson's subculture of violence thesis and its contribution to youth violence research. *Youth Violence and Juvenile Justice,* 2, 303–328.

Çandar, C. (2012). *Leaving the mountain: How may the PKK lay down arms? Freeing the Kurdish question from violence.* Istanbul, TR: Turkish Economic and Social Studies Foundation.

Celebi, E. (2010). Female seperatism: The role of women in the PKK/KONGRA-GEL terrorist organization. *Terrorism and the Internet: Threats—Target Groups—Deradicalisation Strategies,* 67, 105.

Chambliss, W.J. (1990). *Harry King: A professional thief's journey.* New York: Macmillan.

Cline, L.E. (2004). From Ocalan to Al Qaida: The continuing terrorist threat in Turkey. *Studies in Conflict & Terrorism,* 27, 321–335.

Crawford, N.C. (2003). Just war theory and the US counterterror war. *Perspectives on Politics,* 1(1), 5–25.

Daily Sabah. (2017). PKK continues to target civilians, 2 more workers killed. *The Daily Sabah,* September 7. Available at: www.dailysabah.com/turkey/2017/09/07/pkk-continues-to-target-civilians-2-more-workers-killed.

De Bellaigue, C. (2009). *Rebel land: Among Turkey's forgotten peoples.* New York: Bloomsbury.

De Jong, A. (2016). A commune in Rojava? *New Politics,* 15, 69.

Dilulio Jr., J.J. (1995). The coming of the super-predators. *The Weekly Standard,* November 27, pp. 23–28. Available at: www.washingtonexaminer.com/weekly-standard/the-coming-of-the-super-predators.

Düzgün, M. (2016). Jineology: The Kurdish women's movement. *Journal of Middle East,* 12, 284–287.

Entessar, N. (1992). *Kurdish ethno-nationalism.* Boulder, CO: Lynn Rienner Publishers.

Ergil, D. (2000). The Kurdish question in Turkey. *Journal of Democracy,* 11, 122–135.

Eyrice, I.U. (2013). Roots and causes that created the PKK terrorist organization. (Doctoral dissertation). Monterey, CA: Naval Postgraduate School. Available at: https://calhoun.nps.edu/bitstream/handle/10945/37625/13Sep_Eyrice_Idris.pdf?sequence=1.

Feridun, M., & Sezgin, S. (2008). Regional underdevelopment and terrorism: The case of south eastern Turkey. *Defence and Peace Economics,* 19, 225–233.

Flanders News.Be. (2017). Brussels court rules that the PKK is not a terrorist organization, September 16. Available at: http://deredactie.be/cm/vrtnieuws.english/News/1.3066647.

Geoghegan, V. (2003). *Political ideologies: An introduction.* New York: Routledge.

Gibbs, J.P. (2012). Conceptualization of terrorism. In J. Horgan & K. Braddock (Eds.), *Terrorism studies: A reader.* New York: Routledge, pp. 63–76.

Gordon, A. (2006). "Purity of arms," "preemptive war," and "selective targeting" in the context of terrorism: General, conceptual, and legal analyses. *Studies in Conflict & Terrorism*, 29, 493–508.
Gunter, M.M. (2000). The continuing Kurdish problem in Turkey after Ocalan's capture. *Third World Quarterly*, 21, 849–869.
Gupta, D.K. (2008). *Understanding terrorism and political violence: The life cycle of birth, growth, transformation, and demise.* New York: Routledge.
Haner, M. (2018). *The freedom fighter: A terrorist's own story.* New York: Routledge.
Horgan, J. (2003). The search for the terrorist personality. In A. Silke (Ed.), *Terrorists, victims, and society: Psychological perspectives on terrorism and its consequences.* Hoboken, NJ: Wiley, pp. 3–29.
Hurriyet Daily News. (2015). PKK bomb attack hits public offices, hospital in Turkey's southeast. *Hurriyet Daily News*, October 22. Available at: www.hurriyetdailynews.com/pkk-bomb-attack-hits-public-offices-hospital-in-turkeys-southeast-90197.
International Crisis Group. (2012). The PKK and a Kurdish settlement, Europe Report no. 219, September 11. Istanbul/Brussels: ICG.
Izady, M.R. (1992). *The Kurds: A concise history and fact book.* Washington, DC: Taylor & Francis.
Jackson, R. (2010). Critical terrorism studies: An explanation, a defence and a way forward. Paper presented at the International Studies Association meeting, New Orleans, February.
Jongerden, J.P. (2017). Radical democracy and the right to self-determination beyond the nation-state. In G. Stansfield and M. Shareef (Eds.), *The Kurdish question revisited.* London: Hurst Publishers, pp. 245–258.
Kampwirth, K. (2002). *Women and guerrilla movements: Nicaragua, El Salvador, Chiapas, Cuba.* University Park, PA: Penn State Press.
Kaplan, S. (2017). PKK targets innocent civilians in eastern Turkey. *Anadolu Agency*, October 3. Available at: http://aa.com.tr/en/infographics/pkk-targets-innocent-civilians-in-eastern-turkey/926221.
Laciner, S. (2008). Drug smuggling as main source of PKK terrorism. *Journal of Turkish Weekly.* Available at: www.ataa.org/reference/pkk/Drug-Smuggling-as-Main-Source-of-PKK-Terrorism.html.
Levy, B.H. (2014). Stop calling our closest allies against ISIS "Terrorists." *The New Republic*, October 22. Available at: https://newrepublic.com/article/119939/pkk-not-terrorist-organization-theyre-fighting-isis-terrorists.
Luciak, I.A. (2001). *After the revolution: Gender and democracy in El Salvador, Nicaragua, and Guatemala.* Baltimore, MD: JHU Press.
Manafy, A. (2005). *The Kurdish political struggles in Iran, Iraq, and Turkey: A critical analysis.* Lanham, MD: University Press of America.
Marcus, A. (2009). *Blood and belief: The PKK and the Kurdish fight for independence.* New York: New York University Press.
Mason, T.D. (1989). Nonelite response to state-sanctioned terror. *Western Political Quarterly*, 42, 467–492.
Mason, T.D. (1992). Women's participation in Central American revolutions: A theoretical perspective. *Comparative Political Studies*, 25, 63–89.
Mason, T.D., & Krane, D.A. (1989). The political economy of death squads: Toward a theory of the impact of state-sanctioned terror. *International Studies Quarterly*, 33, 175–198.

Masullo, J., & O'Connor, F. (2017). PKK violence against civilians: Beyond the individual, understanding collective targeting. *Terrorism and Political Violence.* Available at: https://doi.org/10.1080/09546553.2017.1347874.

McDowall, D. (2000). *A modern history of the Kurds.* New York: I.B. Tauris.

Nuti, D.M. (2018). The rise and fall of socialism. *DOC Research Institute*, May 18. Available at: https://doc-research.org/2018/05/rise_and_fall_of_socialism/.

Ozkaya, T. (2016). The PKK always targets civilians: A grim timeline. *Anadolu Agency News*, May 20. Available at: http://aa.com.tr/en/todays-headlines/the-pkk-always-targets-civilians-a-grim-timeline/575740.

Philips, D.L. (2017). Remove the PKK from the terror list. *Huffington Post.* Available at: www.huffingtonpost.com/david-l-phillips/pkk-terror-group-status_b_3289311.html.

Rapoport, D. (2012). Fear and trembling: Terrorism in three religious traditions. In J. Horgan & K. Braddock (Eds.), *Terrorism studies: A reader.* New York: Routledge, pp. 3–27.

Reif, L.L. (1986). Women in Latin American guerrilla movements: A comparative perspective. *Comparative Politics*, 18, 147–169.

Richardson, L. (2006). *What terrorists want: Understanding the enemy, containing the threat.* New York: Random House.

Romano, D. (2006). *The Kurdish nationalist movement: Opportunity, mobilization and identity, no. 22.* Cambridge: Cambridge University Press.

Sampson, R.J., & Bean, L. (2006). Cultural mechanisms and killing fields: A revised theory of community-level racial inequality. In R.D. Peterson, L.J. Krivo, & J. Hagan (Eds.), *The many colors of crime.* New York: New York University Press, pp. 8–36.

Sanín, F.G., & Wood, E.J. (2014). Ideology in civil war: Instrumental adoption and beyond. *Journal of Peace Research*, 51, 213–226.

Shaw, C.R. (1930). *The jack-roller: A delinquent boy's own story.* Chicago, IL: University of Chicago Press.

Silke, A. (2003). *Terrorists, victims, and society: Psychological perspectives on terrorism and its consequences.* Hoboken, NJ: Wiley.

Snodgrass, J., Geis, G., Short Jr, J.F., & Kobrin, S. (1982). *The jack-roller at seventy: A fifty-year follow-up.* Lexington, MA: Lexington Books.

Steffensmeier, D.J. (1986). *The fence: In the shadow of two worlds.* Totowa, NJ: Rowman & Littlefield.

Stern, J. (2003). *Terror in the name of god: Why religious militants kill.* New York: Ecco.

Stohl, M. (2008). Old myths, new fantasies and the enduring realities of terrorism. *Critical Studies on Terrorism*, 1, 5–16.

Sucharov, M. (2005). Security ethics and the modern military: The case of the Israel Defense Forces. *Armed Forces & Society*, 31, 169–199.

Sutherland, E.H. (1937). *The professional thief: By a professional thief.* Chicago, IL: University of Chicago Press.

Swartz. K. (2010). Anderson, Elijah: Code of the street. In F.T. Cullen & P. Wilcox (Eds.), *Encyclopedia of criminological theory.* Thousand Oaks, CA: Sage, pp. 46–51.

Swidler, A. (1986). Culture in action: Symbols and strategies. *American Sociological Review*, 51, 273–286.

Thomas, J.L., & Wood, R.M. (2018). The social origins of female combatants. *Conflict Management and Peace Science*, 35, 215–232.

TRT World. (2017a). PKK kills teacher in eastern Turkey: The PKK has killed more than 150 teachers since 1984 and has been responsible for the murders of thousands of civilians, including women and children. *TRT World News*, June 22. Available at: www.trtworld.com/turkey/pkk-kills-teacher-in-eastern-turkey-384643.

TRT World. (2017b). PKK terrorists open fire—targeting civilians on six ambulances in Mardin within last twenty days. *TRT World News*. Available at: www.trtworld.com/turkey/outlawed-pkk-opens-fire-on-6-ambulances-within-20-days-7583.

Viterna, J. (2013). *Women in war: The micro-processes of mobilization in El Salvador.* New York: Oxford University Press.

Wallerstein, I. (1986). Marxism as utopias: Evolving ideologies. *American Journal of Sociology*, 91, 1295–1308.

Weinstein, J.M. (2006). *Inside rebellion: The politics of insurgent violence.* Cambridge: Cambridge University Press.

White, P.J. (2000). *Primitive rebels or revolutionary modernizers? The Kurdish national movement in Turkey.* London: Zed Books.

Worth, R.F. (2016). Behind the barricades of Turkey's hidden war. *The New York Times*. Available at: www.nytimes.com/2016/05/29/magazine/behind-the-barricades-of-turkeys-hidden-war.html.

Yackley, A.J. (2015). Turkey-Kurdish conflict: PKK leader calls on armed followers not to attack security forces. *Independent*, August 25. Available at: www.independent.co.uk/news/world/europe/turkey-kurdish-conflict-pkk-leader-calls-on-armed-followers-not-to-attack-security-forces-10471641.html.

Yahya, H. (2017). The PKK-PYD/YPG are project organizations of the British deep state. *Geopolitica*, June 9. Available at: www.geopolitica.ru/en/article/pkk-pydypg-are-project-organizations-british-deep-state.

Yarkın, G. (2015). The ideological transformation of the PKK regarding the political economy of the Kurdish region in Turkey. *Kurdish Studies*, 3, 26–46.

Yeginsu, C., & Timur, S. (2016). Turkey's Post-Coup Crackdown Targets Kurdish Politicians. *The New York Times*, November 4. Available at: www.nytimes.com/2016/11/05/world/europe/turkey-coup-crackdown-kurdish-politicians.html.

Yeni Safak News. (2017). Around 400 civilians killed in PKK attacks across Turkey: Terrorist organization kills scores of civilians, including politicians, workers and teachers in last 2 years. *Yeni Safak News*, November 30. Available at: www.yenisafak.com/en/news/around-400-civilians-killed-in-pkk-attacks-across-turkey-2849568.

Yesilgazete. (2012). Faşizm TT oldu: "Açılım değil, katliam istiyoruz". *Yesilgazete*, August 6. Available at: https://yesilgazete.org/blog/2012/08/06/fasizm-tt-oldu-acilim-degil-katliam-istiyoruz/.

Part III

Beyond Terrorism

9

Desistance from Terrorism

Daren Fisher

Desistance is one of the primary goals for counterterrorism and is of paramount theoretical importance for the study of terrorism in general. Particularly as recent evidence suggests that the likelihood of recidivism for terrorism is higher than the likelihood of terrorism within the general population (Hasisi et al., 2020), promoting desistance presents a key arm of any comprehensive counterterrorism approach. There are, however, many conceptual and methodological challenges for identifying what desistance is and when desistance from terrorism occurs. Terrorism is a rare event (Arva & Piazza, 2016), and, like crime (Liggins et al., 2019; Sherman, 2007; Wolfgang et al., 1972), it is concentrated within a small number of people (Horgan, 2008) and a small number of places (Fisher & Becker, 2019; LaFree & Bersani, 2014; Perry, 2020). Each of these attributes of terrorism raises their own methodological challenges that need to be accounted for in studying the prevalence of desistance. Especially considering the relative abundance of crime and terrorism opportunities (see Bjørgo, 2005; Clarke & Newman, 2006; Gottfredson & Hirschi, 1990; Klein et al., 2017), there are also numerous challenges for understanding the mechanisms behind why people cease committing these acts after previously offending. Recent research has also produced findings that terrorism desistance varies greatly across study settings (see Altier et al., 2019; Hasisi et al., 2020; Hodwitz, 2019; Schuurman & Bakker, 2016), raising the importance of further exploration into what desistance from terrorism means and what factors influence its likelihood.

It has been a long-standing criticism of criminology that more attention is paid to why people commit crime than why people desist from crime (see Laub & Sampson, 2001). In recent years, many studies have acted to remedy this by providing greater conceptual clarity (see Giordano et al., 2002; Kurlychek et al., 2012) and to expand theoretical understandings of the underlying mechanisms of desistance (see Copp et al., 2020; Giordano et al., 2008; Paternoster et al., 2015, 2016; Rocque et al., 2016). Despite the recent increased interest in studying the prevalence and patterns of terrorism desistance, this area at present is still vastly understudied (Hasisi et al., 2020). As will be further discussed in this chapter, developments in the criminological literature, coupled with greater theoretical understanding of terrorism, provide numerous opportunities for knowledge on desistance from terrorism. Enhanced by methodological and statistical advances, there are increased domains to build off of this previous work that may prove to be pivotal in designing measures that increase desistance from terrorism and reduce the incidence of terrorism within specific individuals and in the aggregate.

> Theorizing and research about desistance from crime is one of the most exciting, vibrant, and dynamic areas in criminology today.
> (Paternoster & Bushway, 2009, p. 1156)

Echoing the above quote from Paternoster and Bushway (2009) regarding criminology in general, there are numerous fertile and vital areas of inquiry within the study of terrorism specifically. To explore these areas, this chapter begins by discussing some of the key perspectives on the nature, definition, and measurement of desistance gleaned from criminology. It then examines some of the theoretical perspectives on desistance from the criminological literature, including deterrence, rational choice theory, control theories, and general strain theory, and explores how these perspectives inform our understanding of desistance from terrorism. The chapter concludes by discussing the empirical literature on desistance from terrorism and provides some guidance on opportunities for future research.

What is Desistance?

Defining desistance poses problems that are unique from understanding the incidence of crime and terrorism. In addition to the greatly discussed definitional disputes surrounding the nature of terrorism (see

Freilich et al., 2009; Schmid & Jongman, 1988; Young & Findley, 2011), Maruna (2001, p. 17) laments that measuring and understanding desistance from any crime adds additional challenges as "it is not an event that happens, but rather it is the sustained absence of a certain type of event." As noted elsewhere in the terrorism literature, the absence of terrorism cannot confirm counterterrorism success (Lynch, 2011), and any observed inaction after a terror attack may be due to planning and preparation for a subsequent attack (Cothren et al., 2008). Consequently, discerning how long the absence of terrorism needs to be before it is considered to be desistance is a central and difficult question to answer. Stemming from these issues, it is unsurprising that the study of desistance within criminology has been impeded by definitional issues, theoretical incoherence, and measurement difficulties (Laub & Sampson, 2001). These issues are exacerbated by many of the intrinsic factors of terrorism, and consequently, it is important to investigate some of these factors in greater detail before examining the applicability of criminological conceptions of desistance to terrorism.

LaFree and Miller (2008) argue that the issues identified by Laub and Sampson (2001) are compounded within the domain of terrorism due to the collective nature of terrorist offending, its covert nature, and its rarity. Taken together, these three factors make having firm definitions of desistance from terrorism vital. The collective nature of terrorism offenses allows for individuals to provide meaningful contribution to an attack, but to potentially not be included among those indicted or recognized as being responsible for an attack. As terrorism is covert and the perpetrators of many attacks are unknown (LaFree & Dugan, 2007), there is potential for false negatives regarding terrorism desistance, whereby previous offenders may be responsible for attacks that are unattributed to any perpetrator. Due to the infrequency of terrorism and the time taken to plan and execute a terror attack (Cothren et al., 2008; Smith & Damphousse, 2009), studies on desistance from terrorism with short temporal horizons could erroneously conclude that an individual had desisted from terrorism despite them actively progressing toward a terror attack in the future, during the observation window. Problematically, all three of these attributes of terrorism lead to the increased likelihood that a person might be judged to have desisted from terrorism when, in reality, they had continued or increased their rate or severity of terrorism offending. Concordantly, many methods that could be used to measure desistance have the potential to produce misleading theoretical inferences through the increased likelihood of erroneously concluding desistance has occurred, resulting in the overestimation of the value and impact of any intervention aimed at increasing desistance.

These factors have led to the argument that desistance from terrorism should be seen to be a process of deradicalization rather than the cessation of participation in terror attacks (Horgan, 2008). This conceptualization has also been observed to have its own challenges. Kruglanski and colleagues (2013) for example note that the inconsistent use of deradicalization, disengagement, and desistance have created a number of conceptual obstacles, and are often used synonymously within the academic literature and beyond. Further, Horgan and Altier (2012) observe that one does not necessarily need to "deradicalize" in order to cease committing terrorism. This renders it important to distinguish whether the focus of desistance within studies of terrorism should be the curtailment of violence or the abandonment of ideologies conducive to terrorism. As former terrorists may wield their former actions to pursue political goals and other nonviolent aims (Cordes, 1987), and can also intentionally conceal their actual beliefs from researchers (Altier et al., 2014), a strong case can be made for focusing on desisting from offending behavior regardless of personal or ideological beliefs. This is reinforced by some criminological theories as well. From the perspective of self-control theory, for example (Gottfredson & Hirschi, 1990), the motivation for crime is invariant across the population as the benefits from crime are abundantly apparent and desirable to all (see Burt & Simons (2013) for an empirical examination of this assumption). If true, then examining the motivations for terrorism would be a moot point where the variation in motivation within a sample could instead be driven by deception, aliases, mistaken identities, and other measurement factors (Miller, 2016). As such, while measuring desistance from terrorism is replete with factors that would lead to over-estimations of the prevalence of desistance, from many theoretical and instrumental perspectives focusing on the cessation of terrorist behavior has greater merit. Concordantly, for the remainder of this chapter, desistance will be viewed in terms of reductions in violent actions rather than in terms of "the elimination of one's violent belief in a violent, extremist ideology" (Altier et al., 2014, p. 647; Kruglanski et al., 2013).

From the criminological literature, desistance has similarly proven difficult to operationalize and measure as "even a five-year or ten-year crime-free period is no guarantee that offending has terminated" (Farrington, 1986, p. 201). In light of these early observations, permanent desistance would only be possible to ascertain after the death of an individual, as the possibility of future offending would otherwise always remain (Huizinga et al., 1989). Given the impracticalities of waiting until the death of all participants in a study (Kazemian & Maruna, 2009), much of the criminological research has essentially equated extended periods of non-offending to desistance (Bushway et al., 2001). This pragmatic approach does raise important concerns that should be noted. As the observation periods and methods of data collection procedures have varied greatly within the criminological empirical literature on desistance, Uggen and Massoglia (2003, pp. 316–317) concluded that "it is difficult to draw empirical generalizations from the growing literature on desistance from crime." Importantly, studies with longer temporal windows of observation would be more likely to see lower levels of desistance as there are increased opportunities to offend. Further, as the aforementioned measurement issues are addressed (see LaFree & Miller, 2008; Miller, 2016), higher quality studies would also be less likely to observe desistance compared to less rigorous studies. In light of this persistent potential for overestimating rates of desistance and the rarity of terrorism, the importance of having an extended follow-up period is vital for future studies. Given the time and resources needed to create such datasets, however, this chapter highlights the importance of triangulating existing findings across methodological approaches and across study contexts to better identify the presence and absence of desistance.

The criminological literature has identified a number of important insights that have revealed much about patterns of desistance. An increasing body of empirical literature has demonstrated that desistance is not uniform. It has been observed that desistance can be an immediate knifing-off of the past from some offenders (Kirk, 2012), and an extended declining process for others that can be influenced by a string of important events (Laub et al., 1998). This has led to those such as Kurlychek et al. (2012) to posit that desistance can be both instantaneous in nature whereby the offender immediately ceases their criminal behavior, and an incremental process where offending declines over a period of time. Evidenced with 18 years of follow-up data on a cohort of felony convicts from the state of New Jersey in the United States, Kurlychek et al. (2012) find that some offenders had already desisted at the beginning of the follow-up period (instantaneous desistance), while others exhibited a more gradual decline in their offending rate (desistance as a process). Although the theoretical explanations for the mechanisms underlying either of these two conceptualizations of desistance differ, as will be discussed in the next section of this chapter, criminological theories and the above compiled evidence from this discipline have already yielded much that can be applied to the understanding of desistance from terrorism.

Theoretical Explanations of Desistance

A range of criminological theories has been applied to understanding desistance and many have contradictory predictions as to the nature, possibility, and mechanisms for desistance. Criminology as a field and its theories have yielded many benefits for the study of terrorism (Fisher & Dugan, 2019a), although much of this has been relatively recent in nature (see Black, 2004). Making greater proportionate use of statistical analyses, systematically collected data, and established theories compared to other approaches (Lum et al., 2006; Silke, 2001), criminological research has helped to dispel intuitively popular but inaccurate theories of terrorism, including personal narcissism and paranoia (Victoroff, 2005). As will be seen in the discussion below, not all criminological theories have been paid equal attention in the extant literature (Freilich & LaFree, 2015), particularly with regard to desistance from terrorism. With this notable limitation, this section provides a brief overview of a range of criminological theories, discusses their predictions for desistance, and summarizes their application with regard to desistance from terrorism.

Deterrence and Rational Choice

Both deterrence and rational choice theories share the underlying assumption that people are rational, and if left to their own devices, would naturally commit crime. This approach stems from the seminal works of Beccaria (1764) and Bentham (1781) who argued that humans are self-interested, possess free will, and seek to maximize their pleasure and minimize their pain through their decisions. Individuals will thus engage in crime, or in this case terrorism, when the expected benefits are greater than the expected risks (Becker, 1968). Empirical research on deterrence and rational choice has revealed that decisions to commit crime are not purely based on incentives and punishments. Clarke and Cornish (1985) along with Loewenstein (1996) have observed that criminal decisions vary greatly across situations and offenses. This avenue of research has led to the present understanding that the perceptions of risks and rewards are often more important than objective probabilities of punishment for decision-making (Nagin, 2013). Rather than possessing pure and objective rationality, people instead practice "bounded rationality" (Simon, 1982), whereby individuals select actions that are "good enough" instead of maximizing their objective utility (Berrebi, 2009, p. 170). This more nuanced understanding of rationality has been observed in a range of terrorism environments, revealing important insights into the strategic calculus of terrorists (Dugan & Chenoweth, 2012; Frey & Luechinger, 2003; Kydd & Walter, 2006; Pape, 2003).

Following the assumptions of rationality, deterrence theory argues for an inverse relationship between the certainty and celerity of punishment and crime in the presence of proportionate punishment (Beccaria, 1764). Deterrence can be general in nature by preventing would-be offenders from offending; or it can be specific by stopping perpetrators from reoffending (Stafford & Warr, 1993). Although general deterrence has been argued to be an essential mechanism for counterterrorism (Fisher & Becker, 2019; Ross & Gurr, 1989), desistance is more directly concerned with specific deterrence. General deterrence may play a role in desistance by advertising the credibility of apprehension and threat of punishment in general, however this influence is likely to be minimal. Instead, the experiences of the individual with their own criminal offending and the experiences of their direct family and peers have a greater impact on one's perceived risk of detection and punishment (van Veen & Sattler, 2020; Wilson et al., 2017). Given that to desist from crime one must have previously committed crime, this evidence suggests that focusing on mechanisms in line with specific deterrence are of greater relevance for understanding desistance from terrorism.

Specific deterrence is a separate mechanism from incapacitation where an individual is deprived from being able to choose to commit a crime (Auerhahn, 1999). Whether death is considered desistance within terrorism is an important question worth its own targeted analysis. Reiss (1989) for example questioned whether desistance need always be a voluntary decision. Particularly as high-risk offenders (Lattimore et al., 1997) are more likely to suffer a premature death, there are important theoretical and practical consequences for whether individuals who desist through death are included in calculations or whether this is considered to be conflating theoretical mechanisms. Targeted killings, imprisonment for one's natural life, and other responses to terrorism aimed at the incapacitation of terrorists are not policies aimed at specific deterrence. If one is concerned with desistance (cessation of violence) through any means, however, then this theoretical distinction would be moot. Theoretically, desistance through death would not diminish the capacity for other terrorists and groups to observe this and desist through general deterrence mechanisms. Nevertheless, recent studies demonstrate that targeted killings, for example, yield negligible general deterrent impacts on terrorism even in the most notable cases (Carson, 2017; Fisher & Becker, 2019). Government actions aimed at achieving specific deterrence also have the potential to incidentally increase terrorism by inciting a violent terrorism backlash (Argomaniz & Vidal-Diez, 2015; Kattelman, 2020; LaFree et al., 2009). To account for this, future studies examining desistance from terrorism, from the perspective of deterrence and/or incapacitation, would benefit from identifying cases of desistance through death within their sample and observing how their inclusion and exclusion within estimates impacts any conclusions. Further, when examining general deterrence as the mechanism for desistance, the deaths of key figures (whether through targeted killings or other sources of premature death) within a terrorist organization provide important opportunities to test hypotheses that are central to desistance through deterrence and distinguishing the impacts of incapacitation.

For many years, the deterrence perspective has been theoretically criticized for its inability to anticipate the complex and variable utility structures of terrorists and the reactions of terrorists to stimuli beyond punishments (Victoroff, 2005). The previously discussed findings supporting backlash hypotheses (see Argomaniz & Vidal-Diez, 2015; Kattelman, 2020; LaFree et al., 2009), also indicate that there are mechanisms beyond deterrence that are important for terrorism. These findings are not without pattern however, indicating that terrorists are not irrational, as has oft been claimed (Abrahms & Lula, 2012; Fisher & Dugan, 2019a). The observable trends within these studies instead indicate that there is a rational component to terrorist decision-making. Indeed, a growing list of studies has provided evidence that terrorist decisions are likely influenced by a broad array of actions, including government incentives for not committing terrorism (Dugan & Chenoweth, 2012), government handling of natural disasters (Fisher & Dugan, 2019b), and that complex rational decision-making is evident for suicide bombers as well (Pape, 2003; Perry & Hasisi, 2015). This suite of findings provides evidence that there are likely rational mechanisms beyond deterrence and incapacitation that could be leveraged to encourage desistance.

The potential for rational choice mechanisms to result in terrorist desistance was discussed and demonstrated in case studies on both terrorist groups and specific terrorists in a special issue of *Dynamics of Asymmetric Conflict* (see Dugan et al., 2008; LaFree & Miller, 2008; McCauley, 2008), and has conceptual roots going back to Ross and Gurr (1989) and Crenshaw (1991). Studies have also provided evidence indicating that there are rational processes that underlie decisions to support or engage in violent extremism (Dhami & Murray, 2016). One of the biggest challenges in this domain, which is holding back systematic and individual-level research on desistance from terrorism, is that "reliable data on recidivism rates among extremists and terrorists tends to be scarce and anecdotal" (Schuurman & Bakker, 2016, p. 66). Databases like the Profiles of Individual Radicalization in the United States (PIRUS, see National Consortium for the Study of Terrorism and Responses to Terrorism (START), 2018) dataset, the American Terrorism Study (ATS), and the Profiles of Perpetrators of Terrorism in the United States (PPT-US), all provide opportunities for testing hypotheses related to rational choice and other theoretical perspectives, especially when integrated with other data sources and analytic techniques (see Becker, 2019). Pursuing data improvements and laying the foundations for the collection of data in line with the Pathways to Desistance dataset (Mulvey et al., 2004), for example, would also help spur along this branch of research. Replicating criminological studies focused on human agency, changing subjective expectations, and changing marginal utilities (see Thomas & Vogel, 2019), and the intersection of identity and rational choice (see Paternoster & Bushway, 2009; Paternoster et al., 2015) provide promising avenues for future terrorism research on desistance from the rational choice perspective.

Control Theories

Control theories differ from all other criminological theories as they ask: why do people not commit crime? Many different control theories have emerged since Reiss (1951), who presented that it was the individual's submission or acceptance of rules that cause their actions to line up with accepted norms, morals, and values of a society. For control theories, crime then results when there is a relative absence of internalized norms and rules governing behavior that conform to socialized norms and rules (Reiss, 1951). There have been numerous iterations within this tradition that have focused upon stakes in conformity (Toby, 1957), techniques of neutralization (Sykes & Matza, 1958), containment (Reckless, 1967), social control (Hirschi, 1969), and self-control (Gottfredson & Hirschi, 1990), and the control theory perspective is the most frequently tested and endorsed theory within criminology (Walsh & Ellis, 1999). Each of these theories offer their own predictions and are worthy of exploration, despite being incorporated into later control theories: notably Hirschi's Social Control Theory (1969), Gottfredson and Hirschi's General Theory of Crime (1990), and in Hirschi's combination of social and self-control (2004). Meta analyses have revealed that self-control is an important predictor of crime (Pratt & Cullen, 2000), providing increased empirical support that low self-control and the absence of other forms of social control predict a range of crimes.

It was previously discussed that the control perspective yields some unique predictions for the motivations and opportunities for crime. Notably within control theory, the motivation to commit crime is ubiquitous (LaFree & Miller, 2008), and the opportunities for crime are omnipresent (Gottfredson & Hirschi, 1990). Previous studies on terrorism do question these assumptions as there is variation in support for violent extremism (Dhami & Murray, 2016; Nivette et al., 2017), and not all practicable opportunities for terrorism have the potential to advance terrorist goals (Asal et al., 2009). As there is also evidence for a diffusion of benefits stemming terrorism interventions rather than a displacement from one terrorist opportunity to another (Hsu et al., 2018), current evidence suggests that there are important differences in opportunities for terrorism that would need to be explained from this perspective (see also Grasmick et al., 1993). At present there is little research directly exploring control theories and terrorism, and direct examinations of these assumptions within the terrorism literature would be of great value. Of the few existing studies, Oliverio and Lauderdale (2005) have also suggested that social control mechanisms could be used to justify terrorism instead of providing the foundation for abstaining or desisting from terrorism, though recent analyses have demonstrated that there is empirical support for social control reducing the likelihood of participating in a violent and ideologically motivated act (Becker, 2019).

These factors do not diminish the potential value of control theories for understanding terrorism, and other important criticisms have led to theoretical advances that may be of great promise for future research. These additional criticisms that have been leveled at control theory include: that it does not explain corporate crime and organizational offending well (Simpson & Piquero, 2002); it does not explain gender differences in crime or changes in crime rates over time well (Tittle et al., 2003); and that it denies the impact of external social factors in later life (Laub & Sampson, 1993). This last criticism is especially important for desistance and is addressed directly by life-course theory (Sampson & Laub, 2003). This theory builds upon social control theory and the age–crime curve, which suggests that all people eventually desist from crime but the rate of desistance differs across the population (Sampson & Laub, 2003). This age-graded theory of informal social control presents that key life "turning points" like marriage, having children, gaining and losing employment, gaining education, and engaging in military service can alter the trajectory of an individual's desistance from crime (Laub & Sampson, 1993, p. 7). Supported by qualitative and quantitative research, Sampson and Laub (2003, pp. 279–280) find that those who desisted from crime had "structures, situations, and persons [that] offered nurturing and informal social control." Research found links between education and terrorism (Brockhoff et al., 2015), although this national-level research was unable to investigate the individual impacts of education as a turning point that leads toward desistance.

Life-course theory also offers an avenue for examination that would be of particular interest to the study of desistance from terrorism. The observation that crime declines with age is one of the most enduring and consistent findings in criminology (Matza, 1964), and was part of the basis for self-control theory (Gottfredson & Hirschi, 1990). According to Gottfredson and Hirschi (1990), changes in criminal offending over a lifetime are likely to be unidirectional, with a peak in offending during adolescence giving way to desistance in adulthood. This theory thus does not allow for adult-onset offenders, otherwise known as late bloomers, whereas life-course theory does allow that traumatic events may also act as turning points that may lead to introductions into crime later in life. Given that it has long been observed that terrorists are typically older than other criminal offenders (Russell & Miller, 1977), identifying the presence of adult-onset terrorists and examining any precursor turning points would yield important insights for desistance from terrorism and for criminology more generally. Particularly as Sohoni and colleagues (2014) found no evidence of true adult-onset offenders, investigations in this area would be particularly fruitful. Considering that control theory has been the most tested criminological theory, there are abundant avenues to replicate previous studies and examine this perspective to better understand desistance from terrorism.

Strain Theories

Based upon the premise that "some social structures *exert a definite pressure* upon certain persons in the society to engage in nonconformist rather than conformist conduct" (Merton, 1938, p. 672, emphasis in original), strain theories within criminology have been among the most prominent criminological theories of the past century. Early strain theories argued that crime results from individuals being structurally precluded from access to culturally approved means (e.g., education and gainful employment) to gain culturally defined aspirations (e.g., the accumulation of wealth or social status) (Merton, 1938). Reformulated by Agnew (1992) as General Strain Theory (GST), this version of strain theory presents that individuals are pressured into crime by the strains and stressors that they experience. Instead of being a result of utilitarian calculus like rational choice theories, Agnew (2006) suggests that individuals engage in crime as a reaction to the strains experienced from the loss of positive stimuli, the experience of negative stimuli, and the inability to achieve desired goals. Also occurring indirectly through experiencing negative emotions like anger and frustration (Agnew et al., 2002), from the perspective of GST, crime is thus a form of corrective action aiming to resolve the perceived source of the strain.

Regarding terrorism, Agnew (2010, p. 131) argues terrorism is most likely to be committed when people experience "collective strains" that are: high in magnitude, with civilians affected; unjust; and inflicted by substantially more powerful others. As strains that fit these criteria are far more common than the incidence of terrorism, the theory in this form would overpredict the incidence of terrorism and suffer from the embarrassment-of-riches problem leveled at earlier conceptions of strain theory (Matza, 1964). Agnew (2010, p. 131) however presents that these conditions will not always lead to terrorism, as "a range of factors condition" the effect of these strains. Although this premise allows GST to avoid overprediction issues in theory, Agnew (2010) does present additional data and methodological issues that would need to be overcome in order to adequately test GST on terrorism. In reviewing previous examinations, Agnew (2010, p. 149) laments in his opinion that previous empirical tests have been too simplistic as "they fail to measure the key dimensions of strain, including magnitude, injustice, and the nature of the source ... [and that] these tests do not examine intervening mechanisms, the subjective interpretation of strain, or conditioning variables."

This lofty data requirement is not beyond the realms of possibility, and important research has begun to rise to this challenge. Testing the key strain hypotheses that "exposure to collective strain is associated with higher support for violent extremism and the effect of collective strain is conditional on perceptions of moral and legal constraints," Nivette et al. (2017, p. 755) find that exposure to collective strains does not have a direct impact on violent extremist attitudes when modeled correctly and that individuals who previously had internalized justifications for violence were more vulnerable to extremist violent pathways after being exposed to stressors. Given that the data from this study come from seven waves of an ongoing prospective longitudinal study based on a stratified random sampling of schools in the Swiss city of Zurich, replication of these findings would be difficult in other contexts. In addition, finding equivalent data on an adult population to meet Agnew's (2010) requirement would pose even greater challenges. Heeding the approach used by Nivette et al. (2017), identifying longitudinal datasets that have been compiled for other means may present opportunities for examining the links between strain and desistance from terrorism as well. While it would be many years before any of the youths in this sample from Zurich engage in terrorism and subsequently desist (if any ever do), investing in this approach would present numerous benefits over analyzing terrorist autobiographies to examine the impact of strain and distress on terrorist engagement and terrorism desistance (see Corner & Gill, 2020).

Support has been found within the criminological literature that the propositions of GST also can predict desistance. Using data from a longitudinal study of males in South Florida, Eitle (2010) found support for a relationship between experiences of strain and desistance from crime (see also Gunnison & Mazerolle, 2007). However, this study also found no support for the claim that changes in self-esteem and social support moderate the relationship between strain and criminal activity (Eitle, 2010), potentially limiting the policy mechanisms that could be used from this perspective to encourage desistance from terrorism. Whether these findings apply to desistance from terrorism remains an open question, and one worthy of exploration. Particularly as some of the potential policy responses from this theoretical perspective include a wide array of options, ranging from the fostering of better coping mechanisms for individuals to the cessation of underlying grievances, this chapter highlights that if appropriate data can be gained, this may prove to be a fruitful theoretical avenue for future research on desistance from terrorism.

Collective Desistance and Terrorist Organizations

Much of the literature discussed above, and in criminology in general, focuses upon individuals and their relationship to crime rather than groups and crime. Criminal gangs, terrorist organizations, and other such organizations may provide pathways for people into crime and may be intrinsic in developing their members' criminal abilities (Decker & Pyrooz, 2011; Miller, 2016; Thrasher, 1927). Terrorist groups may also operate differently and respond differently to a host of stimuli. Atran (2006), for example, argues that group dynamics may supersede individual goals and attributes with regard to terrorism, and the viable strategic options for an organization may differ markedly compared to individuals based upon practical and political realities (DeVore, 2012). Shapiro (2012, p. 5) highlights these internal and external group dynamics as being part of the reasons why "terrorist groups repeatedly take actions that are ultimately politically counter-productive." Exemplified by the overreaching tactics employed by the Armenian Secret Army for the Liberation of Armenia (ASALA), Dugan and colleagues (2008) display how this presents an opportunity for governments to discredit these terrorist organizations specifically and terrorism in general to increase the likelihood of desistance. Combined with the knowledge that government disruptions of criminal networks can also influence group actions, priorities, and patterns of desistance (Fabiani & Behlendorf, 2020), there is growing evidence to suggest that there are policy options that are available to facilitate collective desistance from terrorism that may not exist at the individual level. Indeed, factors unique to the group level for desistance have been identified, including the influence of competition between other terror groups (Young & Dugan, 2014), indicating the need for additional research in this area. Datasets like the Big Allied and Dangerous Version 2 database (Asal & Rethemeyer, 2015) could be used in conjunction with other datasets to test the aforementioned criminological theories to observe whether terrorist groups respond similarly to individual terrorists with regard to desistance.

Studying desistance at the group level does pose its own challenges, with most studies at this point engaging in descriptive analyses. In addition to the aforementioned difficulties with measuring individual-level desistance from terrorism, Miller (2016) provides a key description of some of the additional challenges for measuring the desistance of terrorist organizations. Terrorist groups range in level of organization, level of contact, organizational hierarchy, sophistication, objectives, longevity, and capacity (Miller, 2016). This makes the definition of terrorist groups problematic, with broader definitions suggesting shorter lifespans before desistance (see Rapoport, 1992) compared to longer average lifespans for more conservative terrorism group definitions (Blomberg et al., 2010). In light of these observations, using different definitions of terrorist groups to triangulate findings within a single study would help to provide more nuanced estimates of the impact of different government interventions and other criminological influences on group or collective desistance from terrorism.

When one considers both group and individual desistance simultaneously, a host of new issues emerges. While a terror group may desist, any individual member may then be able to join another terrorist organization as individual allegiances change or as groups splinter into many entities (Gaibulloev & Sandler, 2014). Conversely, a group may persist in terror actions despite the majority of its members individually desisting from terrorism (this may also lead to eventual desistance for the group as well; see Dugan et al., 2008). In either case, should this be considered desistance from terrorism? While sufficient data to test these ideas and their practical implications do not exist at present, this theoretical issue stems back to Plutarch:

> The ship wherein Theseus and the youth of Athens returned had thirty oars, and was preserved by the Athenians down even to the time of Demetrius Phalereus, for they took away the old planks as they decayed, putting in new and stronger timber in their place, insomuch that this ship became a standing example among the philosophers, for the logical question of things that grow; one side holding that the ship remained the same, and the other contending that it was not the same.
> (Plutarch, 1850 [c. 75 AD], p. 26)

The question of identity posed by Plutarch for the ship of Theseus in the above quote has practical implications for understanding desistance within terrorist organizations. For the ship of Theseus, it is debatable whether it is still the same ship after all of the component parts have been replaced. Particularly for organizations that have existed for long periods (more than 40 years) of time like those identified by Miller (2016) in Colombia, Israel and Palestine, Northern Ireland, and Spain, desistance may be occurring while these groups persist. For these few but important terrorist organizations, there may be no original remaining members. In a case like this, is it then possible for a group to persist but for there to be complete individual-level desistance? This may be considered a moot point in research that solely focuses on the persistence and desistance of specific terrorist groups. However, if one is concerned with the profile of terrorism in a nation, globally, or at the individual level, this may be an important dynamic that conditions the incidence and lethality of terrorism. Although a resolution to the paradox posed by the ship of Theseus is unlikely to be forthcoming, parsing out what this means for our understanding of collective desistance from terrorism has theoretical and practical implications for the overall understanding of desistance from terrorism.

Conclusions

Over the past two decades much has been learned about terrorism, and empirical research driven by criminological theories has begun to flourish. This chapter has documented many of these advances, but other theories, including Differential Association/Learning theory, Labeling theory, and to a lesser extent Social Disorganization, provide much untapped potential for understanding terrorism and patterns of desistance. As we improve our descriptive understanding and measurement of terrorism through ground-breaking work on desistance from terrorism (see Altier et al., 2019; Hasisi et al., 2020; Hodwitz, 2019; Schuurman and Bakker, 2016), the value of collecting long-term data on the incidence of terrorism and who commits these acts becomes increasingly evident. It is difficult to generalize findings across these studies due to idiosyncratic difference in study settings and scope, however all of these studies do demonstrate that desistance from terrorism does occur with identifiable factors conditioning its likelihood.

This variation in findings demonstrates the need and the value for increased theoretically driven examinations of desistance from terrorism. The identification of risk factors for recidivism and desistance does have value, and identifying when those who previously committed terrorism return to the same likelihood of offending as the rest of the population would be a major step forward for this literature (see Blumstein & Nakamura, 2009). Incorporating criminological theories to refine these observations and to enable an increased number of testable propositions still marks a key path forward in this domain (Crenshaw, 1981). Employing this theoretical-driven approach, studying desistance from terrorism may prove to be "one of the most exciting, vibrant, and dynamic areas" of terrorism research over the coming years (Paternoster & Bushway, 2009, p. 1156).

References

Abrahms, M., & Lula, K. (2012). Why terrorists overestimate the odds of victory. *Perspectives on Terrorism*, 6(4/5), 46–62.

Agnew, R. (1992). Foundation for a general strain theory of crime and delinquency. *Criminology*, 30(1), 47–88.

Agnew, R. (2006). *Pressured into crime: An overview of general strain theory.* Oxford: Oxford University Press.

Agnew, R. (2010). A general strain theory of terrorism. *Theoretical Criminology*, 14(2), 131–153.

Agnew, R., Brezina, T., Wright, J.P., & Cullen, F.T. (2002). Strain, personality traits, and delinquency: Extending general strain theory. *Criminology*, 40(1), 43–72.

Altier, M.B., Boyle, L.E., & Horgan, J.G. (2021). Returning to the fight: An empirical analysis of terrorist reengagement and recidivism. *Terrorism and Political Violence*, 33(4), 836–860.

Altier, M.B., Thoroughgood, C.N., & Horgan, J.G. (2014). Turning away from terrorism: Lessons from psychology, sociology, and criminology. *Journal of Peace Research*, 51(5), 647–661.

Argomaniz, J., & Vidal-Diez, A. (2015). Examining deterrence and backlash effects in counter-terrorism: The case of ETA. *Terrorism and Political Violence*, 27(1), 160–181.

Arva, B.J., & Piazza, J.A. (2016). Spatial distribution of minority communities and terrorism: Domestic concentration versus transnational dispersion. *Defense and Peace Economics*, 27(1), 1–36.

Asal, V.H., & Rethemeyer, K. (2015). Big Allied and Dangerous Dataset Version 2. Available at: www.start.umd.edu/baad/database.

Asal, V.H., Rethemeyer, R.K., Anderson, I., Stein, A., Rizzo, J., & Rozea, M. (2009). The softest of targets: A study on terrorist target selection. *Journal of Applied Security Research*, 4(3), 258–278.

Atran, S. (2006). The moral logic and growth of suicide terrorism. *Washington Quarterly*, 29(2), 127–147.

Auerhahn, K. (1999). Selective incapacitation and the problem of prediction. *Criminology*, 37(4), 703–734.

Beccaria, C. (1764). *On crimes and punishments.* Indianapolis, IN: Hackett Publishing Company.

Becker, G. (1968). Crime and punishment: An economic approach. *Journal of Political Economy*, 76, 169–217.

Becker, M.H. (2019). When extremists become violent: Examining the association between social control, social learning, and engagement in violent extremism. *Studies in Conflict & Terrorism*. Available at: www.tandfonline.com/doi/abs/10.1080/1057610X.2019.1626093?journalCode=uter20.

Bentham, J. (1781). *The principles of morals and legislation.* Oxford: Clarendon Press.

Berrebi, C. (2009). The economics of terrorism and counterterrorism: What matters and is rational-choice theory helpful? In P.K. Davis & K. Cragin (Eds.), *Social science for counterterrorism: Putting the pieces together.* Santa Monica, CA: RAND Corporation, pp. 151–208.

Bjørgo, T. (Ed.). (2005). *Root causes of terrorism: Myths, reality and ways forward.* London: Routledge.

Black, D. (2004). Terrorism as social control. In M. Deflem (Ed.), *Terrorism and counter-terrorism: Criminological perspectives sociology of crime, law and deviance, Vol. 5*. Oxford: Elsevier, pp. 9–18.

Blomberg, S.B., Engel, R.C., & Sawyer, R. (2010). On the duration and sustainability of transnational terrorist organizations. *Journal of Conflict Resolution*, 54(2), 303–330.

Blumstein, A., & Nakamura, K. (2009). Redemption in the presence of widespread criminal background checks. *Criminology*, 47(2), 327–359.

Brockhoff, S., Krieger, T., & Meierrieks, D. (2015). Great expectations and hard times: The (nontrivial) impact of education on domestic terrorism. *Journal of Conflict Resolution*, 59(7), 1186–1215.

Burt, C.H., & Simons, R.L. (2013). Self-control, thrill seeking, and crime: Motivation matters. *Criminal Justice and Behavior*, 40(11), 1326–1348.

Bushway, S.D., Piquero, A.R., Broidy, L.M., Cauffman, E., & Mazerolle, P. (2001). An empirical framework for studying desistance as a process. *Criminology*, 39(2), 491–516.

Carson, J.V. (2017). Assessing the effectiveness of high-profile targeted killings in the "war on terror": A quasi-experiment. *Criminology & Public Policy*, 16(1), 191–220.

Clarke, R.V., & Cornish, D.B. (1985). Modeling offenders' decisions: A framework for research and policy. *Crime and Justice*, 6, 147–185.

Clarke, R.V.G., & Newman, G.R. (2006). *Outsmarting the terrorists*. Westport, CT: Praeger Security International, p. 144.

Copp, J.E., Giordano, P.C., Longmore, M.A., & Manning, W.D. (2020). Desistance from crime during the transition to adulthood: The influence of parents, peers, and shifts in identity. *Journal of Research in Crime and Delinquency*, 57(3), 294–332.

Cordes, B. (1987). When terrorists do the talking: Reflections on terrorist literature. *The Journal of Strategic Studies*, 10(4), 150–171.

Corner, E., & Gill, P. (2020). Psychological distress, terrorist involvement and disengagement from terrorism: A sequence analysis approach. *Journal of Quantitative Criminology*, 36, 499–526.

Cothren, J., Smith, B.L., Roberts, P., & Damphousse, K.R. (2008). Geospatial and temporal patterns of preparatory conduct among American terrorists. *International Journal of Comparative and Applied Criminal Justice*, 32(1), 23–41.

Crenshaw, M. (1981). The causes of terrorism. *Comparative Politics*, 13(4), 379–399.

Crenshaw, M. (1991). How terrorism declines. *Terrorism and Political Violence*, 3(1), 69–87.

Decker, S., & Pyrooz, D. (2011). Gangs, terrorism, and radicalization. *Journal of Strategic Security*, 4(4), 151–166.

DeVore, M.R. (2012). Exploring the Iran-Hezbollah relationship: A case study of how state sponsorship affects terrorist group decision-making. *Perspectives on Terrorism*, 6(4/5), 85–107.

Dhami, M.K., & Murray, J. (2016). Male youth perceptions of violent extremism: Towards a test of rational choice theory. *Spanish Journal of Psychology*, 19, e51–e83.

Dugan, L., & Chenoweth, E. (2012). Moving beyond deterrence: The effectiveness of raising the expected utility of abstaining from terrorism in Israel. *American Sociological Review*, 77(4), 597–624.

Dugan, L., Huang, J.Y., LaFree, G., & McCauley, C. (2008). Sudden desistance from terrorism: The Armenian secret army for the liberation of Armenia and the Justice Commandos of the Armenian Genocide. *Dynamics of Asymmetric Conflict*, 1(3), 231–249.

Eitle, D. (2010). General strain theory, persistence, and desistance among young adult males. *Journal of Criminal Justice*, 38(6), 1113–1121.

Fabiani, M.D., & Behlendorf, B. (2021). Cumulative disruptions: Interdependency and commitment escalation as mechanisms of illicit network failure. *Global Crime*, 22(1), 22–50.

Farrington, D.P. (1986). Age and crime. In N. Morris & M. Tonry (Eds.), *Crime and justice, Vol. 7*. Chicago, IL: Chicago University Press, pp. 189–250.

Fisher, D., & Becker, M.H. (2021). The heterogeneous repercussions of killing Osama bin Laden on global terrorism patterns. *European Journal of Criminology*, 18(3), 301–324.

Fisher, D., & Dugan, L. (2019a). Sociological and criminological explanations of terrorism. In E. Chenoweth, R. English, A. Gofas, & S.N. Kalyvas. (Eds.), *The Oxford handbook on terrorism*. Oxford: Oxford University Press.

Fisher, D., & Dugan, L. (2019b). The importance of governments' response to natural disasters to reduce terrorist risk. *Justice Quarterly*. Available at: www.tandfonline.com/doi/abs/10.1080/07418825.2019.1685120

Freilich, J.D., & LaFree, G. (2015). Criminology theory and terrorism: Introduction to the special issue. *Terrorism and Political Violence*, 27(1), 1–8.

Freilich, J.D., Chermak, S.M., & Simone Jr., J. (2009). Surveying American state police agencies about terrorism threats, terrorism sources, and terrorism definitions. *Terrorism and Political Violence*, 21(3), 450–475.

Frey, B.S., & Luechinger, S. (2003). How to fight terrorism: Alternatives to deterrence. *Defence and Peace Economics*, 14(4), 237–249.

Gaibulloev, K., & Sandler, T. (2014). An empirical analysis of alternative ways that terrorist groups end. *Public Choice*, 160(1–2), 25–44.

Giordano, P.C., Cernkovich, S.A., & Rudolph, J.L. (2002). Gender, crime, and desistance: Toward a theory of cognitive transformation. *American Journal of Sociology*, 107(4), 990–1064.

Giordano, P.C., Longmore, M.A., Schroeder, R.D., & Seffrin, P.M. (2008). A life-course perspective on spirituality and desistance from crime. *Criminology*, 46(1), 99–132.

Gottfredson, M.R., & Hirschi, T. (1990). *A general theory of crime*. Palo Alto, CA: Stanford University Press.

Grasmick, H.G., Tittle, C.R., Bursik Jr., R.J., & Arneklev, B.J. (1993). Testing the core empirical implications of Gottfredson and Hirschi's general theory of crime. *Journal of Research in Crime and Delinquency*, 30(1), 5–29.

Gunnison, E., & Mazerolle, P. (2007). Desistance from serious and not so serious crime: A comparison of psychosocial risk factors. *Criminal Justice Studies*, 20(3), 231–253.

Hasisi, B., Carmel, T., Weisburd, D., & Wolfowicz, M. (2020). Crime and terror: Examining criminal risk factors for terrorist recidivism. *Journal of Quantitative Criminology*, 36(3), 449–472.

Hirschi, T. (1969). *Causes of delinquency*. Berkeley, CA: University of California Press.

Hirschi, T. (2004). *Self-control and crime*. In: R.F. Baumeister & K.D. Vohs (Eds.), *Handbook of self-regulation: Research, theory, and applications*. New York: Guilford Press.

Hodwitz, O. (2019). The Terrorism Recidivism Study (TRS). *Perspectives on Terrorism*, 13(2), 54–64.

Horgan, J. (2008). From profiles to pathways and roots to routes: Perspectives from psychology on radicalization into terrorism. *The Annals of the American Academy of Political and Social Science*, 618(1), 80–94.

Horgan, J., & Altier, M.B. (2012). The future of terrorist de-radicalization programs. *Georgetown Journal of International Affairs*, 83–90.

Hsu, H.Y., Vásquez, B.E., & McDowall, D. (2018). A time-series analysis of terrorism: Intervention, displacement, and diffusion of benefits. *Justice Quarterly*, 35(4), 557–583.

Huizinga, D.H., Menard, S., & Elliott, D.S. (1989). Delinquency and drug use: Temporal and developmental patterns. *Justice Quarterly*, 6(3), 419–455.

Kattelman, K.T. (2020). Assessing success of the global war on terror: Terrorist attack frequency and the backlash effect. *Dynamics of Asymmetric Conflict*, 13(1), 67–86.

Kazemian, L., & Maruna, S. (2009). Desistance from crime. In M.D. Krohn, A.J. Lizotte, & G.P. Hall (Eds.), *Handbook on crime and deviance*. New York: Springer, pp. 277–295.

Kirk, D.S. (2012). Residential change as a turning point in the life course of crime: Desistance or temporary cessation? *Criminology*, 50(2), 329–358.

Klein, B.R., Gruenewald, J., & Smith, B.L. (2017). Opportunity, group structure, temporal patterns, and successful outcomes of far-right terrorism incidents in the United States. *Crime & Delinquency*, 63(10), 1224–1249.

Kruglanski, A.W., Bélanger, J.J., Gelfand, M., Gunaratna, R., Hettiarachchi, M., Reinares, F., Orehek, F., Sasota, E., & Sharvit, K. (2013). Terrorism: A (self) love story: Redirecting the significance quest can end violence. *American Psychologist*, 68(7), 559–575.

Kurlychek, M.C., Bushway, S.D., & Brame, R. (2012). Long-term crime desistance and recidivism patterns: Evidence from the Essex County convicted felon study. *Criminology*, 50(1), 71–103.

Kydd, A.H., & Walter, B.F. (2006). The strategies of terrorism. *International Security*, 31(1), 49–80.

LaFree, G., & Bersani, B.E. (2014). County-level correlates of terrorist attacks in the United States. *Criminology & Public Policy*, 13(3), 455–481.

LaFree, G., & Dugan, L. (2007). Introducing the global terrorism database. *Terrorism and Political Violence*, 19(2), 181–204.

LaFree, G., & Miller, E. (2008). Desistance from terrorism: What can we learn from criminology? *Dynamics of Asymmetric Conflict*, 1(3), 203–230.

LaFree, G., Dugan, L., & Korte, R. (2009). The impact of British counterterrorist strategies on political violence in Northern Ireland: Comparing deterrence and backlash models. *Criminology*, 47(1), 17–45.

Lattimore, P.K., Linster, R.L., & MacDonald, J.M. (1997). Risk of death among serious young offenders. *Journal of Research in Crime and Delinquency*, 34(2), 187–209.

Laub, J.H., & Sampson, R.J. (1993). Turning points in the life course: Why change matters to the study of crime. *Criminology*, 31(3), 301–325.

Laub, J.H., & Sampson, R.J. (2001). Understanding desistance from crime. *Crime and Justice*, 28, 1–69.

Laub, J.H., Nagin, D.S., & Sampson, R.J. (1998). Trajectories of change in criminal offending: Good marriages and the desistance process. *American Sociological Review*, 63(2), 225–238.

Liggins, A., Ratcliffe, J.H., & Bland, M. (2019). Targeting the most harmful offenders for an English police agency: Continuity and change of membership in the "felonious few". *Cambridge Journal of Evidence-Based Policing*, 3(3–4), 80–96.

Loewenstein, G. (1996). Out of control: Visceral influences on behavior. *Organizational Behavior and Human Decision Processes*, 65(3), 272–292.

Lum, C., Kennedy, L.W., & Sherley, A. (2006). Are counter-terrorism strategies effective? The results of the Campbell systematic review on counter-terrorism evaluation research. *Journal of Experimental Criminology*, 2(4), 489–516.

Lynch, J.P. (2011). Implications of opportunity theory for combating terrorism. In B. Forst, J. Greene, & J. Lynch (Eds.), *Criminologists on terrorism and homeland security*. Cambridge: Cambridge University Press, pp. 151–182.

Maruna, S. (2001). *Making good: How ex-convicts reform and rebuild their lives*, Washington, DC: American Psychological Association.

Matza, D. (1964). *Delinquency and drift*. New York: John Wiley.

McCauley, C. (2008). Group desistance from terrorism: A dynamic perspective. *Dynamics of Asymmetric Conflict*, 1(3), 269–293.

Merton, R.K. (1938). Social structure and anomie. *American Sociological Review*, 3(5), 672–682.

Miller, E. (2016). Patterns of collective desistance from terrorism: Fundamental measurement challenges. *Perspectives on Terrorism*, 10(5), 5–21.

Mulvey, E.P., Steinberg, L., Fagan, J., Cauffman, E., Piquero, A.R., Chassin, L., Knight, G.P., Brame, R., Schubert, C.A., Hecker, T., & Losoya, S.H. (2004). Theory and research on desistance from antisocial activity among serious adolescent offenders. *Youth Violence and Juvenile Justice*, 2(3), 213–236.

Nagin, D.S. (2013). Deterrence: A review of the evidence by a criminologist for economists. *Annual Review of Economics*, 5(1), 83–105.

National Consortium for the Study of Terrorism and Responses to Terrorism (START). (2018). Profiles of individual radicalization in the United States [Data file]. Available at: www.start.umd.edu/pirus. Accessed May 7, 2020.

Nivette, A., Eisner, M., & Ribeaud, D. (2017). Developmental predictors of violent extremist attitudes: A test of general strain theory. *Journal of Research in Crime and Delinquency*, 54(6), 755–790.

Oliverio, A., & Lauderdale, P. (2005). Terrorism as deviance or social control: Suggestions for future research. *International Journal of Comparative Sociology*, 46(1–2), 153–169.

Pape, R.A. (2003). The strategic logic of suicide terrorism. *American Political Science Review*, 97(3), 343–361.

Paternoster, R., & Bushway, S. (2009). Desistance and the "feared self": Toward an identity theory of criminal desistance. *The Journal of Criminal Law and Criminology*, 99(4), 1103–1156.

Paternoster, R., Bachman, R., Bushway, S., Kerrison, E., & O'Connell, D. (2015). Human agency and explanations of criminal desistance: Arguments for a rational choice theory. *Journal of Developmental and Life-Course Criminology*, 1(3), 209–235.

Paternoster, R., Bachman, R., Kerrison, E., O'Connell, D., & Smith, L. (2016). Desistance from crime and identity: An empirical test with survival time. *Criminal Justice and Behavior*, 43(9), 1204–1224.

Perry, S. (2020). The application of the "law of crime concentration" to terrorism: The Jerusalem case study. *Journal of Quantitative Criminology*, 36(3), 583–605.

Perry, S., & Hasisi, B. (2015). Rational choice rewards and the jihadist suicide bomber. *Terrorism and Political Violence*, 27(1), 53–80.

Plutarch. (1850 [c.75 ad]). *Plutarch's lives: Translated from the original Greek.* Translated by J. Langhorne & W. Langhorne. Cincinnati, OH: Applegate Publishers.

Pratt, T.C., & Cullen, F.T. (2000). The empirical status of Gottfredson and Hirschi's general theory of crime: A meta-analysis. *Criminology*, 38(3), 931–964.

Rapoport, D.C. (1992). Terrorism. In M. Hawkesworth & M. Kogan (Eds.), *Encyclopedia of government and politics, Vol. 2*. London: Routledge, pp. 1061–1082.

Reckless, W. (1967). *The crime problem.* New York: Appleton-Century Crofts.

Reiss, A.J. (1951). Delinquency as the failure of personal and social controls. *American Sociological Review*, 16(2), 196–207.

Reiss, A.J. (1989). Ending criminal careers. Final Report prepared for the Desistance/Persistence Working Group of the Program on Human Development and Criminal Behavior, MacArthur Foundation and National Institute of Justice.

Rocque, M., Posick, C., & Paternoster, R. (2016). Identities through time: An exploration of identity change as a cause of desistance. *Justice Quarterly*, 33(1), 45–72.

Ross, J.I., & Gurr, T.R. (1989). Why terrorism subsides: A comparative study of Canada and the United States. *Comparative Politics*, 21(4), 405–426.

Russell, C.A., & Miller, B.H. (1977). Profile of a terrorist. *Studies in Conflict & Terrorism*, 1(1), 17–34.

Sampson, R.J., & Laub, J.H. (2003). Life-course desisters? Trajectories of crime among delinquent boys followed to age 70. *Criminology*, 41(3), 555–592.

Schmid, A., & Jongman, A. (1988). *Political terrorism: A research guide to concepts, theories, databases, and literature.* New Brunswick, NJ: Transaction Books.

Schuurman, B., & Bakker, E. (2016). Reintegrating jihadist extremists: Evaluating a Dutch initiative, 2013–2014. *Behavioral Sciences of Terrorism and Political Aggression*, 8(1), 66–85.

Shapiro, J.N. (2012). Terrorist decision-making: Insights from economics and political science. *Perspectives on Terrorism*, 6(4/5), 5–20.

Sherman, L.W. (2007). The power few: Experimental criminology and the reduction of harm. *Journal of Experimental Criminology*, 3(4), 299–321.

Silke, A. (2001). The devil you know: Continuing problems with research on terrorism. *Terrorism and Political Violence*, 13(4), 1–14.

Simon, H. (1982). *Models of bounded rationality: Empirically grounded economic reason.* Boston, MA: MIT Press.

Simpson, S.S., & Piquero, N.L. (2002). Low self-control, organizational theory, and corporate crime. *Law and Society Review*, 509–548.

Smith, B.L., & Damphousse, K.R. (2009). Patterns of precursor behaviors in the life span of a US environmental terrorist group. *Criminology & Public Policy*, 8(3), 475–496.

Sohoni, T., Paternoster, R., McGloin, J.M., & Bachman, R. (2014). "Hen's teeth and horse's toes": The adult onset offender in criminology. *Journal of Crime and Justice*, 37(2), 155–172.

Stafford, M.C., & Warr, M. (1993). A reconceptualization of general and specific deterrence. *Journal of Research in Crime and Delinquency*, 30(2), 123–135.

Sykes, G.M., & Matza, D. (1958). Techniques of neutralization: A theory of delinquency. *American Sociological Review*, 22(6), 664–670.

Thomas, K.J., & Vogel, M. (2019). Testing a rational choice model of "desistance": Decomposing changing expectations and changing utilities. *Criminology*, 57(4), 687–714.

Thrasher, F.M. (1927). *The gang: A study of 1,313 gangs in Chicago.* Chicago, IL: University of Chicago Press.

Tittle, C.R., Ward, D.A., & Grasmick, H.G. (2003). Gender, age, and crime/deviance: A challenge to self-control theory. *Journal of Research in Crime and Delinquency*, 40(4), 426–453.

Toby, J. (1957). Social disorganization and stake in conformity: Complementary factors in the predatory behavior of hoodlums. *The Journal of Criminal Law, Criminology, and Police Science*, 48(1), 12–17.

Uggen, C., & Massoglia, M. (2003). Desistance from crime and deviance as a turning point in the life course. In *Handbook of the life course.* Boston, MA: Springer, pp. 311–329.

van Veen, F., & Sattler, S. (2020). Modeling updating of perceived detection risk: The role of personal experience, peers, deterrence policies, and impulsivity. *Deviant Behavior*, 41(4), 413–433.

Victoroff, J. (2005). The mind of the terrorist: A review and critique of psychological approaches. *Journal of Conflict Resolution*, 49(1), 3–42.

Walsh, A., & Ellis, L. (1999). Political ideology and American criminologists' explanations for criminal behavior. *The Criminologist*, 24(6), 1–27.

Wilson, T., Paternoster, R., & Loughran, T. (2017). Direct and indirect experiential effects in an updating model of deterrence: A research note. *Journal of Research in Crime and Delinquency*, 54(1), 63–77.

Wolfgang, M.E., Figlio, R.M., & Sellin, T. (1972). *Delinquency in a birth cohort.* Chicago, IL: University of Chicago Press.

Young, J.K., & Dugan, L. (2014). Survival of the fittest: Why terrorist groups endure. *Perspectives on Terrorism*, 8(2), 2–23.

Young, J.K., & Findley, M.G. (2011). Promise and pitfalls of terrorism research. *International Studies Review*, 13(3), 411–431.

10

Terrorism and Deterrence

Pauline L. Moore and Brian A. Jackson

Deterrence is a central feature of counterterrorism. The impossibility of completely eliminating a target's vulnerabilities makes it a necessary component to strategies focused on defeated terrorists; but like many other counterterrorism strategies, including those that focus on prevention and response, the effectiveness of deterrence strategies is difficult to capture and measure.

Traditional concepts of deterrence seek to thwart unwanted terrorist behavior by manipulating the incentives of adversaries: certain strategies seek to raise the costs of particular courses of action, and others seek to deny terrorists the benefits that they might accrue by pursuing these courses of action. Deterrence against terrorist groups, however, is especially fraught with complexity, given the wide variation that exists in terrorist group motivations, among other factors, and in the value that terrorists appear to accrue from actions regardless of the nature of the government response.

This chapter provides an overview of the growing literature examining terrorist decision-making, with an aim to broaden our understanding of deterrence's role in counterterrorism policy. Prior studies have pointed to terrorist groups' dynamic responses to security measures; to further optimize counterterrorism strategies, practitioners need to understand the full spectrum of strategies, and how terrorist groups are likely to respond to them. We discuss the various strategies of deterrence as they apply to countering terrorism, and also provide a discussion of deterrence at the strategic, operational, and tactical levels, and the adaptations that attackers are likely to make in response to these strategies. Ideally, policymakers would be able to design security measures in a way that manipulates terrorist decision-making to produce net security benefits. Our review draws on literature from criminology, economics, and political science, among other disciplines.

The rest of the chapter proceeds as follows. In the next section, we provide a brief discussion of the origins of deterrence theory and its evolution in the context of counterterrorism policy and outline the major assumptions that ground the theory. Following that is a discussion of the three principal strategies of deterrence covered in the literature—deterrence-by-denial, deterrence by punishment, and deterrence through influence. The next section then explains how to think about deterrence across three different levels: strategic deterrence, operational deterrence, and tactical deterrence. The last section concludes with a discussion of deterrence in practice, focusing in particular on measurement challenges involved in determining whether counterterrorism efforts produce their intended effect.

Theoretical Assumptions of Terrorism Deterrence

Classic approaches to deterrence aim to affect the perceived costs of specific behavior (see e.g., Long, 2008; Schelling, 1980). Deterrence theory gained prominence as a military strategy during the Cold War, and emphasized the notion that coercion and intimidation, backed by the destructive power of nuclear weapons, could suffice to dissuade an adversary from engaging in undesirable actions (Brodie, 2015 [1959]; Schelling, 2008 [1966]). Subsequently, a more robust approach to deterrence sought to ensure that would-be attackers would not see a path to victory even if they were willing to incur tremendous costs; this form of deterrence hinged on the notion that adversaries would be discouraged from action because the expected payoffs or rates of success appeared too low. In an age when the risk of global conflict carried existential consequences for the world's two major superpowers, nuclear arsenals created an environment of mutual deterrence that ensured such conflict would not occur.

Across disciplines, deterrence presumes that one party can use threats to convince another party to refrain from initiating a particular course of action (Huth, 1999). A threat works as a deterrent to the extent that it succeeds in convincing its target to not carry out the action; in other words, for a threat to have a deterrent effect, it must sufficiently raise the expected costs of engaging in an action, relative to the expected benefits gained from that action. In the criminology literature, arguments for deterrence make the case that the likelihood and severity of punishment for committing a crime drives the calculus of criminals, and ultimately their behavior (Cook, 1980). Beginning in the 1970s, deterrence theory grew as an explanation for understanding why individuals commit crime (i.e., individuals make decisions based on what will garner them pleasure and avoid pain, and unless deterred they will pursue their desires, even if through committing crimes), and also as a solution to crime (i.e., a targeted message laying out the repercussions of committing a crime is received by the targeted group, who perceives it as a crime, and the group makes rational decisions based on the information received (Pratt et al., 2006)). As we explain later in this chapter, deterrence theory in criminology—as well as other disciplines such as political science—is both a micro- and macro-level theory. The concept of "specific deterrence" contends that individuals who engage in crime will be deterred from future criminal activity when they are apprehended and punished. "General deterrence" suggests that the general population can be deterred from committing offenses when they are aware of the consequences that others have faced after engaging in criminal activity. Specific and general deterrence are both grounded in individual perceptions around the certainty, severity, and celerity of punishment.

Modern deterrence theory is often applied to non- and post-nuclear challenges, including terrorism. That said, deterrence works differently across different types of threats. For example, the strategic-level, deterrence-by-punishment effect that persisted throughout the Cold War is of more limited value against violent non-state groups who maintain little, if any, infrastructure worth protecting against attack, and who are by some accounts prepared to "lose it all" in the service of achieving some broader objective (see e.g., Davis & Jenkins, 2002; Helfstein et al., 2009). Moreover, although concepts of deterrence such as the certainty and severity of punishment can apply as much to terrorists as they do to criminals, important differences between the two types of actors make the deterrence of terrorism unique. The application of deterrence, in other words, shifts with the strategic environment.

Terrorism deterrence models operate under the assumption that terrorist organizations and the individuals who participate in terrorism are rational beings; they make decisions based on the desire to achieve specific goals and weigh different options for pursuing these goals according to a defined value structure. The theory is parsimonious, hence its appeal: actors make decisions to optimize their own well-being while minimizing costs. Contrary to sentimental interpretations that terrorists and the actions in which they engage are "crazy" or "irrational," or that they are ideological fanatics, rational-actor models assume that the choice to use terrorism is calculated, purposeful, and rational in the sense that it helps individuals or the group achieve their objectives at a reasonable cost. For counterterrorism policy, the implication of a rational-actor understanding of terrorism is that terrorists will respond in a calculated way to state actions that sufficiently raise the cost of terrorism.

Deterrence aimed at terrorists—as individuals or groups—is therefore qualitatively different than deterrence of rival nation-states in military conflict. Because terrorist decision-making often involves relatively few individuals, dynamics within the group can shape the perceived costs and benefits of specific actions, and of the risks that are involved in choosing one course of action over another. Rather than seeking to influence the calculus of a rival political system and the actions taken by its military apparatus, deterrence of terrorism may practically involve shaping the decisions of relatively few people.

The circumstances of terrorist decision makers can also mean that human foibles and biases can shape their decisions more generally. These types of dynamics have been the focus of studies grounded in behavioral economics, among other disciplines; they consider how factors such as an individual's enhanced fear of losses, relative to perceptions about the value of gains, or recent experiences, might disproportionately affect risk perception (see e.g., McGill, 2009). Other individual biases, especially when combined with group-level dynamics, can also provide useful levers for deterrence efforts that might not otherwise be available if the target was an entire national government (see e.g., McCauley & Moskalenko, 2008, 2014). A growing number of studies apply criminological theories to better understand how decision-making dynamics at the level of individuals affects the evolution of terrorism and counterterrorism, including efforts to deter terrorists (Freilich & LaFree, 2015; Perry & Hasisi, 2015). And interpersonal interactions like intra- and inter-group competition and the pressures of operating as clandestine groups can also shape how terrorists make choices, potentially providing additional entry points for influence (Perkoski, 2019; Phillips, 2015).

As a counterterrorism strategy, deterrence is a direct practical implication of strategic approaches to understanding terrorism. Such approaches draw on the following set of assumptions to understand terrorist behavior:

- The outcomes of terrorism depend on strategic interactions between the terrorist group and its targeted audience (usually a government);
- Terrorist group preferences are given, ordered, and transitive and stable over time;
- Terrorist groups are unitary actors.

This particular analytical model yields relatively straightforward implications: in general, governments should be able to stop or curb terrorism by imposing high costs on the use of terrorism, and never rewarding terrorist behavior (Kydd & Walter, 2006). A counterterrorism strategy based on the concept of deterrence should be successful as long as it raises the perceived risks and costs associated with engaging in terrorism to sufficiently high levels. For instance, high spending on military campaigns to defeat terrorists abroad and measures imposed to improve homeland security aim to demonstrate to terrorists the futility of planning and attempting terror attacks against the US In short, strategic approaches to terrorism appeal to policymakers because they distill complex problems like terrorism into simple representations that lead to an ideal set of policy responses with estimated likelihoods of success (Chenoweth & Moore, 2018, p. 44).

As we will discuss later in this chapter, there are limitations to strategic approaches to understanding terrorism, which then affect the ability of counterterrorism policies to deter terrorism. First, terrorist organizations are rarely unitary actors (Best & Bapat, 2018; Bueno de Mesquita & Dickson, 2007). Strategic approaches that rely on this assumption to design counterterrorism policies can therefore miss important aspects of groups' incentives and capabilities that lead them to commit terror attacks. Second, the preferences of terrorist groups shift over time (Abrahms, 2008). In the case of Al-Qaeda, for instance, the group has shifted its operations depending on whether its main objective was to wage defensive jihad in Afghanistan and the Balkans in the 1990s, attack the United States, or exploit local conflicts and shore up support in weak states such as Iraq, Syria, and Pakistan after the 2001 and 2003 US invasions of Afghanistan and Iraq, respectively. If terrorist group preferences are not stable, it is difficult to craft coherent policies to deter terrorism, even for single groups. Third, because deterrence policies borne of strategic approaches to understanding terrorism focus singularly on the tactic of terrorism itself, rather than the reasons why people engage in such an extreme form of fighting in the first place, they can be amoral and agnostic to the origins of terrorists' preferences.

Certain approaches to deterrence have had unintended consequences, causing broader counterterrorism efforts to backfire.

Strategies of Deterrence

As noted in the previous section, assumptions that terrorists are rational actors ground deterrence theory and ultimately, deterrence strategies. But strategic approaches to terrorism have drawn criticism, most notably for relying on unrealistic notions of rationality and for lacking empirical support (George & Smoke, 1974; Jervis, 1979). Critics have also questioned the utility of trying to deter the modern terrorist threat, on the basis of this particular adversary's lack of territory, seemingly irrational tactics, and lack of unitary approaches to waging violence (Betts, 2002; Davis & Jenkins, 2002). In fact, the 2002 *National Security Strategy of the United States* embodied these challenges by stating that "Traditional concepts of deterrence will not work against a terrorist enemy whose avowed tactics are wonton destruction ... whose so-called soldiers seek martyrdom in death and whose most potent protection is statelessness" (Bush, 2002a). In the subsequent *2003 National Strategy for Counterterrorism* (Bush, 2002b) the word "deter" did not even appear in the text.[1]

Despite these challenges, the terrorism literature and empirical evidence of past approaches to counterterrorism suggest that certain long-standing strategies of deterrence can in fact work to deter actors from engaging in this form of political contention. We discuss several of these strategies in this section.

Punishment and Denial

Measures that threaten the capability of terrorists to act can be effective approaches to deterrence. In the counterterrorism literature, most policies that aim to punish terrorists for their actions and deny them the possibility of staging attacks fall into the category of so-called "hard-power" approaches to deterring terrorism.

Deterrence through punishment involves the deployment of tangible sources of power—for instance military or police forces—and employs enemy-centric doctrines that consist of specific tactics such as drone strikes to eliminate leaders or armed groups, military interventions or occupations, and increased policing and intelligence operations, among others (Johnston, 2012; Jordan, 2009; Rineheart, 2010). The underlying purposes of deterrence-by-punishment is to impose real costs on groups and individuals that engage in terrorism; the element of coercion is key to such strategies insofar as punishment is calibrated in such a way that terrorism will no longer seem appealing to would-be attackers (Dugan & Chenoweth, 2012). In deterrence-by-punishment, the threat of reprisal is intended to deter the adversary with unacceptable costs.

The effectiveness of deterrence-by-punishment measures varies, and in some cases can depend on factors such as certainty, celerity, and severity of punishment. Nagin (2013a, 2013b), for instance, shows that the certainty of punishment is a more effective deterrent of crime than the severity of punishment: more precise statements establishing the certainty of apprehension for committing a crime is a more effective deterrent than statements expounding on the length of prison sentences. Similar studies also support the finding that individuals are, on average, ambiguity-averse, and therefore less likely to engage in nefarious activity if the consequences of their actions are more explicitly defined (Loughran et al., 2011).

When it comes to combating terrorist groups specifically, however, the objective of raising costs through retaliation can appear intractable when groups seem to benefit from their actions regardless of the nature of the counterterrorism response. This is clear in Kydd and Walter's (2006) elaboration of terrorist motives and strategies, which argues that terrorists are at once motivated to coerce governments into making concessions and to provoke them into draconian responses and overreaction. If a government's punitive responses raise the costs of engaging in terrorism to excessively high levels, the terrorist group has achieved its objective of provoking its adversary to go on the offensive. In other words, the logic suggests that terrorism offers strategic utility in spite of the punishment that it may invite.

Debates over the effectiveness of deterrence-by-punishment strategies also focus on specific tactics of deterrence. For example, studies have shown that the deterrent effect of leadership decapitation is highly dependent on the nature of the group being deterred. Though Radlauer (2006) and other studies find that concerted attacks against specific, traditionally structured hierarchical terror organizations can be effective, it is unclear that eliminating group leaders is an effective deterrent against larger, more networked organizations (Geipel, 2007; Kenney et al., 2017). The removal of one or two highly placed and connected individuals is unlikely to deter the activities of decentralized, "small world" terrorist networks. The threat of drone strikes and other decapitation strategies may therefore fail to deter large terrorist organizations that rely on a broad network of weakly connected operatives. In fact, such strategies might lead certain groups to adapt their recruitment and operating strategies toward flatter structures that are resilient to certain deterrence-by-punishment efforts.

Notably, deterrence-by-punishment strategies also risk failure due to the potential for unintended consequences. This is particularly true in the case of indiscriminate punishment strategies applied to broad populations, which can heighten the perceived illegitimacy of the counterterrorist. In a study of the effectiveness of Israel's policy of house demolitions in response to suicide terror attacks during the Second Intifada, Benmelech et al. (2015) find that demolitions that explicitly targeted the homes of established Palestinian terror operatives were linked to decreases in attacks. Operations that indiscriminately targeted the homes of Palestinians, on the other hand, did not correlate to a decrease in terrorism. Populations often view indiscriminate repression as illegitimate, and its use can cause policies intended to deter terrorism to backfire by drawing more supporters to the terrorists' cause (Argomaniz & Vidal-Diez, 2015).

Deterrence-by-denial strategies seek to make it infeasible or unlikely for terrorism to achieve a particular objective; they focus on denying an attacker the confidence to stage an attack—for instance by increasing the number of operatives or materials required to successfully carry out an attack (Mazarr, 2021).[2] Unlike deterrence-by-punishment strategies, which threaten to impose costs on terrorists for engaging in undesirable courses of action, deterrence-by-denial seeks to deny terrorists any benefits (Snyder, 2015 [1961]).

The objective of denial strategies is not only to defend against attack, but also influence the behavior of an adversary. They send a message to potential attackers that the defender is determined to deny success; unlike deterrence-by-punishment strategies (in which a defender's actions would only take place after an attack has occurred), denial strategies force a defender to make commitments *ex-ante*, before an attacker chooses to attack. The increased emphasis on detection, relative to deterrence-by-punishment strategies, induces a change in the attacker's risk calculus, ultimately decreasing the benefits reaped from an attack and potentially leading the attacker to revise their course of action. Over time, such strategies have become common responses to terrorist desires to delegitimize governments through force and by alienating and frightening their populations; they have included investments in homeland security, such as airport security measures, and other moves to protect critical infrastructure (Stein & Levi, 2020). To some extent, they have been effective: Landes' (1978) landmark study of airline hijackings showed early on that the deployment of metal detectors in airports has a large benefit–cost ratio.

However, not knowing the risk calculus of an attacker poses a significant challenge when it comes to evaluating the effectiveness of a deterrence-by-denial strategy. In the case of a highly motivated attacker, the likelihood of failure may be an acceptable cost. Would-be bombers can frame even unsuccessful attacks as a gain, particularly in a war of attrition against a highly capable enemy (Kydd & Walter, 2006). Moreover, persistent attackers may continually probe the weaknesses of a specific target to identify the weakest links in a security chain, or displace their attacks to lesser protected targets (see e.g., Enders & Sandler, 2004, 2012). In this case, deterrence strategies have not denied terrorism, but rather worked to displace attacks to other locations. We discuss this particular challenge in more detail later in the chapter.

Influence and Conciliation

Strategies of deterrence by influence are a direct response to traditional deterrence concepts—deterrence-by-punishment and deterrence-by-denial—which critics contend are unlikely to be effective against terrorist groups motivated by a wide variety of personal and strategic aims. Influence strategies—even when they employ coercion—aim to push terrorists toward desisting or disengaging from terrorism by broadening the range of counterterrorism targets to include the broader populations from which terrorist groups recruit their members, increase their capabilities, or benefit from other types of support.

Deterrence by influence presumes that the threat of punishment may be able to shape the behavior of non-terrorist populations, and thus affect terrorist behavior indirectly (Davis & Jenkins, 2002). For instance, in the case of global organizations such as the Islamic State of Iraq and Syria (ISIS), which rely on support and action from smaller, locally based "franchise groups" dispersed throughout the world, it may be sufficient to reduce the capabilities of these component groups to disable the overall organization (Davis & Jenkins, 2002; Freedman, 2004). In early work around deterring the global Al-Qaeda terrorist network, Trager and Zagorcheva (2005) also emphasize the value of targeting nonpolitical ends to deter critical elements of terrorist networks from participating in terrorist enterprises; certain essential elements of terrorist support systems are likely to be less motivated than the terrorists themselves, and therefore vulnerable to influence. Strong states such as the United States have the ability to influence terrorists' political aims and to hold these ends at risk if terrorist adversaries cooperate with one another. Deterrence strategies of this nature require attention to the network structures of terrorist organizations, as well as to the processes that lead to attacks.

Other studies point to the value of targeting regimes that harbor terrorists or provide them with other types of support as a means of deterring terrorism; recent US military campaigns in Afghanistan sent a message signaling that the United States and its allies possess the intent, resolve, and capability to unseat regimes that support terrorism (Bowen, 2004). Finally, the finding that terrorist groups have achieved their stated objectives only 7 percent of the time (Abrahms, 2006) suggests that their supporters may be especially deterrable via targeted messages that educate broader populations about the tactic's politically counterproductive effects (Abrahms, 2014).

Other approaches to deterrence by influence rely on soft-power instruments to deter terrorism and focus less on heightening the perceived costs of terrorism than they do on increasing the perceived benefits of abstaining or disengaging from terrorism. Unlike deterrence-by-punishment or denial, these types of strategies take a persuasive approach to countering terrorism and rely on instruments such as political concessions or economic, social, or cultural influence. Though some of these instruments may be punitive in nature, they are by definition noncoercive; some even include rewards or conciliation for individuals or groups that turn away from terrorism.

As an example, many Western states turned to implementing early prevention programs that fall under the banner of countering violent extremism (CVE) in the late 2000s; "terrorism prevention" activities have recently superseded these programs and seek to broaden the options available to address the risk of individual radicalization and mobilizations toward terrorism (and other forms of violence) (Jackson et al., 2019). These broad-brush approaches encapsulate a range of noncoercive tools and programs that engage community leaders and organizations, as well as government leaders, to counter recruiting or radicalization messaging. Their aim is to intervene before individuals carry out serious crimes, including, but not limited to, terrorism.

Other types of "soft-power" deterrence strategies, such as conciliation, can be effective insofar as they carry less potential for engendering the harmful unintended consequences wrought by hard-power approaches to deterrence such as indiscriminate punishment strategies. Conciliatory approaches seek to alter the political context to make terrorism appear less appealing as a form of political contention; Dugan and Chenoweth (2012) explain conciliation as rhetoric and action, to include making concessions to terrorist groups, or action signaling the deterrer's intent to cooperate or negotiate with a terror group. Such approaches may be particularly effective if they are able to convey to terrorist group members, as well as the broader population from which these groups emerge, that engaging in conventional forms of political participation have more benefits than engaging in terrorism. In fact, some groups have made explicit statements speaking to the potential for conciliatory strategies to successfully deter terrorism: Hamas co-founder Mahmud Al-Zahar has been quoted as stating, "we must calculate the benefit and cost of continued armed operations. If we can fulfill our goals without violence, we will do so" (Mishal & Sela, 2006, p. 71).

Importantly, conciliatory approaches also have their place in broader terrorism deterrence strategies that combine a mix of approaches. In the case of counterterrorism approaches against groups active in Europe during the 1970s, for instance, certain forms of conciliation such as conditional leniency with individual prisoners from targeted groups effectively deterred terrorism activity when they were applied in conjunction with preexisting coercive measures and the threat of punishment (Geipel, 2007). Similar studies show that critical infrastructure reinforcement and defense, combined with active military and law enforcement deployments in a time of heightened threat, have also proven themselves as effective terrorism deterrence strategies when they are combined with efforts to increase societal resilience against home-grown terrorists (Gearson, 2012).

As this section makes clear, a critical challenge in the study of counterterrorism deterrence has been the inability to measure the relative effectiveness of different approaches. Obstacles to testing theories of deterrence-by-punishment and denial, as well as softer approaches based on influence and conciliation, are significant. Without systematic access into the thought processes of terrorists and the groups they join, it is difficult to gauge whether periods of inactivity speak to the success of different deterrence strategies; we have little, if any, way of knowing how many would-be attackers have been deterred by the threat of punishment or the opportunity to engage in institutional politics. Although some data do exist that enable us to make linkages between terrorist behavior and certain policies such as target hardening at airports, any inferences that we draw remain limited.

Levels of Deterrence

When considering the role of these various strategies of deterrence in counterterrorism planning, a critical question is how various security measures will affect the perceived cost, utility, and uncertainties associated with specific terrorist operations. A terrorist's perceived enemy—for example the United States—is a collection of varied targets, each one vulnerable to a number of attack modes and unique in terms of associated costs, risks of failure, and potential payoffs. In what follows, we expand the discussion to consider deterrence from the strategic, operational, and tactical levels as viewed from the attacker's perspective.

Strategic-level Deterrence

During the Cold War, which introduced deterrence as a component of military planning, efforts concentrated squarely at the *strategic level*; the goal of deterrence was to influence nations' decision makers to prevent war entirely, and nuclear war in particular. This was an expansive goal for deterrence, which policymakers largely pursued via the mechanism of deterrence-by-punishment by assured retaliation if such a war ever started. For global powers with much at risk from such retaliation, it was reasonable to believe that the deterrent effect produced by mutually assured destruction would be a powerful disincentive to act.

Seeking to achieve this type of deterrence of terrorism is much more difficult. Unlike state actors, the reality behind the aphorism that terrorist attacks often "do not have a return address" limits punishment options (see e.g., Abrahms & Conrad, 2017). Moreover, non-state groups seldom have extensive infrastructures and assets that can be put at direct risk through retaliation in the same way. Though it is less of a feature of contemporary terrorism than it was in some historical conflicts, some groups believe that perceptions that a government actor's security or retaliatory responses to terrorism were excessive can actually attract supporters to their cause—meaning that triggering retaliation and overreaction is actually a goal of terrorist violence (National Research Council, 2002; Kydd & Walter, 2006).

While these factors can limit the deterrent value of direct punishment or retaliation against terrorist groups or their members, non-state groups often rely on support structures or sympathetic populations for material and other support. Other analyses of deterrence—including those discussed above under the broader concept of influence—have suggested such populations might be more susceptible to traditional deterrence-by-punishment strategies (Davis & Jenkins, 2002). In some cases, counterterrorist policies have been designed with that goal in mind: for example, the Israelis attempted to create this type of deterrence through a policy of putting the assets of militants' broader families at risk (Benmelech et al., 2015).

While achieving strategic deterrence from terrorism through punishment might be difficult, would the other strategies of deterrence reviewed above—specifically deterrence-by-denial—be more successful? Deterrence-by-denial seeks to reduce the attractiveness of terrorist action by denying groups the overall benefit accrued from carrying out attacks—either by increasing the costs of staging attacks or by reducing their likelihood of succeeding. Investments in prevention or preparedness are examples of such approaches. While the central challenge of strategic deterrence-by-punishment was that terrorist groups had so few assets to put at risk through retaliation, the challenge to seeking strategic success through deterrence-by-denial is that most societies have so many assets to protect. With many possible targets of terrorism, attempting to protect everything well enough to induce a terrorist group to conclude that no action would be worth trying is prohibitively expensive—both in monetary terms and to the extent that it would impose significant costs on the society attempting deny terrorists the opportunity to attack. For instance, US counterterrorism efforts in the wake of 9/11 to deny Al-Qaeda and other groups the opportunity to stage future attacks involved actions that raised concerns about how those efforts affected society and the rights of the citizens they were designed to protect. Widespread surveillance that sought to intercept Al-Qaeda communications was criticized for collecting data more broadly than intended; subsequent revelations about surveillance efforts spurred numerous critiques surrounding individuals' privacy rights, and the potential for counterterrorism tactics to infringe on these rights (see e.g., Maras, 2012; Risen & Lichtblau, 2005). As a result, while strategic deterrence-by-denial might be an aspirational end goal of an ongoing national effort to strengthen security and preparedness, it is likely not realistic to see it as a practically achievable policy objective.

Nevertheless, even if *strategic* deterrence of terrorism proves elusive, "lower level" deterrence is a key element of security activities focused on non-state groups; the role of deterrence in shaping the choices they make, the actions they take, and the targets they see as attractive is a critical component of security and preparedness to manage the risk of terrorism. As a result, understanding the theory behind less expansive types of deterrence is at least as important as considering whether strategic-level deterrence theory does or does not apply to terrorist actors, and conflicts against non-state groups more generally. Doing so requires applying insights from fields focused on both individual- and group-level decision-making that we discuss above: considering how issues of cost, benefit, and risk shape choices among different types of terrorist activities and might then deter a group from pursuing one or more of these (*operational-level deterrence*); and how shaping the choices that individuals make around specific actions or targets can deter attacks (*tactical-level deterrence*).

Operational-level Deterrence

Deterrence of terrorism at the operational level is best defined as the effect that counterterrorist or security actions can have on groups' pursuit of specific classes of terrorist behavior. These efforts focus on group decision-making processes and group choices about what they will do and how; operational deterrence seeks to shape these choices in a way that is beneficial for security and reduces risk. Specifically, deterrence at this level rests on the notion that a particular type of target that is attractive to terrorist groups can be made less attractive through measures or initiatives that decrease the apparent benefit of attacking that target (e.g., hardening it so that it is less likely to be damaged); increase the cost of attacking that target (e.g., adding security measures that force attackers to devote more time or resources to planning an attack); increasing risk (e.g., changing security measures to make it more likely an attacker will be caught and the operation will fail); or some combination thereof.

For example, in the early history of terrorism, attacks on US embassies abroad involving hostage-taking were attractive operations for some groups. Increases in security to protect embassy buildings reduced the incidence of those attacks, but groups eventually shifted to attacking embassy personnel outside embassy buildings (Enders & Sandler, 1993). In another example, Palestinian terrorist groups that frequently targeted indoor shopping malls in Israel substituted their tactics by staging more outdoor attacks, in response to increases in security to keep attackers out of the interior of malls. While outdoor attacks caused significant damage, the counterterrorism strategy moved the attacks from "a closed area where the impact of the blast would have been very powerful, [to a more open one] where the impact was weaker" (Pedahzur & Perliger, 2006, p. 283). Attacks on the aviation system, including airplanes in flight, provide another salient example of shifts in terrorist operations. The frequency of airplane hijackings, which were very common in the early era of modern terrorism, fell dramatically in response to measures that made it more difficult to bring weapons onto planes. However, terrorists quickly replaced these tactics with others including bombings and hijackings via other means (see e.g., Enders & Sandler, 1993). Other analyses of this facet of terrorist behavior and deterrence have used the term "target-shifting," since causing groups to shift their focus from one target to another is a prominent effect of deterrence at this level (Kessel, 2010).

Efforts to dissuade groups from pursuing specific classes of weapons can also be viewed as operational deterrence. There has been great concern for many years about the potential for terrorist groups to use surface-to-air, man-portable missiles (MANPADs) to strike at civilian aircraft in flight, including concern that efforts to protect the aviation system from other types of attacks would increase the incentive for groups to seek out these particular weapons. Similarly, terrorist group use of unconventional weapons—chemical, biological, radiological, or nuclear (CBRN) weapons—has caused similar levels of consternation (Auerswald, 2006; Stone, 2009). Efforts to deter groups from seeking out such weapons attempt to change the perceived costs, benefits, and risks of doing so. The counterterrorism tools are similar to those used to protect targets— for example, deploying detection technologies that would pick up the use of such weapons or make it easier to discover groups that are trying to build them. For example, putting MANPAD protection technologies on airliners would increase the chance that an attack using one would fail. However, there are other options as well. Perhaps most notably, a terrorist group would need to acquire a MANPAD in order to use one. While intelligence and security organizations could seek to detect and arrest individuals attempting to do so, they could also "participate" in the black market for such weapons, acting as fake sellers in order to discover who was seeking such weapons. If counterterrorists made their tactics known, revealing such information could shift the perceived risk of participating in such markets for many terrorist groups, potentially deterring them from doing so and therefore operationally deterring them from using this particular class of weapons.

Tactical-level Deterrence

While operational-level deterrence focuses on subsets of possible terrorist activities and targets the planning phase of terror group activity, tactical-level deterrence operates at the lowest level, seeking to affect decisions and alter behavior as groups are in the process of acting on their choices. In making a decision to attack a specific target, a terrorist group makes judgments about the costs, benefits, and risks associated with a particular action, and then decides whether these are acceptable; if so, it will move forward with its plans. However, once an attack is underway, the new information that terrorist operatives see and receive can alter these initial judgments and cause them to alter their behavior— for instance they may divert from their originally desired target and move toward a less desirable target, or change when or how they execute an attack. Some will even call off an operation entirely.

Tactical deterrence is most effective when security organizations have enough knowledge about how groups make their cost, benefit, and risk decisions—so that the counterterrorist action has a higher than zero chance of causing a shift in the attacker's judgment. In long-standing terrorist conflicts, security organizations may have enough intelligence on a specific group to engage in this form of deterrence effectively. A well-researched example is the decades-long conflict between the British government and the Provisional Irish Republican Army (PIRA); in that case, security organizations had gained enough intelligence on the PIRA that they learned what sorts of changes—shifts in security deployment, changes in the environment such as staging a traffic jam that would hinder the attackers' chance of escape, among others— would cause the group to abandon an attack (Jackson, 2005; Jackson et al., 2005; Morral & Jackson, 2009). The use of tactical deterrence allowed security agencies to reduce risk based on the information they had about planned attacks, even if that information was not sufficient to take more direct action against the individuals involved.

In the absence of such detailed information about specific groups and their planned activities, classes of less-targeted actions still seek to take advantage of tactical deterrence as a protective strategy. An effective example includes adding an element of randomization to security deployments. Particularly for risk-averse attacker groups, one goal of extensive pre-attack surveillance is building up an understanding of the nature of security and protective measures at their intended target. If there is a random component to security—the numbers of guards change day to day, or their postings or patrol routes shift regularly—then the security the group encounters when they attack will likely look different than what they expected (Arce & Sandler, 2003; Pita et al., 2009). Depending on the group and its tolerance for risk, differences such as these could suffice to deter terrorist operatives from actually carrying out a plan through to completion.

Conclusions: Deterrence in Practice

Though deterrence as a concept has its theoretical origins in the sphere of state–state conflict, specifically in concerns about the prevention of nuclear war between the Soviet Union and the West, theories of deterrence against terrorist or other non-state groups require a different approach, and practical deterrence requires different strategies. Though massive punishment was the foundation for Cold War deterrence, deterrence-by-punishment is much less powerful when the target is not national political decision-making but decisions made by small groups of people or even individual terrorist actors themselves. As a result, terrorism deterrence has much in common with the deterrence of criminal behavior, where the denial of benefits and the certainty of punishment often have more leverage than the severity of punishment when it does occur.

The levels at which deterrence generally operates in the context of terrorism also complicate its role in security planning, and in the design of policy aimed at addressing the risk posed from terrorist violence. Strategic-level deterrence could well be a universal good; deterring terrorism from all potential attackers would benefit most everyone, just as strategic-level deterrence of nuclear war benefited the entirety of the nations in the international system. However, the unintended consequences of some approaches to strategic deterrence—namely indiscriminate approaches that apply punishment or denial strategies to broad populations—risk undermining counterterrorism efforts and contributing to the objectives of some terrorist organizations.

The benefits of operational- and tactical-level deterrence are narrower, and their value may vary a great deal when viewed from different perspectives. For a security planner responsible for securing a particular target or type of target, shifting an attack away from "their target" to a different one is a success—even if it leads to tragic outcomes for targets of the substituted attack. For a higher-level planner (e.g., a national policymaker), whether operational-level deterrence yields tangible security gains depends on a relative comparison of the two targets: if the substitute attack is likely to produce fewer casualties and damage than the originally planned attack, the deterrence strategy might be considered a success from a national perspective. Of course, this will be little consolation to the people or entities who bear the brunt of costs when an attack has simply shifted elsewhere.

A further complication is that the deterrence of terrorist actors is an inherently uncertain task. As is the case in virtually all other facets of human behavior and endeavors, different terrorists and terrorist groups diverge in the levels of cost, benefit, and risk that they are willing to accept. While nearly all such actors meet the definitions of rational decision-making—that is, they make reasoned choices in pursuit of goals they see as desirable—the processes through which they do so and the nature of their goals mean that there is great diversity in the processes they use to make those decisions. As a result, actions that might definitively deter one group may have little or no effect on another—for a security planner or nation seeking to implement a well-defined "deterrence strategy" as part of their response to terrorism, the benefits they can expect from deterrence will almost certainly vary in difficult to predict ways.

Does this unpredictability mean that deterrence does not have a role to play in countering terrorism? We do not think so. However, the role of deterrence must almost certainly be less central than it is in the context of state conflict, and policymakers and those responsible for security should treat deterrence as a contributor to security outcomes, rather than being foundational to achieving them. Any protective or security strategy implemented to defend a vulnerable target has the potential to deter adversaries beyond its direct protective effects. Because different potential attackers use different decision-making processes, a given security approach will deter some but not others. Those who are deterred represent an added security benefit—we should thus view deterrence as a "force multiplier," insofar as it provides levels of protection above what terrorists might otherwise have expected. Since levels of knowledge about the decision-making processes and risk tolerances of all potential adversaries will never be attainable—exceptional situations of long-term conflicts such as the Troubles in Northern Ireland notwithstanding—counterterrorists should not grant deterrence the same weight as they apply to more predictable protective outcomes that also shape a security plan.

Finally, we propose that security planners should also work to understand how successful deterrence at the operational or tactical level could complicate successful security planning. Operational-level deterrence is effective when it shifts adversary decisions about targets and modes of attack. While these shifts *may* produce a net reduction in overall risk, successful deterrence could paradoxically result in an increase in risk if deterrence measures have pushed the adversary toward alternatives that have the potential to cause greater harm (Jackson & LaTourrette, 2015). Such adverse effects mean that understanding the potential paths for deterrence—what an adversary's "next moves" might be in an ongoing conflict over time—is critical to ensuring that actions taken in pursuit of improved security do not result in unintended negative outcomes, even if deterrence is not a primary factor in the design of those actions.

Notes

1 For more information, see https://2001-2009.state.gov/s/ct/rls/rm/2003/17798.htm.
2 See www.rand.org/content/dam/rand/pubs/perspectives/PE200/PE295/RAND_PE295.pdf.

References

Abrahms, M. (2006). Why terrorism does not work. *International Security*, 31(2), 42–78.
Abrahms, M. (2008). What terrorists really want: Terrorist motives and counter-terrorism strategy. *International Security*, 32(4), 78–105.
Abrahms, M. (2014). Deterring terrorism: A new strategy. *Perspectives on Terrorism*, 8(3), 2–15.
Abrahms, M., & Conrad, J. (2017). The strategic logic of credit claiming: A new theory for anonymous terrorist attacks. *Security Studies*, 26(2), 279–304.
Arce, D.G., & Sandler, T. (2003). An evolutionary game approach to fundamentalism and conflict. *Journal of Institutional and Theoretical Economics (JITE)/Zeitschrift für die gesamte Staatswissenschaft*, 159(1), 132–154.
Argomaniz, J., &Vidal-Diez, A. (2015). Examining deterrence and backlash effects in counter-terrorism: The case of ETA. *Terrorism and Political Violence*, 27(1), 160–181.
Auerswald, D.P. (2006). Deterring nonstate WMD attacks. *Political Science Quarterly*, 121(4), 543–568.
Benmelech, E., Berrebi, C., & Klor, E.F. (2015). Counter-suicide-terrorism: Evidence from house demolitions. *The Journal of Politics*, 77(1), 27–43.

Best, R.H., & Bapat, N.A. (2018). Bargaining with insurgencies in the shadow of infighting. *Journal of Global Security Studies*, 3(1), 23–37.

Betts, R.K. (2002). The soft underbelly of American primacy: Tactical advantages of terror. *Political Science Quarterly*, 117(1), 19–36.

Bowen, W.Q. (2004). Deterrence and asymmetry: Non-state actors and mass casualty terrorism. *Contemporary Security Policy*, 25(1), 54–70.

Brodie, B. (2015 [1959]). *Strategy in the missile age*. Princeton, NJ: Princeton University Press.

Bueno de Mesquita, E., & Dickson, E.S. (2007). The propaganda of the deed: Terrorism, counterterrorism, and mobilization. *American Journal of Political Science*, 51(2), 364–381.

Bush, G.W. (2002a). National Security Strategy of the United States of America, Executive Office of the President, Washington, DC. Available at: https://2009-2017.state.gov/documents/organization/63562.pdf.

Bush, G.W. (2002b). National Strategy for Combating Terrorism, Executive Office of the President, Washington, DC. Available at: https://2001-2009.state.gov/s/ct/rls/rm/2003/17798.html.

Chenoweth, E., & Moore, P.L. (2018). *The politics of terror*. New York: Oxford University Press.

Cook, P.J. (1980). Research in criminal deterrence: Laying the groundwork for the second decade. *Crime and Justice*, 2, 211–268.

Davis, P.K., & Jenkins, B.M. (2002). *Deterrence and influence in counterterrorism: A Component in the war on al Qaeda*. Santa Monica, CA: Rand Corporation.

Dugan, L., & Chenoweth, E. (2012). Moving beyond deterrence: The effectiveness of raising the expected utility of abstaining from terrorism in Israel. *American Sociological Review*, 77(4), 597–624.

Enders, W., & Sandler, T. (1993). The effectiveness of antiterrorism policies: A vector-autoregression intervention analysis. *American Political Science Review*, 87, 829–844.

Enders, W., & Sandler, T. (2004). What do we know about the substitution effect in transnational terrorism? In A. Silke (Ed.), *Researching terrorism: Trends, achievements, failures*. Ilford: Frank Cass, pp. 119–137.

Enders, W., & Sandler, T. (2012). *The political economy of terrorism*. New York: Cambridge University Press.

Freedman, L. (2004). *Deterrence*. New York: Polity.

Freilich, J.D., & LaFree, G. (2015). Criminology theory and terrorism: Introduction to the special issue. *Terrorism & Political Violence*, 27(1), 1–8.

Gearson, J. (2012). Deterring conventional terrorism: From punishment to denial and resilience. *Contemporary Security Policy*, 33(1), 171–198.

Geipel, G.L. (2007). Urban terrorists in continental Europe after 1970: Implications for deterrence and defeat of violent nonstate actors. *Comparative Strategy*, 26(5), 439–467.

George, A.L., & Smoke, R. (1974). *Deterrence in American foreign policy: Theory and practice*. New York: Columbia University Press.

Helfstein, S., Meese, M.J., Rassler, D., Sawyer, R., Schnack, T., Sheiffer, M., Silverstone, S., & Taylor, S. (2009). White Paper prepared for the Secretary of Defense Task Force on DoD Nuclear Weapons Management: Tradeoffs and paradoxes: Terrorism, deterrence and nuclear weapons. *Studies in Conflict & Terrorism*, 32(9), 776–801.

Huth, P.K. (1999). Deterrence and international conflict: Empirical findings and theoretical debates. *Annual Review of Political Science*, 2(1), 25–48.

Jackson, B.A. (2005). Provisional Irish Republican Army. In B.A. Jackson, J.C. Baker, K. Cragin, J. Parachini, H.R. Trujillo, & P. Chalk, *Aptitude for destruction, Vol. 2: Case studies of organizational learning in five terrorist groups*. Santa Monica, CA: RAND Corporation, pp. 93–140.

Jackson, B.A., & LaTourrette, T. (2015). Assessing the effectiveness of layered security for protecting the aviation system against adaptive adversaries. *Journal of Air Transport Management*, 48, 26–33.

Jackson, B.A., Baker, J.C., Cragin, K., Parachini, J., Trujillo, H.R., & Chalk, P. (2005). *Aptitude for destruction, Vol. 2: Case studies of organizational learning in five terrorist groups*. Santa Monica, CA: RAND Corporation.

Jackson, B.A., Rhoades, A.L., Reimer, J.R., Lander, N., Costello, K., & Beaghley, S. (2019). *Practical terrorism prevention: Reexamining US national approaches to addressing the threat of ideologically motivated violence*. Santa Monica, CA: RAND Corporation.

Jervis, R. (1979). Deterrence theory revisited. *World Politics*, 31(2), 289–324.

Johnston, P.B. (2012). Does decapitation work? Assessing the effectiveness of leadership targeting in counterinsurgency campaigns. *International Security*, 36(4), 47–79.

Jordan, J. (2009). When heads roll: Assessing the effectiveness of leadership decapitation. *Security Studies*, 18(4), 719–755.

Kenney, M., Coulthart, S., & Wright, D. (2017). Structure and performance in a violent extremist network: The small-world solution. *Journal of Conflict Resolution*, 61(10), 2208–2234.

Kessel, R. (2010). The positive force of deterrence: Estimating the quantitative effects of target shifting. In *2010 International Water Side Security Conference*. Carrara, Italy: IEEE, pp. 1–5.

Kydd, A.H., & Walter, B.F. (2006). The strategies of terrorism. *International Security*, 31(1), 49–80.

Landes, W.M. (1978). An economic study of US aircraft hijacking, 1961–1976. *Journal of Law and Economics*, 21(1), 1–31.

Long, A. (2008). *Deterrence from cold war to long war: Lessons from six decades of RAND research*. Santa Monica, CA: Rand Corporation.

Loughran, T.A., Paternoster, R., Piquero, A.R., & Pogarsky, G. (2011). On ambiguity in perceptions of risk: Implications for criminal decision making and deterrence. *Criminology*, 49(4), 1029–1061.

Maras, M.H. (2012). The social consequences of a mass surveillance measure: What happens when we become the "others"? *International Journal of Law, Crime and Justice*, 40(2), 65–81.

Mazarr, M.J. (2021). Understanding deterrence. *NL ARMS Netherlands Annual Review of Military Studies 2020*, 13–28.

McCauley, C., & Moskalenko, S. (2008). Mechanisms of political radicalization: Pathways toward terrorism. *Terrorism and Political Violence*, 20(3), 415–433.

McCauley, C., & Moskalenko, S. (2014). Toward a profile of lone wolf terrorists: What moves an individual from radical opinion to radical action. *Terrorism and Political Violence*, 26(1), 69–85.

McGill, W.L. (2009). Defensive dissuasion in security risk management. *2009 IEEE International Conference on Systems, Man and Cybernetics*. San Antonio, TX: IEEE, pp. 3516–3521.

Mishal, S., & Sela, A. (2006). *The Palestinian Hamas: Vision, violence, and coexistence*. New York: Columbia University Press.

Morral, A.R., & Jackson, B.A. (2009). *Understanding the role of deterrence in counterterrorism security*. Santa Monica, CA: Rand Corporation.

Nagin, D.S. (2013a). Deterrence in the twenty-first century. *Crime and Justice*, 42(1), 199–263.

Nagin, D.S. (2013b). Deterrence: A review of the evidence by a criminologist for economists. *Annual Review of Economics*, 5(1), 83–105.

National Research Council (2002). *Discouraging terrorism: Some implications of 9/11*. Washington, DC: National Academies Press.

Pedahzur, A., & Perliger, A. (2006). The changing nature of suicide attacks: A social network perspective. *Social Forces*, 84(4), 1987–2008.

Perkoski, E. (2019). Internal politics and the fragmentation of armed groups. *International Studies Quarterly*, 63(4), 876–889.

Perry, S., & Hasisi, B. (2015). Rational choice rewards and the jihadist suicide bomber. *Terrorism and Political Violence*, 27(1), 53–80.

Phillips, B.J. (2015). Enemies with benefits? Violent rivalry and terrorist group longevity. *Journal of Peace Research*, 52(1), 62–75.

Pita, J., Jain, M., Ordónez, F., Portway, C., Tambe, M., Western, C., Paruchuri, P., & Kraus, S. (2009). Using game theory for Los Angeles airport security. *AI Magazine*, 30(1), 43–57.

Pratt, T.C., Cullen, F.T., Blevins, K.R., Daigle, L.E., & Madensen, T.D. (2006). The empirical status of deterrence theory: A meta-analysis. In F.T. Cullen, J.P. Wright, & K.R. Blevins (Eds.), *Advances in criminological theory, Vol. 15. Taking stock: The status of criminological theory*. Piscataway, NJ: Transaction Publishers, pp. 367–395.

Radlauer, D. (2006). Rational choice deterrence and Israeli counter-terrorism. *International Conference on Intelligence and Security Informatics*. Berlin, Heidelberg: Springer, pp. 609–614.

Rineheart, J. (2010). Counterterrorism and counterinsurgency. *Perspectives on Terrorism*, 4(5), 31–47.

Risen, J., & Lichtblau, E. (2005). Bush lets US spy on callers without courts. *The New York Times*, 16, A1.

Schelling, T.C. (1980). *The strategy of conflict: With a new preface by the author*. Cambridge, MA: Harvard University Press.

Schelling, T.C. (2008 [1966]). *Arms and influence*. New Haven, CT: Yale University Press.

Snyder, G.H. (2015 [1961]). *Deterrence and defense, Vol. 2168*. Princeton, NJ: Princeton University Press.

Stein, J.G., & Levi, R. (2020). Testing deterrence by denial: Experimental results from criminology. *Studies in Conflict & Terrorism*, 1–21.

Stone, J. (2009). Al Qaeda, deterrence, and weapons of mass destruction. *Studies in Conflict & Terrorism*, 32(9), 763–775.

Trager, R.F., & Zagorcheva, D.P. (2005). Deterring terrorism: It can be done. *International Security*, 30(3), 87–123.

11

Situational Crime Prevention and Terrorism

Joshua D. Freilich, Jeff Gruenewald, and Steven Chermak

This work summarizes the Situational Crime Prevention (SCP) and terrorism literature, a fairly new, but growing body of research. Clarke and Newman (2006) initiated this research 15 years ago when they extended SCP and applied it to the terrorism context. Historically, most terrorism scholars were psychologists or political scientists, though recently criminologists have also begun to engage terrorism, politically motivated crime and homeland security issues (Freilich & LaFree, 2015; LaFree & Freilich, 2016; for exceptions, see Hamm, 1993; Smith, 1994). Even though these earlier scholars varied in their discipline specific theoretical and methodological approaches, almost all stressed the importance of background factors, ideological grievances, and offender-level dispositions. In the past, some criminologists have concluded that what are considered traditional theories of crime, both sociological and psychological, could also explain terrorism (Agnew, 2016; LaFree & Dugan, 2004; Rausch & LaFree, 2007; Rosenfeld, 2004).

Other criminologists, however, stress the promise of preventing terrorism-related crimes by altering environments to reduce opportunities that make crime increasingly possible. Ecological approaches highlight temporal and spatial characteristics that may impact offender decision-making and victimization patterns, a complementary strategy to confront the myriad complex psychological and social causes and correlates underlying terrorism. These place-based crime models aim to eliminate or reduce situated opportunities for committing crime or at least mitigate the harms from those crimes that still occur. Examples include environmental criminology (Brantingham & Brantingham, 1990), routine activities theory (Cohen & Felson, 1979), hotspot analysis (Sherman et al., 1989; Weisburd & Green, 1995), and crime prevention through environmental design (CPTED) (Cozens, 2011), among others.

Incorporating key tenets of these ecological theories, SCP stresses purposeful or deliberate decision-making occurring across a series of stages (Cornish & Clarke, 2008). It is a practical, policy-oriented approach aiming to prevent or reduce crime in the future (Clarke, 1980). SCP is concerned with *how* offenders commit crime and calls for examining *specific crime types*. Based on particular crime patterns, intervening SCP mechanisms are created and employed to manipulate environments and eliminate the situational opportunities allowing crime to occur (Clarke, 1980; Freilich & Newman, 2017). SCP contends, in other words, that to reduce crime the focus must be on the criminal event, as opposed to distal root causes or structural or cultural dysfunctions that may be too far removed to influence the criminal event.

Importantly, many SCP strategies have been found to reduce crime (Guerette & Bowers, 2009; Weisburd et al., 2006). There are currently five SCP strategies, including 25 techniques that encompass "hard" and "soft" interventions (Center for Problem Oriented Policing, n.d.). Hard strategies increase the difficulty, associated risks, and efforts required to commit a crime, while soft approaches eliminate situational cues that provoke persons to offend and remove excuses justifying crime.

In 2006, Clarke and Newman (2006) published their book *Outsmarting the Terrorists* in which they argued that SCP interventions could be used to reduce terrorist attacks and mitigate the harms caused by those strikes that still occur. Clarke and Newman's (2006) theoretical exposition led to a burgeoning research area that empirically tested, extended, modified, and critiqued their claims. In the last 15 years over 100 works on SCP and terrorism have been published, including MA theses and PhD dissertations, that have tested these ideas.

In reviewing this literature, we focus on authors' backgrounds, their publication outlets, data sources, research focus, research methods, whether they investigate any of the four pillars of terrorism opportunity, and the countries and terrorist groups examined. We also highlight the substantive findings of these studies and note underdeveloped areas that deserve more attention. We end by providing suggestions for future research to address these gaps and extend the application of SCP to terrorism.

Outsmarting the Terrorists through Situational Crime Prevention

Clarke and Newman's (2006) book *Outsmarting the Terrorists* maintains that established techniques of SCP can be applied to terrorism due to its similarities with routine non-ideological crimes like burglary, robbery, white-collar crime, substance abuse, and so on. Both routine crime and terrorism usually implicate mixed motives, a degree of commitment and planning, peer networks, and exploiting opportunities for illegal behavior. Importantly, SCP stresses that those interested in counterterrorism or prevention must focus on the terrorist event itself as opposed to offenders' backgrounds, structural/cultural dysfunctions or other distal issues. Similarly, SCP proponents assume that since there is an unlimited number of potential terrorists, policies that seek to eliminate (i.e., imprison or kill) terrorists, as opposed to removing or reducing situational opportunities, will fail.

Clarke and Newman (2006) note the opportunity structure of terrorism that includes four pillars of targets, weapons, tools, and facilitating conditions. A careful examination of these pillars reveals the opportunities exploited by terrorists and the factors that make it more challenging for terrorists to prepare for and successfully execute attacks. The first pillar of opportunity involves the selection of targets. A common critique of the application of SCP to terrorism is that it is too expensive and taxing to protect all potential targets from a terrorist attack (Mueller, 2010; Stewart, 2008). However, Clarke and Newman (2006) counter that targets vary in their vulnerability; some are more attractive to terrorists, and thus a risk-assessment approach could identify and prioritize at-risk targets. This argument is based upon Clarke and Eck's (2005, pp. 4–5) earlier conclusion about routine crime, that it "is highly concentrated among particular people, places, and things ... [and] as this principle suggests, focusing resources on these concentrations is likely to yield the greatest preventive benefits." Clarke and Newman (2006) built upon prior SCP successes that created templates to identify the products most vulnerable for theft (Felson & Clarke, 1998), to devise a terrorism target risk-assessment template, known by the acronym *EVIL DONE*. Targets that are more *Exposed, Vital, Iconic, Legitimate, Destructible, Occupied, Near* and *Easy* are thought to be more at risk for a terrorist attack.

Those that stand out and are more visible are considered more *exposed* targets. *Vital* targets deliver the necessities that allow society to function such as electrical grids and water supplies. *Iconic* targets are symbolically significant to society (e.g., the Statue of Liberty), while *legitimate* targets are those that are seen as justifiable (e.g., uniformed soldiers on duty) compared to others who are viewed as undeserving of being targeted. Meanwhile, *destructible* targets are easier to destroy than other possible targets. Targets that contain more potential victims, or are more *occupied*, are also more at risk for attack. In addition, targets that are closer, or *nearer*, to the terrorists and easier to travel to are also more at risk. Also, targets that have less security/protection or are *easy* to access, are evaluated as increasingly vulnerable. Finally, in addition to these eight target dimensions, the expected loss, in terms of fatalities and injuries, upon attack must be considered. A thorough assessment of all these dimensions will identify the most vulnerable targets that must be prioritized for situational interventions to protect them from an attack.

The second pillar of opportunity refers to the weapons that terrorists decide to use. Clarke and Newman (2006) contend that just as targets vary in their attractiveness or vulnerability, weapons differ in the likelihood that terrorists will employ them. Clarke and Newman created the acronym *MURDEROUS* to summarize this pillar's dimensions. Terrorists are more likely to rely on weapons that can be employed in a variety of situations (*Multipurpose*), are easy to hide (*Undetectable*), simple to transport (*Removable*), can harm others (i.e., kill or wound) (*Destructive*), are fun to use (*Enjoyable*), usually work and can be counted on (*Reliable*), are easily available for use (*Obtainable*), are simple to use and do not require much training (*Uncomplicated*), and, to the extent possible, minimize the danger to the terrorist using it (*Safe*). Clarke and Newman (2006) suggest that observing and measuring how these particular dimensions are perceived by terrorists to be advantageous for specific types of crimes can be helpful in identifying the weapons that are most sought after by terrorists. Society could then devise intervention strategies that prevent terrorists from obtaining these weapons.

The third pillar of terrorist opportunity according to Clarke and Newman (2006) includes the *tools* that terrorists use to carry out their planned strikes. Common tools include money, which often is used to buy weapons, vehicles, and other travel devices that allow terrorists access to targets, or fraudulent identifications (e.g., passports, social security cards, or driver's licenses) that make it easier to travel without arousing suspicion. Terrorists who have these tools are better positioned to prepare for and then successfully commit their attacks. For example, Timothy McVeigh robbed gun dealers to raise funds to help him acquire the necessary resources to prepare for the 1995 Oklahoma City bombing (Hamm, 1997). Effective SCP strategies would manipulate the opportunity structure to prevent terrorists from accessing these tools.

The final pillar of opportunity is the *facilitating conditions* that allow terrorism to occur. These are more distal factors that have important situational implications in terms of the availability of tools and weapons to the terrorists (Freilich & Chermak, 2009; Wortley 1996, 2002). Clarke and Newman (2006) devised the *ESEER* acronym to summarize this pillar's five dimensions that include *Easy* conditions (e.g., a government rife with corruption where bribery is expected); *Safe* conditions where there is little oversight or few regulations in place (e.g., limited identification regulations); *Excusable* conditions (e.g., overreactions by governments that increase sympathy for the terrorists); *Enticing* conditions (e.g., community support for terrorists actions); and *Rewarding* conditions (e.g., financial, status, or religious rewards). Examples of facilitating conditions include banking, firearms, and immigration laws or policies. Again, these seemingly more distal factors have situational implications in their facilitation of opportunities that make it easier or harder to commit terrorist attacks. Wortley (1996) and Freilich and Chermak (2009) have explained how distal factors like guilt and an extremist political ideology also have important situational influences.

Since terrorists could take advantage of the four pillars of opportunities in many ways, Clarke and Newman (2006) argue that it is important to "think like a terrorist." Those charged with preventing attacks must identify and assess varying crime-specific opportunities available for committing terrorism, as each form of terrorism, whether a suicide bombing, or a targeted shooting assassination, has different opportunity structures. Thus, a successful intervention against one form of terrorism attack will usually not result in displacement to another. Once the opportunities are identified, SCP relies upon its 25 techniques of situational prevention to devise or identify possible interventions to prevent future attacks. SCP proponents endorse using or modifying past successful SCP interventions or innovatively devising novel ones to reduce future attacks (Eck, 2002a, 2002b; Ekblom, 2012).

SCP & Terrorism Literature, 2006–2020

Over 100 articles, chapters, or theses have been published on SCP and terrorism since Clarke and Newman's (2006) book. Two of us with another colleague (Freilich et al., 2019), systematically reviewed 60 articles and chapters that were published between 2006 and 2016. Here we summarize that study and also discuss an additional 27 SCP and terrorism studies that appeared after the previous review was published.

Freilich et al. (2019) examined a number of author-centered issues, such as the academic discipline they were trained in, solo versus collaborative authorship, and their level of publishing in this particular area. They were curious whether only criminologists were employing SCP to understand terrorism, or if trained sociologists, psychologists and others were also interested in this approach. Silke's (2001) classic review of the terrorism literature more generally demonstrated the importance of the latter two questions since academic collaborations often include authors with complementary skills that result in stronger studies than solo-authored works. Similarly, scholars publishing a series of studies in an area often extend their past research to usually create a more sophisticated body of work compared to those only publishing a solitary piece in the area.

Freilich et al. (2019) also captured the type of publication to roughly assess the rigor of these studies. In criminology and criminal justice and related fields, journal articles are usually prioritized over chapters due to being a product of higher levels of peer scrutiny or review. Other examined issues include when the studies were published (to measure the level of output over time); where they appeared (criminal justice outlets vs. other disciplines' periodicals); the type of studies conducted (anecdotal vs. conceptual vs. empirical, with more empirical studies reflecting a more advanced field); the methods used (quantitative vs. qualitative vs. mixed; descriptive vs. multivariate statistics); and data sources relied upon. Importantly, they examined whether the studies focused on any of the four pillars of terrorism opportunity, and empirically tested the *EVIL DONE, MURDEROUS,* and *ESEER* templates' or tools' claims. Finally, which nations and terrorist movements included in the prior studies were examined.

Freilich et al. (2019) identified 60 scholarly journal articles, book chapters, MA theses, and PhD dissertations by systematically searching *EBSCO Academic Search Premier, Criminal Justice Abstracts,* and *Google Scholar* to uncover any SCP and terrorism studies published between March 2006 (when Clarke and Newman's book was published) and spring 2016.¹ Once the correct time period was specified in the searchable indexes, key words like "situational crime prevention", "SCP", "environmental criminology," and "terrorism" were used to identify works. Initially, 69 scholarly works were identified, but nine studies were excluded because they either did not focus on SCP's applications to terrorism, or it was a chapter or PhD dissertation and the majority of the information was included in another article or book. The studies are listed in Appendix 11.1.² For this piece, we used the same search terms they employed to search Google Scholar to identify SCP and terrorism studies published after 2016. We identified 27 studies and they are listed in Appendix 11.2.³

Findings

This section outlines key findings from our previous review of the 60 SCP and terrorism articles published between 2006 and 2016 (Freilich et al., 2019), and discusses the additional 27 SCP and terrorism studies we identified that were subsequently published. Freilich, Gruenewald, and Mandala found that half of the 60 first authors of SCP and terrorism studies reviewed were trained (i.e., received their PhD) in criminal justice (see Table 11.1). Psychology (17 percent) and sociology (10 percent) were the next two most common disciplinary backgrounds of the lead authors. Only four (7 percent) of the first authors were trained

Table 11.1
Lead Author's Disciplinary Background

	Frequency	Percent
Criminal Justice	30	50.0
Psychology	10	16.7
Sociology	6	10.0
Political Science	4	6.7
Anthropology	2	3.3
Engineering	2	3.3
Chemistry	1	1.7
Military Studies	1	1.7
Public Affairs	1	1.7
Religious Studies	1	1.7
Security Studies	1	1.7
Social Work	1	1.7
Total	60	100

political scientists even though historically that field has dominated terrorism studies (Silke, 2004).

This trend accelerated in the period after 2016. Almost 78 percent (n = 21) of the lead authors of the 27 SCP and terrorism studies we identified had criminal justice, criminology, or crime science PhDs, or in one case an MA (highest degree). Only one first author had a Political Science PhD, one had an Anthropology and Sociology PhD, another had a Sociology MA (their highest degree), a fourth had an industrial engineering PhD, and a fifth was an attorney. We were unable to determine what field the remaining first author trained in. None of the first authors we identified were trained psychologists. Thus, as noted previously (Freilich et al., 2019), most scholars applying SCP to terrorism are criminologists, and few from other fields have employed this framework.

Freilich et al. (2019) reported that Silke (2004) found that the vast majority, over 90 percent, of terrorism studies were conducted by one scholar working alone. In other words, there were almost no collaborative research teams publishing terrorism studies. Silke concluded that most terrorism scholars lacked external support and the field was composed of isolated researchers. Conversely, Freilich et al. (2019) found that close to 50 percent of the 60 SCP and terrorism studies reviewed were authored by multiple researchers (see Table 11.2).

This trend also accelerated in the post-2016 period. In fact, over 85 percent (n = 23) of the 27 additional SCP and terrorism studies we identified were co-authored. Only two articles were solo authored and the other two works were a PhD dissertation and an MA thesis that, by nature, were also solo authored. These findings are consistent with studies finding that criminologists are increasingly conducting collaborative projects and co-authoring their studies (Fisher et al., 1998).

Silke (2004) also found that over 80 percent of terrorism studies published during the 1990s were written by "one-time" authors. Merari (1991) concluded this represented a weakness in terrorism studies. He argued that the lack of a solid core of scholars consistently publishing

Table 11.2
Number of Authors

	Frequency	Percent
Single-authored Works	31	51.7
Multiple-authored Works	29	48.3
Total	60	100

Table 11.3
Publication of Multiple Works as Lead Author

	Frequency	Percent
Single Lead-authored Works	50	83.3
Multiple Lead-authored Works	10	16.7
Total	60	100

in the area made it difficult to develop a shared body of findings that the field collectively built upon. Instead, the "coming and going" of scholars resulted in scattered research studies that other scholars rarely extended.

Freilich et al.'s (2019) findings supported Silke's earlier results. Only ten (17 percent) of the studies they reviewed were written by a lead author who was also a lead author on another study examining SCP and terrorism (see Table 11.3). They concluded that the most prolific lead author on the topic of SCP and terrorism was Graeme Newman, co-author of the Clarke and Newman (2006) study, which set the agenda for applying SCP to the study of terrorism. Newman authored four (7 percent) relevant studies; and the only other person who was lead author on more than two studies was Sunniva Frishlid Meyer, who authored three studies related to her doctoral dissertation research.

However, we uncovered a positive development in the more recent, post-2016 period. Over 59 percent (n = 16) of the 27 studies had first authors who were lead authors on more than one SCP and terrorism study. Marchment was the lead author on four works, Hsu was first author on three articles, while Freilich, Gruenewald, Mandala, and Perry were each lead authors on two studies in that period. Romyn was the first author on one article published post March 2016 and was also the lead on an SCP and terrorism study published before March 2016.

Publication Attributes

Freilich et al. (2019) found that two thirds (n = 40) of the 60 studies they reviewed were peer-reviewed articles, another 11 were book chapters (18 percent), four were books (7 percent), three were MA theses (5 percent), and two were PhD dissertations (3 percent) (see Table 11.4).

This trend has also accelerated. Indeed, over 85 percent (n = 23) of the 27 studies we identified post 2016 were journal articles, two were book chapters, another a PhD dissertation, and the fourth was an MA thesis. The PhD dissertation findings for both Freilich and

Table 11.4
Type of Outlet

	Frequency	Percent
Peer-reviewed Journal Article	40	66.7
Book Chapter	11	18.3
Book	4	6.7
Master's Thesis	3	5.0
Doctoral Dissertation	2	3.3
Total	60	100

colleagues, and our findings here, however, are an undercount. Doctoral dissertations (e.g., Henda Hsu; Sunniva Frishlid Meyer) were excluded from Freilich and colleagues' review, and our study here (e.g., Marissa Mandala; Zoe Marchment), if a substantial portion of the content was replicated in another study included in our analysis. In addition, it is likely we would have identified more PhD dissertations post 2016 if we also searched EBSCO and additional web-engines. Our findings suggest that scholars studying SCP and terrorism are largely working via the (blind) peer-review journal processes. This makes sense since we previously demonstrated that most of the scholars conducting these studies are criminologists, and the criminology and criminal justice field prioritizes peer-reviewed journal articles over books and book chapters published in edited volumes.

Not surprisingly, the number of studies applying tenets of SCP to terrorism increased after the publication of Clarke and Newman's (2006) seminal work, though there has not been a precipitous increase of relevant studies over time. Instead, the highest number of studies were published in 2009 due in large part to a special issue volume of *Crime Prevention Studies* focusing specifically on this topic (Freilich & Newman, 2009). The number of relevant studies also increased in 2012 and includes chapters from Lum and Kennedy's (2012) book titled *Evidence-based Counterterrorism Policy*, as well as a series of chapters from Taylor and Currie's (2012) edited volume titled *Terrorism and Affordance*. The 2015 peak in SCP and terrorism studies is due to the publication of many studies in terrorism and criminal justice journals (see Table 11.5).

The post-2016 period reveals a mostly consistent publication rate that seems to be slightly increasing. Five studies were published in 2017, five in 2018, seven in 2019 and another seven in 2020. Three other works appeared online first.

Table 11.5
Year of Publication

Year	Frequency	Percent
2006	1	1.7
2007	4	6.7
2008	3	5.0
2009	11	18.3
2010	3	5.0
2011	6	10.0
2012	10	16.7
2013	6	10.0
2014	3	5.0
2015	9	15.0
2016	4	6.7
Total	60	100

Table 11.6
Types of Peer-reviewed Journal Outlets

	Frequency	Percent
Criminology/Criminal Justice	27	67.5
Security	5	12.5
Terrorism	6	15.0
Public Affairs	2	5.0
Total	40	100

Note: Only studies published in peer-reviewed journals considered.

Freilich et al. (2019) found that approximately two-thirds (67 percent) of SCP and terrorism studies published in peer-reviewed journals appeared in criminology and criminal justice ones, including top-ranked outlets such as *Justice Quarterly*, *Criminology & Public Policy*, and *Journal of Quantitative Criminology* as well as international journals, such as *European Journal on Criminal Policy & Research* (see Table 11.6). The second most common category of scholarly journal outlets were terrorism journals, including the top terrorism journal *Terrorism and Political Violence*, while other studies were published in *Studies in Conflict and Terrorism* and *Behavioral Sciences of Terrorism and Political Aggression*. The third most common journal type, closely behind the terrorism category, was security journals, such as *Security Journal* and *Crime Prevention and Community Safety*.

Our results for the post-2016 period mostly matched these findings. We similarly found that almost 61 percent (n = 14) of the 23 journal articles we identified were published in criminal justice and criminology journals. Importantly, ten of these articles were published in top-tier criminal justice journals with high impact factors and high rejection rates, such as the *Journal of Quantitative Criminology* (n = 3), *Crime and Delinquency* (n = 2), *Journal of Research in Crime and Delinquency*, *Justice Quarterly*, *Criminology and Public Policy*, *Criminal Justice and Behavior*, and *Journal of Experimental Criminology*. An eleventh article appeared in the leading international journal *European Journal of Criminology*.

We similarly found that terrorism journals were another popular option as over 26 percent (n = 6) of the 23 articles we identified were published in these journals. In fact, three were published in *Terrorism and Political Violence*, the top-ranked terrorism studies journal. Two studies appeared in *Studies in Conflict and Terrorism* and *Dynamics of Asymmetric Conflict*, also leading journals in this area, and one appeared in the *Journal of Policing, Intelligence and Counter Terrorism*. However, only one of the 23 articles was published in a security journal, and the remaining two pieces appeared in forensic psychology and geography journals. Thus, it appears SCP and terrorism studies are now consistently being published in the leading journals from both the fields of criminal justice and terrorism studies.

Analytical Attributes

Freilich et al. (2019) also assessed the methodological and analytical features of these works and found that almost half (48 percent) were theoretical works, while another almost 7 percent were critical essays (see Table 11.7). Twenty-eight percent analyzed data quantitatively, and 15 percent did so qualitatively, while one study used mixed methods. Thus, 55 percent of the studies they reviewed were not empirical and did not analyze data.

Once again, though, we found a marked improvement in the time frame after 2016. Around 74 percent (n = 20) of the 27 studies we identified used data and analyzed it quantitatively, including advanced statistical techniques. Another 11 (n = 3) used qualitative techniques such as case studies, the script method, and conjunctive analysis of case configurations. One study was mixed-method, relying on both quantitative and qualitative techniques. Two were review pieces, and another was conceptual as it applied the four pillars of terrorism opportunity to the public mass violence context.

Table 11.7
Type of Publication

	Frequency	Percent
Theoretical	29	48.3
Quantitative	17	28.3
Qualitative	9	15.0
Critical Essay or Review	4	6.7
Mixed-Method	1	1.7
Total	60	100

Table 11.8
Primary Type of Data Used in Empirical Studies

	Percent	Valid Percent
Open-source Data	19	70.4
Official Data	7	25.9
Survey Data	1	3.7
Total	27	100

Note: Only quantitative, qualitative and mixed-method studies considered.

Freilich et al. (2019) documented the type of data the 27 empirical studies used. They found that 70 percent (n = 19) used open-source databases, such as the Global Terrorism Database (LaFree & Dugan, 2007), the US Extremist Crime Database (Freilich et al., 2014) and the American Terrorism Study (Smith, 1994) (see Table 11.8). After the 9/11 attacks, the US government through the Department of Homeland Security, National Institute of Justice, Department of Defense, and the National Science Foundation (and many foreign governments as well), greatly increased their investment in the scientific study of the etiology of, and the responses to, terrorism. As a result, funding for the databases noted above, and other similar efforts, increased. Many scholars turned to databases because typical crime data sources, such as the FBI's Uniform Crime Reports, do not provide details on ideologically motivated crimes (Dugan & Distler, 2016; Freilich & LaFree, 2016). Nonetheless, Freilich and colleagues still found that that 25 percent (n = 7) of studies relied on official data from police agencies (e.g., the Turkish National Police) and publicly accessible military sources. Finally, one study conducted a survey.

Our findings for the post-2016 period were mostly consistent. Three-fourths (n = 18) of the 24 empirical studies we reviewed used data from open-source databases or public information. Nine studies used data from the Global Terrorism Database (GTD) (LaFree & Dugan, 2007), three used data from the Extremist Crime Database (ECDB) (Freilich et al. 2014) and two used data from the American Terrorism Study (ATS). Four studies used newly created open-source databases on loners and the Provisional IRA, among others. Over 16 percent of the studies (n = 4) used official data from police agencies in Great Britain and Israel. Two studies conducted surveys of which one recruited undergraduate students and the other current military personnel.

Freilich et al. (2019) explained that the emergence of systematically collected event-, offender-, and organizational-level databases allowed terrorism scholars to go beyond simply describing data to testing explanatory models as well as making inferences about the situated nature of terrorism. Of the 17 quantitative studies reviewed by Freilich et al. (2019), around 42 percent (n = 7) provided descriptive statistics, and almost 58 percent (n = 10) used more advanced inferential statistics (see Table 11.9).

We again found an improvement for the time frame following 2016. First, we identified 21 studies (20 quantitative, and one mixed-method) that analyzed data quantitatively. In addition, only two of these studies provided bivariate or descriptive findings, while the remaining offered multivariate analyses, or advanced spatial analyses and one employed data mining. Thus, over 90 percent (n = 19) of the 21 quantitative studies we reviewed used advanced quantitative analytical techniques.

Silke's (2004) classic review of terrorism studies published in the mid to late 1990s found that less than 5 percent used statistics which was much less than that found in comparable fields like criminology and forensic psychology. Freilich et al.'s (2019) findings demonstrated that criminologists studying SCP and terrorism were increasingly using advanced statistical methods. Our findings here show that this trend has accelerated, as illustrated by the over 90 percent versus the 58 percent in the earlier period that used advanced quantitative techniques.

Table 11.9
Types of Statistical Approach Used

	Frequency	Percent
Descriptive	7	41.2
Multivariate	10	58.8
Total	17	100

Table 11.10
Primary Country of Conflict Discussed in Study

	Frequency	Percent
United States	20	33.3
No Primary Country	19	31.7
United Kingdom	5	8.3
Iraq	3	5.0
Northern Ireland	3	5.0
Australia	2	3.3
Netherlands	2	3.3
Turkey	2	3.3
Afghanistan	1	1.7
Canada	1	1.7
Israel	1	1.6
Japan	1	1.6
Total	60	100

Freilich et al. (2019) also examined the spatial focus of the studies they reviewed. They found that locations ranged considerably, with some (32 percent) not focusing on terrorism or terrorism prevention in any particular country (see Table 11.10). The remaining studies mostly looked at Western countries, especially the US (33 percent) and the UK (8 percent).

We found similar results for the time frame following 2016. Over 18 percent (n = 5) of the 27 studies focused globally or on Europe as a whole. Nine studies (33 percent) focused on attacks inside the USA, or on its embassies and diplomats. Three studies focused on Israel, two on Australia, two on Great Britain, two on Northern Ireland and one on Turkey. Three studies did not focus on any region.

Freilich et al. (2019) also documented if the studies examined a specific type of movement, or just terrorism overall. They found that 48 percent of the studies focused on terrorism or political violence generally as opposed to a specific terrorist, ideological or extremist movement (see Table 11.11). This is an interesting finding because it may be effective to apply SCP interventions to specific movements. Different movements may confront varying opportunity structures, and individuals may also choose specific crime types (due to varying access to weapons types, resources, and tools, etc.). The second most popular movement examined was the global jihad movement (n = 19, 32 percent). Only 7 percent (n = 4) of the studies focused on the extreme far-right, even though they commit more fatal incidents in the US than left-wing and Al-Qaeda

Table 11.11
Primary Terrorist Movement Discussed

	Frequency	Percent
No Primary Movement	29	48.3
Global Jihad	19	31.7
Far-right	4	6.7
Local Jihad	3	5.0
Left-Wing Separatist	3	5.0
Eco-terrorism	2	3.3
Total	60	100

supporters (Parkin et al., 2017) and American police are concerned about the threat they pose (Carter et al., 2014; Freilich et al., 2009).

Our findings for the time frame following 2016 were similar in some respects but varied in others. Converging with the earlier review, we found that 13 of the 27 studies published after 2016 only looked at terrorism generally and did not examine specific movements or types. However, six studies looked at the extreme far-right, one more than the five investigations that studied Al-Qaeda or similar Islamist extremist movements. One study focused on left-wing terrorists, and another project studied eco-extremists. Six studies examined other movements including the Kurdistan Workers Party (i.e., PKK), the Provisional Irish Republican Army (IRA) (n = 2), and the Israel/Palestine conflict (n = 3). These total numbers come to more than 27 since certain studies investigated more than one movement.

Finally, Freilich et al. (2019) also assessed whether studies investigated the four pillars of terrorism opportunity and empirically tested Clarke and Newman's (2006) risk assessment for targets (*EVIL DONE*), weapons (*MURDEROUS*), or tools, as well as their claims about facilitating conditions (*ESEER*). These prior findings revealed that five works empirically tested *EVIL DONE*, only one tested *MURDEROUS* and, perhaps surprisingly, no studies empirically examined either *ESEER* or their tools claims (see Table 11.12).

Once again, though, our review of the 27 studies published since 2016 reveal a more positive picture. While only two studies formally tested all the *EVIL DONE* dimensions, a third study extended it and offered an updated risk-assessment template for target selection. Further, ten other studies tested target-related hypotheses representing aspects of *EVIL DONE* or SCP claims. Six studies similarly tested weapons hypotheses that also originated from *MURDEROUS* or SCP. Importantly,

Table 11.12
Empirical Tests of *EVIL DONE*, *MURDEROUS*, and *ESEER*

	Frequency	Percent
Tests *EVIL DONE*	5	8.2
Tests *MURDEROUS*	1	0.0
Tests *ESEER*	0	0.0
Tests tools claims	0	0.0

two studies empirically tested tools-related hypotheses and one tested hypotheses representing SCP's facilitating conditions. Another study was conceptual and applied all four pillars of terrorism opportunity to the public mass violence context.

Discussion and Conclusion

Our findings demonstrate that the SCP and terrorism literature has continued to make important strides, especially in the last five years. To begin, we find that a growing number of criminologists and crime scientists have recently embraced Clarke and Newman's (2006) call to apply SCP to the terrorism context. Almost 78 percent (n = 21) of the 27 studies published post 2016 were trained in criminology, criminal justice, or crime science compared to the 50 percent of the 60 studies published between 2006 and 2016. These authors trained at a number of programs, including some of the leading ones today, such as: Australia National University, Claremont Graduate University, University at Albany, University of Cincinnati, Hebrew University, John Jay College of Criminal Justice, University College London, University of Maryland and Michigan State University. On the other hand, fewer scholars from other fields—especially political scientists and psychologists—are employing the SCP framework.

We also found that since 2016, over 85 percent of the 27 studies published in that time were co-authored and over 59 percent of the first authors had also published another SCP and terrorism study compared to the 50 percent and 17 percent respectively of the 60 studies published during the 2006 to 2016 period. Both trends indicate that more ambitious studies are being conducted and more sustained research agendas are being carried out.

Importantly, we found that SCP and terrorism studies are increasingly using more sophisticated analytic techniques and are increasingly being published in the leading criminal justice and terrorism studies journals.

The number of studies that analyzed data quantitatively increased to around 74 percent for the post-2016 period compared to 28 percent from 2006 to 2016. Further, over 90 percent (n = 19) of the 21 quantitative studies published after 2016 used advanced quantitative analytical techniques (i.e., multivariate regression, data mining, etc.) compared to the 58 percent (n = 10) of the 17 studies from 2006 to 2016. Indeed, the more recent time frame's raw number of 19 was almost twice as large as the ten from the earlier period even though its length was less than half the time (less than five years vs. ten years and originated from only 27 studies compared to the 60 in the earlier review).

Similarly, the number of studies published in journals increased from 67 percent of the 60 studies from 2006 to 2016, to over 85 percent of the 27 studies published since 2016. Again, the criminal justice field places a higher premium on journal articles since they are assumed to be of a higher quality due to the presumed rigor of a stricter peer-review process. As noted, most of these journal articles are in criminal justice and terrorism studies outlets, including major tier 1 venues like *Journal of Quantitative Criminology*, *Justice Quarterly*, *Journal of Research in Crime and Delinquency*, *Criminology and Public Policy*, *Terrorism and Political Violence*, *Studies in Conflict and Terrorism*, and *Dynamics of Asymmetric Conflict*. We also found that the number of articles per year since 2016 has been consistent, between five and seven, a year. Significantly, we have documented that since 2006 at least seven PhD dissertations have focused on SCP and terrorism, and there have been additional MA theses during this same period. Collectively, these findings show a robust body of research in this area.

Over two-thirds of all SCP and terrorism studies that used data, draw from publicly available information, especially open-source databases such as the GTD, ECDB, ATS and other recent efforts focused on loners and the Provisional IRA. Initially, it seems surprising that no studies have used the Profiles of Individual Radicalization in the US (PIRUS) database. However, PIRUS is an offender-level database, including attributes capturing many traditional distal criminology theories. SCP focuses on the event, spatial issues, and other attributes that the other open-source databases include. The second most common data source is official data from the police or military. We should note, though, that the number of studies using official sources might be slightly higher since some could classify the ATS as partially official data. The ATS began as a collaboration with the FBI, who provided Dr. Brent Smith with the names of all offenders who were part of their designated terrorism investigations. In addition to using media information, the ATS also draws from court documents for every case.

Both the earlier 2006 to 2016 review, and our post-2016 study here, found that most studies looked at terrorism overall or only at the US and other Western nations. It is possible this is partially the result of data availability issues. Future studies should mimic the SCP and crime literature that has tested its claims around the globe in almost every continent. We also found that even though the 87 SCP and terrorism studies mostly examined terrorism overall or Islamist extremism, they examined other movements too including the extreme far-right, left-wing terrorism (including the PKK, the Provisional IRA, and American leftists), and eco-terrorism.

Another positive development is that in the last five years an increasing number of studies have empirically assessed SCP's four pillars of opportunity. For example, while only five out of the 60 studies published between 2006 and 2016 empirically tested *EVIL DONE*, and only one tested *MURDEROUS*, this increased markedly to 12 studies that assessed target-related hypotheses, and six that examined weapon-related hypotheses in the post-2016 period. What makes these numbers stand out is that they originate from a much smaller pool of studies (27 vs. 60). Further, two studies assessed tools-related hypotheses, one tested facilitating conditions, and another applied all four pillars to the public mass violence context, compared to none that examined tools or facilitating conditions before 2016.

We conclude by briefly highlighting some key substantive content from the SCP and terrorism literature, including important findings and gaps, and set forth additional points for future research to address. As noted, the most commonly tested SCP pillar is *EVIL DONE* and targeted related hypotheses. Romyn and Krebbell (2018, p. 591) concluded that one "problem with the *EVIL DONE* approach is that it assumes that all attributes are equally important … [but we previously found] that the attributes of Occupied, Iconic, Easy and Destructible were the most important when selecting a target, while the attributes Exposed, Vital and Near were less important … [and] Legitimate was extremely subjective." Similarly, Gruenewald et al., (2015) found that for eco-terrorists, target selection seemed to be guided by levels of exposure and legitimacy, while other attributes (i.e., vital, destructibility) were less influential. Their study highlighted the fact that the relevance of opportunity structures to target selection is crime specific.

Freilich et al. (2019) concluded that *EVIL DONE* could be enhanced by adding ideology as a dimension. They noted that while radical Islamist groups, like Al-Qaeda or ISIS, and far-right extremists have frequently attempted to kill as many people as possible, environmental and animal rights extremists have often sought to avoid fatalities, by attacking at night for example, and only aim to cause great property damage. Similarly, terrorism researchers have highlighted how ideology impacts target selection (Drake, 1998). While radical Islamists, left-wing and far-right terrorists have all purposefully targeted the police, extreme far-rightists often attack racial and religious minorities, radical Islamists usually strike military targets or the US population at large, while left-wing terrorists target corporations. Thus, accounting for ideology situationally might enhance *EVIL DONE*'s usefulness.

These findings suggest future research could consider refining *EVIL DONE* by weighting the more important attributes or reconceptualizing the weaker ones. In fact, recently Marchment and Gill (online first) addressed this very issue by building upon *EVIL DONE* to offer an updated risk-assessment model that assumes terrorists' spatial decision-making processes are shaped by how much a potential target is Tolerable, Relevant, Accessible, Close and/or Known (TRACK). They appear to echo Clarke and Newman (2006) who highlighted that interventions must not be static since terrorists adapt.

Marchment and Gill explain their new model "should not be viewed as a criticism of Clarke and Newman's 'EVIL DONE', as its focus on high impact attacks by foreign-based terrorists was appropriate at the time it was introduced. Terrorist strategies are continuously changing in response to increased counterterrorism capability." The TRACK model recognizes that recently terrorists have changed how they operate and some have begun to concentrate on soft targets that are low risk. Thus, *EVIL DONE*'s vital, iconic, and destructible dimensions appear to be less important to the decision-making of terrorists included in their work.

Two other *EVIL DONE*-related issues focus on operationalizing its eight dimensions. First, similar to other phenomena, scholars have operationalized its eight specific dimensions in different ways (see for e.g., Boba, 2008; Gruenewald et al., 2015). While there are good reasons for this, as subsequent scholars extend earlier works, reaching a consensus on how to capture core constructs could move this area of research forward. Doing so would aid replication efforts and allow the field to draw firmer conclusions. Relatedly, while all eight *EVIL*

DONE dimensions are separate constructs, there appears to be overlap in measuring, for example, "exposure" versus "easy." For instance, those targets that are most accessible to the public may also be the least likely to have implemented security measures. In sum, future research could carefully focus on operationalizing and measuring *EVIL DONE* and the other pillars' constructs.

Freilich et al. (2019) noted that scholars seeking to test *EVIL DONE* and the other pillars have often faced challenges in accessing the necessary data. Since *EVIL DONE* is a risk-assessment template, the purest test would compare attacked targets to some type of non-attacked target to determine if they varied on *EVIL DONE*'s dimensions. Since almost all terrorism databases only include attacked targets, to pursue this line of research would require identifying and matching non-attacked targets and then coding them on these attributes. Freilich and colleagues stated this could explain why recent studies (see for e.g., St. George, 2017) had extended *EVIL DONE* (from identifying attacked targets) to instead account for differences across casualty numbers, or financial damage. These studies did not need to identify and include non-attacked targets, but only had to assess the attacked targets on *EVIL DONE*'s dimensions.

Importantly though, St. George's dissertation to some extent tested the efficacy of SCP interventions on harm reduction, or mitigation. While many SCP interventions aim to eliminate, or at least reduce, the number of attacks, another outcome measure many researchers focus on is *mitigating the harms caused* by those attacks that continue to occur. Certain SCP interventions like bullet-proof glass, for instance, or enhanced communication and improved emergency response times, may result in fewer casualties during terrorist attacks. Indeed, Clarke and Newman also crafted a policing terrorism guide that, in its last 15 modules, explained how law enforcement and others could mitigate the harms caused by completed terrorist attacks (Newman & Clarke, 2007). Since it will invariably be local police that are called to a terrorist attack, Newman and Clarke state they must be prepared. These local police must have contingency plans in place for leading and coordinating the response by the various government and private sector institutions (e.g., emergency medical technicians hospitals, trauma centers, etc.), including information-sharing channels. Newman and Clarke maintain that the local police must focus on stopping the perpetrator, quickly providing the victims the aid they need, and communicating with the public to dispel fears and concerns. Future research could empirically test Newman and Clarke's mitigation claims. Scholars could extend St.

George's work by also looking at the other three pillars of terrorism opportunity and the impact of situational interventions in these contexts on harm reduction.

Future research could also consider enhancing Clarke and Newman's pillars of terrorist opportunity by adding a fifth one that assessed the terrorists' expertise. In other words, what skill sets and resources did the terrorists bring with them to the crime scene, and how did these skills and resources (or lack thereof) make a successful attack more or less likely? For example, the 9/11 hijackers took flight lessons to learn how to fly planes and used these skills to carry out the attack. On the other hand, the earlier 1993 World Trade Center bombing failed to destroy the building because the attackers did not know where/how to place the bombs to maximize their impact. Scholar could draw from Ekblom and Tilley's (2000) paper that highlighted aspects of this issue for offenders and regular crime.

We end by noting the common critique leveled against SCP in the criminology literature, specifically that prevention interventions will not reduce crime but will instead displace it elsewhere in terms of geography, time, target selection, tactics, offenders, or crime types (Reppetto, 1976). Terrorism scholars have made similar arguments and referred to displacement as the substitution effect. Hsu and his colleagues have investigated this issue and found that displacement does not always occur and in fact sometimes there is a diffusion of benefits effect. Hsu and Apel (2015), one of the studies we reviewed, used GTD data to examine displacement among terrorist groups that had attacked aviation targets both before and after airport metal detectors were installed. They employed an interrupted time series design and found partial support of SCP claims.

Freilich et al. (2019) concluded that it was encouraging that SCP counterterrorism interventions often did not cause displacement, and sometimes instead led to a diffusion of benefits effect. They noted, though, that Clarke and Newman (2006) had cautioned that some terrorists will "adapt," and create new strategies to overcome SCP interventions (Cornish & Clarke, 2008, pp. 189–190). Freilich et al. (2019) argued that this implicated an understudied issue for SCP and crime overall—the relationship between displacement and adaptation. Displacement is thought to be a short- term effect, while adaptation occurs over a longer time frame. But they also noted that it is unclear when a terrorist group's reaction to an SCP intervention is classified as adaptation as opposed to displacement. Conceptually, this is an important issue since any displacement occurring would undermine SCP's claims, while adaptation would not, and in fact would be expected. Since adaptation may be more expected in the terrorism context than other forms of crime, this is another important point for future research to address.

In sum, SCP's contribution to the scholarly study of terrorism, as well as efforts to protect society by preventing, reducing, and mitigating the harms caused by terrorism, have continued to increase in recent years. We found a burgeoning literature consisting of over 100 studies that have been published in the last 15 years. These studies are more rigorous, are conducted by stronger research teams, and are being published in the leading criminal justice and terrorism studies journals. We also highlighted some underexplored issues, and set forth suggestions for future research to address.

Notes

1. We identified one work, a chapter in Gill's (2015) book on loners that applied SCP to terrorism using script analyses, that Freilich et al. (2019) failed to include in their study.
2. Freilich et al. (2019) detail-coded the 60 works for several attributes into a main database. While one researcher served as the primary coder, two additional coders randomly selected a subsample of publications to review and verify variable-specific coding values, and procedures. The measures included the disciplines of lead authors (or first authors listed), co-authoring patterns (single or multiple), and whether there are multiple publications by the same author. They also coded year of publication, outlet type (book, journal article, chapter, MA thesis, or PhD dissertation), discipline of outlet (criminal justice, sociology, psychology, etc.), type of publication (theoretical, critical essay, quantitative, qualitative, or mixed-method), data source (open-source, official, or survey), method (descriptive or multivariate), primary country of conflict mentioned, and primary terrorist movement (far-right, global jihadi, local jihadi, left-wing/separatist, or eco-terrorism) mentioned. They also captured if the study empirically tested the *EVIL DONE*, *MURDEROUS*, and *ESEER* frameworks or tools claims.
3. In addition to the 87 studies that we reviewed (60 in the earlier review and 27 in this study), 11 other studies were excluded since they were PhD dissertations or chapters that were similar to published journal articles. As noted, Freilich et al. (2019) excluded nine such works, and as we explain below, we excluded two others. Again, Freilich et al. (2019) also failed to include the chapter from Gill's (2015) loner book. Finally, we did not include either the earlier review, or this current review in our analyses.

References

Agnew, R. (2016). General strain theory & terrorism. In G. LaFree & J. Freilich (Eds.), *The handbook of the criminology of terrorism*. New York: John Wiley, pp. 119–132.

Boba, R. (2008). A crime mapping technique for assessing vulnerable targets for terrorism in local communities. In S. Chainey & L. Tompson (Eds.), *Crime mapping case studies: Practice and research*. Chichester: John Wiley, pp. 143–151.

Brantingham, P.J., & Brantingham P.L. (1990). *Environmental Criminology* (2nd Edn.). Long Grove, IL: Waveland Press.

Carter, D., Chermak, S., Carter, J., & Drew, J. (2014). *Understanding law enforcement intelligence processes*. College Park, MD: START. Available at: www.start.umd.edu/pubs/START_UnderstandingLawEnforcementIntelligenceProcesses_July2014.pdf.

Center for Problem Oriented Policing. (n.d.). 25 techniques grid. Available at: https://popcenter.asu.edu/sites/default/files/library/25%20techniques%20grid.pdf.

Clarke, R.V.G. (1980). Situational crime prevention: Theory and practice. *British Journal of Criminology*, 20(1),136–147.

Clarke, R.V.G., & Eck, J.E. (2005). *Crime analysis for problem solvers in 60 small steps*. Washington DC: US Department of Justice. Office of Community Oriented Policing Services. Center for Problem Oriented Policing.

Clarke, R.V.G., & Newman, G.R. (2006). *Outsmarting the terrorists*. Westport, CT: ABCCLIO Praeger Security International.

Cohen, E., & Felson, M. (1979). Social change and crime rate trends: A routine activity approach. *American Sociological Review*, 44, 588–605.

Cornish, D.B., & Clarke, R.V. (2008). Opportunities, precipitators, and criminal decisions: A reply to Wortley's critique of situational crime prevention. *Crime Prevention Studies*, 16: 41–96.

Cozens, P. (2011). Crime prevention through environmental design. In R. Wortley & L. Mazerolle (Eds.), *Environmental criminology and crime analysis*. London: Routledge, pp. 153–177.

Drake, C.J.M. (1998). The role of ideology in terrorists' target selection. *Terrorism and Political Violence*, 10(2), 53–85.

Dugan, L., & Distler, M. (2016). Measuring terrorism. In G. LaFree & J.D. Freilich (Eds.), *Handbook on the criminology of terrorism*. Hoboken, NJ: Wiley-Blackwell, pp. 198–205.

Eck, J.E. (2002a). Preventing crime at places. In L. Sherman, D. Farrington, B. Welsh, & D. Mackenzie (Eds.), *Evidence-based crime prevention*. New York: Routledge, pp. 241–294.

Eck, J.E. (2002b). Learning from experience in problem-oriented policing and situational prevention: The positive functions of weak evaluations and the negative functions of strong ones. *Crime Prevention Studies*, 14, 93–118.

Ekblom, P. (2012). Happy returns: Ideas brought back from situational crime prevention's exploration of design against crime. In G. Farrell & N. Tilley (Eds.), *The reasoning criminologist: Essays in honor of Ronald V. Clarke*. New York: Routledge, pp. 52–64.

Ekblom, P., & Tilley, N. (2000). Going equipped. *British Journal of Criminology* 40(3), 376–398.

Felson, M., & Clarke, R.V. (1998). Opportunity makes the thief: Practical theory for crime prevention. Police Research Series, Paper 98. London: Home Office.

Fisher, B.S., Vander Ven, T.M., Cobane, C.T., Cullen, F.T., & Williams, N. (1998). Trends in multiple authored articles in criminology and criminal justice. *Journal of Criminal Justice Education*, 9(1), 19–38.

Freilich, J.D., & Chermak, S.M. (2009). Preventing deadly encounters between law enforcement and American far-rightists. *Crime Prevention Studies*, 25, 141–172.

Freilich, J.D., & LaFree, G. (2016). Measurement issues in the study of terrorism: Introducing the special issue. *Studies in Conflict and Terrorism*, 39(7–8), 569–579.
Freilich, J.D., & LaFree, G. (2015). Criminology theory and terrorism: Introduction to the special issue. *Terrorism and Political Violence*, 27(1), 1–8.
Freilich, J.D., & Newman, G.R. (Guest Eds.). (2009). *Crime prevention studies, Vol. 25: Reducing terrorism through situational crime prevention.* Boulder, CO: Lynne Rienner Publishers.
Freilich, J.D., & Newman, G.R. (2017). Situational crime prevention. In H. Pontell (Ed.), *Oxford research encyclopedia of criminology and criminal justice.* New York: Oxford University Press. Available at: https://doi.org/10.1093/acrefore/9780190264079.013.3.
Freilich, J.D., Chermak, S., Belli, R., Gruenewald, J., & Parkin, W. (2014). Introducing the extremist crime database (ECDB). *Terrorism & Political Violence*, 26(2), 372–384.
Freilich, J.D., Chermak, S.M., & Simone Jr., J. (2009). Surveying American state police agencies about terrorism threats, terrorism sources, and terrorism definitions. *Terrorism and Political Violence*, 21(3), 450–475.
Freilich, J.D., Gruenewald, J., & Mandala, M. (2019). Situational crime prevention and terrorism: An assessment of 10 years of research. *Criminal Justice Policy Review*, 30(9), 1283–1311.
Gill, P. (2015). *Lone actor terrorists: A behavioural analysis.* London: Routledge.
Gruenewald, J., Allison-Gruenewald, K., & Klein, B.R. (2015). Assessing the attractiveness and vulnerability of eco-terrorism targets: A situational crime prevention approach. Studies in Conflict & Terrorism, 38(6), 433–455.
Guerette, R.T., & Bowers, K.J. (2009). Assessing the extent of crime displacement and diffusion of benefits: A review of situational crime prevention evaluations. *Criminology*, 47(4), 1331–1368.
Hamm, M.S. (1993). *American skinheads: The criminology and control of hate crime.* Westport, CT/London: Praeger.
Hamm, M.S. (1997). *Apocalypse in Oklahoma: Waco and Ruby Ridge revenged.* Boston, MA: Northeastern University Press.
Hsu, H.Y., & Apel, R. (2015). A situational model of displacement and diffusion following the introduction of airport metal detectors. *Terrorism and Political Violence*, 27(1), 29–52.
LaFree, G., & Dugan, L. (2004). How does studying terrorism compare to studying crime? In M. Deflem (Ed.), *Terrorism and counter-terrorism: Sociology of crime, law and deviance, Vol. 5.* Bingley: Emerald Group Publishing Limited, pp. 53–74.
LaFree, G., & Dugan, V. (2007). Introducing the global terrorism database. *Terrorism & Political Violence*, 19(2), 181–204.
LaFree, G., & Freilich, J.D. (2016). Bringing criminology into the study of terrorism. In G. LaFree & J.D. Freilich (Eds.), *Handbook on the criminology of terrorism.* Hoboken, NJ: Wiley-Blackwell, pp. 3–14.
Lum, C., & Kennedy, L.W. (Eds.). (2012). Evidence-based counterterrorism policy. In *Evidence-based counterterrorism policy.* New York: Springer, pp. 3–9.
Merari, A. (1991). Academic research and government policy on terrorism. *Terrorism and Political Violence*, 3(1), 88–102.
Mueller, J. (2010). Assessing measures designed to protect the homeland. *Policy Studies Journal*, 38(1), 1–21.

Newman, G.R., & Clarke, R.V. (2007). *Policing terrorism: An executive's guide*. Washington, DC: US Department of Justice, Office of Community Oriented Policing Services (COPS), Center for Problem Oriented Policing (POP).

Parkin, W.S., Gruenewald, J., Klein, B.R., Chermak, S.M., & Freilich, J.D. (2017). Countering all violent extremism. *Conversation*. Available at: https://theconversation.com/threats-of-violent-islamist-and-far-right-extremism-what-does-the-research-say-72781.

Rausch, S., & LaFree, G. (2007). The growing importance of criminology in the study of terrorism. *The Criminologist*, 32(6), 1, 3–5.

Reppetto, T.A. (1976). Crime prevention and the displacement phenomenon. *Crime and Delinquency*, 22(2), 166–177.

Romyn, D., & Kebbell, M.R. (2018). Mock terrorists' decisions concerning use of the internet for target selection: A red-team approach. *Psychology, Crime & Law*, 24(6), 589–602.

Rosenfeld, R. (2004). Terrorism and criminology. *Sociology of Crime, Law and Deviance*, 5, 19–32.

Sherman, L.W., Gartin, P.R., & Buerger, M.E. (1989). Hot spots of predatory crime: Routine activities and the criminology of place. *Criminology*, 27(1), 27–56.

Silke, A. (2001). The devil you know: Continuing problems with research on terrorism. *Terrorism and Political Violence*, 13(4), 1–14.

Silke, A. (2004). Terrorism and the blind man's elephant. In A. Silke (Ed.), *Research on terrorism: Trends, achievements and failures*. London: Frank Cass, pp. 186–213.

Smith, B.L. (1994). *Terrorism in America: Pipe bombs and pipe dreams*. New York: State University of New York Press.

Stewart, M.G. (2008). Cost-effectiveness of Risk Mitigation Strategies for Protection of Buildings against Terrorist Attack. *Journal of Performance of Constructed Facilities*, 22(2), 115–120.

St. George, S. (2017). Assessing the vulnerability in targets of lethal domestic extremism. (PhD Dissertation). Michigan State University, East Lansing, MI.

Taylor, M., & Currie, P.M. (Eds.). (2012). *Terrorism and affordance*. London: Bloomsbury Academic.

Weisburd, D., & Green, L. (1995). Policing drug hotspots: The Jersey City drug market analysis experiment. *Justice Quarterly*, 12(4), 711–735.

Weisburd, D., Wycoff, L.A., Ready, J., Eck, J.E., & Hinkle, J.C. (2006). Does crime just move around the corner? A controlled study of spatial displacement and diffusion of crime control benefits. *Criminology*, 44(3), 549–592.

Wortley, R. (1996). Guilt, shame and situational crime prevention. *Crime Prevention Studies*, 5, 115–132.

Wortley, R. (2002). *Situational prison control: Crime prevention in correctional institutions*. Cambridge: Cambridge University Press.

Appendix 11.1

Publications Reviewed by Freilich, Gruenewald, & Mandala (2019), 2006–2016

1. Belli, R., & Freilich, J.D. (2009). Situational crime prevention and non-violent terrorism: A "soft" approach against ideologically motivated tax refusal. *Crime Prevention Studies*, 25, 173–206.
2. Bjørgo, T. (2013). *Strategies for preventing terrorism*. New York: Springer.
3. Bjørgo, T. (2016). Counter-terrorism as crime prevention: A holistic approach. *Behavioral Sciences of Terrorism and Political Aggression*, 8, 25–44.
4. Block, M.M. (2016). Applying situational crime prevention to terrorism against airports and aircrafts. (Doctoral dissertation). University of Louisville, Louisville, KY.
5. Boba, R. (2009). EVIL DONE. *Crime Prevention Studies*, 25, 71–91.
6. Borrion, H., Tripathi, K., Chen, P., & Moon, S. (2014). Threat detection: A framework for security architects and designers of metropolitan rail systems. *Urban, Planning & Transport Research*, 2, 173–194.
7. Braithwaite, A., & Johnson, S.D. (2015). The battle for Baghdad: Testing hypotheses about insurgency from risk heterogeneity, repeat victimization, and denial policing approaches. *Terrorism and Political Violence*, 27, 112–132.
8. Cave, B. (2012). Counterinsurgency and criminology: Applying routine activities theory to military approaches to counterterrorism. In C. Lum & L.W. Kennedy (Eds.), *Evidence-based counterterrorism policy*. New York: Springer, pp. 323–349.
9. Clare, J., & Morgan, F. (2009). Exploring parallels between situational crime prevention and non-criminological theories for reducing terrorist risk. *Crime Prevention Studies*, 25, 207–228.
10. Clark, W. (2009). Bioterrorism: A situational crime prevention approach. *Crime Prevention Studies*, 25, 93–110.
11. Clarke, R.V., & Newman, G.R. (2006). *Outsmarting the terrorists*. New York: Praeger.
12. Clarke, R.V., & Newman, G.R. (2007). Police and the prevention of terrorism. *Policing*, 1(1), 9–20.
13. Currie, P.M. (2012). Affordance as an inferred opportunity. In M. Taylor & P.M. Currie (Eds.), *Terrorism and affordance*. New York: Continuum International Publishing Group, pp. 157–170.
14. De Bie, J.L., de Poot, C.J., & van der Leun, J.P. (2015). Shifting modus operandi of Jihadist foreign fighters from the Netherlands between 2000 and 2013: A crime script analysis. *Terrorism and Political Violence*, 27, 416–440.
15. Donkin, S. (2014). *Preventing terrorism and controlling risk: A comparative analysis of control orders in the UK and Australia*. New York: Springer.
16. Duguay, R. (2015). Threats of radiological terrorism and the securing of radioactive sources. *Journal of Physical Security*, 8, 55–68.
17. Ekblom, P. (2012). Conceptual and methodological explorations in affordance and counter terrorism. In M. Taylor & P.M. Currie (Eds.), *Terrorism and affordance*. New York: Continuum International Publishing Group, pp. 33–48.
18. Ekblom, P., & Hirschfield, A. (2014). Developing an alternative formulation of SCP principles—the Ds (11 and counting). *Crime Science*, 3, 1–11.

19. Ekici, N., Ozkan, M., Celik, A., & Maxfield, M.G. (2008). Outsmarting terrorists in Turkey. *Crime Prevention & Community Safety*, 10, 126–139.
20. Fahey, S., LaFree, G., Dugan, L., & Piquero, A.R. (2012). A situational model for distinguishing terrorist and non-terrorist aerial hijackings, 1948–2007. *Justice Quarterly*, 29, 573–595.
21. Freilich, J.D., & S.M. Chermak. (2009). Preventing deadly encounters between law enforcement and American far-rightists. *Crime Prevention Studies*, 25, 141–172.
22. Fussey, P. (2007). Observing potentiality in the global city: Surveillance and counterterrorism in London. *International Criminal Justice Review*, 17, 171–192.
23. Fussey, P. (2011). An economy of choice? Terrorist decision-making and criminological rational choice theories reconsidered. *Security Journal*, 24, 85–99.
24. Gibbs, S. (2010). Applying the theory and techniques of situational criminology to counterinsurgency operations: Reducing insurgency through situational prevention. (Doctoral dissertation). Naval Postgraduate School, Monterey, CA.
25. Greene, J.R. (2009). Weapon choice and American political violence. *Criminology & Public Policy*, 8, 647–654.
26. Gruenewald, J., Allison-Gruenewald, K., & Klein, B.R. (2015). Assessing the attractiveness and vulnerability of eco-terrorism targets: A situational crime prevention approach. *Studies in Conflict & Terrorism*, 38(6), 433–455.
27. Hsu, H.Y. (2013). Post-9/11 U.S. airport security changes and displacement. In S.G. Shoham & J.D. Freilich (Eds.), *Policing & preventing terrorism around the globe*. Ontario, Canada: de Sitter.
28. Hsu, H.Y., & Apel, R. (2015). A situational model of displacement and diffusion following the introduction of airport metal detectors. *Terrorism and Political Violence*, 27, 29–52.
29. Johnson, S.D., & Braithwaite, A. (2009). Spatio-temporal modeling of insurgency in Iraq. *Crime Prevention Studies*, 25, 9–32.
30. Jones, M. (2011). Can railway station design reduce the risk of a terrorist attack or the impact of an incident? Proceedings of the Institution of Mechanical Engineers, Part F. *Journal of Rail and Rapid Transit*, 225, 351–357.
31. Klein, B.R., Gruenewald, J., & Smith, B.L. (2016). Opportunity, group structure, temporal patterns, and successful outcomes of far-right terrorism incidents in the United States. *Crime & Delinquency*, 63(10), 1224–1249.
32. Legault, R.L., & Hendrickson, J.C. (2009). Weapon choice and American political violence: A comparison of terrorists in federal custody to other felons. *Criminology & Public Policy*, 8, 531–559.
33. Lulham, R., Duarte, O.C., Dorst, K., & Kaldor, L. (2012). Designing a counterterrorism trash bin. *Crime Prevention Studies*, 27, 131–146.
34. Lum, C., & Koper, C. (2011). Is crime prevention relevant to counterterrorism? In B. Forst, J.R. Greene, & J.P. Lynch (Eds.), *Criminologists on terrorism and homeland security* New York: Cambridge University Press, pp. 129–150.
35. Lum, C., Gill, C., Cave, B., Hibdon, J., & Weisburd, D. (2012). Translational criminology: Using existing evidence for assessing TSA's comprehensive security strategy at airports. In C. Lum & L.W. Kennedy (Eds.), *Evidence-based counterterrorism policy*. New York: Springer, pp. 209–251.
36. Lynch, J.P. (2011). Implications of opportunity theory for combatting terrorism. In B. Forst, J.R. Greene, & J.P. Lynch (Eds.), *Criminologists on terrorism and homeland security*. New York: Cambridge University Press, pp. 151–181.

37. Meyer, S. (2012). Reducing harm from explosive attacks against railways. *Security Journal*, 25, 309–325.
38. Meyer, S. (2013). Impeding lone-wolf attacks: Lessons derived from the 2011 Norway attacks. *Crime Science*, 2(1), 1.
39. Meyer, S., & Ekblom, P. (2012). Specifying the explosion-resistant railway carriage: A "bench" test of the security function framework. *Journal of Transportation Security*, 5, 69–85.
40. Morris, N.A. (2015). Target suitability and terrorism events at places. *Criminology & Public Policy*, 14, 417–426.
41. Newman, G.R. (2009). Reducing terrorist opportunities: A framework for foreign policy. *Crime Prevention Studies*, 25, 33–60.
42. Newman, G.R., & Clarke, R.V. (2007). Commentary: The situational prevention of terrorism: Some ethical considerations. *Criminal Justice Ethics*, 26, 2–66.
43. Newman, G.R., & Clarke, R.V. (2010). Terrorism. In M. Natarajan (Ed.), *International criminal justice*. Cambridge: Cambridge University Press.
44. Özer, M.M., & Akbaş, H. (2011). The application of situational crime prevention to terrorism. *Turkish Journal of Police Studies*, 13, 179–194.
45. Paton, S. (2013). EVIL DONE vulnerability assessment: Examining terrorist targets through situational crime prevention. (Doctoral dissertation). Florida Atlantic University, Boca Raton.
46. Perry, S., & Hasisi, B. (2015). Rational choice rewards and the Jihadist suicide bomber. *Terrorism and Political Violence*, 27, 53–80.
47. Perry, S., Apel, R., Newman, G.R., & Clarke, R.V. (2017). The situational prevention of terrorism: An evaluation of the Israeli West Bank Barrier. *Journal of Quantitative Criminology*, 33, 727–751.
48. Prenzler, T. (2014). Re-thinking counter-terrorism and crime prevention strategies from a harm perspective. *Australasian Policing*, 6(2), 15.
49. Roach, J. (2012). Affordance, terrorism and the overestimation of offender homogeneity. In M. Taylor & P.M. Currie (Eds.), *Terrorism and affordance*. New York: Continuum International Publishing Group, pp. 141–156.
50. Roach, J., Ekblom, P., & Flynn, R. (2005). The conjunction of terrorist opportunity: A framework for diagnosing and preventing acts of terrorism. *Security Journal*, 18(3), 7–25.
51. Romyn, D., & Kebbell, M. (2014). Terrorists' planning of attacks: A simulated "redteam" investigation into decision-making. *Psychology, Crime & Law*, 20, 480–496.
52. Rorie, M.L. (2008). Communicating through violence: An application of rational choice theory to terrorist claims of responsibility. (Master's thesis). University of Maryland, College Park, MD.
53. Ross, N. (2009). How to lose the war on terror: Lessons of a 30-year war in Northern Ireland. *Crime Prevention Studies*, 25, 229–244.
54. Safer-Lichtenstein, A. 2015. Incorporating ideas of displacement and diffusion of benefits into evaluations of counterterrorism policy. (Doctoral dissertation). University of Maryland, College Park, MD.
55. Shaftoe, H., Turksen, U., Lever, J., & Williams, S.J. (2007). Dealing with terrorist threats through a crime prevention and community safety approach. *Crime Prevention & Community Safety*, 9, 291–307.
56. Silke, A. (2010). Understanding terrorist target selection. In A. Richards, P. Fussey, & A. Silke (Eds.), *Terrorism and the Olympics: Major event security and lessons for the future*. New York: Routledge, pp. 49–71.

57. Townsley, M., Johnson, S.D., & Ratcliffe, J.H. (2008). Space–time dynamics of insurgent activity in Iraq. *Security Journal*, 21, 139–146.
58. Weenink, A.W. (2012). Situational prevention of terrorism: Remarks from the field of counterterrorism in the Netherlands on Newman and Clarke's *Policing Terrorism*. *Trends in Organized Crime*, 15, 164–179.
59. Wortley, R. (2012). Affordance and situational crime prevention: Implications for counter terrorism. In M. Taylor & P.M. Currie (Eds.), *Terrorism and affordance*. New York: Continuum International Publishing Group, pp. 17–32.
60. Yun, M. (2009). Application of situational crime prevention to terrorist hostage taking and kidnapping: A case study of 23 Korean hostages in Afghanistan. *Crime Prevention Studies*, 25, 111–139.

Appendix 11.2

SCP & Terrorism Studies Published Post March 2016

1. Berkell, K.A. (2020). A criminological approach to preventing terrorism: Situational crime prevention and the crime prevention literature. In A.P. Schmid (Ed.), *Handbook of terrorism prevention and preparedness*. The Hague, Netherlands: The International Centre for Counter-Terrorism—The Hague (ICCT), pp. 51–78.
2. Duru, H., Onat, I., Akyuz, K., & Akbas, H. (2020). Microcycles of terrorist violence in Turkey: A spatio-temporal analysis of the PKK attacks. *Asian Journal of Criminology*. Available at: https://doi.org/10.1007/s11417-020-09326-z.
3. Freilich, J.D., Bejan, V., Parkin, W.S., Chermak, S.M., & Gruenewald, J. (2020). An interventions analysis of fatal U.S. far-right extremist violence within a vector-autoregressive framework. *Dynamics of Asymmetric Conflict*, 13(2), 143–171.
4. Freilich, J.D., Chermak, S.M., & Klein, B.R. 2020. Investigating the applicability of situational crime prevention to the public mass violence context. *Criminology and Public Policy*, 19(1), 271–293.
5. Gill, P., Horgan, J., & Corner, E. (2019). The rational foraging terrorist: Analysing the distances travelled to commit terrorist violence. *Terrorism and Political Violence*, 31, 929–942.
6. Gruenewald, J., Drawve, G., & Smith, B.L. (2019). The situated contexts of American terrorism: A conjunctive analysis of case configurations. *Criminal Justice & Behavior*, 46(6), 884–901.
7. Gruenewald, J., Klein, B., Parkin, W., Freilich, J.D., & Chermak, S. (2019). A situated comparison of suicide and non-suicide terrorist plots and homicides in the United States, 1990–2014. *Crime & Delinquency*, 65(9), 1187–1217.
8. Hasisi, B., Perry, S., Ilan, Y., & Wolfowicz, M. (2020). Concentrated and close to home: The spatial clustering and distance decay of lone terrorist vehicular attacks. *Journal of Quantitative Criminology*, 36, 607–645.
9. Hsu, H.Y., & McDowall, D. (2017). Does target-hardening result in deadlier terrorist attacks against protected targets? An examination of unintended harmful consequences. *Journal of Research in Crime and Delinquency*, 54(6), 930–957.
10. Hsu, H.Y., Vasquez, B.E., and McDowall, D. (2018). A time-series analysis of terrorism: Intervention, displacement, and diffusion of benefits. *Justice Quarterly*, 35(4), 557–583.

11. Hsu, H.Y., Vasquez, B.E., & McDowall, D. (2019). A deadlier post-9/11 terrorism landscape for the United States abroad: A quasi-experimental study of backlash effects of terrorism prevention. *Journal of Experimental Criminology*, 16(4), 607–623.
12. Lasley, J., & Guffey, J. (2017). A U.S. military perspective on the promise of situational crime prevention for combatting terrorism. *Journal of Policing, Intelligence and Counter Terrorism*, 12, 85–104.
13. Mandala, M., & Freilich, J.D. (2017). Preventing successful assassination attacks by terrorists: An environmental criminology approach. *Journal of Criminological Research, Policy and Practice*, 3(3), 173–191.
14. Mandala, M., & Freilich, J.D. (2018). Disrupting terrorist assassinations through situational crime prevention. *Crime and Delinquency*, 64(12), 1515–1537
15. Marchment, Z., & Gill, P. (2018). Terrorists are just another type of criminal. In R. Wortley, A. Sidebottom, N. Tilley, & G. Laycock (Eds.), *Routledge handbook of crime science*. London: Routledge.
16. Marchment, Z., & Gill, P. (2019). Modelling the spatial decision making of terrorists: The discrete choice approach. *Applied Geography*, 104, 21–31.
17. Marchment, Z., & Gill, P. (2020). Spatial decision making of terrorist target selection: Introducing the TRACK framework. *Studies in Conflict and Terrorism*. (Online first) DOI: 10.1080/1057610X.2020.1711588.
18. Marchment, Z., Bouhana, N., & Gill, P. (2020). Lone actor terrorists: A residence-to-crime approach. *Terrorism and Political Violence*, 32(7), 1413–1438.
19. Mudgett, E. (2020). Extreme ideologies, situational factors, and terrorists' target selection. (MA thesis). University of Arkansas, Fayetteville, AR.
20. Perry, S. (2020). The application of the "law of crime concentration" to terrorism: The Jerusalem case study. *Journal of Quantitative Criminology*, 36, 583–605.
21. Perry, S., Hasisi, B., & Perry, G. (2019). Lone terrorists: A study of run-over attacks in Israel. *European Journal of Criminology*, 16(1), 102–123.
22. Robinson, A., Marchment, Z., & Gill, P. (2019). Domestic extremist criminal damage events: Behaving like criminals or terrorists. *Security Journal*, 32, 153–167.
23. Romyn, D., & M.R. Kebbell. (2018). Mock terrorists decisions' concerning use of the internet for target selection: A red-team approach. *Psychology, Crime & Law*, 24, 589–602.
24. Singer, G., & M. Golan. (2019). Identification of subgroups of terror attacks with shared characteristics for the purpose of preventing mass-casualty attacks: A data-mining approach. *Crime Science*, 8, 14. Available at: https://crimesciencejournal.biomedcentral.com/track/pdf/10.1186/s40163-019-0109-9.pdf.
25. St. George, S. (2017). Assessing the vulnerability in targets of lethal domestic extremism. (Doctoral dissertation). Michigan State University, East Lansing, MI.
26. Williams, A., Corner, E., & Taylor, H. (2020). Vehicular ramming attacks: Assessing the effectiveness of situational crime prevention using crime script analysis. *Terrorism and Political Violence*. (Online first, September) DOI: 10.1080/09546553.2020.1810025.
27. Yang, S.-M., & I.-Chin, J. (2018). An evaluation of displacement and diffusion effects on eco-terrorist activities after police interventions. *Journal of Quantitative Criminology*, 34, 1103–1123.

12

Fear of Terrorism
Extent, Sources, and Reactions

Heejin Lee, Brooke Miller Gialopsos, and Cheryl Lero Jonson

"The Day That Shook America," "America's Darkest Day," "Bastards!" (Abadi, 2020). Each of these jarring headlines were scrawled across the front page of newspapers in the aftermath of the September 11th terrorist attacks. Before noon that day, nearly 3,000 innocent lives were cut short,[1] the Twin Towers had crumbled, the Pentagon was burning, and heroic passengers fought back against four terrorist hijackers crashing a plane into a field rather than its intended target (9/11 Memorial and Museum, 2021). However, the reverberations of the events extended well beyond the loss of life and the destruction of property. As tragedy unfolded in New York City, Washington, DC, and Shanksville, Pennsylvania, millions of people across the globe watched in horror as America was under attack by 19 militants associated with Al-Qaeda (Schuster et al., 2001).

Although prior attacks had occurred on American soil, the scope and the incomparable loss of life made the September 11th attacks a defining moment in American history. In the immediate aftermath, fear and worry gripped Americans, skyrocketing from 24 percent of the public expressing worry about terrorism in the year prior to the attacks to 58 percent on the day of the attacks (Gallup, 2021). And, unlike after the 1995 Oklahoma City Bombing, this increased level of worry has continued almost two decades later as slightly more than 40 percent of the public continues to express concern about terrorism (Brenan, 2019; Lewis, 2000). While Americans have been experiencing a chronic level of fear over the past 20 years, a different form of terrorism is beginning to capture the attention of the public. In light of the events at the U.S. Capitol Building on January 6, 2021, a spotlight has been focused on domestic terrorism, with FBI director Christopher Wray warning the threat is "metastasizing across the country" (Goldman, 2021). As a result, Americans are now navigating a world with an acute awareness of threats coming from both home and abroad.

Given this new American reality, fear of terrorism will continue to be an issue the public grapples with in the years ahead. To promote further understanding of the fear–terrorism relationship, this chapter is comprised of four sections. First, it will highlight the complexity in defining terrorism and the common motivations for carrying out such acts of violence (LaFree & Dugan, 2009). Second, it will review the previous literature that examined the extent of public fear associated with terrorism, focusing on two types of terrorism—international and domestic. Third, it will examine the individual factors related to greater fear of terrorism and whether they are unique to terrorism or applicable to fear of crime in general. Finally, the last section will discuss the reactions of this fear—both individually and on a policy level.

What's in a Name? Defining Terrorism and its Motives

Despite its undeniable impact on millions of people around the world, the study of terrorism is a challenging endeavor. Contributing to this difficulty is the lack of a universally accepted definition (Becker & Rubinstein, 2011; Haner, 2017; LaFree & Dugan, 2009; Ruby, 2002; Shanahan, 2016). As a result, there is currently a surplus of over 250 academic and governmental definitions with broad disagreement on what exactly constitutes terrorism (Aly & Balnaves, 2007; Easson & Schmid, 2011; LaFree & Dugan, 2009; Schmid, 2011; Schmid & Jongman, 1988; Stampnitsky, 2017). The definitions vary on a multitude of factors including, but not limited to, victim and target characteristics, the purpose of the violence, and the chosen tactics (Weinberg et al., 2004). Furthermore, even among those engaging in terrorist activity, there is not a consensus: They rarely identify as a "terrorist," rather viewing themselves as a revolutionary, freedom fighter, martyr, or soldier (Schmid, 2016).

Officially, the United States government has defined "international terrorism" as:

> activities that—(A) involve violent acts or acts dangerous to human life that are a violation of the criminal laws of the United States or of any State, or that would be a criminal violation if committed within the jurisdiction of the United States or of any State; (B) appear to be intended—(i) to intimidate or coerce a civilian population; (ii) to influence the policy of a government by intimidation or coercion; or (iii) to affect the conduct of a government by mass destruction, assassination, or kidnapping; and (C) occur primarily outside the territorial jurisdiction of the United States, or transcend national boundaries in terms of the means by which they are accomplished, the persons they appear intended to intimidate or coerce, or the locale in which their perpetrators operate or seek asylum.
> (18 U.S.C. §2331, 2018)

Similarly, the United States has defined "domestic terrorism" using the same definition above with a slight variation. Section C is replaced with "(C) occur primarily within the territorial jurisdiction of the United States." Thus, unlike international terrorism, domestic terrorism involves "homegrown" elements. Accordingly, in the United States, these attacks involve "Americans who commit ideological driven crimes in the United States but lack foreign direction or influence" (Sacco, 2021, p. 1; see also Graham, Chapter 4 of this volume).

Sifting through these definitions, four commonalities begin to emerge. First, terrorism involves the use of violence or illegal force, often politically motivated. Second, the violence is directed at noncombatant, "soft" targets, including attacks on civilians as well as military targets during peacetime (Ruby, 2002; Stern, 2003). Third, the violence is committed by clandestine or subnational actors. This criterion excludes from terrorist activity any announced conflicts or declared war. Thus, terrorist acts are, in their very nature, unannounced surprise attacks making a defense all but impossible (Ruby, 2002). Fourth, the violence aims to purposefully affect an audience and often an audience that extends beyond the immediate victims of an attack (Becker & Rubinstein, 2011; Haner, 2017; Oots, 1990; Ruby, 2002).

Just as there is considerable variation in the definitions of terrorism, there is also substantial diversity in the motives for carrying out such acts. Recently, Wojciechowski (2017), building off the work of Sterling (1981), categorized six reasons for terrorist activity: (1) religious and cultural sources, (2) territorial and ethnic sources, (3) socio-economic conditions, (4) politico-historical reasons, (5) psychological sources, including hatred and revenge, and (6) other selected reasons, encompassing a variety of motives from globalization to terrorism encouraged by leaders and elites. However, underlying each of these motives is one other fundamental goal of terrorism—to "terrorize" or instill extreme fear in a wider audience (Aly & Balnaves, 2007). As a result, terrorists often use the deaths of innocent and seemingly random victims as a means to wage "psychological warfare" on the larger society in order to obtain their intended objective (Ganor, 2004, p. 38; see also Ben-David & Cohen-Louck, 2010). The randomness and the often public location—our workplaces, airports, sporting events—of such attacks give the appearance that no one is safe from this violence, increasing alarm and anxiety well beyond the people immediately harmed by the attack. Although the likelihood of dying from a terrorist attack on American soil is minute, the psychological impact is extensive with three out of five American adults expressing stress about terrorism (APA, 2019; START, 2017). To gain a better insight of the impact of this psychological warfare resulting from terrorism, the following sections will examine the extent, sources, and reactions to this fear of terrorism.

Extent of Fear

Between 1995 and 2016, 3,277 Americans lost their lives to terroristic violence on U.S. soil. However, the vast majority of deaths—3,070 to be exact—occurred from two specific events: (1) the 1995 bombing of the Alfred P. Murrah Federal Building in Oklahoma City, an act of domestic terrorism, and (2) the 2001 September 11th attacks, an act of international terrorism (START, 2017). When removing these two outliers, the number of individuals murdered by both international and domestic terrorists over the course of 21 years falls to 207. As a result, in an *average* year, the percentage of deaths attributed to terrorism has consistently been less than 0.01 percent (Ritchie, 2018a, 2018b), with Americans significantly more likely to die from cardiovascular diseases, motor vehicle accidents, and suicide (Ruby, 2002). To elevate terrorism into the top 10 causes of death in the United States, more than 30,000 people would need to die in a *single* year at the hands of terrorists (Ritchie, 2018a; START, 2017). Given that there have only been three years since 1970 when the number of terrorist attacks *worldwide* exceeded 30,000, it is highly improbable that the United States will ever experience terrorist activity of that magnitude (Global Terrorism Database, 2021).

Terrorists and terrorist organizations often use fear as a conduit for achieving their ultimate goal of political, social, or religious change. Although the risk of death is exceptionally low, terrorists and terrorist organizations have had "success" in inducing fear and anxiety among a wider audience— with Americans and the international community substantially overestimating their risk of being a victim of this type of violence (Haner et al., 2020; Sloan et al., 2020). This inflated perception of risk and exaggerated feeling of fear from the public is not surprising as terrorism and the media have a sort of "symbiotic relationship" (Spencer, 2012, p. 6).

Immediately after an attack, the media rushes to "break the news," broadcasting images of the devastation into our homes and across our social media feeds in an attempt to earn much sought-after ratings for their network or organization (Hoffman, 2006; Spencer, 2012). However, this saturation of media coverage comes at a cost as it simultaneously provides the terrorist actors or organizations the desired public attention needed to reach a broader audience and spread fear and anxiety beyond the immediate victims of the attack (Ganor, 2004; Hoffman, 2006; LaFree & Dugan, 2004; Spencer, 2012). Thus, while the media snags their ratings and the terrorists have their message amplified, the public is left listening, watching, and reading the horrific details of the attack (Altheide, 2017; Nellis & Savage, 2012; Sloan et al., 2020).

This resultant fear is a powerful emotion. As will be described later in the chapter, it has the ability to impact our physical, emotional, and mental well-being, alter our individual behavior, and influence our support for various policy preferences (Aly & Balnaves, 2007; Haner et al., 2019; Neria et al., 2011; Sloan et al., 2020). Although terrorism has some features that might depress fears in the United States—it is infrequent and tends to occur in certain locations (e.g., large metropolitan areas), it has numerous features that might inspire fear—it is unpredictable, targets random innocent civilians, and inflicts a high level of harm when it occurs. Even with fear recognized as a fundamental goal of terrorism, the extent of the public's fear has received limited scholarly attention (Haner et al., 2019, Haner et al., 2020; Sloan et al., 2020). Instead, much of what we know about the public's fear has been derived from public opinion polls (APA, 2019; Brenan, 2019; Chapman University, 2019; Pew Research Center, 2019).

Before reviewing what is known about the extent of fear, one issue must be taken into consideration. The vast majority of polls on this topic often use the term "terrorism" generally, asking questions such as, "To what degree are you worried about the following: A terrorist attack?" (World Values Survey, 2020). Due to the imagery of the September 11th attacks forever etched into the minds of millions of people, the term "terrorism" is likely interpreted by most Americans as international terrorism, and more specifically, acts perpetrated by radical Islamic extremists (Gruenewald et al., 2019). However, this exclusive focus on international terrorism does not fully capture the extent of the terrorist threat in the United States (Parkin et al., 2017). Between 1990 and 2019, removing the outliers of Oklahoma City and September 11th, 154 deaths over 47 incidents were attributed to Islamic extremists compared to 345 people killed in 217 attacks carried out by far-right domestic terrorists (Gruenewald et al., 2019). Due to the events at the U.S. Capitol Building in January 2021, this latter category is beginning to receive more attention by the American public. However, given these considerations, it becomes necessary to distinguish between foreign and domestic terrorists when assessing the public's fear of terrorism.

A review of numerous public opinion polls illustrates that the concern about terrorism in general is a reality for a substantial proportion of Americans. For example, in a 2018 survey, Haner and colleagues (2019) discovered that roughly 45 percent of the American public is fearful of a terrorist attack. These findings are consistent with the majority of polls conducted in the past five years. In 2017 and 2019 Gallup polls, 42 percent and 46 percent of the public, respectively, expressed worry about terrorism (Brenan, 2019; McCarthy, 2017). Although there have been spikes in reported worry after specific incidents of terrorism (e.g., the London transit bombings, the Paris shootings), the average level of worry about terrorism among the American public has been relatively stable over the past two decades, with slightly more than 4 in 10 individuals indicating they are worried about terrorism generally.

Additionally, these findings mirror the most recent Chapman University Survey of American Fears (2019). This annual survey found that 43.4 percent of the public is afraid or very afraid of terrorism in general, with 51.4 percent being afraid specifically of a terrorist attack that might occur in the near future. Interestingly, this level of fear exceeds the percentage of Americans reporting they are fearful of theft of property (38.2 percent) and break-ins (37.6 percent), being murdered by a stranger (31 percent) or someone they know (22.2 percent), muggings

(30 percent), abductions/kidnappings (27.1 percent), sexual assault by a stranger (26.2 percent) or someone they know (20.3 percent), gang violence (26 percent), and stalking (24.1 percent). Even with Americans having an increased likelihood of experiencing these more common crimes, they still express an exaggerated level of fear compared to their relative risk, with slightly more than half of the population fearful of terrorist acts occurring in the near future.

Not only does the public worry about terrorism, but they also view it consistently as one of the top issues facing the country. In their annual surveys, Pew Research Center asks respondents from across the globe how much they perceive a variety of issues as being major threats to their country's well-being. When specifically inquiring about ISIS, a slight majority (53 percent) of Americans considered the group a threat to the United States in 2019 (Pew Research Center, 2019). However, this is a substantial decline since 2015 when more than 80 percent identified ISIS as a substantial threat (Pew Research Center, 2019).

In 2020, Pew Research Center significantly altered this question, removing any mention of a specific terrorist organization or group. Instead, the question now simply inquires if individuals believe that "terrorism" generically is a major threat facing the United States. As a result, there was a 20 percentage point jump in Americans viewing terrorism as a major issue, rising from 53 percent seeing ISIS as a threat in 2019 to 73 percent viewing terrorism in general as a threat in 2020 (Pew Research Center, 2019, 2020). A potential factor in this increase could be new awareness surrounding the threat of domestic terrorism. Given this consideration, future polls should seek to isolate the impact of both international and domestic terrorist threats.

One such study simultaneously assessed the public's view of domestic and international terrorism to allow for comparisons of the public's perception between the two acts of violence. Haner et al. (2020) surveyed roughly 1,000 Americans about how likely they believed a terrorist attack would occur in their community. Unlike most other surveys on the topic, the researchers specifically delineated the nationality of the perpetrators by indicating the attack was committed "by someone born in the U.S." or "by a radical Islamist born in a Muslim country" (Haner et al., 2020, p. 1613). This differentiation had a substantive influence on perceived likelihood of an attack, with almost half (46 percent) believing a terrorist attack was likely to occur by a person born in United States, but only a quarter (26 percent) feeling an attack was likely by a radical Islamic terrorist. Thus, the threat of "homegrown" terrorism appears to be weighing more heavily on the minds of Americans than the threat of international terrorism (Haner et al., 2020).

This differentiation will likely become even more important in the near future. It is probable that, with the considerable attention given to domestic terrorist threats (e.g., the storming of the U.S. Capitol), larger numbers of Americans will begin to fear this form of violence (Goldman, 2021). With groups such as the Proud Boys and Oath Keepers garnering a national spotlight and, in some cases, being designated as terrorist organizations (Coletta, 2021; Graham, Chapter 4 of this volume), Americans are now seeing the images of their fellow countrymen and women, not the faces of foreign nationals, attacking symbolic buildings and other citizens. In fact, in a 2021 poll by Monmouth University, a staggering 83 percent of the public considered domestic terrorism a very or extremely important issue for the federal government to address, only being surpassed by jobs/unemployment and education/schools. Furthermore, the threat of domestic terrorism was perceived as more important than the raging coronavirus pandemic, healthcare, election laws, taxes, and racial inequality (Monmouth University, 2021). As a result, to truly understand the impact of terrorism on the psyche of the American public, future research must make clear distinctions between the threats coming from both within and outside our national border.

Sources of Fear

With an understanding of the definitions, motives, and extent of fear stemming from terrorism, it is important to dissect the sources of fear. The fear of crime literature has long argued for crime-specific measures (e.g., are you afraid of being a victim of sexual assault?) over broad, general explorations into fear of crime (e.g., are you afraid of crime?) (Ferraro & LaGrange, 1987; Warr & Stafford, 1983), and fear of terrorism fits the bill. Although the information discussed below is not an exhaustive list of all predictors of fear of terrorism, it captures the primary factors explored empirically by researchers. While many of these variables are consistent with the larger fear of crime framework and deal with perceived vulnerability (e.g., media consumption, gender, age, prior victimization), there are some that deviate from this prior context and warrant more attention moving forward (e.g., religion, ideology, political views).

However, before this exploration begins, it is necessary to differentiate between two conceptually distinct phenomena. Though similar, there is a firm understanding among victimologists that fear is separate from risk perceptions (DuBow et al., 1979; Ferraro, 1995; Ferraro & LaGrange, 1987). Whereas fear of crime tends to be an affective, emotional response, perceived risk is more of a cognitive judgment (Ferraro & LaGrange, 1987) or a recognition of potential danger in a situation (Ferraro, 1995). In the broader fear of crime literature, these concepts are often linked (Tillyer et al., 2011; Warr, 1987; Wilcox et al., 2005) and an investigation of fear of terrorism would be incomplete without taking perceived risk of terrorism into account. Further, these two separate constructs often produce different outcomes (see Wilcox Rountree & Land, 1996) and likely unique policy implications.

Media

Paralleling the fear of crime and perceived risk literature (Gerbner & Gross, 1976; Gomme, 1988), it is believed that consumption of mass media and other media related variables influence fear and perceived risk of terrorism. Terrorism studies by Elmas (2020) and Wilcox et al. (2009) have found support for this notion. There are many reasons why media consumption may increase one's fear and risk perceptions, with one of the more prominent ideas known as the cultivation hypothesis. The cultivation hypothesis purports that emotions and attitudes become distorted by the frequency of media consumption (Gerbner, 1969). Essentially, individuals who consume large amounts of media are taking in more events that are violent and/or extreme, which eventually alters their perceptions of reality.

Using interviews of adults residing in New York City and Washington, DC, Nellis and Savage (2012) examined whether the cultivation hypothesis extends to fear and perceived risk of terrorism. In doing so, they also explored whether altruistic fear (i.e., fear for others, particularly loved ones) is different from fear for self (see also Warr, 2000). Nellis and Savage's (2012) work showed that the effect of media consumption might vary on personal fear, altruistic fear, and risk perceptions. For example, the amount of television news consumption had a significant and positive effect on fear of a family member becoming a victim of a terrorist attack, but its relationship with fear for self was not significant (Nellis & Savage, 2012). Thus, their findings yield partial support for the cultivation hypothesis.

Beyond the frequency of media consumption, Williamson et al.'s (2019) work included whether the media sources were actively or passively accessed. This classification was dependent on the amount of effort used to access the source and its information. While passive sources include television and radio, active sources are those accessed through the Internet or via newspapers. Using the Australian National Security and Preparedness Survey, Williamson et al. (2019) found that consuming multiple media sources resulted in a greater fear of terrorism, but that passively accessed sources were not as influential in cultivating fear compared to actively accessed ones. In addition, they explored whether self-reported knowledge of terrorism factored into respondents' fear (see also Warr, 1990). Their results indicated that individuals with self-reported knowledge of terroristic activities or events worried more about terrorism. Moreover, this self-reported terrorism knowledge served to partially mediate the relationship between fear of terrorism and the number of media sources accumulated.

As much as the media coverage of terrorism and terrorists has had a marked impact on the general public's fear, politicians have been able to capitalize on the extreme fear or panic (e.g., De Castella & McGarty, 2011). Applying Cohen's (1972) stages of moral panic to terrorism, Rothe and Muzzatti (2004) conclude that the portrayal of these terrorist acts has created an "us or them" mentality that has resulted in excessive levels of fear and panic. Due to the level of coverage in the media, terrorism is consumed in a brand-like fashion similar to McDonald's or Coca-Cola (Recuber, 2009). Recuber (2009) argues the portrayal and consumerism around these "terrorist folk devils" impact the authenticity of these threats and the public's calculation of risk. According to Altheide (2006), this mass-mediated fear has expanded the discourse on crime to include terrorism largely though victimization narratives. The resulting "politics of fear" impacts assumptions regarding risk and danger, preoccupies us with the idea of future victims (i.e., anyone is a potential victim of terrorism), and allows decision makers to advance their agenda (Altheide, 2006). Therefore, just like crime, the media has played a significant role in socially constructing fear of terrorism (Gadarian, 2010).

Gender

Most studies assessing gender differences find that women are more fearful of terrorism (e.g., Haner et al., 2019; Shechory-Bitton & Cohen-Louck, 2018) or report being more worried about it (e.g., Haner et al., 2019; Nellis & Savage, 2012; Williamson et al., 2019). The fear of crime literature has long grappled with the discrepancy between women's elevated fear of crime and their lower rates of victimization (see Ferraro, 1995, 1996). Known as the shadow of sexual assault hypothesis, the general idea is that women tend to fear all crime because of the potential for any victimization to lead to a sexual assault. Nevertheless, the fact that terrorist attacks tend to be nondiscriminatory and threaten men and women equally is an important theoretical consideration (Ben-David & Cohen-Louck, 2010; Nellis, 2009).

While the paradox itself may not apply in terroristic situations, the sentiment that women feel more vulnerable and, thus, more fearful appears to remain (Ben-David & Cohen-Louck, 2010). Nellis (2009) examined whether this paradox of fear holds when examining fear of terrorism and found support for gender-specific differences. However, she proposed that women's elevated fear may be driven by feelings of both social and physical vulnerability, rather than the shadow of sexual assault. In addition, Ben-David and Cohen-Louck (2010) attribute women's more generalized concern for others, their perceptions of terrorist attacks being more dangerous, and their lower sense of controllability to explain why women remain more fearful of terrorism than men.

In their cross-national study, Hong and colleagues (2020) uncovered that female college students from both the United States and South Korea were more worried about a terrorist attack in their country *and* the victimization of themselves and their family members than their fellow male students. Likewise, female students exhibited more social anxiety on the Liebowitz Social Anxiety Scale and lower levels of aggression on the Buss–Perry Aggression Questionnaire than their male counterparts (Hong et al., 2020).

Wilcox and colleagues (2009) discovered that female high school students in Turkey remained more fearful of terrorism in the region than male students when controlling for individual-level and contextual factors. They speculated that this gendered fear of terrorism may be explained by perceived risk. These findings align with other studies such as Nellis and Savage (2012) reporting higher perceptions of terrorism risk among women compared to men.

Similarly, the work of May et al. (2011) on perceived risk of terrorism in Kentucky used geography-specific measures by asking respondents to indicate the likelihood of a terrorist attack in the state within the next year as well as within their community. They explored several types of fear, which included one measure of personal fear and three measures of altruistic fear (i.e., being afraid that someone in their family, community, and state would be a victim of a terrorist attack). As a result, females revealed more fear and greater perceived risk than males, and these gender differences might be attributable to the socialization of women and men.

Age

Several studies found that older respondents are more fearful of crime (see Clemente & Kleiman, 1976; Weinrath & Gartrell, 1996) and have higher perceived risk (see Franklin et al., 2008). These findings can be understood from a vulnerability standpoint. In this vein, a positive relationship between age and worry about terrorism was identified by Williamson et al. (2019). Examining fear of terrorism among individuals in Israel, Shechory-Bitton and Cohen-Louck (2020) found a similar result with age. For perceptions of risk, May et al. (2011) found older respondents in Kentucky perceived a greater risk of terrorism.

However, not all studies have found a positive relationship, indicating that the relationship between age and fear of crime is not conclusive. For example, Nellis's (2009) work revealed that younger women were more worried about terrorism than their older counterparts. This finding mimics some work in the broader fear of crime literature with younger individuals reporting more worry and/or fear (e.g., Ferraro, 1995). Nellis and Savage (2012) found this applied for personal fear but not altruistic fear of terrorism. Elmas (2020) also reported that younger college students were more fearful of terrorism than older students. In addition, Haner et al. (2019) found that older respondents were less worried about terrorist attacks than younger respondents.

Race and Nationality

The prior research has indicated that Black, Indigenous, People of Color (BIPOC) respondents are often more fearful of crime (e.g., Ferraro, 1995; Warr & Ellison, 2000) and perceive more risk than their White counterparts (e.g., Ferraro, 1995; LaGrange & Ferraro, 1989). This, too, has been conceptualized in terms of perceived vulnerability (Miethe & Lee, 1984). Examining the role of race on fear and perceived risk of terrorism, Nellis and Savage (2012) found that White respondents were less fearful and had lower risk perceptions than non-White respondents. Similarly, Haner et al. (2019) uncovered that non-White respondents were more likely to express both fear and worry about a terrorist attack than White respondents. Additionally, the level and type of fear might be variant across different national settings. For example, Hong et al.'s (2020) study of college students revealed that American respondents expressed more worry about an attack happening in their country, whereas South Koreans tended to worry about threats to themselves or their families. In another study by Christensen and Aars (2019), terrorist fear was more prevalent among citizens in nondemocratic countries than citizens under democratic governments.

Education

Previous studies are not consistent regarding the association between education and fear of crime in general, with some studies suggesting an inverse relationship (Ferraro, 1995; Weinrath & Gartrell, 1996) and others failing to find a significant relationship (Warr & Ellison, 2000). The concept of vulnerability can be applied again as lack of education (an index of low socioeconomic status) can represent individual, social, and/or situational vulnerability (see Donnelly, 1989). Williamson et al. (2019) revealed a negative relationship between educational attainment and being worried about terrorism. Similarly, Haner et al. (2019) showed that less educated individuals were more likely to be afraid of a terrorist attack, although education did not have a significant effect on worry. Aly and Balnaves (2007) also found individuals with lower educational attainment scored higher on the fear of terrorism.

Prior Victimization and Exposure to Terrorist Threat

Prior victimization appears to be a strong covariate for both fear of crime and perceptions of risk (see Ferraro, 1995; Weinrath & Gartrell, 1996; Wilcox Rountree & Land, 1996). Typically, the fear and risk literature includes both one's own victimization (i.e., direct victimization) and vicarious victimization (i.e., indirect victimization). And Nellis and Savage (2012) suggest that the same framework can be extended to personal and altruistic fear of terrorism, showing that prior victims of terrorism (both direct and indirect victims) were more afraid of terrorism. Individuals victimized by terrorist attacks also reported higher perceived risk for self and others. Consistently, Elmas's (2020) work on college students revealed that indirect victimization increased fear of terrorism.

Relatedly, exposure to terrorist threat might affect fear of terrorism, although research is lacking to draw a definitive conclusion. Shechory-Bitton and Cohen-Louck (2018) found that exposure to terrorism (as measured by living near hotspots of terrorism) heightened fear of terrorism, as did neighborhood disorder. In contrast, May et al.'s (2011) work in Kentucky revealed that respondents in urban areas (commonly assumed to be at a greater risk of terrorist attacks) reported lower levels of perceived risk than those living outside of urban areas.

Emotional Vulnerability

Haner et al. (2019) measured emotional vulnerability by using an abbreviated Center for Epidemiologic Studies Depression (CES-D) Scale. They found that respondents who were more depressed or distressed on this scale expressed great fear and worry about terrorist attacks. Though studied to a lesser extent, this finding is also in line with the larger fear of crime literature (see Cossman & Rader, 2011; Jackson & Stafford, 2009).

Perceived Risk

The work of May et al. (2011) revealed, that compared to demographic variables, including gender, perceived risk of terrorism was a much stronger predictor of fear of terrorism. Individuals who perceived a greater likelihood of a terrorist attack occurring in their community and in Kentucky had higher levels of fear (i.e., personal and altruistic fear combined). Nellis (2009) and Nellis and Savage (2012) both found a significant positive relationship between fear of terrorism and risk perceptions among a sample of adults living in Washington, DC and New York City. Similar findings are also observed in the larger fear and perceived risk literature (see e.g., Ferraro & LaGrange, 1992; LaGrange & Ferraro, 1989). Thus, future studies should continue to tap into the relationship between risk perceptions and fear of terrorism.

Moving Forward: Politics, Religion, and Ideological Beliefs

Although the covariates of fear of terrorism are similar to those of fear of crime in general, several other constructs merit further attention.

First, Andersen and Mayerl (2018) suggest that the fear of crime framework is insufficient to explain fear of terrorism because the strongest predictors of fear of terrorism are unfavorable attitudes toward Muslims. Thus, in their view, studies that fail to account for Islamophobia are spurious and incomplete.

Second, political attitudes might be associated with fear of terrorism. In this regard, existing research is inconsistent. Nellis (2009) failed to find a significant relationship between political conservativism and fear of terrorism, while other studies found respondents who were more worried about terrorism tended to be politically conservative (e.g., Williamson et al., 2019). Haner et al. (2019) uncovered a similar result, finding that those who identified as politically conservative were more likely to be afraid of and worry about terrorist attacks.

Third, as argued by Shechory-Bitton and Cohen-Louck (2018), additional theoretical constructs such as ideology and religion might be added, as traditional demographic factors alone appear inadequate to explain the complexities of fear of terrorism. Using a sample of adults from various locations in Israel, their results showed that nonreligious participants expressed more fear of terrorism than their religious counterparts. Although ideology was not specifically explored, they instead focused on geographical areas within Israel, which is largely divided by ideology and/or religion. Drawing from a national sample of Americans, Haner et al. (2019) found that identifying as Christian increased respondents' fear and worry about a terrorist attack. Similarly, Elmas (2020) also found higher fear among Protestant and Catholic Christians. Thus, more research is needed to better understand the role that these variables play.

To date, it appears that while who you are matters, what you believe could matter even more when examining fear and perceived risk of terrorism. Support for theoretical constructs that involve vulnerability (e.g., gender, age) exists, but it is also mixed (Nellis, 2009; Sloan et al., 2020) and limited (May et al., 2011; Shechory-Bitton & Cohen-Louck, 2018). Future researchers should continue to break out of the traditional fear-of-crime mold and emphasize the importance of variables like political beliefs, ideology, and religion when examining fear of terrorism. Additionally, most of these measures only captured terrorism in a general sense without differentiating between domestic or foreign terrorism. Future researchers should consider more purposefully exploring this distinction (see Haner et al., 2020).

Reactions to Fear of Terrorism

With terrorism causing fear for a substantial number of individuals, the following section will review what types of individual and policy responses are employed in reaction to that fear. The first part will discuss how people cope with fear of terrorism for themselves or for family members. The second part will explore how the public's fear affects the policies they favor to reduce the threat of terrorism.

Personal Reactions

Both direct and vicarious experiences of a terrorist attack arouse feelings of fear, which can have lingering effects. As a response, individuals make necessary adaptations to cope with distress associated with terrorist threats. Personal reactions to fear of terrorism manifest in different forms of emotional, psychological, and behavioral responses.

Emotional and Psychological Responses

Emotional and psychological effects of terrorist acts have been extensively studied after the September 11th attacks—particularly in the field of medicine. Although there is a dearth of research that specifically examines the effect of terrorism-related fear on mental health outcomes (because fear itself can be considered the outcome of terrorist events), there is a consensus in the prior research. The literature has consistently found an increase in the reporting of depression, anxiety, post-traumatic stress disorder (PTSD), and substance use (e.g., alcohol, cigarettes, marijuana) following the September 11th terrorist attacks (Boscarino et al., 2006; Centers for Disease Control, 2002; Richman et al., 2004; Richman et al., 2008; Richman et al., 2009; Schuster et al., 2001; Vlahov et al., 2002).

The threat of terrorism tends to cause lasting emotional and psychological distress, often accompanied by increases in substance use. According to the report from the Centers for Disease Control (2002) drawing from 3,512 residents of three states (Connecticut, New Jersey, New York) immediately after the September 11th attacks, "3% of alcohol drinkers reported increased alcohol consumption, 21% of smokers reported an increase in smoking, and 1% of nonsmokers reported that they started to smoke after the attacks" (Centers for Disease Control, 2002, p. 1468).

Vlahov et al. (2002) analyzed the prevalence of cigarette smoking, alcohol consumption, and marijuana use five to eight weeks after September 11th. Among 988 adults who lived in Manhattan south of 110th Street,[2] the overall use of three substances increased by 28.8 percent after the September 11th attacks. To be specific, the percentage of individuals smoking cigarettes increased from 22.6 percent to 23.4 percent (9.7 percent increase), the percentage of individuals drinking alcohol increased from 59.1 percent to 64.4 percent (24.6 percent increase), and the percentage of individuals smoking marijuana increased from 4.4 percent to 5.7 percent (3.2 percent increase). Similarly, using a random sample of 1,681 New York City adults, Boscarino et al. (2006) revealed that greater exposure to the World Trade Center disaster (i.e., four or more stressful events experienced during the attacks) increased the odds of binge drinking and alcohol dependence by two to three times both one year and two years after the September 11th attacks.

However, the effects of the events of September 11th went beyond the residents of New York City and surrounding communities. A review of previous studies suggests that emotional vulnerability (or the extent of stress response to begin with) associated with a terrorist attack is highly variable among individuals—such that objective measures of exposure or loss cannot fully explain the degree of response (Silver et al., 2001; see also Sloan et al., 2020). Thus, emotional and psychological costs of terrorism (e.g., depression, anxiety, PTSD, cigarette smoking) can be borne by both victims and non-victims.

Using a longitudinal mail survey of employees at a Midwestern university (N = 1453), Richman et al. (2008) employed a 12-item index to measure negative beliefs and fears related to terrorism (e.g., "feel less safe than before September 11th," "remain fearful of potential attacks in future"). They found negative beliefs and fears in 2003 predicted increased escapist motives for drinking among both men and women and drinking to intoxication among men in 2005. Using the 2003 wave from the same dataset, Richman and colleagues (2009) showed statistically significant associations of negative beliefs and fears with increased symptoms of depression, anxiety, hostility, somatization, and PTSD.

Schuster et al. (2001) conducted a national-level survey of adults (N = 560) three to five days after the September 11th attacks. The results showed that the respondents experienced substantial stress symptoms such as feeling very upset when something reminds of what happened (30 percent), having repeated, disturbing memories, thoughts, or dreams about what happened (16 percent), having difficulty concentrating

(14 percent), trouble falling or staying asleep (11 percent), and feeling irritable or having angry outbursts (9 percent). As a total, 44 percent of the sample reported suffering from at least one of the stress symptoms.

Behavioral Responses

Emotional and psychological responses to a terrorist attack affect attitudes and decision-making, thereby prompting subsequent behavioral changes (Maguen et al., 2008; see also Denovan et al., 2017; Henson & Reyns, 2015; Huddy et al., 2002). Thus, as argued by Kirschenbaum (2006), various forms of behavioral adaptation are used as a "survival strategy" against terrorism, and these adaptations derive from the cognitive acceptance that terror will be part of daily life. For example, using a national-level survey of 560 adults two months after the September 11th attacks, Stein and colleagues (2004) uncovered that Americans significantly altered their behavior in response to that fateful day. Among the 16 percent of the sample who reported persistent distress symptoms, a majority talked with family and friends about terrorism (75 percent), turned to religion (75 percent), accomplished less at work (65 percent), and made donations (56 percent). A lesser extent of change was reported for feeling unable to share their terrorism-related thoughts and feelings with others (43 percent), using alcohol, medications, or other drugs because of worries about terrorism (32 percent), avoiding public gathering places (24 percent), and consulting with general medical providers (11 percent).

The behavioral changes did not only occur in the months immediately following September 11th. Torabi and Seo (2004), using a national sample of 807 adults, found that about 3 in 10 Americans maintained changes to their behaviors or life routines 10 to 12 months after the September 11th attacks. Specifically, changes were reported for the following behaviors: watching TV more often (47 percent), talking more with others about terrorism (30 percent), limiting outside activities (25 percent), turning to prayer, religion, or spirituality (24 percent), changing mode of transportation (23 percent), improving home security (21 percent), gathering emergency supplies (15 percent), considering buying a weapon (10 percent), and spending more time volunteering (10 percent). Notably, this study supported that demographic characteristics were related to the extent and type of behavioral change endorsed (see also Kirschenbaum, 2006). For example, except for purchasing a firearm, behavioral changes were more likely to be reported by vulnerable populations (e.g., women, BIPOC). In addition, young (ages 18 to 29) and old (65 and above) individuals and those living in rural areas reported making fewer life changes compared to the reference group (those aged 45 to 64 and living in medium-sized cities).

However, the studies that assessed various behavioral changes after the terrorist attacks are limited in delineating the relationship between fear and behavioral responses. In this regard, two other studies are noteworthy. First, Lerner and colleagues (2003) examined whether fear and anger related to terrorism affect the perceived likelihood of experiencing risky events and taking precautionary measures. Between September and November 2001, a national sample of 973 adults completed two surveys, and for the second survey, each respondent was randomly assigned to one of the three emotion conditions (fear, anger, sadness). Experimental manipulation was employed to evoke the target emotion by exposing the respondent to relevant media portrayals (e.g., for fear, the text warned of anthrax and bioterrorism and the picture showed postal workers wearing flimsy masks). The results from this study supported that those more fearful of terrorist attacks engaged in more precautionary actions such as traveling less than usual and screening mail carefully for suspicious items.

Second, Sloan et al. (2020) examined behavioral responses to the threat of terrorism using a 2018 national-level survey of 1,068 American adults. Drawing from the fear of crime literature (e.g., Liska et al., 1988), this study suggested two types of behavioral coping: restrictive behaviors and assertive behaviors. Restrictive (also called avoidance) behaviors refer to when people constrain their behaviors to avoid unsafe situations, whereas assertive (also called protective) behaviors involve taking actions to protect oneself (see also Aly & Balnaves, 2007). Examples of restrictive behaviors are staying home, reducing leisure activities, avoiding public events, and not flying on airplanes. Examples of protective behaviors include raising awareness of surroundings and buying self-defense supplies.

They found that fear of terrorism was associated with two types of avoidance behaviors—not flying on planes and not using public transportation—after controlling for gender, age, existing emotional vulnerability, political orientation, and attitudes toward Muslims. However, those who were fearful of terrorism were not statistically different in their willingness to attend public events, enter skyscrapers, and travel overseas. In comparison, worry about terrorism significantly predicted the five avoidance behaviors examined. Regarding protective behaviors, fear of crime resulted in a greater likelihood of voting participation, but not purchasing a gun. Worry about terrorism did not have a significant influence on any protective behavior. In sum, research is lacking on clarifying the effect of terrorism-related fear on different types of behavioral responses. Thus, more research is needed to further pursue this line of inquiry.

Policy Reactions

After the September 11th attacks, most Western countries, including the United States, expanded restrictive counterterrorist regulations such as limiting procedural rights of terror suspects, making immigration laws stricter, and increasing spending on national defense (Epifanio, 2011; Guiora, 2005; Leavitt & Beacham, 2002). While the overall influence on terrorist attacks on policy change is quite expansive—spanning the areas from national security (for a review, see Guiora, 2005), international relations (Bassiouni, 2002), to public health (Leavitt & Beacham, 2002)—extant studies focused on whether emotions, such as fear and anger, affect public attitudes toward foreign policies that are considered aggressive/confrontational/hawkish or conciliatory/defensive/dovish (Gadarian, 2010; Huddy & Feldman, 2011; Huddy et al., 2005; Sadler et al., 2005; Skitka et al., 2006; Wetherell et al., 2013).

For example, Huddy and colleagues (2005) examined the effects of anxiety and anger on support for anti-terrorism policies using a random-digit-dial survey (Threat and National Security Survey) of 1,549 U.S. adults between October 2001 and March 2002. The results showed that anxiety of terrorism in the months after the September 11th attacks decreased support for President Bush's handling of the terrorist crisis and aggressive policies such as U.S. military intervention in Afghanistan and overseas involvement.

The findings were consistent with those of other national samples. In Lerner et al.'s (2003) survey of a nationally representative sample of U.S. adults (N = 973) between September and November 2001, they found those with greater anger related to the September 11th attacks supported punitive policies (e.g., deporting foreigners in the U.S. who lack valid visas). Additionally, those who perceive a greater fear endorsed conciliatory policies (e.g., investing in general capabilities, such as stronger public health, more than a specific solution such as smallpox vaccinations). In a similar vein, Skitka et al. (2006) surveyed a nationally representative sample (N = 550) between December 2001 and January 2002, finding that anger was positively associated with greater support for expanding the war on terrorism beyond Afghanistan, and fear increased support for deporting Arab Americans, Muslims, or first-generation immigrants.

Finally, a similar finding was observed in the work conducted by Sadler and colleagues (2005). Using a convenient sample of 120 adults in Colorado immediately after the September 11th attacks, the survey examined the effects of three emotions (anger, sadness, and fear) on preferences for four types of policies that the United States might undertake in response to terrorist attacks: (1) a strong military intervention (e.g., "All-out conventional war against any country that harbors or protects terrorists, including Iran, Iraq, Afghanistan, or Libya, even if it means U.S. military casualties"); (2) a moderate military intervention (e.g., "Use of special troop forces in Afghanistan to collect information on terrorist whereabouts"); (3) surveillance of people within the United States (e.g., "Relax constraints on law enforcement: make it easier to obtain warrants for searches, seizures and surveillance"); and (4) humanitarian aid (e.g., "Offer more foreign aid to poor countries"). The findings indicated distinct effects of emotions on policy preferences regardless of sampling designs. Those fearful of terrorism decreased their support for strong military policies, although their support was not statistically different for the other three policy types (moderate military, surveillance, humanitarian aid). In comparison, those angry about terrorism enhanced their support for strong military responses and surveillance within the United States but undercut support for humanitarian aid for poor countries such as Afghanistan. And those who were sad about terrorism expressed less support for strong military intervention and surveillance but instead endorsed humanitarian aid.

Regarding these findings, studies explained that fear is associated with a greater level of pessimism, external attributions (i.e., blaming the situation), and high risk-appraisals; as a result, those more fearful are more likely to take preventive measures and provide stronger support for conciliatory or defensive policies (Huddy & Feldman, 2011; Huddy et al., 2005; Lerner et al., 2003; Skitka et al., 2006; Wetherell et al., 2013). In contrast, anger corresponds with a greater level of optimism, internal attributions (i.e., blaming the actor), and low risk-appraisals; thus, those experiencing more anger prefer vengeful reactions and aggressive or confrontational policies (Huddy & Feldman, 2011; Huddy et al., 2005; Lerner et al., 2003; Sadler et al., 2005; Skitka et al., 2006;

Wetherell et al., 2013). Of note, emotions were stronger predictors of policy preferences than political orientation (Sadler et al., 2005; Skitka et al., 2006). In sum, emotions, such as fear, are a powerful precedent of counterterrorism policy preference, exerting both direct effects and indirect effects through attribution and appraisal processes.

Conclusion

Terrorism, both committed by those within and outside our borders, has weighed heavily on the minds of Americans during the past several decades. As long as its history attests, also complex is defining the act of terrorism. Across more than 250 existing definitions, the common elements of terrorism include (1) the use of violence or threatened violence, (2) noncombatant targets, (3) clandestine or subnational actors, and (4) the targeting of an audience often beyond its direct victims. Motivations for terrorism are also diverse, spanning the sources of religion, culture, territoriality, ethnicity, socioeconomic conditions, politics, and history. Regardless of its manifestation, however, the ultimate goal of terrorism is simple and straightforward: to inspire "terror" or extreme fear among the public or any section of the public to win political concessions (Aly & Balnaves, 2007). It is in this context that this chapter examined the extent, sources, and reactions of terrorism-induced fear.

Based on a review of previous findings, there are several key takeaways and implications for future research. First, according to recent national polls, the threat of terrorism is a stressor to many Americans in everyday life. About 4 in 10 Americans reported fear of or worry about terrorism, and more than 7 in 10 considered terrorism as a general threat facing the United States. To put in perspective, a greater number of Americans are fearful of a terrorist attack than falling victims to other crimes—including murder or robbery. However, considering the miniscule likelihood of a terrorist event—even lower than that of being killed by lawnmowers (Ritchie, 2018a), the findings clearly demonstrate the disproportionately high fear of terrorism prevalent among the public. Furthermore, there is a growing concern over a new form of terrorism occurring within national boundaries. For example, as of the writing of this chapter, the United States is wrought with events of domestic terrorism such as the January 2021 events at the U.S. Capitol and hate crimes dubbed as "male supremacy terrorism" (e.g., *The New York Times*, 2021). Thus, terrorism studies should pay more attention to this less explored type of terrorism.

Second, mostly aligned with the fear of crime literature, fear of terrorism tends to be stronger among demographic groups that are deemed physically, psychologically, or socially vulnerable. Therefore, a greater level of fear is reported among females, BIPOC, direct and indirect victims of previous terrorist attacks, individuals with emotional disorders (e.g., depression) or high perceived threats, and those exposed to a greater amount of media coverage on terrorism-related issues. In addition, some studies find that those who are older or lacking education are more frightened of terrorism, although the evidence is less consistent. Diverging from the fear of crime literature, however, several other covariates might be uniquely relevant to fear of terrorism. In this regard, future studies need to account for the effects of political, ideological, religious beliefs as well as the attitudes toward groups symbolically associated with terrorists (e.g., Muslims). More research is also warranted to examine whether the effects of these covariates on fear are moderated by whether a terrorist threat is domestic or international.

Third, in response to a terrorist threat, individuals make emotional, psychological, and behavioral adaptations in an effort to exert control over situations appraised as stressful (Maguen et al., 2008). For example, in the months and years following the September 11th attacks, studies evidenced an increase in cases of psychological distress (e.g., depression, anxiety, PTSD) and substance use (e.g., alcohol consumption, cigarette smoking, marijuana use)—not only in communities directly affected by the attacks but also across the nation. Moreover, fear of terrorism has led individuals to engage in behavioral changes, including restrictive (or avoidance) behaviors and assertive (or protective) behaviors. Although not enough studies exist to draw a definitive conclusion, existing research indicates that fear of terrorism is associated with certain restrictive behaviors (e.g., not flying on planes or public transportation) and protective behaviors (e.g., voting participation, screening mail for suspicious items).

Beyond personal reactions, there are political consequences resulting from public fear of terrorism. Fear of terrorism anchors individuals' policy preferences to reduce the threat of terrorism by influencing the perceptions of attribution and risk appraisal. Thus, in contrast to anger, the feelings of fear prime individuals to endorse conciliatory or defensive policies (e.g., investing in general capabilities), rather than aggressive or confrontational policies (e.g., military intervention). Given that fear of terrorism is associated with various demographic and attitudinal characteristics, future studies might need to unpack the relationship between these individual-level variables, emotion, and policy preferences using appropriate research designs (e.g., mediation analysis).

In closing, terrorism will continue to be an issue facing our nation for the foreseeable future. With threats coming from both abroad and home, the fear associated with international and domestic terrorism will continue to influence the lives of millions of Americans in a multitude of ways, affecting our emotional and psychological well-being, behaviors, and political and policy preferences. Due to this broad impact, more research is needed to discern not only the impact that this threat of terrorism and its associated fear has on us individually and as a nation, but also how international and domestic terrorist threats have differential impacts on both fear and its responses.

Notes

1 This count does not include the individuals who have died from health complications resulting from working on or around Ground Zero (Never Forget Project, 2021).
2 This location is within eight miles of the World Trade Center.

References

18 U.S. Code. §2331 (2018).
9/11 Memorial and Museum. (2021). September 11 attack timeline. New York: Author. Available at: https://timeline.911memorial.org/#FrontPage.
Abadi, M. (2020). "America's darkest day": See newspaper headlines from around the world 24 hours after 9/11. *Insider*, September 11. Available at: www.businessinsider.com/september-11-911-newspaper-headlines-2018-9.
Altheide, D.L. (2006). Terrorism and the politics of fear. *Cultural Studies Critical Methodologies*, 6(4), 415–439. Available at: https://doi.org/10.1177/1532708605285733.
Altheide, D.L. (2017). *Terrorism and the politics of fear*. Lanham, MD: Rowman & Littlefield.
Aly, A., & Balnaves, M. (2007). "They want us to be afraid": Developing a metric for the fear of terrorism. *The International Journal of Diversity in Organisations, Communities, & Nations*, 6(6), 113–122.
Andersen, H., & Mayerl, J. (2018). Attitudes towards Muslims and fear terrorism. *Ethnic and Racial Studies*, 41(15), 2634–2655.
APA (American Psychological Association). (2019). *Stress in America 2019*. Washington, DC: Author.
Bassiouni, M.C. (2002). Legal control of international terrorism: A policy-oriented assessment. *Harvard International Law Journal*, 43(1), 83–103.

Becker, G.S., & Rubinstein, Y. (2011). Fear and the response to terrorism: An economic analysis. CEP Discussion Paper No. 1079. London: Centre for Economic Performance.

Ben-David, S., & Cohen-Louck, K. (2010). Fear of terrorism and the coping paradox. In W. Benedek, C. Daase, V. Dimitrijević, & P. van Duyne (Eds.), *Transnational terrorism, organized crime and peace-building*. New York: Palgrave Macmillan, pp. 66–80.

Boscarino, J.A., Adams, R.E., & Galea, S. (2006). Alcohol use in New York after the terrorist attacks: A study of the effects of psychological trauma on drinking behavior. *Addictive Behaviors*, 31(4), 606–621.

Brenan, M. (2019). Americans equally worried about mass shooting and terrorism. *Gallup*, October 11. Available at: https://news.gallup.com/poll/267383/americans-equally-worried-mass-shooting-terrorism.aspx.

Centers for Disease Control. (2002). Psychological and emotional effects of the September 11 attacks on the World Trade Center—Connecticut, New Jersey, and New York, 2001. *JAMA*, 288(12), 1467–1468.

Chapman University. (2019). Survey of American Fears: America's top fears 2019. Irvine, CA: Author. Available at: www.chapman.edu/wilkinson/research-centers/babbie-center/_files/americas-top-fears-2019.pdf.

Christensen, D.A., & Aars, J. (2019). Does democracy decrease fear of terrorism? *Terrorism and Political Violence*, 31(3), 615–631.

Clemente, F., & Kleiman, M.B. (1976). Fear of crime among the aged. *The Gerontologist*, 16(3), 207–210.

Cohen, S. (1972). *Folk devils and moral panics: The creation of the Mods and the Rockers*. Oxford: MacGibbon and Kee.

Coletta, A. (2021). Canada declares Proud Boys a terrorist group. *The Washington Post*. February 3. Available at: www.washingtonpost.com/world/the_americas/canada-proud-boys-terrorist-capitol-siege/2021/02/03/546b1d5c-6628-11eb-8468-21bc48f07fe5_story.html.

Cossman, J.S., & Rader, N.E. (2011). Fear of crime and personal vulnerability: Examining self-reported health. *Sociological Spectrum*, 31(2), 141–162.

De Castella, K., & McGarty, C. (2011). Two leaders, two wars: A psychological analysis of fear and anger content in political rhetoric about terrorism. *Analyses of Social Issues and Public Policy*, 11(1), 180–200.

Denovan, A., Dagnall, N., Drinkwater, K., Parker, A., & Clough, P. (2017). Perception of risk and terrorism-related behavior change: Dual influences of probabilistic reasoning and reality testing. *Frontiers in Psychology*, 8, 1721.

Donnelly, P.G. (1989). Individual and neighborhood influences on fear of crime. *Sociological Focus*, 22(1), 69–85.

DuBow, F., McCabe, E., & Kaplan, G. (1979). *Reactions to crime: A critical review of the literature*. Washington, DC: US Government Printing Office.

Easson, J.J., & Schmid, A.P. (2011). Appendix 2.1: 250-plus academic, governmental, and intergovernmental definitions of terrorism. In A.P. Schmid (Ed.), *The Routledge handbook of terrorism research*. New York: Routledge, pp. 99–157.

Elmas, M.S. (2020). Perceived risk of terrorism, indirect victimization, and individual-level determinants of fear of terrorism. *Security Journal*. Advance online publication. doi: 10.1057/s41284-020-00242-6.

Epifanio, M. (2011). Legislative response to international terrorism. *Journal of Peace Research*, 48(3), 399–411.

Ferraro, K.F. (1995). *Fear of crime: Interpreting victimization risk*. New York: State University of New York Press.
Ferraro, K.F. (1996). Women's fear of victimization: Shadow of sexual assault? *Social Forces*, 75(2), 667–690.
Ferraro, K.F., & LaGrange, R. (1987). The measurement of the fear of crime. *Sociological Inquiry*, 57(1), 70–101.
Ferraro, K.F., & LaGrange, R.L. (1992). Are older people most afraid of crime? Reconsidering age differences in fear of victimization. *Journal of Gerontology: Social Sciences*, 47(5), S233–S244. Available at: https://doi.org/10.1093/geronj/47.5.S233.
Franklin, T.W., Franklin, C.A., & Fearn, N.E. (2008). A multilevel analysis of the vulnerability, disorder, and social integration models of fear of crime. *Social Justice Research*, 21(2), 204–227.
Gadarian, S.K. (2010). The politics of threat: How terrorism news shapes foreign policy attitudes. *Journal of Politics*, 72(2), 469–483.
Gallup. (2021). *Terrorism*. Author. Available at: https://news.gallup.com/poll/4909/terrorism-united-states.aspx.
Ganor, B. (2004). Terrorism as a strategy of psychological warfare. *Journal of Aggression, Maltreatment, & Trauma*, 9(1–2), 33–43.
Gerbner, G. (1969). Toward cultural indicators: The analysis of mass mediated message systems. *AV Communication Review*, 17(2), 137–148.
Gerbner, G., & Gross, L. (1976). Living with television: The violence profile. *Journal of Communication*, 26(2), 172–199.
Global Terrorism Database. (2021). *Global terrorism database*. College Park, MD: National Consortium for the Study of Terrorism and Responses to Terrorism. Available at: www.start.umd.edu/data-tools/global-terrorism-database-gtd.
Goldman, A. (2021). Domestic terrorism threat is "metastasizing" in U.S., F.B.I. Director says. *The New York Times*, March 2. Available at: www.nytimes.com/2021/03/02/us/politics/wray-domestic-terrorism-capitol.html.
Gomme, I.M. (1988). The role of experience in the production of fear of crime: A test of a causal model. *Canadian Journal of Criminology*, 30(1), 67–76.
Gruenewald, J., Freilich, J.D., Chermak, S., & Parkin, W. (2019). 19 years after 9/11, Americans continue to fear foreign extremists and underplay the dangers of domestic terrorism. *The Conversation*, September 10. Available at: https://theconversation.com/19-years-after-9-11-americans-continue-to-fear-foreign-extremists-and-underplay-the-dangers-of-domestic-terrorism-145914.
Guiora, A.N. (2005). Legislative and policy responses to terrorism: A global perspective. *San Diego International Law Journal*, 7(1), 125–172.
Haner, M. (2017). The freedom fighter: A terrorist's own story. (Unpublished doctoral dissertation). Cincinnati, OH: University of Cincinnati.
Haner, M., Sloan, M.M., Cullen, F.T., Kulig, T.C., & Jonson, C.L. (2019). Public concern about terrorism: Fear, worry, and support for anti-Muslim policies. *Socius: Sociological Research in a Dynamic World*, 5, 1–16.
Haner, M., Sloan, M.M., Pickett, J.T., & Cullen, F.T. (2020). Safe haven or dangerous place? Stereotype amplification and Americans' perceived risk of terrorism, violent street crime, and mass shootings. *British Journal of Criminology*, 60(6), 1606–1626.
Henson, B., & Reyns, B.W. (2015). The only thing we have to fear is fear itself ... and crime: The current state of the fear of crime literature and where it should go next. *Sociology Compass*, 9(2), 91–103.

Hoffman, B. (2006). *Inside terrorism* (2nd Edn.). New York: Columbia University Press.
Hong, F., Lin, Y., Jang, M., Tarullo, A., Ashy, M., & Malley-Morrison, K. (2020). Fear of terrorism and its correlates in young men and women from the United States and South Korea. *Journal of Aggression, Conflict and Peace Research*, 12(1), 21–32.
Huddy, L., & Feldman, S. (2011). Americans respond politically to 9/11: Understanding the impact of the terrorist attacks and their aftermath. *American Psychologist*, 66(6), 455–467.
Huddy, L., Feldman, S., Capelos, T., & Provost, C. (2002). The consequences of terrorism: Disentangling the effects of personal and national threat. *Political Psychology*, 23(3), 485–509.
Huddy, L., Feldman, S., Taber, C., & Lahav, G. (2005). Threat, anxiety, and support of antiterrorism policies. *American Journal of Political Science*, 49(3), 593–608.
Jackson, J., & Stafford, M. (2009). Public health and fear of crime: A prospective cohort study. *British Journal of Criminology*, 49(6), 832–847.
Kirschenbaum, A. (2006). Terror, adaptation and preparedness: A trilogy for survival. *Journal of Homeland Security and Emergency Management*, 3(1), 1–33.
LaFree, G., & Dugan, L. (2004). How does studying terrorism compare to studying crime? In M. Deflem (Ed.), *Terrorism and counter-terrorism: Criminological perspectives (Sociology of Crime, Law and Deviance), Vol. 5*. Bingley: Emerald Group Publishing Limited, pp. 53–74.
LaFree, G., & Dugan, L. (2009). Research on terrorism and countering terrorism. In M. Tonry (Ed.), *Crime and justice: A review of research, Vol. 38*. Chicago, IL: University of Chicago Press, pp. 413–477.
LaGrange, R.L., & Ferraro, K.F. (1989). Assessing age and gender differences in perceived risk and fear of crime. *Criminology*, 27(4), 697–719.
Leavitt, J.K., & Beacham, T.B. (2002). The effects of September 11 on health policy. *American Journal of Nursing*, 102(9), 99–102.
Lerner, J.S., Gonzalez, R.M., Small, D.A., & Fischhoff, B. (2003). Effects of fear and anger on perceived risks of terrorism: A national field experiment. *Psychological Science*, 14(2), 144–150.
Lewis, C.W. (2000). The terror that failed: Public opinion in the aftermath of the bombing in Oklahoma City. *Public Administration Review*, 60(3), 201–210.
Liska, A.E., Sanchirico, A., & Reed, M.D. (1988). Fear of crime and constrained behavior specifying and estimating a reciprocal effects model. *Social Forces*, 66(3), 827–837.
Maguen, S., Papa, A., & Litz, B.T. (2008). Coping with the threat of terrorism: A review. *Anxiety, Stress, & Coping*, 21(1), 15–35.
May, D.C., Herbert, J., Cline, K., & Nellis, A. (2011). Predictors of fear and risk of terrorism in a rural state. *International Journal of Rural Criminology*, 1(1), 1–22.
McCarthy, J. (2017). Seven in 10 trust the U.S. government to protect against terrorism. *Gallup*, June 19. Available at: https://news.gallup.com/poll/212558/seven-trust-government-protect-against-terrorism.aspx.
Miethe, T.D., & Lee, G.R. (1984). Fear of crime among older people: A reassessment of the predictive power of crime-related factors. *The Sociological Quarterly*, 25(3), 397–415.
Monmouth University. (2021). National: Public wants GOP to work with Biden. Author, January 27. Available at: www.monmouth.edu/polling-institute/reports/monmouthpoll_us_012721/.

Nellis, A.M. (2009). Gender difference in fear of terrorism. *Journal of Contemporary Criminal Justice*, 25(3), 322–340.

Nellis, A.M., & Savage, J. (2012). Does watching the news affect fear of terrorism? The importance of media exposure on terrorism fear. *Crime & Delinquency*, 58(5), 748–768.

Neria, Y., DiGrande, L., & Adams, B.G. (2011). Posttraumatic stress disorder following the September 11, 2001, terrorist attacks: A review of the literature among highly exposed populations. *American Psychologists*, 66(6), 429–446.

Never Forget Project. (2021). Statistics from 9/11 and 15 years later. Author. Available at: http://neverforgetproject.com/statistics.

Oots, K. (1990). Bargaining with terrorists: Organizational considerations. *Terrorism*, 13(2), 145–158.

Parkin, W., Klein, B., Gruenewald, J., Freilich, J.D., & Chermak, S. (2017). Threats of violent Islamist and far-right extremism: What does the research say? *The Conversation*, February 21. Available at: https://theconversation.com/threats-of-violent-islamist-and-far-right-extremism-what-does-the-research-say-72781.

Pew Research Center. (2019). *Climate change and Russia are partisan flashpoints in public's views of global threats*. Washington, DC: Author. July 30. Available at: www.pewresearch.org/politics/2019/07/30/climate-change-and-russia-are-partisan-flashpoints-in-publics-views-of-global-threats/.

Pew Research Center. (2020). *Americans see disease as top international threat along with terrorism, nuclear weapons, cyberattacks*. Washington, DC: Author. April 13. Available at: www.pewresearch.org/global/2020/04/13/americans-see-spread-of-disease-as-top-international-threat-along-with-terrorism-nuclear-weapons-cyberattacks/.

Recuber, T. (2009). The terrorist as folk devil and mass commodity: Moral panics, risk and consumer culture. *Journal of the Institute of Justice and International Studies*, 9, 158–170.

Richman, J.A., Cloninger, L., & Respenda, K.M. (2008). Macrolevel stressors, terrorism, and mental health outcomes: Broadening the stress paradigm. *American Journal of Public Health*, 98(2), 323–329.

Richman, J.A., Shannon, C.A., Respenda, K.M., Flaherty, J.A., & Fendrich, M. (2009). The relationship between terrorism and distress and drinking: Two years after September 11, 2001. *Substance Use & Misuse*, 44(12), 1665–1680.

Richman, J.A., Wislar, J.S., Flaherty, J.A., Fendrich, M., & Respenda, K.M. (2004). Effects on alcohol use and anxiety of the September 11, 2001, attacks and chronic work stressors: A longitudinal cohort study. *American Journal of Public Health*, 94(11), 2010–2015.

Ritchie, H. (2018a). Is it fair to compare terrorism and disaster with other causes of death? *Our World in Data*, February 14. Available at: https://ourworldindata.org/is-it-fair-to-compare-terrorism-and-disaster-with-other-causes-of-death.

Ritchie, H. (2018b). What do people die from? *Our World in Data*, February 14. Available at: https://ourworldindata.org/what-does-the-world-die-from.

Rothe, D., & Muzzatti, S.L. (2004). Enemies everywhere: Terrorism, moral panic, and U.S. civil society. *Critical Criminology*, 12(3), 327–350.

Ruby, C. (2002). The definition of terrorism. *Analyses of Social Issues and Public Policy*, 2(1), 9–14.

Sacco, L.N. (2021). *Domestic terrorism and the attack on the U.S. Capitol*. January 13. Washington, DC: Congressional Research Service.

Sadler, M.S., Lineberger, M., Correll, J., & Park, B. (2005). Emotions, attributions, and policy endorsement in response to the September 11th terrorist attacks. *Basic and Applied Social Psychology*, 27(3), 249–258.

Schmid, A.P. (2011). The definition of terrorism. In. A.P. Schmid (Ed.), *The Routledge handbook of terrorism research* New York: Routledge, pp. 39–98.

Schmid, A.P. (2016). The way forward on counter-terrorism: Global perspectives. *Strathmore Law Journal*, 2(1), 49–73.

Schmid, A.P., & Jongman, A.J. (1988). *Political terrorism: A new guide to actors, authors, concepts, databases, theories, and literature.* New Brunswick, NJ: Transaction Books.

Schuster, M.A., Stein, B.D., Jaycox, L.H., Collins, R.L., Marshall, G.N., Elliott, M.N., Zhou, A.J., Kanouse, D.E., Morrison, J.L., & Berry, S.H. (2001). A national survey of stress reactions after the September 11, 2001, terrorist attacks. *New England Journal of Medicine*, 345(20), 1507–1512.

Shanahan, T. (2016). The definition of terrorism. In R. Jackson (Ed.), *Routledge handbook on critical terrorism studies.* New York: Routledge, pp. 103–113.

Shechory-Bitton, M., & Cohen-Louck, K. (2018). Does fear of terrorism differ from fear of crime and sexual assault: A question of geographical location and residential area. *International Journal of Offender Therapy and Comparative Criminology*, 62(3), 806–826. Available at: https://doi.org/10.1177%2F0306624X16658472.

Shechory-Bitton, M., & Cohen-Louck, K. (2020). An Israeli model for predicting fear of terrorism based on community and individual factors. *Journal of Interpersonal Violence*, 35(9–10), 1888–1907.

Silver, R.C., Holman, E.A., McIntosh, D.N., Poulin, M., & Gil-Rivas, V. (2001). Nationwide longitudinal study of psychological responses to September 11. *JAMA*, 288(1), 1235–1244.

Skitka, L.J., Bauman, C.W., Aramovich, N.P., & Morgan, G.S. (2006). Confrontational and preventative policy responses in terrorism: Anger wants a fight and fear wants "them" to go away. *Basic and Applied Social Psychology*, 28(4), 375–384.

Sloan, M.M., Haner, M., Cullen, F.T., Graham, A., Aydin, E., Kulig, T.C., & Jonson, C.L. (2020). Using behavioral strategies to cope with the threat of terrorism: A national-level study. *Crime & Delinquency*. Advance online publication. Available at: https://doi.org/10.1177/0011128720940984.

Spencer, A. (2012). *Lesson learnt: Terrorism and the media.* Swindon: Arts and Humanities Research Council.

Stampnitsky, L. (2017). Can terrorism be defined? In M. Stohl, R. Burchill, & S. Englund (Eds.), *Constructions of terrorism: An interdisciplinary approach to research and policy.* Oakland, CA: University of California Press, pp. 11–20.

START (National Consortium for the Study of Terrorism and Responses to Terrorism). (2017). American deaths of terrorist attacks, 1995–2016: Fact sheet. College Park, MD: National Consortium for the Study of Terrorism and Responses to Terrorism. Available at: www.start.umd.edu/pubs/START_AmericanTerrorismDeaths_FactSheet_Nov2017.pdf.

Stein, B.D., Elliott, M.N., Jaycox, L.H., Collins, R.L., Berry, S.H., Klein, D.J., & Schuster, M.A. (2004). A national longitudinal study of the psychological consequences of the September 11, 2001 terrorist attacks: Reactions, impairment, and help-seeking. *Psychiatry*, 67(2), 105–117.

Sterling, C. (1981). *The terror network: The secret war of international terrorism.* New York: Henry Holt & Company.

Stern, J. (2003). *Terror in the name of God: Why religious militants kill.* New York: Ecco.

The New York Times. (2021). 8 dead in Atlanta spa shootings, with fears of anti-Asian bias. March 19. Available at: www.nytimes.com/live/2021/03/17/us/shooting-atlanta-acworth.

Tillyer, M.S., Fisher, B.S., & Wilcox, P. (2011). The effects of school crime prevention on students' violent victimization, risk perception, and fear of crime: A multilevel opportunity perspective. *Justice Quarterly*, 28(2), 249–277.

Torabi, M.R., & Seo, D.-C. (2004). National study of behavioral and life changes since September 11. *Health Education & Behavior*, 31(2), 179–192.

Vlahov, D., Galea, S., Resnick, H., Ahern, J., Boscarino, J., Bucuvalas, M., ... Kilpatrick, D. (2002). Increased use of cigarettes, alcohol, and marijuana among Manhattan, New York, residents after the September 11th terrorist attacks. *American Journal of Epidemiology*, 155(11), 988–996.

Warr, M. (1987). Fear of victimization and sensitivity to risk. *Journal of Quantitative Criminology*, 3(1), 29–46.

Warr, M. (1990). Dangerous situations: Social context and fear of victimization. *Social Forces*, 68(3), 891–907.

Warr, M. (2000). Fear of crime in the United States: Avenues for research and policy. In D. Duffee (Ed.), *Measurement and analysis of crime: Criminal Justice 2000, Vol. 4*. Washington, DC: United States Department of Justice, Office of Justice Programs, pp. 451–489.

Warr, M., & Ellison, C.G. (2000). Rethinking social reactions to crime: Personal and altruistic fear in family households. *The American Journal of Sociology*, 106(3), 551–578.

Warr, M., & Stafford. M. (1983). Fear of victimization: A look at the proximate causes. *Social Forces*, 61(4), 1033–1043.

Weinberg, L., Pedahzur, A., & Hirch-Hoefler, S. (2004). The challenges of conceptualizing terrorism. *Terrorism and Political Violence*, 16(4), 777–794.

Weinrath, M., & Gartrell, J. (1996). Victimization and fear of crime. *Violence and Victims*, 11(3), 187–197.

Wetherell, G., Weisz, B.M., Stolier, R.M., Beavers, A.J., & Sadler, M.S. (2013). Policy preference in response to terrorism: The role of emotions, attributions, and appraisals. In S.J. Sinclair & D. Antonius (Eds.), *The political psychology of terrorism fears*. New York: Oxford University Press, pp. 125–136.

Wilcox, P., Campbell Augustine, M.C., Bryan, J.P., & Roberts, S.D. (2005). The "reality" of middle-school crime: Objective vs. subjective experiences among a sample of Kentucky youth. *Journal of School Violence*, 4(2), 3–27.

Wilcox, P., Ozer, M.M., Gunbeyi, M., & Gundogdu, T. (2009). Gender and fear of terrorism in Turkey. *Journal of Contemporary Criminal Justice*, 25(3), 341–357.

Wilcox Rountree, P., & Land, K.C. (1996). Perceived risk versus fear of crime: Empirical evidence of conceptually distinct reactions in survey data. *Social Forces*, 74(4), 1353–1376.

Williamson, H., Fay, S., & Miles-Johnson, T. (2019). Fear of terrorism: Media exposure and subjective fear of attack. *Global Crime*, 20(1), 1–25.

Wojciechowski, S. (2017). Reasons of contemporary terrorism: An analysis of main determinants. In A. Sroka, F.C.-R. Garrone, R.D.T. Kumbrián (Eds.), *Radicalism and terrorism in the 21st century: Implications for security, Vol. 9*. Frankfurt, Germany: Peter Lang Edition, pp. 49–70.

World Values Survey. (2020). World Values Survey, Wave 7. Vienna, Austria: Author. Available at: www.worldvaluessurvey.org/WVSOnline.jsp.

13

How Terrorism Ends

Leonard B. Weinberg

The title of this commentary presupposes that terrorism does end. We should not take this as a given. Various groups, movements, and "lone wolves" engaging in terrorist violence have certainly suffered defeat and passed from the scene. Some, though, have succeeded and then turned their attention to other pursuits. Today, few remember Germany's Red Army Faction or Italy's Red Brigades, although at one point in the 1970s they were widely believed to pose major threats to their countries' democracies. At the international level the same applies to the Abu Nidal organization and the Popular Front for the Liberation of Palestine (PFLP); once regarded as major threats to international security, they faded into oblivion. They were, of course, succeeded by new generations of terrorists with different agendas operating at different times and in different parts of the world. As we shall see, terrorist groups do indeed come to an end. "Lone wolves" come and go. What seems highly unlikely though is that terrorism as a tactic will disappear any time soon.

To begin, it may be helpful to provide several examples of what we have in mind when we apply the term "terrorism" to different violent incidents.

April 1934—Marseilles—while on a state visit to France, King Alexander of Yugoslavia was assassinated, along with the French foreign minister Barthou, by members of Ustacha, a Croat nationalist group (Laqueur, 1977).

August 15, 1980—Neo-Fascist militants belonging to the Nuclei of Revolutionary Action (NAR) detonated a bomb in the waiting room of the Bologna (Italy) railway station killing 85 vacation-bound passengers and injuring hundreds more.

March 20, 1995—members of a Japanese religious cult, Aum Shinrikyo, staged a poison gas attack in the Tokyo subway, during rush hour. Over 50 passengers are injured and 13 are killed.

April 18, 1995—Timothy McVeigh detonated a truck bomb in front of the Murrah Federal Building in Oklahoma City (USA) that destroys the building and kills 169 occupants, including a dozen children attending a day-care facility.

July 22, 2011—Anders Breivik, a 41-year-old Norwegian, killed eight fellow countrymen in Oslo and a further 69 on a close-by island, who are members of a Social Democratic youth group, because he believed they were encouraging a Muslim invasion of this Nordic country.

April 2, 2015—Gunmen belonging to the Somali terrorist group Al-Shabaab attacked Garrisa University in northern Kenya. Their targets are Christian university students; during the incident 48 students are killed and many more are injured.

November 13, 2015—Paris—"A series of attacks occurred simultaneously in a bar and restaurant in the 10th Arrondissement where 15 were killed and many more injured. A bomb was detonated at Bataclan theater during a rock concert. Dozens were killed, and approximately 100 hostages were taken. Another bombing took place in the Stade de France stadium in the suburb of Saint-Denis during a football game, and their last attack took place in Les Halles mall." (BFMTV, "EN Direct—Fusillades a Paris: au moins 120 morts dans les attaques")

April 21, 2019—Easter Sunday, Sri Lanka—Three churches across Sri Lanka and three luxury hotels in Colombo were bombed. Later in the day, there are smaller explosions at a housing complex and a guest house, killing mainly police investigating the situation and raiding suspect locations ... 258 people are killed, including at least 35 foreign nationals, and around 500 are injured. ("Sri Lanka attacks: Death Toll soars to 290" (BBC, April 22, 2019).

What, if anything, do these violent events have in common? They were all spectacular murders which drew the attention of news' media and their audiences throughout the world. To the extent the perpetrators sought publicity, they certainly achieved their aims. Their long-term goals are another matter. The perpetrators were members of what observers of international politics label "non-state actors." In two cases,

Timothy McVeigh and Anders Breivik, we are dealing with "lone wolves," individuals unattached to a formal organization. In the other episodes, the killers are acting as agents of politically or religiously inspired organizations. How do such terrorist groups and "lone wolves" meet their demise?

We begin this assessment by noting that the modern study of terrorism began during the late 1960s and early 1970s. Before the explosion of terrorist activity in these years, terrorist violence was of limited interest to academics and journalists: a largely marginal phenomenon. Thanks to the Cuban Revolution, the Vietnam War and the various insurgencies underway in Latin America (South America's northern cone especially), both observers and practitioners were focused on guerrilla warfare and the tactics employed by insurgents, operating in the countryside, to topple the governments they targeted. Fidel Castro famously observed that cities were the "graveyards of revolution." The idea of the "urban guerrilla" appeared a contradiction in terms (Laqueur, 1977). The French writer Regis Debray's (2017) widely read *Revolution in the Revolution* provided an inspiration to those who believed the road to revolution passed through the countryside.

In the context of the Cold War and the popularity of Mao's ideas about revolution, American policymakers and their advisers focused on counterinsurgency techniques. How, for example, can governments go about winning the "hearts and minds" of farmers and peasants to make them unresponsive to the appeals of pro-communist insurgents? At the same time, the Kennedy administration (1961–1963) created the "Alliance for Progress" in Latin America, aimed at promoting land reform in Venezuela, Colombia, and other Latin American countries. At the time, the Shah of Iran was regarded as a major success story because he promoted land reform measures through his "White revolution," which supposedly insulated Iranian peasants from the allure of the Tudeh Party (Marxist–Leninist) revolutionaries. (The fact that much of the land redistributed to the peasants was taken from Iran's religious establishment was not thought to pose a serious problem at the time.)

We should also remember that the Kennedy administration's initial commitment to defend South Vietnam (1961–1962) against the Viet Cong insurgency was really an attempt to apply counterinsurgency theory to Southeast Asia. The massive troop deployments came later under President Johnson.

Phase 1—The Initial Terrorist Campaigns of the Late 1960s and 1970s

The shift in attention from guerrilla warfare to political terrorism was the result of developments from the late 1960s on (Bell, 1978). Three developments in particular come to mind.

First, there was the aftermath of the June 1967 Arab–Israeli war. Before the fighting there was widespread belief among Palestinians that a war between Israel and the Arab states surrounding it would result in the destruction of the Jewish state and much of its population. To the surprise of many onlookers, the six-day war resulted in a decisive Israeli victory and its occupation of the West Bank (1967) (including all of Jerusalem), the Golan Heights, the Gaza Strip, and the Sinai desert. With their hopes dashed, the Palestinians turned to self-help. The result of this recalculation was the proliferation of terrorist groups most, though not all, under the umbrella of the Palestine Liberation Organization (PLO).

At first these groups confined their operations to targets inside Israel and the occupied West Bank. Soon though their terrorist attacks on civilian targets spread to Western Europe. The "skyjacking" of commercial airliners on their way to Tel Aviv became a common phenomenon. Citizens of countries thought to be sympathetic to Israel became fair game, particularly the United States.

The most spectacular of the Palestinian terrorist attacks during this early era involved the kidnapping and subsequent killing of Israeli athletes at the 1972 Munich Olympics. The murder of 11 Israeli competitors was the work of "Black September," an arm of Al Fatah, the largest of the PLO organizations.

The appearance of Palestinian terrorism from the late 1960s forward coincided with rise of "urban guerrilla" groups throughout Latin America. Originally, young Latin American revolutionaries were enthralled by Castro's achievements in Cuba. They came to believe that they could be replicated throughout the Continent. They also came to regard Che Guevara, one of Castro's lieutenants, as a romantic figure who would show them the way. In practice, that way involved Che and a small band of fellow revolutionaries staging guerrilla attacks in the Andes of Bolivia. In 1967, this effort to duplicate the Cuban Revolution failed. The Bolivian army (with some assistance from the United States) killed Che and eliminated his band.

Enter the "urban guerrilla": If rural-based guerrilla warfare did not work, what would? In Uruguay, Brazil, Argentina, and other Latin

American countries, the answer was urban terrorism. The Brazilian Communist, Carlos Marighella's *Minimanual of the Urban Guerrilla* (1969) offered a framework. Marighella reasoned that Latin America's vast urban conurbations offered fertile terrain for revolutionary activity. Among other things, their enormous slums offered anonymity to revolutionaries after staging hit-and-run attacks on government targets. For another, cities were the headquarters for the mass media, television stations especially. Attacks in rural areas might go unnoticed, attacks staged in cities guaranteed publicity.

In any event, "urban guerrilla" groups soon proliferated throughout the Continent. The Tupamaros in Uruguay, the Montoneros, and Trotskyite ERP (People's Revolutionary Army) in Argentina (Gillespie, 1983) captured the most publicity initially. In virtually all the cases where the urban guerrilla groups represented more than a minor annoyance to the powers that be, the military seized power and quickly put an end to the various armed struggles.

The third contribution to the advent of the terrorist age came from the wealthy democracies of Western Europe, Japan, and the United States and took the form, some would argue, of a generational rebellion (Feuer, 1969) against the bourgeois liberal democratic order. More than anything else it was the Vietnam War that triggered mass protests and the subsequent outbreaks of terrorism.

In the years following the massive American military commitment to South Vietnam, there were widespread young peoples' protests against the United States and the collaboration, real or imagined, of their own countries' support for this "neo-colonial" adventure.

There was also the matter of the "New Left." In Italy, West Germany, France, Japan, and elsewhere thousands of university students and young workers became radicalized to believe that the conventional left-wing political parties (e.g., the Italian Communist Party) and labor unions had become too satisfied with the political and economic status quo. For many young people dreaming of radical change in their societies, direct action seemed the answer. For some of them, Frantz Fanon's *The Wretched of the Earth* (1961) provided a source of inspiration—particularly since the French philosopher Jean-Paul Sartre wrote the introduction.

These perceptions gave rise to a politics of contestation accompanied by cycles of mass protest (Tarrow, 1994). The former World War II Axis countries—Italy, the German Federal Republic (FRG), Japan— appeared to lead the way. In Japan, the university student movement, the Zengakuren, took to the streets of Tokyo to protest against the government's renewal of a mutual defense treaty with the US. In the FRG, thousands joined in protest against the state visit of the Shah of Iran—regarded as a criminal because the Savak, Iran's security agency, engaged in the widespread use of torture against dissidents. Italy experienced the "hot autumn" of 1969. In Milan, Turin, and other northern cities, the Student Movement activists joined together with young workers (often newly arrived from the country's impoverished South) to stage mass marches, rallies, and wildcat strikes against Fiat, Pirelli, Sit-Siemens, and other manufacturing firms.

Similar mass protests occurred in France in 1968 and the United States from that year through 1970. In both cases, their focus was on the respective governments. In the French case their target was De Gaulle and the country's antiquated university system. In America, the opposition to the Vietnam War was the dominant cause.

In general, as the mass protest movements lost momentum—a result of repression by the authorities or their own internal dynamics—small bands of terrorists appeared in their wake; groups whose militants were unwilling to abandon the revolutionary cause. Accordingly, in Italy the Red Brigades and the Nuclei of Armed Revolutionaries (NAP) launched violent campaigns aimed at toppling the country's corrupt political order and capitalist economic order. Likewise, in the FRG, the Red Army Faction (aka the Baader-Meinhoff Gang) and the June 2 movement engaged in the kidnapping and assassination of German businessmen and politicians with similar aims in mind. In Japan, as the Zengakuren protests subsided, the United Japanese Red Army surfaced to launch terrorist attacks on symbols of the country's political institutions (leaders of this band believed North Korea offered a Marxist–Leninist model!).

The German and Japanese stood out because they defined themselves as groups acting on behalf of an international struggle against Western neo-imperialism and racism. Consequently, units of these terrorist bands staged operations in conjunction with the nominally Marxist–Leninist Palestinian groups. So the famous skyjacking of an Air France jet liner and compelling its pilot to land in Entebbe in Uganda (July 1976) was a joint German–Palestinian operation, one among several.

Nationalism also became a significant cause of terrorism in this era. In Spain, still under Franco (until his death in 1975) members of the country's long-repressed Basque community formed Basque Homeland and Liberty (ETA), which began to launch attacks on government targets. In Ulster or Northern Ireland, the development of a peaceful Catholic civil rights movement produced a violent Protestant backlash which, in turn, led to the revival and radicalization of the Irish Republican Army (IRA) with its demand for Ireland's unification and the advent of two decades of "The Troubles."

The cause of Croat independence from Marshall Tito's Yugoslavia also became a source of terrorism. The most spectacular episode in this connection was the skyjacking, by Fighters for a Free Croatia, of a Trans World Airlines (TWA) flight bound from Chicago to New York and diverting it to Paris. In exchange for the passengers' lives, *The New York Times* agreed to publish the group's manifesto.

The terrorism involved in the struggles for Basque and Croat independence and the status of Ulster as part of the UK were the most dramatic episodes of nationalist terrorism in the 1970s. But they were not alone. Canada, widely regarded as the "peaceable kingdom," had a modest terrorist campaign launched by the Front for the Liberation of Quebec (FLQ), aimed at independence for that French-speaking Province. In the United States, Puerto Rican nationalists sought independence for their home island by staging terrorist attacks on civilian targets in Chicago and New York.

By the middle of the 1970s, and the years thereafter, terrorism had become a major concern for many governments throughout the Western World and the international community more generally. What were their initial responses?

We should start by pointing out that in these years the Western democracies were relatively isolated at the United Nations and other international forums in their efforts to curtail international terrorism during the 1970s, especially insofar as the Palestinian groups were concerned. Not only did the Palestinian cause win the sympathy of many Third World countries, but also a number of UN member states—Syria, Iraq, Libya—actively sponsored one or another of the Palestinian groups (Livingstone & Arnold, 1986). Some journalists even suspected the Soviet Union of providing covert support for some of the revolutionary groups that surfaced in Europe. The Turkish People's Liberation Army (TPLA), and more modest groups in Greece and Italy, came under suspicion. The Russian aim was to weaken NATO at its most vulnerable points (Sterling, 1981).

The early years of the terrorist era produced different reactions among the democracies. The Israeli reaction was unambiguous: No concessions, no negotiations. In 1973, the Nixon administration adopted the same uncompromising policy after two American diplomats were murdered by Black September militants while attending a reception at the Saudi embassy in Khartoum.

The logic of "no concessions, no negotiations" was based upon the idea of deterrence. If those planning terrorist attacks on civilian targets were aware they could not extract any concessions from the countries whose citizens they were holding hostage, they would be deterred from carrying out new operations. (The evidence in support of this response is mixed.)

The other Western democracies' responses to the initial terrorist threats were more uncertain. France, Germany, and Austria were confronted by the problem of the "poisoned pawn." When they arrested and detained members of a terrorist group in Paris, Bonn, or Vienna, they became aware that in so doing they were guaranteeing that other members of the same group would stage another attack, seize more hostages, and demand the release of those already in custody. The affected governments then had a strong incentive to release the terrorists in custody. Few governments were looking for trouble if it could be avoided.

By the second half of the 1970s, the French, German, Austrian, and other Western governments concluded that, whatever the immediate threat, making concessions to terrorist demands rarely brought peace. Accordingly, most democracies enacted anti-terrorism legislation, often loosening restrictions on personal privacy (e.g., wiretapping) and the length of pre-trial detention for those arrested for terrorism-related crimes. The democracies—particularly those like Italy and Great Britain, confronted by domestic terrorism threats—formed specialized anti-terrorism units within their police forces. In general, as the decade progressed the democracies shifted from regarding terrorism as a law enforcement problem to a military one, and changed policy accordingly.

During these early years of the terrorist era, the United Nations' General Assembly, dominated by Third World and Soviet Bloc states, failed to condemn terrorism, much less take any concrete measures aimed at criminalizing the conduct. A week after the September 1972 Munich Olympic Games massacre, Kurt Waldheim, the UN's Secretary General, urged the Assembly to "take adequate measures to prevent acts of violence against innocent people in the future" (Weinberg, 2013). Based on Waldheim's urging, the Assembly created an ad hoc committee to investigate the matter. Over the next few years, the committee discussed but failed to define terrorism. Lacking a definition, the committee members nonetheless went ahead and defined its "root" causes.

These were identified as "colonial, racist, and alien regimes," which, in turn were held responsible for causing "poverty, misery and despair." In case anyone missed the point, the General Assembly went ahead in 1975 and passed a resolution defining "Zionism" as racism and invited PLO leader Yasser Arafat to address the body. The PLO itself was offered "observer" status. PLO terrorism had worked in the sense that at least it had called worldwide attention to the Palestinian cause and offered some support for PLO violence against civilian targets.

In short, throughout the 1970s the United Nations chose to ignore the terrorist problem or, worse, in the case of the General Assembly, offered moral support for one of its principal perpetrators. This is not to say, however, that the international community more generally was inert.

First, there was the matter of the "political exemption" in international law. Based upon legal precedents dating back to the nineteenth century, states were normally obliged to extradite individuals upon the request of another state, if the latter could supply some evidence that the suspect had committed a crime within the state seeking to return him/her to face prosecution. If, however, the individual involved had committed a politically motivated "crime," for example speaking out against dictatorial rule, demanding greater freedom, the state receiving the extradition request was under no obligation to comply.

The advent of the terrorist era posed a dilemma. Were countries to which terrorists fled or allegedly fled under any obligation to extradite these persons to the countries where they had carried out acts of politically motivated violence? To complicate matters INTERPOL (the international police agency) at first refused to issue international arrest warrants for individuals who had committed politically motivated violent crimes.

By the end of the 1970s, INTERPOL's practice and the "political exemption" rule had been toppled. Legally, at least, states were now obliged to grant extradition. In practice, though, the new regime had a limited effect. The Germans might return some of its own citizens to Sweden to face prosecution for their seizure of the FRG embassy in Stockholm. On the other hand, there was the case of Colonel Ghaddafi's Libya. On March 21, 1975 a half-dozen Arab terrorists, led by "Carlos the Jackal" (the Venezuelan Vladimir Ilyich Sanchez) seized control of OPEC (Organization of the Petroleum Exporting Countries) headquarters in Vienna, killing several guards in the process. They then took OPEC's oil ministers hostage and demanded a large payment in exchange for their freedom. The Austrian government caved in immediately. The

OPEC countries agreed to pay the ransom. The ministers and their captors were then flown to Tripoli, where the officials were freed and the terrorists were paid-off. Carlos the Jackal and his confederates were given a hero's welcome by Libyan crowds. Carlos took some of the proceeds, nominally intended to aid the Palestinian cause, from this operation and bought a seaside villa on the Mediterranean Coast.

Air piracy was another subject which attracted the attention of the international community. During this first wave of terrorism in the 1970s it became common for skyjackers to take over a commercial airliner in mid-flight and fly it to a destination they demanded. Almost always the terrorists threatened to kill the passengers if their demands were not met. The most dramatic episode, among many, occurred in the summer of 1970 when members of a Palestinian group seized three commercial airliners in mid-flight and had them flown to an abandoned airstrip in the Jordanian desert. The skyjackers demanded Israelis free Palestinians they held in prison in exchange for the passengers' lives. Negotiations led the terrorists to free their captives. But in full view of an international television audience, the skyjackers blew up all three airliners.

These and other skyjacking episodes led to international conventions on airline safety. The Tokyo (1969) and Hague (1971) conventions defined air piracy as an international crime and obligated all countries either to extradite or prosecute individuals who had committed this offense. Furthermore, the International Airline Pilots' Association decided to boycott countries whose authorities declined to adhere to this convention.

Phase 2—Globalization of Terrorism and the Role of Religious Extremism

The perpetrators and targets of terrorism underwent major changes during the 1980s and thereafter. Religious groups became major fomenters of terrorism as the leftist revolutionary groups in Western Europe and the United States faded into insignificance, as did their careers in violence, voluntarily or otherwise. The cause of some type of Marxist or Maoist revolution grew increasingly remote as post-Mao China embarked on an economic development policy that bore a striking resemblance to Western-style capitalism ("socialism with Chinese characteristics"). Also, by the 1980s few would-be revolutionaries in the West could view the Soviet Union or the communist regimes in Eastern Europe with much sympathy as the Cold War drew to a close.

Latin America offered a few exceptions, Peru most conspicuously. There, after years of internecine struggle among far-left political parties, the Shining Path (Sendero Luminoso) under the leadership of Abimael Guzman, a philosophy professor at a provincial university, initiated a terrorist campaign in Lima and other Peruvian cities which, by the end of the decade, had achieved some notable tactical successes. The same was true to a lesser extent in Colombia with FARC (the Revolutionary Armed Forces of Colombia) and a handful of other groups; one of which, M19, managed to murder members of the country's supreme court in 1985 after seizing control of the Palace of Justice in Bogota.

The major developments in the evolution of terrorism occurred elsewhere. These developments were set in motion by the Soviet invasion of Afghanistan, the Iranian revolution and, to a lesser extent, the brief seizure of the Holy Mosque in Mecca by a Salafist band lead by a man whose followers regarded him as the Mahdi (the Holy One, the Redeemer). All three events occurred in 1979 and had profound influences on the bases of terrorist activity.

Up until these events, terrorism had been, by and large, a secular activity based upon revolutionary or nationalist goals (Northern Ireland was something of an exception). We should remember, for example, that the PLO's 1964 Charter had called for the replacement of Israel by a "democratic secular state."

The events of 1979 set in motion an extended period of religious excitation among both Sunni and Shiite Muslims. The Soviet invasion of Afghanistan was in defense of a secular pro-communist regime in Kabul that faced defeat at the hands of Muslim (largely Pashtun) guerrillas. Sunni religious leaders in Saudi Arabia, Pakistan, Egypt, and elsewhere declared the resistance to the Soviet presence a defensive holy war (intifada) and urged all Believers to aid in the defense of the country against the invaders. Within a short time, young jihadis from Egypt, Saudi Arabia, and other parts of the Muslim world made their way to the Pakistani city of Peshawar close by the Afghan border (Gunaratna, 2002) in the hope of aiding in the resistance against the Soviets and their Afghan supporters. Among the fighters who answered the call were the Egyptian physician Dr. Ayman al-Zawahiri, leader of the violent al-Jihad organization, Abdullah Azzam, a Palestinian teacher, and the young Saudi millionaire Osama bin Laden.

In addition to providing assistance to young holy warriors on their way to the fighting across the border in Afghanistan, Azzam and his collaborators formed "the Base" or Al-Qaeda (Wright, 2006). Its ambitious purpose was to act as the spearhead for a "holy war" to purify the House of Islam from its corrupt rulers and compel the United States to leave the region.

And following the American-led effort to expel Iraqi forces from the occupation of Kuwait in 1990–1991, bin Laden, now Al-Qaeda's leader, identified America as the "Great Satan" and declared a jihad aimed at expelling the United States from the region.

The other transformative event of 1979 was the Iranian revolution that toppled the Shah from power and led, after some years of struggle, to the formation of the Islamic Republic, headed by the uncompromising Shiite cleric the Ayatollah Ruhollah Khomeini. During the course of the Revolution, Khomeini's young followers seized control of the American Embassy in Tehran and held its personnel captive for close to two years. Despite the profound differences between Sunni and Shiite, both Al-Qaeda and the followers of the Ayatollah identified the United States as the source of corruption throughout the Muslim world and committed their movements to its expulsion from the region—by all means available.

These events had profound ramifications in terrorist activity throughout much of the world. What had been a largely secular pursuit based on nationalist and left-wing revolutionary causes became, in the 1980s and thereafter, a largely religion-driven activity. As Bruce Hoffman and other analysts pointed out, terrorists animated by secular causes had to be sensitive to the reactions of the population they hoped to mobilize. With few exceptions the intended audiences reacted negatively to acts of indiscriminate violence causing mass casualties. Often, the authorities were only too happy to blame such attacks on nationalist or secular revolutionary organizations.

Religiously inspired terrorists had no such inhibitions. Their audience, or imagined audience, was divine. Acting in the name of God gave them a justification for killing as many people as the terrorists thought necessary to advance the divine intent.

It is at this point that suicide terrorism appears on the scene. To be sure, terrorism has always possessed a suicidal element. In the nineteenth century, before the invention of dynamite, bomb-throwers seeking to assassinate a monarch or president had to rely on fulminate of mercury, a highly unstable compound. So, there was a strong chance the bomb thrower would kill himself in the process—and was aware of this likelihood.

Martyrdom has always been a powerful element in Shiite doctrine. It was put into practice during the Iran/Iraq war (1980–1989) when members of the Basij, youths belonging to the Islamic Revolutionary Guards Corp (IRGC), volunteered to walk through Iraqi minefields in advance of the Iranian armed forces, based upon the belief that they would be assured a place in Heaven for their self-sacrifice.

Lebanese Shiites followed this example. In 1982, Israeli forces invaded Lebanon, intent on eliminating the Palestinian organizations that had repeatedly launched terrorist attacks inside Israel from southern Lebanon. During these years a bloody civil war was underway (1975–1990) in Lebanon. Israel's military presence did not help matters. Eventually, the United States, France, and Italy (the Multi-National Force) sent peace-keeping forces to Beirut with the intent of strengthening the government and restoring order. This effort did not succeed. The American and French military became drawn into the fighting and were widely perceived as supporting the country's Christian militias.

At this point, an Iranian-backed group, soon to become Hezbollah, launched suicide attacks on American and French targets. The most lethal of these martyrdom operations was the October 1983 bombing of the US Marine Corps barracks near the Beirut airport, an attack that killed close to 307 Marines.

These suicide attacks worked. Within a few face-saving months, the Americans and their two allies withdrew their forces and Hezbollah ("the Party of God") became a major force in Lebanese political/military life. It took somewhat longer but these suicide missions also succeeded in driving the Israelis out of the country.

What began as a distinctively Shiite tactic was soon adopted by violent Sunni groups, most conspicuously by Palestinian ones. By the 1990s the Palestinian struggle to destroy the state of Israel was taken up by religious groups. Both Hamas and Palestinian Islamic Jihad (PIJ) began as outgrowths of Egypt's Muslim Brotherhood (Alexander, 2002). The Brotherhood was a long-standing organization strongly influenced by the writings of Sayyid Qutb. Qutb, an Egyptian school administrator, advocated holy war against corrupt Arab regimes and the elimination of the Jews from Dar al-Islam. He was imprisoned and then executed (1966) by Gamal Nasser's Egyptian dictatorship. His writings lived on and became a key component of Islamist/Salafist challenge to the prevailing order.

Following the 1994 Oslo peace agreement between the Palestinian Authority and Israel, which returned most of the West Bank to the latter's control, Hamas and PIJ launched a series of suicide attacks aimed at sabotaging the agreement. Crowded buses, restaurants, and shopping malls were favorite targets. By the early years of the twenty-first century, particularly during the al Aqsa Intifada, the suicide bombing campaign had worked. The Israeli government had made a sharp turn to the right (under Ariel Sharon) and the Oslo principles disintegrated.

Like the world economy and mass communications, terrorism underwent a process of globalization. Regions that had been largely free of terrorism became venues for the violence. In Sri Lanka, the Hindu Tamil Tigers initiated a terrorist campaign against the Buddhist government in Colombo. In India, a Sikh separatist group carried out terrorist attacks on civilian targets, including detonating a bomb aboard an Air India flight over the Atlantic, which killed several hundred passengers. In the Philippines, the government in Manila confronted a terrorist campaign initiated by Abu Sayyaf, a Salafist band intent on separating the country's largely Muslim populated southern islands from the rest of the country.

In Algeria, the military government agreed to hold democratic elections in 1992. When the Islamic Salvation Front (FIS) showed substantial voter support at the first turn at the ballot, the government cancelled the second turn and declared FIS illegal. In the aftermath, Islamists formed the Armed Islamic Group (GIA) and began staging terrorist attacks in Algiers and other cities. A virtual civil war ensued, leaving the military in control but with GIA evolving into an affiliate of Al-Qaeda in the Islamic Maghreb (AQIM).

In 1998, bin Laden issued a declaration of Jihad, a holy war, against Crusaders and Jews, promising to drive them out of the House of Islam. What followed from this declaration was a series of dramatic attacks on American targets. Some months after Al-Qaeda's declaration, jihadis bombed the American embassies in Nairobi Kenya and Dar al Salam Tanzania. Then, in October 2000, suicide bombers, using a small boat, detonated a bomb against the side of an American destroyer, the US Cole, while at anchor in the port of Aden.

The following year, on September 11, 2001, well-trained Al-Qaeda terrorists skyjacked and then crashed two airliners into the twin towers of the World Trade Center in New York; a third was flown into the Pentagon in Washington. The death toll was close to 3000, killing more people than died at the Japanese attack on Pearl Harbor.

The enormity of 9/11 had profound ramifications on a worldwide basis. America's NATO allies invoked the relevant article in the Charter and offered military assistance to the US. The United Nations Security Council passed Resolution 1373 making terrorism an international crime and requiring all member states to adopt domestic legislation criminalizing terrorist activities, including their support and financing. To monitor compliance, the Council created a Counter Terrorism Committee (CTC) (Oudraat, 2004).

For its part, the United States declared a "war on terrorism." From an organizational perspective, the Bush administration reorganized the federal bureaucracy in ways not seen since World War II. The Department of Homeland Security was created by merging several theretofore independent agencies; a new center for counterterrorism was established within this framework. To better coordinate intelligence, President Bush appointed a "director of national intelligence" to help the CIA, the National Security Agency (NSA), the Military Intelligence Agency (MIA), and the FBI to provide a comprehensive picture of the terrorist threat. In addition, the US Congress enacted the "Patriot Act" which, among other things, made it easier for the relevant federal agencies to monitor the communications of individuals suspected of planning terrorist attacks.

What followed was a successful military effort by American and other NATO forces to topple the Islamist regime in Kabul and compel Al-Qaeda's departure from Afghanistan by the end of 2001. Almost needless to say, this was hardly the end of the matter. The core Al-Qaeda leadership—bin Laden, al-Zawahiri (Azzam had been assassinated under mysterious circumstances)—reestablished itself in Pakistan's largely ungoverned tribal areas (evidently with the consent of Pakistan's security service, the ISI).

In conformity with the globalization phenomenon, Al-Qaeda developed "franchises" throughout much of the House of Islam. In Algeria (other locales in the Maghreb), Indonesia (Bali), Saudi Arabia, Yemen, the Sudan, and eventually northern Nigeria, Islamist/Salafist groups surfaced and undertook "holy wars" against various "near enemies." In most cases the attacks took the form of mass bombings, carried out by "martyrs" designed to kill as many people as possible.

Western countries did not emerge from this virtually worldwide terrorist campaign unscathed. The sons (for the most part) of Middle Eastern, North African, and South Asian immigrants to Britain, France, Spain, and the United States became susceptible to the appeals of Al-Qaeda and one or another of its franchises. Oftentimes the recruitment campaign was aided by the sermons, either delivered online or in person, of Islamist preachers.

Among the most lethal of the ensuing attacks occurred in Madrid, with the March 11, 2004 bombing of four commuter trains as they approached the Atocha railway station, leaving a death toll of close to 200 passengers. The following year, on July 7, 2005, Al-Qaeda followers killed 52 passengers when they detonated bombs at several London Underground stations during the always busy rush hour. This was just one of various terrorist attacks initiated by jihadists in these years.

In response, Britain's Home Office developed a counterterrorism policy known by the acronym CONTEST—which encompasses Prevent, Pursue, Protect, and Prepare. In place since 2006, elements of CONTEST have been challenged in the courts and the Commons on civil liberties grounds (what were known as "control orders" were found to be particularly objectionable)—not unlike challenges to the Patriot Act in the United States, and were then subject to multiple revisions.

Hezbollah, the Shiite "Party of God," supported by Iran's Islamic Republic, also carried out a number of outstanding terrorist attacks. In addition to kidnapping and sometimes assassinating Western academics and journalists living in Lebanon (e.g., the 1984 murder of Malcolm Kerr, the president of the American University of Beirut), its operatives carried out two major bombings in Argentina. In March 1992, Hezbollah agents set off a bomb at the Israeli Embassy in Buenos Aires that killed 29 civilians, and two years later (October 2006), acting in coordination with Iranian agents, bombed the Jewish Community Center in the same city, an attack in which 85 Argentines were killed.

The March 2003 decision by the Bush administration and the Blair government to invade Iraq, ostensibly to eliminate its non-existent weapons of mass destruction, upset the country's ethnic/religious balance. The overthrow of Saddam Hussein's Sunni-based regime shifted the country's religious balance in favor of the majority Shiite population. The southern part of the country, along with South Baghdad, became centers of Shiite dominance. The Kurdish population in northern Iraq, after being targeted by poison gas attacks, sought to go its own way.

The, now subordinate, Sunni community quickly became hostile to the Anglo-American occupation and the elevated status enjoyed by the Shia. The response was not long in coming. The result was Al-Qaeda in the Arabian Peninsula (AQAP) which began carrying out terrorist attacks on Anglo-American targets and Shiite holy sites in Najaf and Karbala.

AQAP was led for some time by Abu Musab al-Zarqawi, a former petty criminal from Jordan. Despite having pledged his loyalty to bin Laden and Al-Qaeda, al-Zarqawi ignored requests from al-Zawahiri to avoid exceptionally cruel attacks on Sunni tribesmen, involving the beheading of hostages and indiscriminate attacks on Shiite pilgrims. Al-Zarqawi was eventually tracked down by the Americans and killed in June 2006. His death, though, did not end Sunni-based terrorism.

Phase 3—Cyberspace

This distinction may seem somewhat arbitrary, catching the Salafist campaign against the Anglo-American presence in midstream as it were. But terrorist activity seems to have developed a new wrinkle during the second decade of the twenty-first century. A comment by Singer and Brooking captures the development: "From the world's most powerful nations to the pettiest flame war combatants, all of today's fighters have turned social media into a weapon in their own national and personal wars ... They all fight to bend the global information environment to their will ... The Internet ... has become weaponized" (Singer & Brooking, 2018, p. 19). In short, access to, and the adroit use of, the Internet has become a central component of terrorist operations.

Or, as Cass Sunstein writes: "Terrorist leaders for Al-Qaeda, ISIL, and others act as polarization entrepreneurs. They create enclaves of like-minded people. They stifle dissenting views and take steps to ensure a high degree of internal solidarity" (Sunstein, 2018, p. 238).

It was against this background that the Islamic State (ISIS) emerged following the death of al-Zarqawi. The region also was the site of the Arab Spring of 2011, a brief period in which there were popular uprisings against authoritarian rulers throughout the Middle East, including and especially Bashar al-Assad's Syria.

After an initial period of uncertainty following al-Zarqawi's death, his successors proclaimed the formation of a new Islamic State, a development that came as a surprise to the Al-Qaeda leadership of bin Laden and al-Zawahiri (McCants, 2015). The latter had expected to wait until American forces had been driven from the region before proclaiming such an entity. This new "state" was to operate independently, not acting at the direction of Al-Qaeda.

Within a short time, this new Islamic State came under the direction of a relatively obscure young Iraqi, Abu Umar al-Baghdadi, whose followers identified him as the "Commander of the Faithful," to whom unqualified obedience was owed. ISIS rapidly became a substantial operation. Thanks to its adroit use of cyberspace (including the publication of its online commentaries and recruitment videos) it was able to recruit members from around the world. It had its greatest successes in North Africa and Western Europe. Thousands of young men and women traveled, usually through Turkey, to ISIS venues in Iraq and, later, sections of Syria.

ISIS specialized in highly publicized acts of cruelty (Stern & Berger, 2015). In territory, it managed to seize from the weak Shiite-dominated government in Baghdad and ungoverned areas of Syria (after the 2011 rebellion against al-Assad's regime); the Islamic State's jihadists specialized in beheading captives, both Westerners and locals. Raping and selling women (members of the Yazidi religion, in particular) became common practices as well. Unlike Al-Qaeda and most other terrorist organizations (the Tamil Tigers in Sri Lanka would be another exception), ISIS managed to conquer and govern a significant and contiguous territory, cutting across Iraq and Syria. Its major achievement in this regard was the capture in 2014 of Mosul, a city of over 1 million inhabitants.

For some ISIS followers, the holy war against the West spread to Europe. France with its large Muslim population became the favorite venue for ISIS attacks. The most spectacular of these attacks occurred in 2015. In January, ISIS followers murdered 12 journalists at the offices of Charlie Hebdo, a satirical weekly, because they had insulted the Prophet. Later in the year in the Paris area, there were three separate explosions, one in front of France's crowded soccer stadium, and six mass shootings, including attacks at a theater and night club. The Islamists' attacks left 130 people dead.

The following year, on Bastille Day (July 14, 2016) in Nice, another ISIS militant commandeered a truck (killing the driver in the process) and drove it through a crowd of holiday celebrants. Eighty-six French citizens were murdered in the process.

The conquest of territory by ISIS was a mistake. It provided its, by now numerous, enemies with a name and address. This was made to order for the use of conventional military forces. Accordingly, over the next few years American and Iraqi forces recaptured the ISIS enclave. Al-Baghdadi was killed by an American air strike at the end of October

2019. So, ISIS persists but it seems unlikely it will be able to reassert itself as a territorial formation.

Terrorist attacks carried out by single individuals certainly pre-date the arrival of the various cyberspace platforms. Timothy McVeigh's bombing of the Murrah Federal Building in Oklahoma City in 1995 may serve as an example (observers report McVeigh spent long hours watching violent TV shows while preparing himself at a hotel in Kingman Arizona). The neo-Nazi figure William Pierce's second novel *Hunter* (1989) involving a single individual traveling throughout the US killing inter-racial couples would be another case in point. Though a work of fiction, *Hunter* was based on a real-life person, Joseph Paul Franklin.

In recent decades, though, cyberspace has become an indispensable element in the planning and execution of "lone wolf" terrorist attacks, especially ones involving mass casualties. Often, though not always, these single actor killings have targeted members of racial and religious minorities. The presence of a large and growing Muslim population in Europe has ignited a violent backlash by individuals who have learned to believe that the followers of the Prophet will shortly turn what had been a largely Christian region into another part of Dar al-Islam. The 2011 case of the Norwegian Anders Breivik, mentioned at the beginning of this commentary, would be a case in point. So would the murder of 51 Muslim worshippers at two mosques in Christchurch New Zealand on March 15, 2019 by a young Australian man Brenton Tarrant. Thanks to the Internet, Tarrant was inspired by Breivik's murders and the Manifesto the Norwegian published online justifying them. He also went one step further in live-streaming his murders as he committed them.

Lone actor and cyberspace-aided killers have been active in the United States as well. For example, Patrick Crusius, a 21-year-old Texan who acquired his hatred of Mexican immigrants online, wrote his own online "manifesto," expressing his worries about the Hispanic invasion (he was evidently influenced by Donald Trump's views on the subject). On August 3, 2019 Crusius drove from his home to El Paso where he shot and killed 23 Walmart shoppers, many of whom were people of Hispanic origin.

These lone wolf terrorist killers are hard for law enforcement agencies to identify and then anticipate their behavior. Hard, but not impossible. Researchers have produced profiles of these individuals (Bouhana et al., 2018). The general profile that emerges from a number of studies yields the following attributes:

1. They tended to be unattached single males, usually without close family ties, even as adults
2. Despite having acquired relatively high levels of education, lone actors tended to be unemployed
3. A significant proportion of lone wolves had criminal records
4. A record of mental illness was not uncommon—relative to the general population.

Also, to the extent lone actor terrorists are radicalized or seek to radicalize others via the Internet, their "signals" make them visible to law enforcement agencies.

Endings

Almost from the beginning of the terrorism era, the word and the phenomenon it seeks to capture have been "essentially contested." Over the, now approximately, 50 years since acts of terrorism have drawn the attention of mass publics and government officials there has been a struggle over language and who gets to define the term "terrorism." No universally acceptable definition has been forthcoming. A significant part of the problem is that most Western governments have enacted laws and established special agencies aimed at preventing or defeating terrorist activities. Many academics have been drawn into, or have drawn themselves into, the anti-terrorism cause. Instead of scholarly neutrality, many scholars have become part of the struggle in the fight against terrorist organizations. One result of these practices has been the appearance of "critical terrorism studies." According to this perspective, one based on critical theory on the analysis of "texts," what we label "terrorism" is a social construct designed by those in power to preserve their hegemony over political life. Of course, there is a certain sleight of hand involved in this "critical" outlook, in that it provides a "progressive" rationale to justify most forms of politically motivated violence if perpetrated by groups and individuals with whom these "critics" have an affinity (since 2008 a journal *Critical Studies in Terrorism* has been published by Taylor & Francis in the UK).

Another way of grappling with the problem of terrorism analysts' pro-government bias has been to relabel the activity as "clandestine political violence" thereby defining the activity without attaching the disputed word (Della Porta, 2013). This suggestion certainly has considerable merit. On the other hand, it would require some language stretching. For instance, insurgents engaged in a guerrilla warfare campaign do not routinely announce their presence before they are ready to attack their enemy. And, on the other side of the ledger, "terrorists" not uncommonly issue warnings publicizing their operations before, during, and after their commission. The Provisional IRA's active service units did this on a routine basis.

It is worth calling attention to "propaganda by deed." The Italian revolutionary Carlo Pisacane coined the term in 1857. Shortly afterward the Russian revolutionary group the People's Will adopted the idea in its struggle to overthrow the Czar (Hoffman, 1998). The logic was that terrorist attacks would generate publicity to groups and causes that would otherwise be unable to achieve much public notice. Since that era, the last third of the nineteenth century, spokespersons for terrorist organizations have claimed their violence was necessary to call attention to their cause. This certainly worked in the case of the Palestinians, at least up to a point.

If one of the major reasons for staging terrorist attacks is to win public attention for groups and causes that would otherwise be little noticed, the purpose seems to have been overtaken by more recent developments. Cyberspace with its various social media platforms appears tailor-made for groups and individuals with various political grievances. No bombs and guns seem necessary to reach a significant audience. Terrorism seems likely to persist but its original rationale—publicizing a cause—no longer applies in the era of cyberspace.

For the most part, the study of terrorism has meant the study of groups. Before we seek to investigate how these groups end or change tactics, we should call attention to the fact that terrorist attacks may also be staged by violent crowds. Lynch mobs in the American South come to mind. But this is not necessarily ancient history. In recent years Hindu mobs in India have run amok looting, killing, and terrifying Muslims in their neighborhoods. In 2016, mobs in Germany surrounded asylum hostels containing recent immigrants and set them on fire. And following the 2004 murder of Dutch film-maker Theo Van Gogh by a young Islamist (Van Gogh had made a film about Muslim mistreatment of women), there were retaliatory attacks on mosques in Amsterdam and elsewhere in the Netherlands.

In addition to the use of terrorism by relatively spontaneous mobs, we should also note the role of terrorism in what some have labelled "hybrid" or Fourth Generation warfare (Kilcullen, 2013; Martin & Weinberg, 2016). Most armed conflicts in the twenty-first century have involved the contestants employing multiple means to achieve their objectives. These means include conventional battlefield tactics but also include computer attacks on the enemy's infrastructure, disinformation campaigns, guerrilla warfare and terrorist attacks on civilian populations. As the long-term war in Afghanistan suggests, terrorism has become part of the repertoire armed groups now employ to defeat their enemies.

If we confine our analysis to groups that rely predominantly on terrorism as a tactic, we can make a number of defensible generalizations. First, there is the matter of durability: in general, how long do terrorist groups persist?

Several data collections are available. One widely used by terrorism analysts is the list of Foreign Terrorist Organizations (FTO) compiled by the US Department of State. Such leading terrorism observers as Audrey Cronin (2009), Martha Crenshaw (2011) and Max Abrahms (2006) rely on it in making their evaluations. Based on the FTO database, Cronin estimates the median lifespan of terrorist groups as between 19 and 20 years. This is a good long time. But it probably overestimates their durability. Groups that surface, carry out a few attacks, and then disperse or disappear would not be included. Crenshaw and others believe the FTO underestimates the number of far-right (White supremacist, neo-fascist) organizations. Groups that do not pose a threat to the United States and its interests are likely undercounted as well.

Do terrorist groups get what they want, or say they want? Here, there is a distinction to be made between tactical and strategic success. For example, in 1978 a "column" of the Italian Red Brigades (BR) kidnapped former Italian Prime Minister Aldo Moro. They held him hostage for 55 days before killing him and leaving his body in the trunk of a car in downtown Rome. All this was done while thousands of police sought to find the location where Moro was being held, and despite appeals from the Pope and the UN Secretary General to spare his life.

In tactical terms the BR had achieved an outstanding success, showing the impotence of the Italian government and the BR's agility. In strategic terms, however, the Moro case turned out to be a defeat. The Italian public became increasingly hostile to the BR and its revolutionary agenda. The Italian authorities focused their attention on the BR and created a special unit to defeat it. By 1982–1983 the terrorist group had suffered a fatal defeat, as many of its members surrendered and then informed on their fellow Brigade comrades.

Years ago, now, the terrorism analyst Max Abrahms compiled a list of 28 terrorist groups culled from the FTO list active from 1978 through

2001 (Abrahms, 2006). He makes his evaluation based on what the groups' statements said they wanted to achieve through their violent operations (see Table 13.1) Did they succeed or fail in achieving these goals? Or were there some limited successes?

Table 13.1
The Outcome of Terrorist Campaigns

Group	Objective	Outcome
Abu Nidal Organization	Destroy Israel	No Success
Abu Sayyaf Group	Establish Islamic State in the Philippines	No Success
Al-Qaeda	Expel US from Persian Gulf	Limited success
Al-Qaeda	Sever US–Israel Relations	No Success
Al-Qaeda	Sever US–Apostate Relations	No Success
Al-Qaeda	Spare Muslims from Crusader wars	No Success
Armed Islamic Group	Establish Islamic State in Algeria	No Success
Aum Shinrikyo	Establish utopian state in Japan	No Success
Egyptian Islamic Jihad	Establish Islamic state in Egypt	No Success
Fatherland and Liberty	Establish Basque State	No Success
Hamas	Establish state in historic Palestine	Limited success
Hamas	Destroy Israel	No Success
Harakat ul-Mujahidin	Rule Kashmir	No Success
Harakat ul-Mujahidin	Eliminate Indian Insurgents	No Success
Hezbollah	Expel Peacekeepers	Total success
Hezbollah	Expel Israel	Total success
Hezbollah	Destroy Israel	No Success
Islamic Group	Establish Islamic state in Egypt	No Success
Islamic Jihad	Establish state in historic Palestine	Limited success
Islamic Jihad	Destroy Israel	No Success
Islamic Movement in Uzbekistan	Establish an Islamic State in Uzbekistan	No Success
Kach	Transfer Palestinians from Israel	No Success
Kurdistan Workers' Party	Establish Kurdish State	No Success
Kurdistan Workers' Party	Establish communism in Turkey	No Success
Mujahideen-e-Khalq	End clerical rule in Iran	No Success
National Liberation Army	Establish Marxism in Colombia	No Success
November 17	Establish Marxism in Greece	No Success
November 17	Sever US–Greek relations	No Success
Palestine Liberation Front	Destroy Israel	No Success
Palestine Liberation Front	Establish Marxism in Turkey	No Success
Palestine Liberation Front	Sever US–Turkish Relations	No Success

(*continued*)

Table 13.1
Cont.

Group	Objective	Outcome
Popular Front for the Liberation of Palestine (PFLP)	Destroy Israel	No Success
Popular Front for the Liberation of Palestine (PFLP)	Establish Marxist Palestine	No Success
PFLP General Command	Destroy Israel	No Success
PFLP General Command	Establish Marxist Palestine	No Success
Real Irish Republican Army	Establish Irish Unification	No Success
Revolutionary Armed Forces of Colombia	Establish Peasant rule in Colombia	Limited success
Revolutionary Nuclei	Establish Marxism in Greece	No Success
Revolutionary Nuclei	Sever US–Greece Relations	No Success
Shining Path	Establish communism in Peru	No Success
Tamil Tigers	Establish Tamil state	Partial success
United Forces of Colombia	Eliminate left-wing insurgents	No Success

Source: Abrahms (2006, pp. 49–50).

According to Abrahms' calculation, none of the 28 terrorist groups got what they said they wanted. A few of them enjoyed limited successes, for example, Hamas and Palestinian Islamic Jihad succeeded in seizing control of the Gaza Strip from the Palestinian Authority but made no observable headway in their overall goal of destroying Israel. He records the Tamil Tigers in Sri Lanka as experiencing a "partial success" in maintaining control of the Jaffna Peninsula and the eastern part of the country. But this "partial success" did not last. A few years after Abrahms' work, the Sinhalese-dominated government in Colombo launched a full-scale invasion of Tamil territory, with little regard for the civilian population, killing hundreds, and completely destroyed the Tamil Tiger organization.

Terrorist campaigns enjoyed some successes in the post-World War II era when the British and French Empires collapsed. Terrorist groups such as the National Liberation Front (FLN) in French Algeria and the Irgun in Britain's Mandate in Palestine helped encourage the departure of the colonial powers. The same might be said about the 1955 withdrawal of British control of Cyprus in favor of a Greek-Cypriot government in Nicosia. It may be argued that the maintenance of colonial empires was becoming increasingly expensive and that their support

Table 13.2
Insurgencies and the Use of Terrorism

Outcome	Indiscriminate	Mutual Atrocities	Discrete	Little or None
Government wins	11	3	8	4
Mixed outcome	5	3	6	4
Government loses	5	2	14	4
Ongoing	7	4	1	1

Source: Connable & Libicki (2010, p. 109).

was waning at home, especially when the casualties mounted. So, the terrorist groups may have provided a push, while the public back in the metropole offered a pull.

Does the type of terrorist attack make a difference in the outcome of wider-scale insurgencies? These insurgencies are episodes in which challenging groups mount violent campaigns against incumbent governments (see above). The Rand Corporation analysts, Ben Connable and Martin Libicki (2010) developed evidence (see Table 13.2) about the results of some 88 insurgencies launched between the last half of the twentieth century and the first decade of the twenty-first.

Bearing in mind our focus now is insurgencies which employ a variety of tactics in seeking to defeat an incumbent political regime, the picture of virtually complete defeat, as painted by Abrahms, changes significantly. Illustratively, in Afghanistan the Taliban have made extensive use of terrorism along with an array of other tactics in seeking to defeat the government in Kabul and its American supporters.

Of the 89 insurgencies Connable and Libicki examined, they found 28 victories for the incumbents and 26 for the insurgents (the balance was unresolved or produced ambiguous results). In other words, if opposition groups are able to mount a substantial insurgency, they stand a good chance of defeating the government—unlike stand-alone terrorist campaigns, as were mounted by the Italian Red Brigades and the German Red Army Faction.

Terrorism was employed in the majority of cases Connable and Libicki investigated. There were only 17 instances in which terrorism played no role in the conflict. Terrorist violence was employed not only by the insurgents but also by the government in power. So, in the case of Central American conflicts, for example Nicaragua and Guatemala, the governments made extensive use of "death squads" in seeking to destroy the insurgents' support among the rural populations.

The type of terrorism insurgents and government forces employ appeared to make a difference in terms of the conflicts' outcomes. The use of indiscriminate violence by insurgents is strongly linked to defeat. The evidence is hardly overwhelming but suggests nonetheless that "discrete" forms of terrorism by the challengers go together with improved chances of their winning power.

Terrorist groups end their campaigns in several ways (for detailed discussions, see Cronin, 2009; Weinberg, 2013). Defeat seems to be the most obvious. Defeat, though, may be the result of different considerations.

At present, political Islam seems increasingly to be a spent force. In the first decade of the twenty-first century violent Islamist groups—Hamas, PIJ, ISIS, Al-Qaeda, Lashkar-e-Taiba—appeared to pose a significant challenge to international security. Suicide bombing campaigns against American, European, Israeli, and Indian targets achieved major disruptions. Today Hamas, for example, has been reduced to sending incendiary balloons across the Gaza border with Israel.

Earlier in the evolution of modern terrorism it was some version of Marxism/ Leninism or Maoism that excited the cause of political revolution throughout much of the West. Today it would be hard to find more than handfuls of individuals in Latin America or elsewhere prepared to sacrifice their lives in the name of revolutionary communism.

What happened?

One answer is that a sense of futility and exhaustion set in. What appeared to be a cause worthy of self-sacrifice or martyrdom lost its salience. Younger generations of potential recruits to the cause, no longer see the point. Quantifying the *zeitgeist* is not all that easy. But it should at least be given some consideration.

Decapitating a group's leaders has been employed as one means of defeating terrorist groups. "Decapitation" typically involves two alternatives: capture alive or kill. Illustratively, the arrest of Abimael Guzman at a dance studio in Lima in 1992 drained the energy from Peru's Shining Path's revolutionary passions. Other analysts assert that killing a terrorist group leader is likely to be counterproductive. The contention here is that killing the leader, making him into a martyr, is an effective recruiting tool for winning new members and redoubling the commitment of those already wedded to the cause (Bjørgo & Horgan, 2008; Cronin, 2008). Further, oftentimes killing the terrorist leaders means the use of missiles fired from drones (e.g., America Reapers). In turn, this usually means the death of innocent bystanders (Boyle, 2020) whose family and friends then become bitter enemies of the Americans or whoever was responsible for the missile strike. Perhaps. But we should ask ourselves if Al-Qaeda after bin Laden, or ISIS after al-Baghdadi, were ever the same.

The careers of individuals engaged in terrorism are relatively short. There is need then for generational replacement. If the terrorist group is unable to recruit successor generations it will, in all likelihood, wither away. For the authorities, finding ways of insulating vulnerable youths from the appeals of terrorism should be a high priority. In recent years, it has become possible to do battle, figuratively at least, through cyberspace. Just as ISIS and its cohorts use the Internet to spread its message, so, too, can anti-terrorists launch online attacks against them through mockery and ridicule.

Members of terrorist groups vary in the intensity of their commitments and in regard to their outlook on the likely outcome of their violence. In other words, terrorist groups, like extreme political parties, are prone to factionalism and splitting. Basque Homeland and Liberty (ETA) for example went through multiple divisions, how much violence versus how much politics, over the course of its long struggle to create a separate state—ultimately abandoning terrorism.

Most terrorism analysts in the US and other Western democracies tend to be defenders of democratic values and constitutional rule. In fact, for many that is the purpose of their work—how best to defend democracy against terrorist threats. In some cases, though, that leads them to ignore one seemingly obvious way of defeating terrorist groups: brute force. Consider the case of revolutionary Iran (1979–1983). After the Shah was overthrown in 1979 it was by no means clear what type of regime would replace the monarchy. A variety of groups contended for power. The winners were the Islamists led by the Ayatollah Khomeini. But during this struggle of succession a number of Marxist revolutionary groups fought for dominance. The most vigorous was the Mujahedin-e-Khalq. To prevent a victory for Khomeini's supporters the Mujahedin launched a terrorist campaign against the cleric and his followers. Among other things, they assassinated Iran's incoming president and bombed the headquarters of the ruling Islamic Republican Party, killing a significant number of Islamists elected to the Majlis.

The new Islamic republic reacted with great brutality. The Islamic Revolutionary Guards (IRGC), along with special revolutionary tribunals, reacted by torturing and executing members of the Mujahedin when they had been captured. In some cases, wounded Mujahedin were dragged from hospitals and then killed—on the grounds they did not deserve medical care.

Suffice it to say that within a few years of this treatment, the Mujahedin-e-Khalq was completely repressed. Their surviving leaders were in exile, living in Paris.

Terrorist groups may cease and desist their campaigns as the result of negotiations with the authorities. Successful negotiations require certain crucial elements. The "armed struggle" itself should have reached a point of stalemate, where neither side is willing to bear the cost of overwhelming the other. The willingness of intermediaries to mediate may be essential, given the high level of mistrust and suspicion that typically prevails between the contenders. The 1998 "Good Friday" agreement between Britain and the Provisional IRA would probably not have succeeded without the involvement of American and other outside parties. But there are no guarantees of success.

In Sri Lanka, the government in Colombo engaged in a long series of negotiations with the Tamil Tiger leadership ultimately to no avail. The Indian government sought to help, even stationing peace-keeping forces on the Island. This goodwill effort not only failed but also led to the 1991 assassination of Prime Minister Rashid Gandhi by Tamil militants.

Negotiated settlements of terrorist campaigns have some built-in problems. From the point of view of the terrorist group, "negotiations" implies compromise. More militant members of the group may reject this approach, denounce the negotiators as betraying the cause and split off to create their separate terrorist group, for example, "The Real IRA" after the Good Friday Agreement. By entering into negotiations with terrorists, the government may be viewed as conferring legitimacy on the group, recognizing it as something more than bandits and outlaws. The recognition may then meet opposition by the government's military or security services—who have suffered casualties at the hands of the terrorists—or by the families the terrorists have killed.

Terrorist groups may also end their careers in violence by undergoing a transformation (Weinberg, 1991). Given the appropriate circumstances, they may become political parties campaigning for votes and seeking to elect their candidates to public office. If a country undergoes a transition from military or some other type of authoritarian rule to an open democracy, clandestine terrorist groups may surface, express their commitment to democratic rule, and resurface as political parties. For example, in the British Mandate of Palestine, the Irgun under the leadership of Menachem Begin operated as a terrorist group, blowing up a wing of Jerusalem's King David Hotel in the process (1946). After Israel's independence in 1948, Begin transformed his followers into the Herut political party, achieved representation in the Knesset, the country's parliament. Eventually, of course, Begin became Israel's prime minister following the 1976 general election and later was a co-winner of the Nobel Peace Prize along with PLO leader Yasser Arafat, another former terrorist leader!

Another way in which terrorist groups may transform themselves is a straightforward change into common criminality. Terrorist groups normally engage in criminal activities—robbing banks, kidnapping, drug-dealing, murder—that are politically motivated. Not uncommonly, members of terrorist groups have backgrounds in common criminality who have been politicized while serving prison sentences. This is true, for example, of various White supremacist groups in the US and Protestant paramilitaries in Northern Ireland, or "revolutionary" groups in Colombia. At some point the groups' political rhetoric simply becomes a rationale to justify organized crime, pure and simple.

Conclusion

It seems pretty clear that terrorism, as we have come to know it, is unlikely to disappear, particularly in the developing countries of Africa, the greater Middle East and South Asia. At present, the Sahel (the African countries stretched along the southern rim of the Sahara—Mali, Niger, South Sudan). Here religious and tribal differences are the principal drivers. The same elements are at play in South Asia.

The Western World provides us with a different picture. In Europe and North America, the major causes that produced terrorism in the past have largely played themselves out. What we have witnessed in recent years, and continue to witness today, is the emergence of violent right-wing organizations—ones active especially in the United States, Germany, and Sweden—that see Western civilization as threatened by immigrants from the Middle East, South and East Asia, and Latin America. In the face of what they perceive as mortal threats, "lone wolves" and White supremacist organizations are prepared to kill.

References

Abrahms, M. (2006). Why terrorism does not work. *International Security*, 31(2), 42–78.

Alexander, Y. (2002). *Palestinian religious terrorism: Hamas and Islamic jihad*. Leiden: Brill Nijhoff.

BBC (2019). Sri Lanka attacks: Death toll soars to 290 after bombings hit churches and hotels. *BBC News*. Available at: www.bbc.com/news/world-asia-48008073.

Bell, J.B. (1978). *A time of terror: How democratic societies respond to revolutionary violence*. New York: Basic Books, p. 173.

Bjørgo, T., & Horgan, J.G. (Eds.). (2008). *Leaving terrorism behind: Individual and collective disengagement*. New York: Routledge.

Bouhana, N., Corner, E., Gill, P., & Schuurman, B. (2018). Background and preparatory behaviours of right-wing extremist lone actors: A comparative study. *Perspectives on Terrorism*, 12(6), 150–163.

Boyle, M.J. (2020). Weapon of choice: Terrorist bombings in armed conflict. *Studies in Conflict & Terrorism*, 1–21.

Connable, B., & Libicki, M.C. (2010). *How insurgencies end, Vol. 965*. Santa Monica, CA: Rand Corporation.

Crenshaw, M. (2011). *Explaining terrorism: Causes, processes and consequences*. London and New York: Routledge.

Cronin, A.K. (2008). *Negotiating with groups that use terrorism: Lessons for policymakers*. Geneva, Switzerland: HD Centre for Humanitarian Dialogue.

Cronin, A.K. (2009). How terrorist campaigns end. In T. Bjørgo, & J. Horgan (Eds.), *Leaving terrorism behind: Individual and collective disengagement*. London: Routledge, pp. 49–65.

Debray, R. (2017). *Revolution in the revolution? Armed struggle and political struggle in Latin America*. New York: Verso Books.

Della Porta, D. (2013). *Clandestine political violence*. New York: Cambridge University Press.

Fanon, F. (1961). *The wretched of the earth*. New York: Grove/Atlantic, Inc.

Feuer, L.S. (1969). *Conflict of generations: The character and significance of student movements*. New York: Basic Books.

Gillespie, R. (1983). *Soldiers of Peron: Argentina's Montoneros*. Oxford: Clarendon Press.

Gunaratna, R. (2002). *Inside Al Qaeda: Global network of terror*. New York: Columbia University Press.

Hoffman, B. (1998). *Inside terrorism*. New York: Columbia University Press.

Kilcullen, D. (2013). *Urbanization and the future of conflict*. London: Chatham House. www.chathamhouse.org/events/view/193549.

Laqueur, W. (1977). Interpretations of terrorism: Fact, fiction and political science. *Journal of Contemporary History*, 12(1), 1–42.

Livingstone, N.C., & Arnold, T.E. (1986). The rise of state sponsored terrorism. In N.C. Livingstone & T.E. Arnold (Eds.), *Fighting back: Winning the war against terrorism*. Lexington, MA: Lexington, pp. 11–24.

Marighella, C. (1969). *Minimanual of the urban guerrilla*. Ravensdale, WA: Praetorian Press LLC.

Martin, S., & Weinberg, L. (2016). *The role of terrorism in twenty-first-century warfare*. Manchester: Manchester University Press.

McCants, W. (2015). *The believer: How an introvert with a passion for religion and soccer became Abu Bakr al-Baghdadi, leader of the Islamic State*. Washington, DC: Brookings Institution Press.

Oudraat, C.D.J. (2004). The United Nations and the campaign against terrorism. *Disarmament Forum*, 1(January), 29–37.

Pierce, W.L. (1989). *Hunter*. Charlottesville, VA: National Vanguard Books.

Singer, P.W., & Brooking, E.T. (2018). *Like War: The weaponization of social media*. New York: Eamon Dolan Books.

Sterling, C. (1981). *The terror network: The secret war of international terrorism*. London: Weidenfeld and Nicolson, p. 55.

Stern, J., & Berger, J.M. (2015). *ISIS: The state of terror*. New York: Ecco, HarperCollins Publishers.

Sunstein, C.R. (2018). *#Republic: Divided democracy in the age of social media*. Princeton, NJ: Princeton University Press.

Tarrow, S. (1994). *Social movements in Europe: Movement society or Europeanization of conflict?* Florence: European University Institute.

Weinberg, L. (1991). Turning to terror: The conditions under which political parties turn to terrorist activities. *Comparative Politics*, 23(4), 423–438.

Weinberg, L. (2013). *The end of terrorism?* New York: Routledge.

Wright, L. (2006). *The looming tower: Al-Qaeda and the road to 9/11*. New York: Alfred A. Knopf Incorporated.

Index

9/11: clash of civilizations theory 59, 139; fear 315–316, 320, 330–333, 334–335; focus on individual psychology 9; focus on insurgent terrorism 34; focus on Islamic terrorism 55, 72, 320; increase in suicide bombings 176; masculinity 122–124; moral indignation 49; as outlier 318, 320; preparations 305; scale of 315, 358; strategic rationale 158; as suicide attack 174

Abdulmutallah, Umar Farouk 41
abortion 88, 140
Abrahms, Max 366–368
Abu Ghraib 49
Abu Nidal organization 345
Abu Sayyaf 41, 358
adolescence 13, 91, 249
Afghanistan: Al-Qaeda 52, 266, 359; Soviet invasion 64, 355; Taliban 52, 369; terrorist attacks 176, 366, 369; US military intervention 52, 271, 334, 335, 359
African National Congress 39
Al-Assad, Bashar 361, 362
Al-Awlaki, Anwar 70
Al-Baghdadi, Abu Bakr 160, 362, 371
Al-Barnawi, Abu Musab 156
Algeria 63, 151, 358, 359, 368
algorithms 11, 12, 102–103
Al-Maliki, Nouri 71
Al-Nusra Front 161
Al-Qaeda: affiliates 191, 195, 358, 359–360; Afghanistan 52, 266, 359; declaration of Jihad 356, 358; deterrent strategies 270–271, 274; goals 57, 62, 179, 266; and ISIS 69, 156, 194, 361, 362; origins 356; recruitment of women 128; status 122–123; suicide bombings 179, 181–182, 183, 191, 195, 358, 360; targeting strategy 151, 155–156, 158, 162, 181–182, 303, 361
Al Shabaab 158, 346
Al-Zarqawi, Abu Musab 155, 160, 162, 361
Al-Zawahiri, Ayman 155–156, 158, 162, 355, 359, 361
American Civil Liberties Union (ACLU) 106
anger 91, 92, 142, 225, 250, 334–336
Anti-Defamation League (ADL) 100, 101
anti-Semitism 80, 83–84, 85, 94
anti-social behavior 133, 141–142
anti-terrorism legislation 352, 359
Apo 199–200, 202, 205, 214
apocalypticism 57, 59–60
Arab Spring 361
Arafat, Yasser 119, 128, 353, 373
Argentina 68, 69, 348–349, 360
Armed Islamic Group (GIA) 69, 151, 160, 358
Aryan Brotherhood 40
Asch, Solomon 6–7
atheism 58, 59
audience, of terrorism 36–37, 43
Aum Shinrikyo 40, 41, 51, 346
Australia 52
Austria 352, 353
Autism Spectrum Disorder (ASD) 21
aviation safety 69, 270, 276, 305, 354
Azzam, Abdullah 355, 356, 359

Baader-Meinhof group 126, 345, 350
Balkans 266
Bamboo United 39
Begin, Menachem 373
Bhartiya Janata Party 55

Bin Laden, Osama: background 41, 355; death 70, 371; declaration of Jihad 356, 358; and ISIS 361; Pakistan 359; publicity 122; views 151, 152, 158, 161
biological weapons 107, 276
Black September 348, 352
Blair, Tony 360
Boko Haram 126, 156, 158, 186
Brazil 348–349
Breivik, Anders 38, 346, 363
Bronfenbrenner, Urie 14, 15
Buddhist terrorism 55, 56, 72
Buenos Aires 360
Burma 38, 55, 56
Bush, George W. 123, 124, 140, 334, 360
Bush, Laura 139–140
Butler, Richard G. 88, 89

Cambodia 46, 51–52
Canada 57, 351
Capitol attack (January 2021) 17, 38, 320, 322
Captagon 25
captives *see* hostages
Carlos the Jackal 353, 354
Castro, Fidel 39, 347, 348
Center for Strategic Counterterrorism Communications (CSCC) 164, 165
Central African Republic 56
Central America 369
Chechens 126, 133, 137
chemical weapons 107, 217, 276, 346, 360
child terrorists 131, 186, 193, 194
China 51, 52, 69, 354
Christian Identity 81, 82, 83, 85, 88–89
Christian terrorism 55, 57
CIA 4, 39, 359
civilian attacks: avoidance of 204–205, 206, 214–215, 217; effect on political engagement 184, 215; leadership opposition to 151, 160–163, 165, 361; motivation 154–155, 157, 158, 173, 185
civil liberties, restriction of 69–70, 360
codes: enforcement 161–162, 224–227; military 209–210; street 200, 201; terrorist 160–161, 200, 201, 210–224

coercive diplomacy 44–46
Cold War 347, 351, 355; deterrence 51, 263, 264, 273, 278
Colombia 355, 373
Colombian National Liberation Army 160
colonial rule 49, 63, 368–369
Communist Party of India-Maoist (CPI-Maoist) 161
conspiracy theories 83–84, 89–90, 94
control theory 247–249
Copeland, David 38
Countering Violent Extremism (CVE) 13, 71, 142, 271
counterterrorism: challenging radicalization 71–72, 163–164; effectiveness 52–53; effect on women 138–139; homeland security strategies 69–70; importance of structural conditions 47; military strategies 70–71; restriction of civil liberties 52, 69–70; safe havens 50; strategic 164–165; suicide bombings 184–187. *See also* deterrence
Creativity Movement 84, 89
Crusius, Patrick 363
Cuban Revolution 347, 348
Cyprus 368

databases 106–107, 247, 296–297, 301–302, 304, 366
Dawkins, Richard 58
Dawson, Shepard 29
Debray, Regis 347
decapitation strategies 70–71, 163, 245, 246, 268–269, 370–371
dehumanization 18, 44, 96, 228
deradicalization 13, 71, 242
desistance: collective 252–254, 345, 371, 372–373; control theories 247–249; defining 239, 240–244; measuring 241–242; rational choice theory 244–245, 246–247; strain theories 250–251; through incapacitation 245–246, 268–269, 370–371; from white supremacy 98–99
deterrence: by conciliation 272; by denial 269–270, 274, 278; general

and specific 245, 246, 264; by influence 270–271; operational-level 275–277, 278–279, 280; by punishment 244–245, 264, 267–269, 273–274, 278; rational choice theory 264–265; strategic-level 263, 264, 273–275, 278; tactical-level 277–279, 280; theoretical assumptions 263–267
dictatorships 39, 64
Dilulio, John 227
domestic terrorism 35; data and research 106–109; definition 78–79, 107, 317; infiltration 103–106; law enforcement strategies 99–101, 108; perception of threat from 316, 320, 321–322; rising threat 316, 336. *See also* white supremacy
Domestic Terrorism DATA Act 106

Earth Liberation Front (ELF) 154
Ecological Systems Theory 14, 15
economic conditions, effect on terrorism 41, 47
economic sanctions 43, 45
eco-terrorism 154, 302, 303
Egypt 64, 69, 355, 357
Erdogan, Recep Tayyip 228, 229
ERP (People's Revolutionary Army) 349
ETA (Basque Homeland and Liberty) 37, 350, 371
European Union (EU) 45, 208
extortionists 40, 119
extradition 353, 354

factionalism 155–156, 371
Fanon, Franz 349
FARC (Revolutionary Armed Forces of Colombia) 160, 355
FBI 11, 97, 99, 100, 103, 301–302, 316
fear: age differences 326; as aim of terrorism 36, 129–130, 318; caused by "ordinary" crime 39–40; caused by suicide attacks 173, 315–316; education level 327; emotional vulnerability 328; extent of 319–322, 336–337; gender differences 139, 324–326; impact of media coverage 319, 323–324; perceived risk 328; personal beliefs 329; prior vicimization 327–328; race and nationality 326–327; reactions to 330–336, 337–338
Fighters for a Free Croatia 351
Ford, Gerald 46
France 350, 352, 357, 359; state terrorism 38; terrorist attacks 79, 345, 346, 362
freedom fighters, distinction from terrorists 35–36, 119
French Revolution 35
Freud, Sigmund 8
Front for the Liberation of Quebec (FLQ) 351
Fuerzas Armadas Revolucionarias de Colombia (FARC) 160, 355

Gandhi, Rajiv 126
Gandhi, Rashid 372
gangs 10, 23, 24, 119, 252
gender: counterterrorism measures 138–140; crime 125; fear of terrorism 139, 324–326; involvement in terrorism 13, 125–129, 141, 142; masculinity status 121–124, 128, 129; media coverage 130–133; motivations 133–136, 142; PTSD 21–22; stereotypes 129–130, 132–133; theories 120–121, 127, 135–136, 140–143; unequal consequences 136–138
General Strain Theory (GST) 141–142, 250–251
Germany 38, 126, 349, 350, 352, 365
globalization of terrorism 358–361
Goldman, David 102
Good Friday Agreement 37, 51, 372
Guantanamo Bay 49
guerrilla warfare 210–227, 347, 348–349, 355, 364–365
Guevara, Che 348
Guzman, Abimael 355, 370

Hacker, Frederick 47–48
Hamas 128, 357, 358, 368, 370
hate-crime laws 100
Hatewatch 102

Hezbollah: attacks 160, 175, 178, 192, 357, 360; as target of attacks 176, 192–193
hijacking *see* skyjacking
Hindu terrorism 55, 56, 72, 365
Holocaust denial 85, 86
homophobic violence 35
hostages 220–222, 275, 352, 353–354, 362; killings 155–156, 361, 362, 366
human rights 25, 201, 208, 211; violations 43, 203, 228
Huntington, Samuel 58–59
Hussein, Saddam 360
hybrid terrorism 39, 365–366

Idris, Wafa 128, 132, 137
immigration 84, 373
India 55, 72, 126, 358, 372
Indonesia 37, 359
Inkatha Freedom Party 39
insurgencies 71, 206, 347, 369–370
Interactional Theory 23
internet: anti-terrorism 371; content filtering 102–103; mental ill health 21; terrorist propaganda 152, 360, 362, 365; white supremacy 90, 91, 92–94, 102, 105, 363
INTERPOL 353
intersectionality theory 135–136, 141
Iran 64, 151, 175, 347, 350, 355, 356, 360, 371; Revolution 356; suppression of terrorism 371–372
Iran/Iraq War 357
Iraq 49; 2003 invasion 176, 360; invasion of Kuwait 64, 356; sectarian conflict 71, 360–361; suicide bombings 180, 181
Irgun 368, 373
Irish Republican Army (IRA): disarming 37, 183, 184, 372; motivations 56, 350–351; tactical deterrence 277; warnings 365
ISIS: and Al-Qaeda 69, 156, 194, 361, 362; civilian attacks 158, 160; drug use 25; ideology 67; origins 69, 71, 361–362; perception of threat from 321; propaganda 152, 194, 362; suicide bombings 67, 179, 186, 194–195; territories 362–363; women and minors 126

Islam 59, 65, 72; Salafist ideology 67, 192, 355, 357, 359; Shiite doctrine 357
Islamic Jihad 128
Islamic Revolutionary Guards Corp (IRGC) 357, 371–372
Islamic Salvation Front (FIS) 358
Islamic State (IS) *see* ISIS
Islamist terrorism: focus on 37, 55, 72, 320; goals 57, 67, 192; history 355–363, 370; lethality 67, 154–155, 303; risk to United States 97, 321–322
Islamophobia 94, 329
Israel: counterterrorism 52, 181, 187–190, 269, 274, 276; fear of terrorism 329; independence 373; invasion of Lebanon 357; no negotiation policy 351; Six-Day War 64, 348; suicide bombings 128, 175, 176, 181, 358
Italy 345–346, 349, 350, 351, 352, 357, 366

Jackson, Henry 35–36
Japan 349–350
Jewish terrorism 55, 57, 72
Johnson, Daryl 98

Kaczynski, Theodore 38
Karayılan, Murat 160
Karma, Mahendra 161
Kennedy, John F. 347
Kenya 63, 160, 181, 346, 358
Kenya Land and Freedom Army 160
Khomeini, Ruhollah 356
Kissinger, Henry 46
Klassen, Ben 84, 85, 89
Ku Klux Klan 80, 81, 82, 87–88; in law enforcement 104, 105
Kurdistan Workers' Party *see* PKK
Kurds: Iraq 360; Turkey 126, 201–203, 214, 228–229, 230
Kuwait 64, 356

Lane, David 83
Laqueur, Walter 131
large group identity 17–18
Latin America 347, 348–349, 355
Lebanon 175, 181, 190–192, 357, 360

leftist terrorism 154, 348–350, 354–355, 366, 370. *See also* eco-terrorism; PKK
Liberation Tigers of Tamil Eelam (LTTE) *see* Tamil Tigers
Libya 38, 335, 351, 353, 354
life histories 206–209
Lockerbie bombing 38
London 38, 183, 320, 360
"lone wolves" 20, 38, 154, 345, 347, 363–364, 373
lynching 34–35, 80, 81, 365

Madrid 360
Mafia 40, 52
MANPADs 276
Maoism 161, 354, 370
marginalization 41, 47, 134, 135
Marighella, Carlos 349
Marxism-Leninism 63, 347, 350, 354, 370, 371; PKK 201, 203–204, 205
McCord, Mary 80, 81, 82, 97, 107
McVeigh, Timothy 38, 288, 346, 347, 363
Mecca 355
media coverage 37, 124, 130–133, 199–200, 201; perception of risk 323–324, 333; as terrorist goal 122, 130–131, 164, 180, 194–195, 319, 346
mental ill health 9–10, 18–22, 24, 25, 132
Merari, Ariel 17, 41, 48
Metzger, Tom 103
military occupation 49, 61
mob violence 365
Mogadishu 35
Montoneros 69, 349
moral indignation 49
Moro, Aldo 366
Mujahedin-e-Khalq 151, 371–372
Munich Olympic Games 1972 158, 348, 352
Muslim Brotherhood 357

Nasser, Gamal Abdul 64, 357
National Alliance 86–87
National Consortium for the Study of Terrorism and Responses to Terrorism (START) 106, 107
nationalism 134, 350–351
National Liberation Front (FLN) 368
National Socialist Movement (NSM) 87
National Tawheed Jamaat 192–193
NATO 351, 359
Nazzaro, Rinaldo 103
negotiations: discredited by violence 159, 180–181, 184, 195; effectiveness 372; hostage 354; policy against 351–352; religious terrorism 67, 73
neo-Nazism 38, 86–87, 96, 105
Nepalese Communist Party 160
Netherlands 365
"New Left" 349–350
New People's Army 161
"new terrorism" 63–64, 119, 121, 125, 126, 141
New Zealand 90, 93, 363
Nice 362
Nigeria 41, 126, 156, 176, 359
Nixon, Richard 351–352
Nixon, Robert 45–46
nonviolent political action 154, 158, 183, 202; transition to 179, 184, 190–191, 192, 195
Northern Ireland: drug use and trade 24–25; Good Friday Agreement 37, 51, 372; nationalism 350–351; psychological effects of conflict 10; religious terrorism 56
North Korea 38, 45, 51, 350
Norway 38, 79, 176, 346, 363
nuclear weapons 51, 263, 273, 276, 278
Nuclei of Revolutionary Action (NAR) 345–346, 350

Obama, Barack 82, 164
Ocalan, Abdullah 199–200, 202, 205, 214
Odinism 89–90
O'Hare, Brian 100
Oklahoma City bombing 38, 82, 87, 318, 320, 346, 363
OPEC (Organization of the Petroleum Exporting Countries) 353–354
Organisation Armée Secrète 51

organized crime: intelligence agencies 39; links to terrorism 20, 40, 119–120, 373
Oslo Accords 176, 187, 358
outcomes of terrorist campaigns 366–370

Pakistan 37, 161, 176, 186, 355; Al-Qaeda 70, 266, 359
Palestine 52, 128–129, 138, 368
Palestine Liberation Organization (PLO) 128, 348, 353, 355
Palestinian Islamic Jihad (PIJ) 357, 368
Palestinian territories 175, 176, 181, 186
paramilitary groups: drug use and trade 24–25; psychopathology 19; state terrorism 43
Paris 25, 320, 346, 362
Parler 93–94
Peru 68, 69, 355, 370
Philippines 37, 41, 161, 358
Pierce, William 86, 87, 363
Pisacane, Carlo 365
PKK (Kurdistan Workers' Party): avoidance of civilian attacks 160, 161, 204–205; code of ethics 200, 201, 210–224, 229, 230; discipline 206; enforcement of code 161, 224–227; political goals 201–202, 203–204, 216, 230, 231; portrayal of 199–200, 203, 228, 229; suicide bombings 179; Western perception of 230
pluralism 61, 72
Plutarch 253
political terrorism: and crime 39–40; definition of 35–37; hybrid 39; lethality 67–68; motivation 41, 46–51; non-state actors 37–38; results of 51–52; state actors 38–39, 42–46
Popular Front for the Liberation of Palestine (PFLP) 345
population growth 47
prediction 11–13, 48
prisoner exchange 221
prisons: white supremacy 40, 94, 373
propaganda 164, 165, 221–222, 365; online 152, 163, 194, 360, 362, 365

Provisional Irish Republican Army *see* Irish Republican Army
psychology of terrorism: Ecological Systems Theory 14, 15; extremism 25–28; focus on the individual 9, 13–14, 15; fundamental attribution error 5–6; impact on perpetrators 21–22, 44; large group identity 17–18; mental health disorders 9–10, 18–22, 24, 132; personality characteristics 12, 47–48; prediction 11–13; problematic assumptions 4–6, 7–8; psychoanalytic explanations 8–9, 16–18; research process 6–7, 28–29; suicide attacks 17, 19, 41, 48, 132
PTSD 21–22, 330, 331, 337
punishment, as deterrent 244–245

Qutb, Sayyid 357

radicalization: and military operations 71; online 92–94, 126; paths to 48–49; in prisons 94, 373; societal factors 47
Rainbow Warrior 38
Real IRA 37, 372
Red Army Faction 126, 345, 350, 369
Red Brigades 51, 345, 350, 366, 369
Reicher, Stephen 5–6, 29
religious freedom 61, 72
religious terrorism: combating 69–72; compared with secular terrorism 67–68, 73–74; definition of 56; faith-based 57, 58–60; group identity 56–57; increase in 55, 63–65, 154, 354, 355–356; intersection with politics 34, 60–63, 64–65; resilience 68–69, 73; ruthlessness 65–68, 155; secularist view of 61–63
Rockwell, George Lincoln 86
Rohingya Muslims 55
"root-causes" 46–47, 285, 352–353
Russia 39, 45, 365
Rwandan genocide 21–22

Sahel 373
Salafi-jihadism 67, 155, 192, 355–358, 359–363
Saudi Arabia 355, 359

Schelling, Thomas 45
secularism, political 64–65
sexual assault 222, 325, 362
Shah of Iran 347, 350, 356, 371
Sheehan, Michael 62
Shekau, Abubakar 156
Shining Path 51, 69, 158, 355, 370
Sikh terrorism 72, 358
Sinn Fein 160, 184
Situational Crime Prevention (SCP): application to terrorism 284–285, 286–289, 302–306; literature 289–305
Six-Day War 64, 348
skinheads 90
skyjacking 348, 350, 351, 354; deterrent measures 53, 270, 276
smartphone data 12
social media 93–94, 319, 361, 365
Sontag, Susan 123
South Africa 38–39, 45
Southern Poverty Law Center (SPLC) 100, 101, 102
Soviet Union: Cold War 51, 278, 351, 354–355; collapse 204; invasion of Afghanistan 64, 355; state terrorism 38, 51
Spain 63, 350, 359, 360
Sri Lanka 56, 358; negotiations 372; repression of terrorism 69–69, 187, 192, 368; suicide bombings 175, 183, 192–193, 346
state terrorism 7, 20, 38–39, 42–46, 50, 51
Stormfront 92, 93
Strategic Model of Terrorism 157–160, 165
substance use 13, 24–25, 186, 330–331, 332
Sudan 352, 359, 373
suicide attacks: abstention from 182–183, 193–194, 195; by children 156, 186, 193; definition 174; fear caused by 173, 180, 185; as group phenomenon 176–179; history 34, 175–176, 356–357, 358; jihadist 155; lethality 172, 173, 179; and masculinity 122; motivations 134, 135, 136, 179–182; psychology 17, 19, 41, 48; stopping 184–192; by

women 126, 128, 129, 130, 131, 132, 134, 135, 137, 186
Sun Tzu 38
surveillance: civil liberties 52, 70, 274; hindering 278; support for 335; target hardening 184, 188; women 138
Syria: Al-Qaeda 191, 266; ISIS 156, 191, 362; 2011 rebellion 361, 362; sanctions 45; state sponsorship 191, 351; terrorist attacks 161, 176

Taiwan 39
Taliban 52, 158, 160, 161, 186, 369
Tamil Tigers 358, 362; defeat of 192, 368; goals 37, 158; ideology 56, 69; negotiations with 372; suicide bombers 126, 175, 186, 192
Tanzania 181, 358
targeted killings 70–71, 163, 245, 246, 268–269, 370–371
target hardening 69, 164, 184–185, 187, 275–276
target selection: civilian targeting 157, 158, 159, 160–163; ideological 153–157; importance of research into 151–152, 165; inconsistent with propaganda 152–153; strategic 157–160
Tarrant, Brenton 363
Tehrik-e-Taliban 161
terrorism, definition of 35–37, 119–120, 151, 316–317, 364–365
Thornberry, Terence 23
Thucydides 45–46
Trump, Donald 101, 163, 363
Tupamaros 69, 349
Turkey: civilian attacks 161; 1980 coup 202; 2016 coup attempt 228; EU accession 208; fear of terrorism 325; military bases 216–217; rangers 212–213; suppression of the Kurds 202–203, 228–229. *See also* PKK
Turkish People's Liberation Army (TPLA) 351

Unabomber 38
unemployment 47, 322
United Japanese Red Army 350

United Kingdom 38, 90–91, 183, 352, 360; CONTEST policy 360
United Nations 45, 53, 351, 352–353, 359
United Red Army 158
United States: Center for Strategic Counterterrorism Communications (CSCC) 164, 165; civil rights movement 81, 103; counterinsurgency techniques 347; definition of terrorism 317; Department of Homeland Security 69, 101, 106, 359; Department of Justice 81–82, 100, 101; domestic terrorism 78, 79, 99–101; Domestic Terrorism DATA Act 106; invasion of Iraq 176, 360; military intervention in Afghanistan 52, 271, 334, 335, 359; *National Security Strategy of the United States* 267; *National Strategy for Counterterrorism* 163–164, 267; "Patriot Act" 359; risk of terrorism 97, 318–319; state terrorism 51; 1970s terrorist attacks 351; "War on Terror" 49, 124, 139–140, 176, 334–335, 359
urbanization 47
Uruguay 68, 69, 348–349
USS Cole 181, 358
Ustacha 345

values: ideological 87, 93, 95, 128; organizational 211, 225; religious 65, 87; social 27, 47, 200, 247
Van Gogh, Theo 365

Vienna 353
Vietnam War 45–46, 347, 349, 350

Waldheim, Kurt 352
"War on Terror" 49, 124, 139–140, 176, 334–335, 359
white supremacy: civil litigation 101–103; data and research 106–109; entry into 91–96; groups 85–91; ideology 79–80, 83–85; infiltration 103–106; law enforcement strategies 99–101, 108; online 91, 92–94, 102–103; in prisons 94, 373; religious aspects 57, 87, 88–90; rising threat 37–38, 373; UK 90–91; US history 80–83; violence, extent of 96–98, 303; women 95–96
Whitmer, Gretchen 82, 98
women: as captives 222; crime 125; fear of terrorism 139, 324–326; media coverage 130–131, 132–133; rights of 139–140; as terrorists 125–130, 134–135, 141, 142; unequal consequences 136–139; white supremacy 95–96
World Trade Center attack 2001 *see* 9/11
World Trade Center bombing 1993 305
WWII 51

Yazidis 362
Yemen 70, 181, 359
Yugoslavia 345, 351

Zetas 40
Zouabri, Antar 160

For Product Safety Concerns and Information please contact our EU representative GPSR@taylorandfrancis.com
Taylor & Francis Verlag GmbH, Kaufingerstraße 24, 80331 München, Germany

www.ingramcontent.com/pod-product-compliance
Ingram Content Group UK Ltd.
Pitfield, Milton Keynes, MK11 3LW, UK
UKHW021855271025
464395UK00011B/425